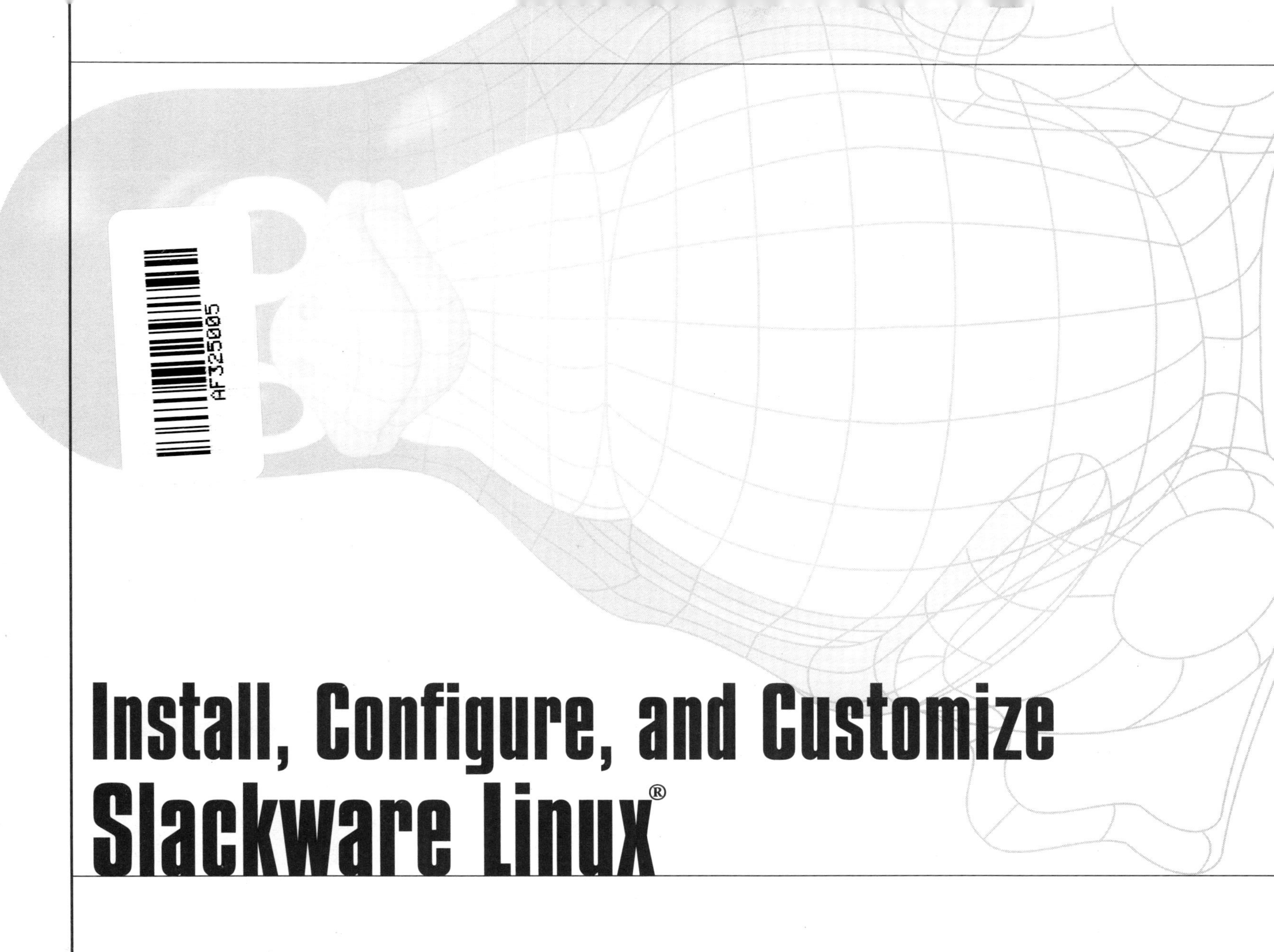

Install, Configure, and Customize
Slackware Linux®
AF325005

Send Us Your Comments:

To comment on this book or any other PRIMA TECH title, visit PRIMA TECH's reader response page on the Web at **www.prima-tech.com/comments**.

How to Order:

For information on quantity discounts, contact the publisher: Prima Publishing, P.O. Box 1260BK, Rocklin, CA 95677-1260; (916) 787-7000. On your letterhead, include information concerning the intended use of the books and the number of books you wish to purchase. For individual orders, visit PRIMA TECH's Web site at **www.prima-tech.com**.

Slackware Linux®

Install, Configure, and Customize

Joe "Zonker" Brockmeier

Jacek Artymiak, et al.

A Division of Prima Publishing

© 2000 by Prima Publishing. Appendix A, "A Linux Primer," may be distributed only subject to the terms and conditions set forth in the Open Publication License, vX.Y or later (the latest version is presently available at http://www.opencontent.org/openpub/). With the exception of Appendix A, "A Linux Primer," all rights reserved. No part of this book may be reproduced or transmitted in any form or by any means, electronic or mechanical, including photocopying, recording, or by any information storage or retrieval system without written permission from Prima Publishing, except for the inclusion of brief quotations in a review.

 A Division of Prima Publishing

Prima Publishing and colophon are registered trademarks of Prima Communications, Inc. PRIMA TECH is a trademark of Prima Communications, Inc., Roseville, California 95661.

Linux is a registered trademark of Linus Torvalds. The Linux penguin, Tux, is used with permission from Larry Ewing (lewing@isc.tamu.edu). Ewing created this image using *The GIMP* (http://www.gimp.org). Modifications to Tux were made by Jim Thompson.

Microsoft and Windows are registered trademarks of Microsoft Corporation. Mac and Macintosh are trademarks or registered trademarks of Apple Computer, Inc.

Prima Publishing and the authors have attempted throughout this book to distinguish proprietary trademarks from descriptive terms by following the capitalization style used by the manufacturers.

Important: If you experience problems running or installing Slackware Linux 7, go to Slackware's Web site at http://www.slackware.com for support and technical information. Prima Publishing cannot provide software support.

Information contained in this book has been obtained by Prima Publishing from sources believed to be reliable. However, because of the possibility of human or mechanical error by our sources, Prima Publishing, or others, the Publisher does not guarantee the accuracy, adequacy, or completeness of any information and is not responsible for any errors or omissions or the results obtained from the use of such information. Readers should be particularly aware of the fact that the Internet is an ever changing entity. Some facts may have changed since this book went to press.

ISBN: 0-7615-2616-1
Library of Congress Catalog Card Number: 99-06894
Printed in the United States of America

00 01 02 03 04 II 10 9 8 7 6 5 4 3 2 1

Publisher
Stacy L. Hiquet

Marketing Manager
Judi Taylor

Associate Marketing Manager
Jody Kennen

Managing Editor
Sandy Doell

Acquisitions Editor
Kim Spilker

Developmental Editor
Charles Coffing

Project Editor
Melody Layne

Copy Editor
Kate Welsh

Technical Reviewer
Van Hendrickson

Proofreader
Kate Talbot

Interior Layout
Marian Hartsough

Cover Design
Prima Design Team

Indexer
Johnna VanHoose

*This book is dedicated to everyone
who makes and uses
open-source software.*

Acknowledgments

There are a lot of people I've always wanted to thank in print for their contributions to my life in big and small ways. My family, of course; my friend Denise and her family; Hannah; my instructors at East Central Community College; and many, many others.

This book has been a long time in the making, much longer than my wonderful acquisitions editor, Kim Spilker, would have liked. I'd like to thank her for her patience, and for not sending a couple of guys to my house to break my knees.

Thanks to the folks at Atipa for loaning me the dual-processor machine—it was a big help while writing the book.

I'd also like to thank everybody at LinuxMall.com, especially my boss, Mark Bolzern, for hiring me and being a really good guy. He's one of the Linux old-timers, and without Mark and others like him Linux would not be the success that it is today. Since I started working at LinuxMall.com I've had a ton of opportunities that I never would have had otherwise, and I'm very grateful I've had the opportunity to make money working with Linux.

I've met a lot of people in the Linux community over the past year whom I consider to be friends, especially the gang at *Linux Magazine*, who gave me my first crack at writing about Linux. Adam, Lara, Bob—you guys are awesome.

Finally, a big thanks to Patrick Volkerding, the guy who is primarily responsible for Slackware. When I first started using Slack, I had some trouble getting *XFree86* to work with my video card and I sent an email to the support address for Slackware. Many companies would probably have never responded, but I got a response directly from Pat that was helpful and gracious. Had I not received a response, I probably would have decided to forget about using Linux, but instead I kept plugging away and finally got the hang of (almost) everything.

—Joe "Zonker" Brockmeier

Joe "Zonker" Brockmeier is vice president of marketing for LinuxMall.com. He has two and a half years experience with Slackware Linux and has written and edited publications for LinuxMall.com, as well as for broadcast news.

Jacek Artymiak is a freelance consultant, journalist, and writer who has used various flavors of UNIX and Linux since 1994. He has collaborated on books for other publishers and has helped numerous businesses integrate their IT solutions.

Brian Proffitt is a professional author and computer consultant. He consults in the areas of desktop application training, documentation, and configuration management. He is the author of Prima Tech's *Sun™ StarOffice® 5.1 for Linux* and Prima Tech's *Sun™ StarOffice® 5.1 for Windows*.

William Schaffer is an embedded firmware engineer by trade and a wandering UNIX Sysadmin by moonlight. Introduced to UNIX in 1988, he has been using Linux since late 1992 and tries to help others make the change.

Charles Coffing received his bachelor's and master's degrees in computer science from MIT in 1999. He currently works in Provo, Utah, as a software engineer for Novell. His special interests include operating system design, encryption, and the interactions between new technologies and personal liberties.

Andy Harris is a computer science instructor for Indiana University/Purdue University at Indianapolis. His interests are beginner-level computer science, Web design, and programming, with specialties in Perl, Javascript/DHTML, Java, and Visual Basic.

Keith E. Pettit is a freelance writer, IT solutions consultant, and software beta tester. He's worked with Linux for over two years and has published numerous articles on the Web.

Chapter 12: New Directions 291

Chapter 13 Introduction to Emacs 323

Part III
Appendixes 361

Appendix A: A Linux Primer 363

Welcome to *Install, Configure, and Customize Slackware Linux 7*. This book is designed to help you get the Slackware Linux operating system up and running on your computer, as well as to help you start being productive once you have Slackware installed.

It is my hope that this book makes installing and using Slackware easy for people who haven't used Linux before.

What This Book Is About

This book covers, in great detail, the basics of installing and configuring Slackware Linux 7. It is written for the beginner, not the expert user. It's our hope that this book makes Linux seem less intimidating and allows more people to experience the benefits of using a Linux distribution. (Okay, we'd also like to sell quite a few copies of the book....)

The authors of this book have taken great pains to write to the average computer user, not to other geeks. We do assume that the reader has used a computer before and that you have a general understanding of how to use a mouse, turn on your computer, and that sort of thing.

Who Should Read This Book?

As the author of the book, I really feel everyone should read this book. Buy one for yourself and everyone else that you know. (It's worth a try....)

Okay, actually, the people who should buy this book are people who want to try running Linux on a desktop or workstation computer. We don't address, in great detail, running servers or using Linux to do exotic tasks. We do explain how to get Slackware installed and tweaked for the end user who wants to use Linux to be productive.

If you've already gotten Slackware installed, this book can help you become more familiar with Linux, as well as guide you through a number of common customizations. Although you might not be a Linux guru by the time you finish this book, you'll certainly know a lot more.

If you're already an expert Linux user, this book can help you get to know the Slack-ware Linux distribution a bit better, but probably won't teach you anything you don't already know about Linux in general. The book is primarily aimed at the user who is new to Linux.

What You Need to Begin

To use this book you need an Intel-based or Intel-compatible computer that has a 386 or better processor. You need at least 8MB of RAM and up to 700MB of hard disk space free to install Linux. If you don't have a computer, ICC Slackware might make for interesting reading, but probably won't be very useful.

The book includes the download version of Slackware Linux on CD-ROM and detailed instructions on how to install Linux.

How This Book Is Organized

The book is organized in a chronological fashion, assuming that you begin with installing Slackware and then proceed to fine-tuning your installation. If you've already installed Slack, then you probably want to skip the first part of the book that deals exclusively with preinstallation and installation.

- **Part I: Installing Slackware 7**

  This part of the book covers making sure that your computer is ready for Slackware, installing Slackware Linux, and what to do immediately after installing Slackware.

- **Part II: Configuring and Customizing Slackware**

  Once you've gotten Slackware installed, Part II covers everything from configuring X to getting your sound card, printing, and networking up and running. Part II also covers recompiling the Linux kernel and working with KDE, GNOME, and other window managers that come with Slackware Linux.

- **Part III: Appendixes**

  Appendix A, "A Linux Primer," covers the basics of using Linux from the command line. Sure, these days you could get around in Linux from the graphical interface only, but why? It also briefly discusses the philosophy behind the Linux operating system and editing text in Linux using vi.

  Appendix B, "Linux Resources," lists the best of the best about Linux on the Web.

  Appendix C, "Hardware Compatibility Journal," provides you a space to record important data you find.

Special Elements in This Book

Cautions generally tell you how to avoid problems.

Notes provide additional helpful or interesting information.

Tips often suggest techniques and shortcuts to make your life easier.

Terms and phrases that geek-like people toss around.

A Brief History of Linux

What is generally known as the Linux operating system is actually a compilation of software, including the Linux kernel. The Linux kernel is the core of the operating system, but alone it would be pretty useless. The kernel handles lower-level operations and would not provide much end-user functionality by itself.

The Linux kernel was developed by Linus Torvalds in 1991. At the time, Linus was a student at the University of Helsinki who really wanted to play with something like UNIX on a 386 PC. Not realizing the trouble he would cause, he started working on Linux and made the code available on the Internet to anyone who wanted to work on the OS.

The Free Software Foundation

The history of Linux, told chronologically, actually begins before Linus Torvalds wrote the Linux kernel. Many of the tools used in a Linux system are actually tools produced by the Free Software Foundation's GNU (GNU's Not UNIX) project. The C compiler, shell, and most of the UNIX-like utilities that are used with Linux existed before Linus started working on the first version of the Linux kernel.

Not only did the Free Software Foundation make code available for a project such as Linux, but it also made an important philosophical contribution, without which Linux and most tools used with Linux would not be possible. That contribution is the GPL, or General Public License. The GPL is a nonrestrictive license that allows anyone to use, modify, and redistribute code that is GPL'ed. Without the ability to do that, Linus could never have used the GNU utilities to write the Linux kernel, and if Linus had not chosen to license the kernel under the GPL, Linux could not have grown so explosively or benefited from the contributions of people around the world who have been hacking on the kernel since its release.

The Other Bits

As mentioned before, a Linux distribution is a conglomeration of open-source software. A typical distribution, such as Slackware, includes software from the XFree86 Project, Apache, Samba, countless GNU utilities, and window managers and desktop environments such as KDE, GNOME, and Enlightenment. The success of Linux would not be possible without the contributions of thousands of people all over the world who have put time and effort into writing code for various open source projects.

What Is a Distribution?

Because Linux is not a commercial venture in and of itself, Linux was originally available only as a download of source code. This wasn't particularly useful if you weren't a computer guru, so several groups started packaging precompiled bits of software, including the Linux kernel, GNU utilities and compilers, and various other necessities such as installers and package-management utilities.

The collection of software that you get came to be known as a distribution. In addition to Slackware Linux, there are dozens, if not hundreds, of other distributions of Linux. Some of these, such as Red Hat, SuSE, Caldera, and Linux Mandrake, are commercial ventures. Others, such as Debian, are put together by nonprofit groups.

Why Use Slackware?

Once you've made the decision to use Linux, how do you pick a distribution? One of the most frequently asked questions about Linux is, Which one do I use?

The somewhat flippant answer is that Linux distributions are a bit like underwear—you never know what makes you comfortable until you try them all. It's kind of a boxers or briefs type of question.

If you're thinking to yourself that people using Windows don't have to make this kind of complicated decision, ask yourself whether you would choose to use Windows 9x, Windows 2000, or Windows CE. 'Nuff said.

The reason that I use Slackware is twofold. For one thing, Slack is the first distribution I ever used, so I'm the most comfortable with it. I've tried a lot of others since I started using Linux, but I've never really liked any of the others as much as Slackware.

The second reason is that I've always found Slackware to be extremely stable and fairly bug-free. Slackware is very reliable and tends to get very high marks from system administrators who know UNIX.

Patrick Volkerding is the original founder and maintainer of Slackware Linux, and he still maintains Slackware today along with a small staff. Many of the Linux distributions that are popular today, including Red Hat, were originally based on Slackware. (SuSE Linux, for example, was occasionally billed as "Slackware with RPMs.")

The Slackware Distribution Included with This Book

The distribution included with this book is the downloadable version available from Slackware's Web site (http://www.slackware.com). You might want to check and see if a newer version has been released since this book was published. The majority of this book should apply to future versions of Slackware, as the installation tools and package-management software have not changed significantly over time.

The version included with this book is all you need to get a Linux system up and running. However, if you like Slackware, I encourage you to buy the full distribution from one of the many vendors that carry Slackware. This will allow Patrick and the gang to continue to spend their time maintaining Slackware Linux and making it the best it can possibly be.

Contacting the Author

If you'd like to send an e-mail telling me how wonderful the book is or report an error in the text, please write me at Zonker@LinuxMall.com. I don't promise to respond to all e-mails, but I will try.

I hope that you find this book enlightening and very useful. Suggestions on how to make future versions of the book more useful are greatly appreciated.

Thanks for reading, and good luck with Linux!

1 Before You Install: Getting to Know Your Hardware

2 Partitioning Your Hard Drive

3 Installing Slackware

4 After the Installation

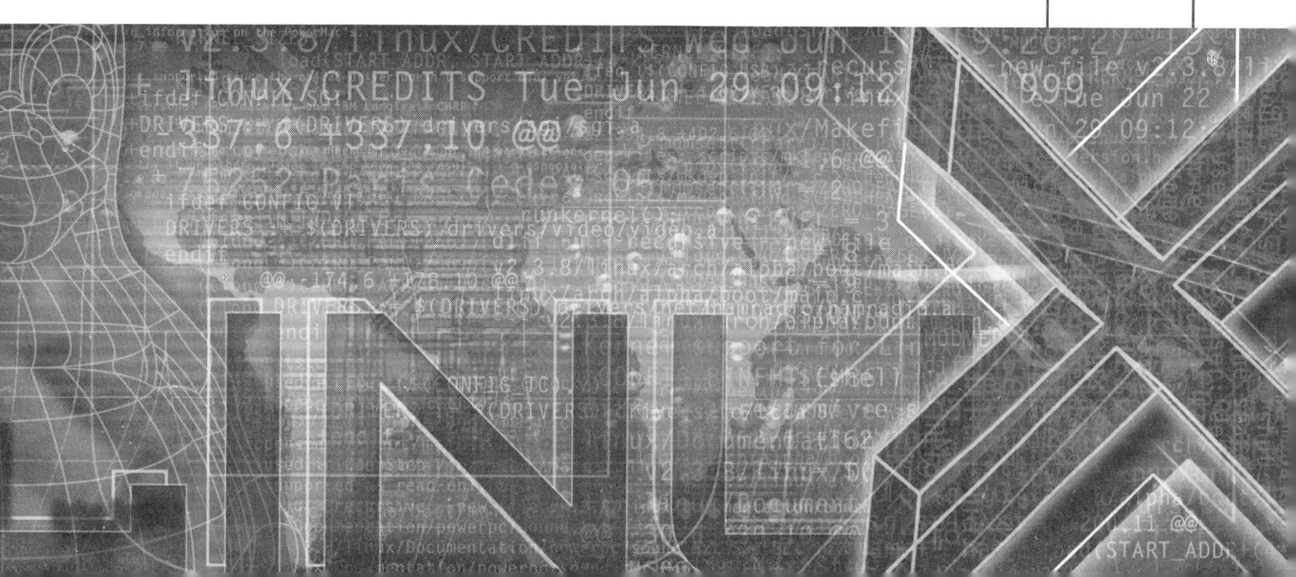

Jacek Artymiak

Chapter 1: Before You Install: Getting to Know Your Hardware

Hardware Requirements for Installing Slackware Linux

Is My Hardware Compatible?

Other Considerations: What to Do When Your Hardware Isn't Compatible

Linux is one of the most flexible computer operating systems available on the market today and can be easily adapted to run on a wide range of computers from old Intel 386-based PCs, to multiprocessor Intel Pentium workstations and servers, through the latest Transmeta Crusoe processors.

Although support for the original Intel and Intel-compatible chips is most widespread at the moment, Linux, including the Slackware Linux 7 distribution, can be easily recompiled to run on computers powered by Motorola 680x0, PowerPC, Digital/Compaq Alpha, MIPS, ARM, Sun Sparc and many other processors. You don't even have to obtain additional licenses.

No other operating system is currently available for so many hardware platforms, and none is as scalable as Linux, which can power small embedded systems, desktop workstations, and powerful supercomputing installations. Naturally, such advantages must be accompanied by some disadvantages, such as the need to know the hardware you plan to install Linux on a little better than users of other operating systems such as Microsoft Windows, but this can only be a good thing—knowing your tools can only help you get the most out of them.

In this chapter I talk at length about Slackware Linux 7 hardware requirements and about various internal and external devices with which this distribution of Linux can communicate. No Ph.D. in supercomputer design is required to understand the material presented on this and the following pages.

Hardware Requirements for Installing Slackware Linux

One of the reasons Linux can be so easily configured to run on a wide range of hardware is the simple fact that its creators (Linus Torvalds and his many supporters) did not have unlimited cash resources to buy tons of memory or the latest hardware. Instead, they had to make the system run on inexpensive PC computers powered by slower Intel 386 chips and equipped with totally different network adapters, video cards, hard disk drives, and other devices. That is why today, even though you can get a Pentium-based PC for next to nothing, Linux can still run on computers with very limited resources, such as those described in the next section.

Minimum Requirements

Just like its earlier versions, the Slackware Linux 7 distribution has very modest hardware requirements and can run on any PC-compatible computer with the following parameters:

- **Intel 386SX processor**. The speed it is running at does not matter, and no math coprocessor is necessary to run Linux (the system has a built-in emulator).

- **4MB of RAM**. You might have to jump through a few extra hoops to get Slackware installed on a machine with only 4MB of RAM, but it is possible. Once installed, this should be enough to run basic system services.

- **50MB of free space on a hard disk drive**. This should be enough to install basic software.

- **5.25-inch floppy disk drive**. A 3.5-inch disk drive is better, though.

That is some pretty ancient hardware; you would have problems finding such a configuration today, unless you have a job at an organization that is still using such computers or if you found one at an old computer equipment sale. My advice is to avoid such hardware unless it is possible to add at least another 4MB of RAM and a hard disk drive with at least 300MB of free space. Only then can Linux show what it is capable of.

Believe it or not, even a lowly 386 can be used as a low-volume network server or a workstation for people who want to learn Linux. The processor speed does not matter that much when you are just learning Linux, and when you don't expect it to run the graphical user interface (the X Window System). The X Window System requires at least 16MB of RAM, a fast 486 processor, and much more free space on a hard disk drive.

One particular segment of the computing industry where current configurations meet or only slightly exceed the basic hardware requirements given in this section is industrial PCs. They are highly modular systems used to control construction machinery, air-conditioning systems, and other similar contraptions that most of us usually do not have to deal with in real life. These things are governed by entirely different rules, and an operating system with low resource requirements, such as Linux, might be just what the designers of such machines are looking for. (More information about using Linux in embedded systems can be found at http://www.pc104.org).

Fortunately, most of you don't have to deal with such old hardware; the majority of Intel-based PCs manufactured during the past five years are likely to be equipped with a Pentium (or compatible) processor; at least 16MB of RAM; a 1GB or larger hard disk drive; a 3.5-inch floppy drive; and a CD-ROM drive, which comes in handy when you want to install Slackware Linux 7 from a CD-ROM (the most convenient method). This is enough to install and comfortably run Slackware Linux 7 for all but the most graphically or computationally intensive tasks.

Is My Hardware Compatible?

The main problem with computer hardware is that you might have problems finding out whether it can run happily with a particular piece of software. The Microsoft Windows or Apple Mac OS users have it easy—manufacturers usually print basic information about compatibility with these operating systems on the packaging or at least mention it in the documentation.

Linux users still have to wait for the day when they can walk into a shop and ask for a Linux-compatible modem or video card, although this situation is rapidly changing. For now, the majority of manufacturers do not mention compatibility under Linux, even if their product is compatible, often because they do not know how to test for it yet. So, before you install Slackware Linux 7 on your computer, or before you add or exchange a particular hardware component, you need to do some investigative work on your own. To make it a relatively painless job, arm yourself with the following tools:

- **A copy of this book.**
- **Original documentation.** User manuals, technical guides, data sheets, specifications, factory test printouts, leaflets, and so on.
- **Copies of inscriptions on labels and other information printed directly on each hardware component.** Manufacturer's name, model name and number, serial number, and so on.
- **Copies of messages displayed during boot sequence after you switch the computer on or after you reset it.** You might have to press Ctrl+Alt+Del or the reset button several times in order to copy all information.
- **Various HOWTO and mini-HOWTO documents (for example, Hardware-HOWTO).** You can find these documents at http://www. linuxdoc.org (the Linux Documentation Project), on the official Slackware Linux Web site (it's part of the howto.tgz package from the F series of Slackware Linux 7 packages), and on every Slackware Linux 7 CD-ROM disc in the /docs/Linux-HOWTO and /docs/Linux-mini-HOWTO directories. (After installation they are copied to the /usr/doc/Linux-HOWTOs and /usr/doc/Linux-mini-HOWTOs directories. See Chapter 3, "Installing Slackware," for more details.)
- **The online database of Linux-compatible hardware located at http://lhd.datapower.com.**
- **One Philip's-head screwdriver.** This is in case you need to open the computer when you cannot find necessary information any other way. Remember that opening the computer's case might invalidate the warranty.

Remember to unplug the computer and all other devices connected to it from the power source!

If you have never opened a computer case before, ask someone who has for help!

Checking a computer's compatibility under Linux is much easier for the owners of portable computers than it is for those who own desktop PCs, mainly because the configuration options are more limited on portable PCs. If you want to install Slackware Linux 7 on a portable computer, visit http://www.linux.org/hardware/laptop.html and http://www.cs.utexas.edu/users/kharker/linux-laptop, where you will find plenty of information and detailed installation guidelines. (Keep in mind that some of these Web sites might not describe installing Slackware Linux 7 on a particular computer, but the general rules still apply.) You can also check out *Prima Tech's Linux for Your Laptop.*

Hardware Checklist

It is a good idea to keep a paper log (I use a simple spiral-bound notebook) where you can record all pieces of information about the main components of your computer and any external devices you want to connect to it. Once you have done that, read the following sections, checking to make sure your computer's components match Slackware Linux 7 requirements. I begin with one of the most important pieces of silicon—your computer's processor.

Processors

Slackware Linux 7 is a distribution for the Intel family of processors and runs on any PC computer powered by chips from the list below:

- **386.** All models with or without a math coprocessor, including (but not limited to) 386SX, 386DX, 386SL, 386DXL, and 386SLC. Linux can emulate a math coprocessor if your model doesn't have one.

- **486.** All models with or without a math coprocessor including (but not limited to) 486SX, 486DX, 486SL, 486SX2, 486DX2, 486DX4. The lack of the math coprocessor is not a problem; Linux can emulate it.

- **Pentium (also known as 586).** All models from the Pentium, Pentium MMX, Pentium Pro, Pentium II, Pentium III, Celeron, Xeon, and others. These chips have a built-in math coprocessor.

None of these chips cause problems under Linux. Also, if you are planning to run Slackware Linux 7 on a computer with more than one processor, Intel chips are currently your best choice. Information regarding multiprocessor computers is available in the Hardware-HOWTO and Parallel-Processing-HOWTO documents available on the CD-ROM. You can view these documents under Windows in Wordpad after you place the Slackware Linux 7 CD-ROM in your computer's CD-ROM drive. The HOWTO documents can be found in the D:\DOCS\LINUX-HO directory. If you cannot find them, choose Search from the Windows's Start menu and type their names into the Search dialog box.

One big disadvantage of using Intel chips is their relatively high price. Less expensive alternatives are available from AMD, Cyrix, and IDT; they make good replacements for Intel chips and cost considerably less, which is important when you want to upgrade your old computer without parting with too much of your hard-earned cash. You should be warned that some Intel and Intel-compatible chips, especially early versions of older chips (386, 486, and early Pentium clones), might have bugs that could cause problems. Fortunately, the current version of the Linux kernel already compensates for most of these flaws. Very few of these chips do not work under Linux. Up-to-date information about processor compatibility can be found in the Hardware-HOWTO document (D:\DOCS\LINUX-DO\HARDWARE or /cdrom/docs/Linux-HOWTO/Hardware-HOWTO under Linux).

If you have a non-Intel processor, check the Hardware-HOWTO to see what it says about that particular chip. Then, check the Linux Hardware Database located at http://lhd.datapower.com. If no information about compatibility problems is listed there, you can safely assume that your processor does not cause problems under Linux.

When you suspect that the processor you are using might be causing problems, ask other Linux users about their experiences with that particular chip on one of the Linux Usenet newsgroups (comp.os.linux.hardware and comp.os.linux.slackware are good places to start). Alternatively, try the linux-newbie mailing list (see the "Further Info" section near the end of this chapter for details on how to join it). Remember to always specify the Linux kernel version (in the case of Slackware Linux 7, it is Linux kernel 2.2.13), the distribution version (Slackware Linux 7), and the make, type, and speed of the processor on which you are trying to make Slackware Linux 7 run. Make sure you thank people who answer your questions, because they do it for free and sometimes spend a lot of their spare time looking for answers.

Although Slackware Linux 7 is available in precompiled form for the Intel family of processors, it does not necessarily mean that you cannot run Slackware Linux 7 on computers powered by other chips. However, you have to reconfigure and recompile the kernel (necessary sources are available in the lx2213.tgz archive included in the K1 package set) and the rest of the software, possibly making a few changes along the way. In the end you might have a different Linux distribution that can no longer be called Slackware Linux 7.

Which Processor Do I Have?

The type and speed in MHz (megahertz) of your processor are usually displayed during boot sequence after you switch on the power supply or reset the computer. Make note of that information and compare it with the list of processors given earlier in this chapter. Remember, though, that this information might not be correct for processors other than Intel, and in some cases even those can be identified incorrectly. Under Windows you can find this information in the System dialog box (choose Start, Settings, Control Panel, System).

The correct information about the type of processor installed in your computer should be given in the computer's documentation. If the information is not available, the best way to find out the type of processor installed in your computer is to open the box and read the markings on the chip. (As stated earlier, doing so might invalidate the warranty.)

If you are planning to upgrade your processor, remember that in some cases you might have to buy a new motherboard, new memory chips, or other internal components. Upgrading PCs is a huge topic. I'm not going to cover it here, but if you are interested in finding out more information about Intel and Intel-compatible processors, visit these sites:

- http://webopedia.internet.com/TERM/C/CPU.html
- http://users.erols.com/chare/cpu_gen.htm
- http://www.ugeek.com/procspec

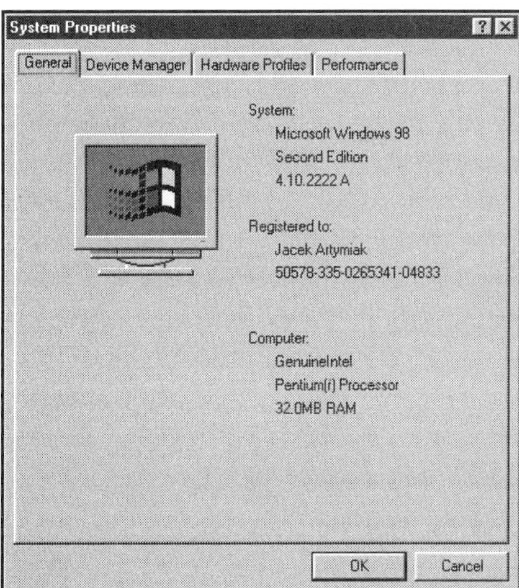

Figure 1.1 *The Windows System Control Panel*

More information about Linux ports to other processors and computer architectures can be found at these addresses:

- **ARM.** http://www.arm.uk.linux.org/~rmk/armlinux.html
- **Alpha (AXP) Project.** http://www.alphalinux.org
- **Intel 8086, 80186, 80286, and other pre-386 Intel chips.** http://www.uk.linux.org/ELKS-Home
- **MIPS R2000, R3000, and R4000.** http://www.linux.sgi.com
- **Motorola 68000.** http://ryeham.ee.ryerson.ca/uClinux
- **Motorola 680x0.** http://www.linux-m68k.org
- **PA-RISC.** http://www.thepuffingroup.com/parisc
- **PowerPC.** http://www.ppc.kernel.org
- **Sun Sparc.** http://www.ultralinux.org

> You can find many more pointers to various Linux ports and projects at http://www.linux.org/projects/ports.html.

Motherboards

Motherboards are large printed circuits to which every piece of hardware inside (and outside of) your computer connects. There are two major types of motherboards: AT and ATX—they can be only used with AT or ATX cases. It does not matter which standard your computer is based on; Linux does not care.

The major communication routes on motherboards, or buses, as they are usually called, can be designed in one of many standardized ways called architectures. Slackware Linux 7 runs on motherboards equipped with ISA, EISA, PCI, and AGP buses. The only visible sign of implementation of these architectures on your computer's motherboard is the expansion card connectors used to plug in video cards, sound cards, SCSI interface cards, modems, and other useful bits of hardware. When you are buying an expansion card, check which architecture it works with and which architectures your motherboard supports. That information ought to be included in the computer or motherboard documentation; if you don't have it, check the BIOS messages and markings on the largest chips located on the motherboard and search the Internet using one or more search engines for information. It is worth mentioning that ISA and EISA cards are slowly disappearing from the market, and new motherboards no longer have necessary connectors.

Some PCs, IBM's PS/2 in particular, use the MCA or MicroChannel bus architecture, which is also supported by Linux, but you might have to recompile the kernel in order to get it working. You can find more information at http://www.dgmicro.com/.

Problems with motherboards usually crop up at the beginning when you are trying to install Slackware Linux 7 or when you are upgrading the processor. It is impossible to know whether your motherboard is compatible under Linux unless you've tried to install the system, but the good news is that only a few motherboards refuse to work under Linux. Some of them are mentioned in the Hardware-HOWTO and in the Linux Hardware Database located at http://lhd.datapower.com. If you are still not sure, ask on one of the Linux newsgroups or mailing lists (see the "Further Info" section near the end of this chapter).

Sometimes a motherboard compatibility problem can be fixed by changing BIOS settings or changing the BIOS itself. This is a job for an experienced person and you should not attempt it if you do not know what you are doing. Otherwise, you can end up with a dead motherboard. It is almost always a good idea to let a more qualified person do this for you.

For more information about motherboards, visit these sites:

- http://www.motherboards.org
- http://www.sysopt.com/mboard.html
- http://x86.ddj.com/intel.doc/intelmotherboards.htm

Memory

Although Slackware Linux 7 can be installed on a computer with only 4MB of RAM, I advise all users to install at least 8MB of RAM if they are not going to use the X Window System for the graphical user interface, or at least 16MB of RAM if they are.

Memory modules installed in your computer should be of the same type (in a majority of new computers that means EDO SIMM or DIMM modules), the same frequency, and if possible, the same make. Before you buy memory, check your motherboard's memory requirements (for online guides, see the URLs listed earlier in the "Motherboards" section).

Remember that physical RAM is not the only kind of memory available under Linux. When you are running out of memory, parts of data and program code are moved to a special place on your computer's hard disk drive called swap space. This swap space on your hard drive acts like virtual memory. Because the swap space might be included in the total memory count, you often can run applications that have higher memory requirements if you have enough swap space. I cover configuring swap space and virtual memory in Chapter 2, "Partitioning Your Hard Drive."

If you are interested in learning more about computer memory, visit the memory page at PCWebopedia located at http://www.pcwebopedia.com and search for these keywords: memory, EDO, SIMM, DRAM, SDRAM. Also, do not forget to read the Hardware-HOWTO.

Hard Drives

Hard drives connect to the rest of the system through a dedicated controller. There are two popular families of controllers that Linux can work with: ATA (all variants, including IDE, EIDE, Ultra ATA/33, and Ultra ATA/66) and SCSI (in many variations, including SCSI-1, SCSI-2, SCSI-3, and all the Fast, Wide, and Ultra versions of these). In general, if Linux supports the controller, and the disk works with the controller, then you will be okay. Only a few kinds of drives will not work. For more information, read the Hardware-HOWTO and check the Linux Hardware Database at http://lhd.datapower.com. Other documents worth reading are Hard-Disk-Upgrade, Large-Disk, and Ultra-DMA mini-HOWTOs.

Additional documents worth reading are the Root-RAID-HOWTO and the DPT-Hardware-RAID mini-HOWTO (they explain how to set up a RAID system under Linux). As for online resources, one of the best sources of information about hard disk drives is the ATA FAQ (ATA drives) located at http://members.aa.net/~obata/atafaq.htm. Also check out Gary Field's SCSI Info Central (SCSI drives) at http://www.scsifaq.org and the Storage Review site at http://www.storagereview.com.

CD-ROM Drives

Most of the CD-ROM drives with IDE or SCSI interfaces, or those that connect to the CD-ROM interface on a sound card, work under Linux. The Hardware-HOWTO lists both supported and unsupported CD-ROM drives, but don't worry if your drive is not listed as supported—there are so many of them that it is hard to keep this list current. If it is an IDE (or EIDE) or SCSI drive, then it should work under Linux. More information about CD-ROM drive support in Linux can be found in the CD-ROM-HOWTO. If you are looking for information about CD-ROM drives in general, visit the PCWebopedia located at http://www.pcwebopedia.com and search for CD-ROM.

Some CD-R and CD-RW drives are also supported for read and write operations, although the latter must be done with additional software (just like in Microsoft Windows or Apple Mac OS, but the software is free). Supported drives (IDE, EDIE, and SCSI) are listed in the Hardware-HOWTO, and information about hardware and software requirements for CD-R and CD-RW writing is given in the CD-Writing-HOWTO.

Kernel documentation can sometimes be of help as well; have a look inside the /docs/linux-2.2.13/cdrom/ directory on the Slackware Linux 7 CD-ROM (after you install the lx2213.tgz file from the k1 package set, you can find these files in the /usr/src/linux-2.2.13/Documentation/cdrom/ directory).

SCSI Cards

Most Linux users are quite happy with the speed of ordinary IDE and EIDE hard drives, but those who need top performance will want to use the SCSI interface cards to connect fast SCSI hard disks, CD-ROM/CD-RW/CD-R drives, tape streamers, or removable media. Also, if you want to use a scanner under Linux, it is best to use one with a SCSI interface, which currently has the best support.

Information about SCSI cards supported by Linux is given in the Hardware-HOWTO.

Additional information about SCSI cards can be obtained online at these addresses:

- **Gary Fields' SCSI Info Central.** http://www.scsifaq.org
- **Adaptec Home Page (Adaptec SCSI cards are among those supported under Linux).** http://www.adaptec.com
- **A Visual Guide to SCSI Connectors (pictures of various SCSI connectors).** http://www.scsita.org/Pictures.html

Video Cards

Video cards (or video adapters, as some people prefer to call them) are responsible for generating text and graphics on your monitor. Linux supports all VGA-type video cards in text mode (MDA, CGA, EGA, SVGA, and XGA should be okay as well). Things get complicated when you want to use the X graphical user interface. Then you must check if your card is supported by *XFree86*—the free implementation of the X Window System. In the case of *XFree86*, the most important information you must know is the name of the chipset that is used in a card—not the name of the card itself. This means that the video adapters integrated with motherboards should work as well. All chipsets supported in Linux have their own X servers (they are a special type of a video card driver).

Once you know the name of the chipset, you can check if an appropriate server exists in the *XFree86* documentation. You can find lists of supported chipsets in the xdoc.tgz archive in the X1 package set (after you install the xdoc.tgz archive on your computer, these documents are available in the /var/X11R6/lib/doc directory). Unfortunately, finding that the chipset driving your video card is supported under Linux does not automatically mean that your card works; this can only be checked by installing Linux. You can find necessary information in Chapter 5, "Configuring the X Window System." One typical problem that still sometimes prevents video cards from working under *XFree86* is non-linear addressing used in cheap cards. You can find more information about *XFree86* at http://www.xfree86.org.

The 3-D cards that have become so popular in recent years are also supported if their chipsets are supported. You can find lists of supported chipsets in the mesa.tgz archive in the X1 package set (after you install that archive on your computer, these documents will be available in the /usr/doc/Mesa-3.0/ directory). More information about Mesa software can be found at http://www.ssec.wisc.edu/~brianp/Mesa.html.

Another interesting development is the various combo video cards incorporating 2-D and 3-D graphics, teletext, TV tuners, radio tuners, TV/video signal recording, video phones, and Web cam interfaces in many different configurations. All these add-ons are usually supported by the Video4Linux software. Again, your card is considered compatible if the chipset it uses is supported by Video4Linux. Switching on support for that kind of video card is done through kernel reconfiguration and recompilation. More information about Video4Linux can be found in the /docs/linux-2.2.13/video4linux directory (or D:\DOCS\LINUX-2_.13\VIDEO4LI for Windows) on the Slackware Linux 7 CD-ROM that comes with this book and at the official Video4Linux page, http://roadrunner.swansea.uk.linux.org/v4l.shtml or http://www.metzlerbros.de/bttv.html.

Whatever kind of video card you want to use under Linux, remember that the monitor you connect it to must be at least as recent. You can't hook an old VGA monitor to a new video card, for example.

Additional information about video cards can be found in these documents:

- XFree86-HOWTO
- XFree86-Video-Timings-HOWTO
- XWindow-User-HOWTO
- 3Dfx-HOWTO
- Hardware-HOWTO

Sound Cards

Virtually all sound cards are compatible with Linux. In general, if you stick to Sound-Blaster or compatible cards, you will be okay although some chips on these cards are not supported (for example, the ASP chip on Sound Blaster 16 cars and the E-mu MIDI synthesizer chip on AWE32 boards). Other supported cards include Aztech, Gravis, and Logitech. Because sound support is implemented in the Linux kernel itself, it might be necessary to either reconfigure and recompile the kernel or just add sound support modules.

Although it does not seem natural at first, a video adapter is optional after you configure and install Slackware Linux 7 on a computer that acts as a server. Such computers are called *headless boxes*. The lack of a monitor or even a keyboard is not a big problem because you can manage such servers via a network connection from another computer.

More information about sound support in Linux can be found in the Hardware-HOWTO, Sound-HOWTO, and Sound-Playing-HOWTO documents.

Keyboards

There are no problems with any PC-compatible keyboards under Linux. When buying a new keyboard for your computer, just make sure you check that the keyboard plug matches the keyboard socket on the back of your computer (some manufacturers add necessary adapters at no additional cost).

Note that only a limited number of the latest USB keyboards are currently compatible under Linux. For more information about using keyboards under Linux, read the Keyboard-and-Console-HOWTO, XFree86-HOWTO, and XWindow-User-HOWTO documents.

Mice and Other Pointing Devices

Mice, 2-D digitizers, and joysticks are well supported under Linux, and you should not have any problems using any kind of mouse, joystick, or trackball currently available on the market. Configuration of these devices for text mode and X is explained in Chapters 3 and 5. You might also want to read the Hardware-HOWTO and Busmouse-HOWTO documents.

Modems

Modems are devices that brought inexpensive Internet access to hundreds of millions of households all over the world. They are relatively easy to install and use. Make sure you get one that supports the AT set of commands and the following communication and data compression protocols: Group 3, V.22bis, V.29, V32, V.32bis, V.34, V.42, V.42bis, and V.90 (some manufacturers label their products V.*everything* to indicate support of all protocols). Also, make sure you pick up an external modem—a lot of internal modems, especially cheap ones, do not work under Linux (they are known as Winmodems).

Linux does support fax and voice functions in modems if the right software is installed (mvm or vgetty for voice and hylafax, mgetty+fax, or efax for fax sending and reception).

More information can be found in the Hardware-HOWTO and the Modem-HOWTO or on the Web at http://www.linmodems.org and http://www.o2.net/~gromitkc/winmodem.html.

Cable Modems

Cable modems allow you to access the Internet via the popular cable networks. More information about cable modems that are compatible with Linux can be found at http://www.cablemodeminfo.com/linbasics.x.html-ssi.

ISDN Modems

ISDN modems are a combination of ordinary modems and ISDN adapters. They connect to your computer just like ordinary external modems, and you use standard modem software (not ISDN) to connect and send and receive data. See also the section about "ISDN Cards" later in this chapter.

> Please note that some ISPs, such as CompuServe and AOL, do not support Linux and force you to use their proprietary access software that runs only under Windows. You need an account at an ordinary ISP that supports Linux.

Network Cards

Because Slackware Linux 7 is a living, breathing networking system, it is not surprising that it can work with almost every network adapter imaginable. Those not supported are rather hard to find. To see if your card is supported, check the Hardware-HOWTO. If you cannot find your card there, check its documentation for information about compatibility with other cards and start from there. Network configuration is covered in Chapter 6, "Configuring Your Computer to Work on a Network."

Other Peripherals

There are many other peripheral devices that can be used under Linux. There is no space to describe all of them here, but the following pointers should help you find the necessary information.

Printers

Almost all printers are compatible under Linux. The only ones that need special treatment under Linux are Windows-only printers. These are usually very inexpensive because they do not contain some of the typical bits of hardware and software found in standard printers, leaving the computer to do the dirty work. The software that does this dirty work is available for Linux, but you are really better off buying a standard printer. More information about printing under Linux can be found in the Printing-HOWTO and Printing-Usage-HOWTO documents.

Scanners

Scanner support under Linux used to be rather poor, but it is improving at a fast pace, thanks to the team behind the SANE scanner driver project (visit its home page at http://www.mostang.com/sane). As a general rule, you are able to use your scanner if it is a SCSI device. This means that the scanner must be attached to a SCSI card supported by Linux. Some scanners come with cut-down versions of SCSI cards that can only work with one device. If you know which SCSI card it was cut down from, you might be able to persuade Linux to talk to your card. Otherwise, buy an additional SCSI card (this is a good investment anyway).

Uninterruptible Power Supplies

Power outages and other power failures are extremely dangerous to any multitasking system; I advise everyone to buy at least a dumb UPS for workstation use or a smart UPS for server use. A dumb UPS warns you about power outages and keeps supplying the power to the computer for a few minutes, whereas a smart UPS can shut down the system without human intervention. More information about configuring a UPS and the smart models that work best under Linux can be found in the UPS-HOWTO document.

PCMCIA Cards

PCMCIA cards found on many laptop computers are supported as long as their manufacturers supply information necessary to write Linux drivers. For a list of currently supported PCMCIA cards and tips on PCMCIA driver configuration, see the Hardware-HOWTO, or check out http://pcmcia.sourceforge.org and http://pcmcia.sourceforge.org/ftp/SUPPORTED.CARDS.

If you cannot find your card on the list, do not despair—your card might use the chipset of one of the supported cards. Also, you might have to try a few drivers to see if they might work. A search on the manufacturer's site for the Linux keyword might help as well.

USB Devices

USB support in Linux is a new thing, and not a lot of drivers exist for various USB devices yet. However, development is continuing for various digital audio devices, cameras, MIDI devices, hubs, keyboards, mice, printers, interface converters, scanners, and many other kinds of devices. For now, it is better to choose similar devices that do not use the USB interface. More information can be found at http://www.linux-usb.org.

IrDA Devices

Infrared communications devices are usually found on laptops, palmtops, and other portable devices like cell phones, as well as on some printers. They allow fast communication without cables, and are really useful to people who are constantly on the move. In general, if you can install and run Linux on a laptop equipped with an IrDA port, you can use that port without problems after enabling it by configuring the kernel (see Chapter 8 "Recompiling the Kernel" for more information). To find out which other IrDA devices are compatible under Linux, check out the Linux IrDA project page at http://www.cs.uit.no/linux-irda. You can find more information about IrDA protocol support in Linux in the Hardware-HOWTO and IR-HOWTO documents.

Parallel Interface Devices

Parallel interface is most often used to connect printers, but there is no reason it cannot be used to communicate with other kinds of devices, such as the popular parallel port version of the Iomega Zip removable disk drive. Information about parallel port devices that work under Linux can be found in the Hardware-HOWTO and at http://www.torque.net/parport.

PalmPilot

The famous USRobotics/3Com PalmPilot personal organizer is very well supported on Linux. You can find software to exchange and edit data stored in your PalmPilot, or if you want, you can write your own software for PalmPilot. That software is not included in the Slackware Linux 7 distribution, but you can easily download and install it at a later date after you install your basic Slackware Linux 7 configuration.

The PalmOS-HOWTO contains detailed information about downloading and installing PalmPilot productivity and development software.

Zip, Jaz, and LS Removable Media Drives

All kinds of Zip, Jaz, and LS drives using IDE or SCSI interfaces are currently supported under Linux. Some parallel port devices work, too (see the "Parallel Interface Devices" section earlier in this chapter). Also, you can look for information about Iomega Zip and Jaz drives in the Zip-Drive and Jaz-Drive mini-HOWTOs.

Tape Streamers

Tape streamers are used for making backup copies of data on magnetic tapes. Because they are considered to be one of the most essential groups of hardware products for Linux, there are only a few that are not supported. Most popular streamers connecting through the IDE or SCSI interface are supported. Also, some of the streamers connecting through the parallel port are supported.

More information about these devices can be found in the Hardware-HOWTO and Ftape-HOWTO. Additional sources of information about tape streamers of al kinds can be found at http://www.seagate.com/support/tape/scsiide/sublinks/tape_frequently_asked_questions.shtml.

Smart Card Readers and Writers

Smart card readers and writers could work under Linux, but they need appropriate drivers. The efforts to port smart card development tools and hardware drivers to Linux are coordinated by the members of the MUSCLE Smart Card Developers Project. See the project's home page at http://www.linuxnet.com/smartcard/index.html.

FM Radio Tuner Cards

I mentioned that FM radio tuners can be integrated with sound or TV cards (including mixed video/TV/radio cards), but they can also be purchased as standalone cards. Again, it is irrelevant who manufactures the radio card you want to use under Linux as long as Linux supports that radio chip. For more information, visit the Video4Linux home page located at http://roadrunner.swansea.uk.linux.org/v4l.shtml.

ISDN Cards

ISDN adapters are another type of communication device that are becoming popular because they can send data at higher speeds, and it takes them less time to connect to the networks. Linux drivers for many of these cards are already available. You can find more information about ISDN support in Linux in the Hardware-HOWTO and at http://www.muc.de/~hm/linux/linux-isdn.html.

Digital Cameras

Digital cameras can be supported through many interfaces; finding out which devices are supported requires more detective work. Check the Video4Linux documents and links mentioned in the "Video Cards" section, along with the documents and links mentioned in the "USB Devices" and "Scanners" sections in this chapter.

2-D Digitizers (Wacom)

Support for 2-D digitizers from Wacom and other manufacturers is included in XFree86, and you should have no problems using them under Linux. There might not yet be many programs available that can use all the features of your 2-D digitizer, but that should change soon.

Multifunction (Printer, Scanner, Fax, and Modem)

These devices combine many functions in one box. Most of them are targeted at Microsoft Windows users, and the software drivers are available almost exclusively for that system. Some functions, such as printing, might work under Linux, but scanning probably will not. This situation might change in the future, but no hard facts are available yet.

Amateur Radio Transceivers

Linux is the only operating system to support the AX.25 packet radio protocol that allows TCP/IP networking using radio waves. Although I am not aware of any amateur radio transceivers on a card that could be installed inside a computer, you can find a full range of such devices that connect to the parallel (printer) or serial (the same that you usually connect a modem to) port on your computer. They are available from many well-known manufacturers such as Yaesu and others. The best place to start looking for information about the AX.25 protocol and all matters related to AX.25 support in Linux is the AX25-HOWTO. Also, check this site for links to all sorts of amateur radio information: http://www.meaning.com/pointers/wwwvl-ham.html.

3-D Digitizers, Virtual Reality Devices (Gloves, Body Suits, and Motion Trackers)

These devices are used to read three-dimensional coordinates of points on surfaces of human bodies and other physical objects. The software that reads and processes data collected by such devices has almost always been written for UNIX workstations; therefore, Linux is a natural platform for these applications. At the time of writing, I could find no freely available software for Linux, but if you are interested in using 3-D hardware under Linux, you should get in touch with the manufacturers. Also, if you want to write the software yourself, you might want to check the manufacturers' Web sites—they often publish necessary specifications and sample software on their Web sites. If you are interested in learning more about these devices and want to get in touch with these companies, try these addresses:

- **Ascension Technology Corporation.** http://www.ascension-tech.com
- **Cyberware.** http://www.cyberware.com

- **Faro.** http://www.faro.com
- **Immersion Corporation.** http://www.immerse.com
- **Polhemus.** http://www.polhemus.com
- **X-ist Realtime Technologies.** http://www.x-ist.de

Lego Mindstorm Robots

These educational toys from Lego are currently not supported under Linux, but judging by their popularity, it is probably only a matter of time before someone ports necessary software to Linux.

Further Info

What if you are still not sure if your hardware is compatible with Slackware Linux 7? Try zipslack or bigslack! You can unzip the zipslack distribution on a Zip disk or a DOS partition and run it from there without making any changes to your current system. If Slackware runs without problems from a Zip disk or a DOS partition, you can safely assume that it will run okay after you perform a full installation. The bigslack distribution is similar to zipslack, but contains more packages and must be copied to a hard disk with a few hundred megabytes of free space.

If you can't find information about a particular piece of hardware at addresses mentioned in this chapter, try looking for it in different places on the Internet. Popular search engines should be the first resource you turn to. I usually use the following search engines:

- http://www.yahoo.com
- http://www.google.com
- http://www.excite.com
- http://www.hotbot.com
- http://www.lycos.com

Also, if you know the name of the manufacturer of a particular component or the chipsets used in that component, try typing it into the URL field of your Web browser. For example, typing **http://www.ibm.com** takes you to the IBM Web site. This simple trick can save you a lot of time.

If your searches fail, try asking for help on one of the following Usenet newsgroups:

- alt.os.linux.slackware
- comp.os.linux.hardware
- comp.os.linux.setup
- comp.os.linux.answers
- comp.os.linux.announcements

You might also try posting your questions on one of the Linux mailing lists. The linux-newbie list on http://vger.rutgers.edu seems to be one of the best places to ask such questions. To subscribe to this list, send a message with the words "subscribe linux-newbie" in the body of the message to majordomo@vger.rutgers.edu, leaving the subject field empty, and wait for the confirmation of your subscription, which is sent to your mailbox. It might take a while. Always be polite and thank the people who help you; they do it for free. When you are no longer interested in subscribing to this list, send a message with the words "unsubscribe linux-newbie" to majordomo@vger.rutgers.edu, and the messages will stop arriving in your mailbox shortly after.

Other obvious sources of information are the manufacturers themselves and the people who sold you the hardware you are trying to learn more about.

Other Considerations: What to Do When Your Hardware Isn't Compatible

If one of the hardware components is incompatible with Slackware Linux 7, you have two choices: Look for Linux kernel patches that remove incompatibilities, or change the offending component. You might also have to wait a few months until a support for it is added. Alternatively, you could trade it with a Microsoft Windows user. The last resource could be to list it on eBay.

Summary

Slackware Linux 7 runs on any Intel microprocessor from 386 to the latest Pentium chips and can support more than one processor. Most of the popular standard external devices work under Slackware Linux 7 without problems. Quite a lot of nonstandard devices work as well. Make sure to collect as much information about your hardware as possible; this can save you a lot of time later. In a majority of cases, if your computer worked under other operating systems and meets the basic hardware requirements for Slackware, you should be able to install at least the basic system. When you have doubts about compatibility and do not want to proceed with full installation, use the zipslack or bigslack distributions to see if your computer cooperates with Slackware Linux 7.

Chapter 2: Partitioning Your Hard Drive

Jacek Artymiak

What Is Partitioning and Why Do You Do It?

The Linux Filesystem

Partitioning Strategies

Using FDISK.EXE to Partition a Hard Drive

Using fdisk to Partition a Hard Drive

Troubleshooting

Every operating system has its own unique way of organizing data on a hard drive. Slackware Linux 7 (and Linux in general) is no exception; it requires you to prepare the hard drive on which you choose to install it according to its expectations. Doing so is not very difficult, and anyone who follows the directions in this chapter can perform the necessary steps without breaking anything. By the way, if you think that other operating systems are easier to install, think again—in the majority of cases, you are either buying them already installed, or the hard drives are preformatted in the way that the operating system bundled with your computer expects it. That is why it seems so easy to install MS Windows. Do not worry! In this chapter, you learn not only how to install Linux on a hard drive previously "held hostage" by Microsoft, but you also learn how to install Linux so it happily coexists on the same drive with Windows!

This chapter consists of two parts. The first teaches you how to use different tools to make space for Linux on your existing Windows (or other) system. The second part—the actual creation of the Linux partitions—must be done during the installation of Linux. So you refer back to the second half of this chapter later.

Preparing a hard drive for installing a new operating system almost always involves partitioning the drive. I discuss partitioning in the next section.

What Is Partitioning and Why Do You Do It?

As you probably already know, once you install an operating system on your hard drive, it can be divided into directories (or folders, as some prefer to call them). These are used to organize data. For example, system files go into one directory, your own programs go into another, and yet another directory is used to store the files you create (wordprocessing documents, spreadsheets, databases, images of your family, and so on).

Dividing your hard drive into smaller pieces with directories is easy and flexible, but not very secure if your data resides on the same drive as your system and other applications. Why? Every operating system sets aside a special region on the hard disk for a table that holds the information about the location of each file stored on the disk. If a program wipes out this table, or if it damages a part of it, the system does not know where your files are located. In addition, when you install a new program, there is always the danger that it might erase or modify some files without asking for your permission. Of course, there are special tools that try to recover lost files, but they rarely recover all files.

A good way to solve this problem is to place system files and your own files on separate drives. This might not necessarily protect your data against all the above-mentioned hazards, but at least your own files are safe if the system drive's file location information is destroyed. (Of course, the opposite may occur, leaving your system files safe but destroying your personal files; this is why it is important to make regular backups, but I talk about that later.)

This is all very well, but what if you cannot afford to buy an additional hard drive, or what if there is no space left inside the computer for another drive? In that case, you can partition the drive, divide it into a series of smaller logical drives by adding entries to another table that stores the list of all partitions created on that drive. By a widely respected convention, operating systems usually cannot modify that table directly and do not allow other programs to modify it. Each partition is seen by the system as a separate drive, and all programs see them as such because they get all information about disks, directories, and files directly from the operating system itself. Therefore, if one partition is damaged, others are not—even if they reside on the same physical drive. Unlike directories, there are limits to how many partitions you can create, but that is rarely a problem.

> You can think of directories as name tags attached to each file, whereas partitions are more like reinforced concrete shelters. Even when a bomb destroys one, the others are likely to survive without damage.

Linux needs at least two partitions: one for its filesystem (that is the name by which experienced Linux users call any systematic way of arranging files on a hard drive or a floppy drive), and the other to store data and programs temporarily moved from the computer's memory to the hard drive to make room for additional programs or data when they all do not fit into the physical memory installed in your computer. That second partition is called the swap partition and is invisible to your programs (which is a good thing). One particularly interesting feature of Linux is that every directory in the Linux filesystem can be located on a different partition, which is often used to add more storage as the number of users on a system and their space requirements grow. I return to that subject in a while, but for now I want to talk about the tools necessary to partition your drive so it can be used under Linux.

What You Need to Partition the Hard Drive

Before you begin partitioning your hard drive, make sure you have the following tools. (If you are installing a Linux-only system, with no regard to any operating system or data already on your hard drive, you only need the Slackware CD-ROM. You do not need to do any of this preparation.)

- **SCANDISK.EXE**. This is a standard MS-DOS/MS Windows utility for checking hard drives for errors.

- **FDISK.EXE**. This is a standard MS-DOS/MS Windows hard drive partitioning utility sold with every copy of the MS-DOS or MS Windows operating systems. This is the simplest (as in not very smart) partitioning tool, but it works and is quite dependable.

- **fdisk or cfdisk**. These are Linux equivalents of FDISK.EXE.

- **FIPS.EXE or Partition Magic**. These drive-partitioning utilities can resize existing partitions to make room for the Linux filesystem without danger of data loss (there is still danger of losing data, but much less than in case of FDISK.EXE and fdisk, which destroy all data stored in partitions on which they operate). Make sure you unpack the FIPS20.ZIP archive into one of the directories on your hard drive before you start the rest of the preparations for repartitioning. The FIPS utility can be downloaded from http://www.igd.fhg.de/~aschaefe/fips/.

- **Backup software**. If you are using Microsoft Windows, make sure you install the Microsoft Backup utility or any other backup utility you might prefer. Microsoft Backup can create backup copies of your data and applications on floppy disks, tapes, and other media. If you are using other operating systems, you need to find an appropriate backup utility for your operating system.

- **Backup media**. You need floppy disks, Zip drives, Jaz drives, tape drives, or another hard disk.

- **Original copies of software**. You need original versions of your operating system, drivers, service packs, and applications (in the form of floppy disks, CD-ROM discs, or other media) to reinstall software in case you lose data during partitioning.

- **Registration keys**. You need these to reinstall the software. They are usually printed on separate cards or on labels on floppies or CD-ROMs.

- **Software installation documentation**. It is always a good idea to keep various installation guides and manuals handy, even if the installation is relatively simple.

Once you have these tools, you should check the disk, clean it up, defragment, and make backup copies of all data, even if you are planning to use FIPS.EXE or Partition

Magic, both of which try very hard to preserve your data. I am going to focus on tools available for MS-DOS/Microsoft Windows; other operating systems usually have their equivalents.

Checking Your Disk for Errors

Before you start making any modifications to hard drives, check them for errors with ScanDisk. You can run it from the MS-DOS command line. Just type **SCAN-DISK.EXE** and press Enter. Alternatively, choose Start, Programs, Accessories, System Tools, ScanDisk. You should see a window similar to the one shown in Figure 2.1.

If there are errors, ScanDisk describes them and gives you a chance to fix them. You can find necessary information about using ScanDisk and interpreting its messages in the Microsoft Windows Help. Once you are done with ScanDisk, you can begin cleaning up the disk.

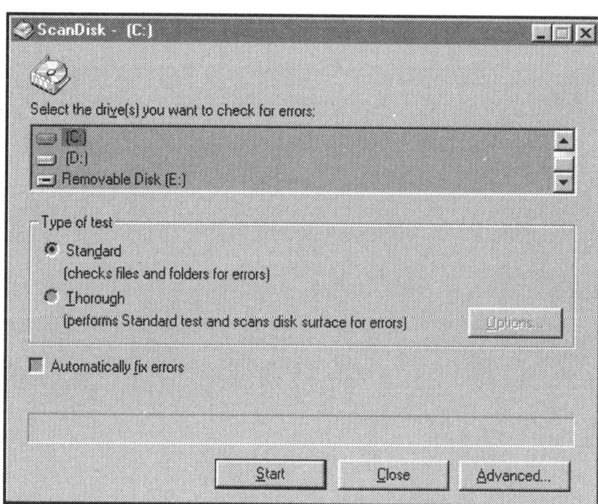

Figure 2.1 *The Microsoft Windows ScanDisk utility is used to check for low-level disk errors.*

Cleaning Up Your Disk

The second step before partitioning your disk is cleaning it up. You would be surprised how much digital grime fills your hard drive after a few months of mild use—temporary files, backups of files you were working on, ScanDisk reports, and megabytes of data gathered in cache directories during Web surfing. Cleaning out such files is only necessary if you don't think you have enough free space to install Linux otherwise, but it's not a bad idea, regardless.

No tool can replace a human being in this job, but you can make your job easier under Microsoft Windows 98 with the Disk Cleanup tool. To activate it, choose Start, Programs, Accessories, System Tools, Disk Cleanup. You ought to see a window similar to the one shown in Figure 2.2.

You can find more information about this tool in the Microsoft Windows Help system. Files not removed by Disk Cleanup must be removed by hand; select them and press the Delete key. Empty the Trash afterwards. Once you are done cleaning up the hard drive, you should back up your important files.

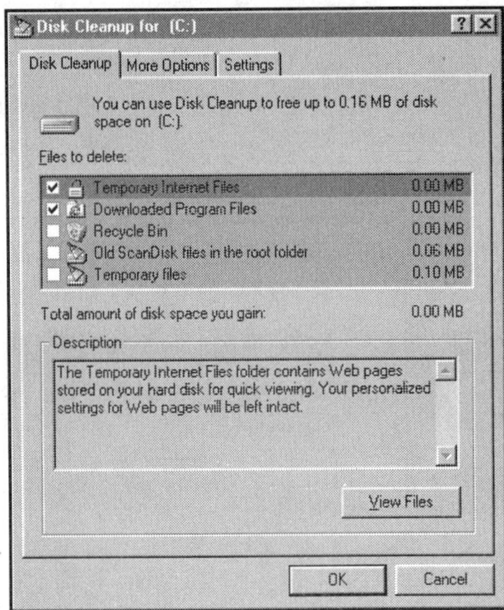

Figure 2.2 *The Microsoft Windows Disk Cleanup utility is used to remove unwanted files.*

Backing Up Your Data

Creating backup copies of data is one of the least exciting jobs you can do, but it is very important. Without it, you risk losing a lot of time, money, and the results of your hard work. So instead of dismissing it as boring, just do it.

The first thing you need to think of before you start making backups is what really needs to be backed up and what can be restored from original media. In most cases, you can restore the system and various applications from floppy disks and CD-ROMs. That leaves you to decide which files created by you have to be backed up.

> You might need to back up the whole contents of the drive if the vendor who sold you the computer already installed the operating system and applications on the hard drive but did not give you copies of that software on a CD-ROM or on floppy disks.

Obviously, that includes all files created with applications such as word processors, spreadsheets, imaging tools, databases, and so on, as well as Web links and address books. Even network connection settings need to be copied so you can re-create them quickly later. If you used a limited number of applications, finding appropriate files is not a problem. In most cases, you need to make copies of the following files and directories:

- **The My Documents directory and its subdirectories**. This is the place where most of your documents, images, and other files (usually) reside.

- **Messages and address books from Microsoft Outlook**. Use the File, Export menu to make copies of your mail messages, address book, appointments, and other important data.

- **Favorites**. These are links stored inside the C:\WINDOWS\FAVORITES directory.

- **Any additional files located outside the My Documents folder**.

To save space, compress data before making backup copies. This can easily decrease the size of the files by half.

The next step is choosing the right backup media. At present, you have the following options:

- **Floppy disks**. Use them only if you must, and for archives that do not exceed 20MB (that is about 15 floppy disks, about the limit that any sane person can bear). Always remember to buy one extra pack of floppies in case one of them fails. To save time, buy preformatted floppies.

- **Zip or LS-120 disks**. These can handle 100MB (old Zip), 120MB (LS-120), or 250MB (new Zip) of data, which should be enough for most home or office users. Drives are available in internal and external configurations. External is better if you want to move data between computers.

- **CD-R, CD-RW discs**. These can store up to 640MB of data. The disadvantage of CD-R drives is that they can only be written to, but the prices of CD-R media are currently very low. The majority of these drives are internal devices, but there are some external ones as well.

- **Optical disks**. Several models can store from 200MB to a few gigabytes of data on a single disk. Both internal and external versions are available.

- **Jaz cartridges**. These can store between 1GB and 2GB of data (depending on which version you buy). Both internal and external versions are available.

- **Tape drives**. These beauties can store between hundreds of megabytes and dozens of gigabytes of data—probably overkill for home or office use, but an excellent choice for network servers.

- **DVD-RAM discs**. Relatively new and expensive, these discs can store a few gigabytes of data.

- **Another hard drive**. This is an option if you have another hard drive that you do not want to repartition.

- **Network or Internet**. Do this if you have a fast connection to the Internet or if you are on a network and there is enough space to store your data files. This is practical for a few dozen megabytes of data.

Whatever backup medium you choose, make sure you buy the appropriate backup software for it or make sure it works with Microsoft Backup (see Figure 2.3), a standard backup utility that comes with every copy of Windows 95 and 98 (choose Start, Programs, Accessories, System Tools, Backup). If you cannot find Microsoft Backup on your hard drive, install it from the Microsoft Windows 95 or 98 CD-ROM.

The last step in preparing for repartitioning is to defragment your disk.

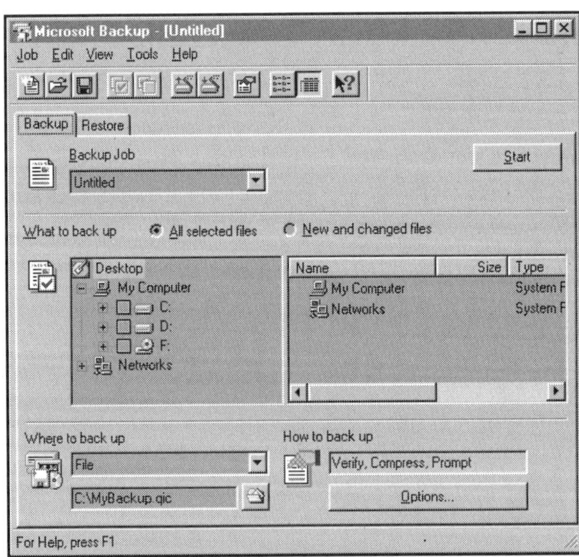

Figure 2.3 *Microsoft Backup is good enough in most cases.*

Defragmenting Your Disk

Defragmenting is used to reorganize files within a partition so all of their parts reside next to each other instead of being scattered all over the place. This is important because partitions must be continuous regions of a disk. Therefore, even if you free up a lot of space on the disk, it might not be fit for repartitioning if even a few kilobytes of data are saved near the end of the disk. Defragmenting the disk moves files so they are near the beginning of the disk, freeing up space at the end that can be used by a second partition.

Microsoft Windows comes with a tool called Disk Defragmenter, which does the job quite nicely. To start it, choose Start, Programs, Accessories, System Tools, Disk Defragmenter. You should see a window like the one shown in Figure 2.4. Simply follow the onscreen instructions, or search for additional information in Microsoft Windows Help.

Once you have completed all the steps above, take a break and learn a few rudimentary things about the Linux filesystem.

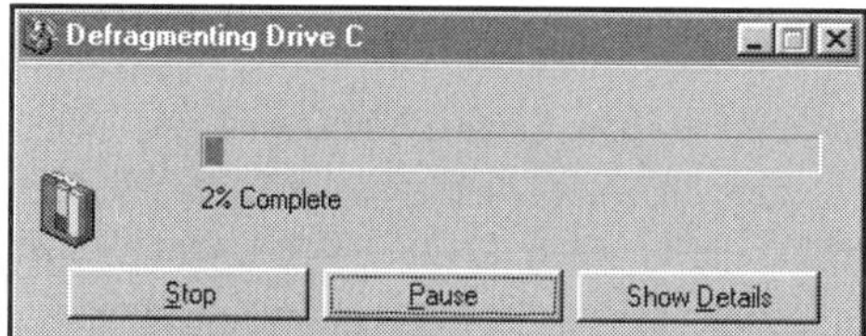

Figure 2.4 *The Microsoft Windows Disk Defragmenter utility is used to remove unwanted files.*

The Linux Filesystem

The Linux filesystem, known as ext2, has a classic UNIX-like structure of a tree with one root (the / directory) and many branches arranged as shown in Figure 2.5.

When you want to point a program to a particular file, simply give it its full access path. For example, the notation /usr points to the file or directory named usr stored in the root (/) directory. Likewise, /usr/bin points to the file or directory called bin stored in the directory named usr, which is in turn stored in the root directory. As you can see, the slash (/) symbol, when it does not appear at the very beginning of an access path, is used to separate directories.

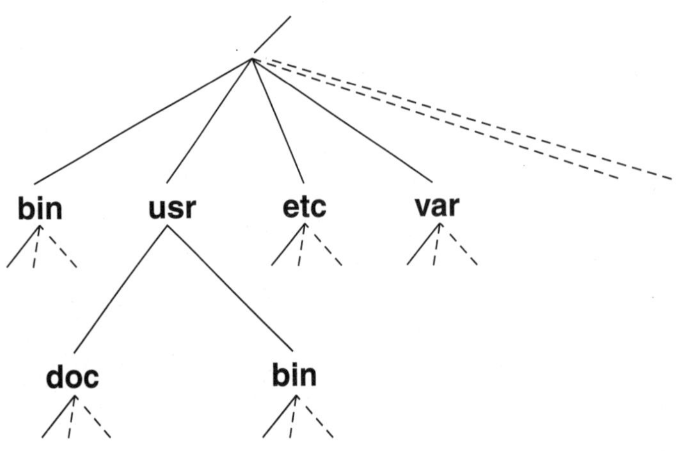

Figure 2.5 *The structure of the Linux filesystem*

Ext2 versus FAT 16/FAT 32

The ext2 filesystem is incompatible with the FAT12, FAT16, and FAT32 filesystems used by MS-DOS and Microsoft Windows, which means that once you install ext2 on its separate partition, that partition is not visible from DOS, Windows, or any other operating system (besides Linux, of course). This is good for data protection, but not so good for data sharing. Fortunately, you can mount foreign partitions under Linux as directories (but you cannot mount Linux partitions under MS Windows or MS-DOS, which is probably a good thing anyway). For example, you can create a directory called /mnt/c and use the *mount* command to make drive C available under Linux. (This is explained in Chapters 3, "Installing Slackware," and 4, "After the Installation.")

Single Partition versus Multiple Partitions

If you have been using popular Microsoft-made operating systems, you might have not heard of multiple partitions on a single drive because usually every fixed drive has only one primary partition. This is a deliberate design feature to simplify installation of these systems, but it results in less data safety, something that is very important under Linux. It also severely limits the filesystem expansion possibilities.

Partitions can be either primary or extended, but there can only be four primary partitions on any single physical hard drive. There are no such limits on the number of extended partitions.

Now that you know that Linux needs more than one partition, you can consider some partitioning scenarios:

- Partitioning a single drive
- Partitioning large drives
- Partitioning multiple drives

Partitioning a Single Drive

The vast majority of people installing Slackware Linux 7 have computers equipped with a single hard disk drive; it must be large enough to cope with the demands of the existing system (usually Microsoft Windows 98) and Linux. You can safely assume that you need between 1GB and 2GB of space for Microsoft Windows and Microsoft Office and about 1GB of free space to install and comfortably use Linux. Therefore, you need a disk with at least 3GB of space (you might get away with 2GB, but the comfort of work is not the same). As I mentioned before, your FAT partitions are visible under Linux and you can read and write to them freely. On the other hand, Microsoft Windows and MS-DOS do not see your Linux partitions.

Of course, if you plan to get rid of other operating systems and install only Linux, you can do this on a smaller disk. One with only 500MB of total space works, but 1GB gives you more elbowroom.

Partitioning Large Drives

Large drives with capacity over 6GB are becoming a standard. Although modern operating systems can use all of their capacity, it is still a good idea to partition them into smaller chunks, even if you are planning to install only one operating system.

Partitioning Multiple Drives

If your computer has more than one hard drive, you have more freedom. It does not matter on which drive you are installing Linux, as long as there is enough space.

Partitioning Strategies

As I mentioned, there are a few partitioning strategies that you can follow, depending on how much you need to use another operating system. I discuss them now, starting with the easiest solution.

Partitioning for a Linux-Only System

This is the only advisable option if you want to use your computer as a server. You need to delete all partitions on a hard drive and create two (or more) partitions for Linux. One partition must be used to store the Linux filesystem; the other must be a swap partition. You can create even more partitions so that users have their accounts stored on a separate partition, and you can have more than one swap partition.

Partitioning for a Dual-Boot System

If you want to use two operating systems on the same hard drive, you need to divide it into three or more partitions: one for the old operating system, one for the Linux ext2 filesystem, and one for use as virtual memory (the swap partition). For disks already used by the MS-DOS/Microsoft Windows operating systems, you can use the FIPS.EXE utility or a commercial tool, such as Partition Magic, to make room for the Linux partitions.

Using Fips to Resize MS-DOS/Windows Partitions

Once you finish cleaning up and repartitioning the hard drive, and only after you have made backup copies of all important data, you can try to split your existing MS-DOS/Microsoft Windows partition into smaller ones. To make sure that everything goes smoothly, follow these steps:

1. Insert one clean 1.44MB floppy disk into the floppy disk drive.

2. Switch to MS-DOS mode—in Windows 98, choose Start, Programs, MS-DOS, or shut down the system and tell it to go into MS-DOS mode.

If you do not own a copy of MS-DOS or Microsoft Windows, you must repartition your hard drive from under Linux using *cfdisk* (it is a more user-friendly version of *fdisk*).

Additional information about partitioning hard disks can be found in the Linux Partition HOWTO located in the D:\docs\Linux-mini-HOWTO\ Partition file.

3. Type **format a:** /s. This makes the floppy disk bootable.

4. Copy files /FIPS.EXE, /RESTORRB.EXE, and /ERRORS.TXT from the FIPS directory (I mentioned that in the section "What You Need to Partition the Hard Drive" earlier in this chapter).

5. Press Ctrl+Alt+Del to reboot the computer.

6. Type **FIPS**, press the Enter key, and wait for a welcome message (shown below):

```
FIPS version 2.0. Copyright (C) 1993/94 Arno Schaefer
    FAT32 Support Copyright (C) 1997 Gordon Chaffee


DO NOT use FIPS in a multitasking environment like Windows, OS/2, Desqview,
Novell Task Manager or the Linux DOS emulator: boot from a DOS boot disk
first.


If you use OS/2 or a disk compressor, read the relevant sections in FIPS.DOC.


FIPS comes with ABSOLUTELY NO WARRANTY, see file COPYING for details
This is free software, and you are welcome to redistribute it
under certain conditions: again see file COPYING for details.


Press any Key
```

7. Press any key. FIPS.EXE displays the partition table shown below (the numbers are different in your case). If you see a message about no free partitions, you must use FDISK.EXE to delete some of them (see the "Using Fdisk to Partition a Hard Drive" section later in this chapter).

```
        |    |         Start         |    |         End        | Start  |
Number of| Part.|bootable|Head Cyl. Sector|System|Head Cyl. Sector|
Sector |Sectors  |  MB
—-+——+———+———+——+————+——-+—
1 | yes  |   0    0    1|  06h|   31   825    63|    63|   1665153|3815
2    no  |   0    0    0|  00h|    0    0     0|     0|     0|     0
3    no  |   0    0    0  00h|    0    0     0|     0|     0|     0
4    no  |   0    0    0|  00h|    0    0     0|     0|     0|     0
Checking root sector ... OK
Press any key
```

8. Press any key; you should see a long list of parameters (shown below), which are important only if you are interested in technical details:

```
Bytes per sector: 512
Sectors per cluster: 8
Reserved sectors: 1
Number of FATs: 2
Number of rootdirectory entries: 512
Number of sectors (short): 0
```

```
Media descriptor byte: f8h
Sectors per FAT: 145
Sectors per track: 63
Drive heads: 16
Hidden sectors: 63
Number of sectors (long): 141057
Physical drive number: 80h
Signature: 29h
```

9. FIPS.EXE runs additional checks on your hard drive, and if the results are positive, you should see these messages:

```
Checking root sector ... OK
Checking FAT ... OK
Searching for free space ... OK
```

10. If all goes well, you should be able to resize the partition.

```
Enter start cylinder for new partition (713-825):
Use the cursor keys to choose the cylinder, <enter> to continue
Old partition              Cylinders              New Partition
   705.8 MB                   717                    107.3 MB
```

11. Use the left and right cursor keys to change the size of a new partition. When you are happy with the results, press the Enter key.

12. FIPS.EXE asks if you want to save the old disk structure to a floppy drive—answer yes (you can recover the old disk structure using RESTORRB.EXE if anything goes wrong) and let FIPS.EXE modify your drive. Once it is finished, reboot the computer by pressing Ctrl+Alt+Del and run ScanDisk on your old partition to make sure it is okay.

13. You can later split the new partition (one for the Linux filesystem and one for swap) with Linux *fdisk*, or you can create another partition (the swap partition) using FIPS.EXE. Simply repeat the whole procedure, beginning with step 5.

For more information about FIPS.EXE, read the /FIPS.DOC file in the FIPS20.zip archive.

Partition Magic/Partition Commander

If you are not too happy with the basic functionality of FIPS.EXE, you might want try one of the commercial tools like Partition Magic or Partition Commander, or a low-cost Partition Manager. For more information, visit these Web sites:

- **Partition Magic.** http://www.powerquest.com
- **Partition Commander.** http://www.v-com.com
- **Partition Manager.** http://www.users.intercom.com/~ranish/part/VRH

Using an Existing MS-DOS Filesystem

If you do not want to make the commitment of repartitioning so that you can install Linux on your hard drive, you can use a special UMS-DOS filesystem that piggybacks on an existing MS-DOS filesystem. This results in slightly slower performance than repartitioning and using the native Linux ext2 filesystem, but it's a low-risk way to try Linux.

UMS-DOS: Running Linux on FAT Filesystems

To run Linux on FAT filesystems, you need to use the UMS-DOS filesystem, which is a replacement for the traditional Linux ext2 filesystem. This requires the use of a special kernel during installation (to learn how it is done, see Chapter 3). The UMS-DOS filesystem is a quite robust filesystem, but I do not advise that you use it for anything but the simplest tasks, such as learning the system, commands, and command-line applications. It is great for demonstration purposes, but if you are thinking of using Linux for serious purposes, install it on a separate partition.

When you install Linux on an MS-DOS partition, its entire filesystem is exposed to MS-DOS or Microsoft Windows, and you can read files that belong to the UMS-DOS filesystem directly. You can also write to those files or delete them, both of which are dangerous things to do, because they can corrupt the Linux installation.

Using FDISK.EXE to Partition a Hard Drive

When you do not want to use FIPS.EXE or you want to erase all existing partitions from your disk and start from scratch, you can repartition your hard drive using FDISK.EXE. Remember to always boot into MS-DOS (not the MS-DOS window under Microsoft Windows) before running it.

FDISK.EXE cannot create more than one primary partition, so it should be used only to remove old partitions from a hard drive or to create the first primary partition for MS-DOS or Microsoft Windows in a dual-boot configuration. The remaining space on disk is configured under Linux during system installation.

Displaying Partitions

To display the partition information about your hard drive, follow these steps:

1. Type **FDISK** and press the Enter key. You should see the FDISK Options menu, similar to the one shown in Figure 2.6. (If you see a long message explaining the advantages of converting your disk into a more efficient file allocation table system, type **N** for now. You can always do this later.)

2. Type **4** to display the partition table; you should see a table similar to the one shown in Figure 2.7. If you have any logical drives defined on your system, you might see them as well (see Figure 2.8).

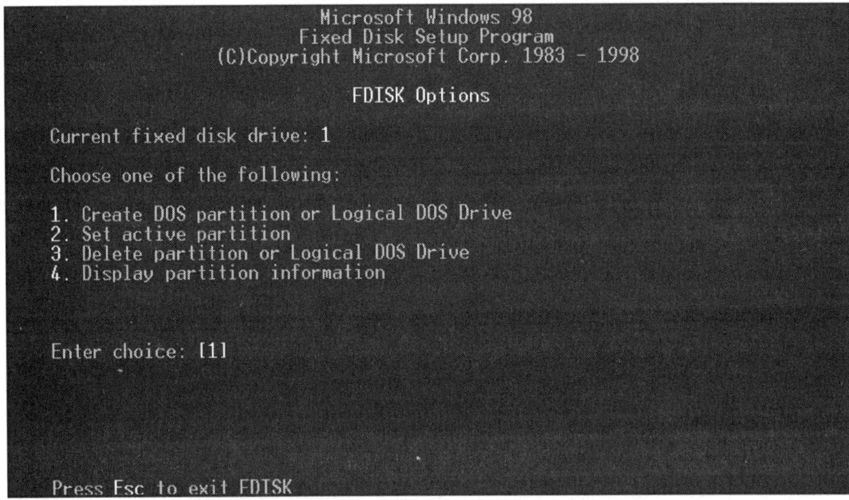

Figure 2.6 *The FDISK.EXE main menu*

```
                    Display Partition Information

Current fixed disk drive: 1

Partition  Status   Type    Volume Label   Mbytes   System   Usage
C: 1         A     PRI DOS                  1028     FAT16  *  27%
   2               EXT DOS                   803              21%
   3               Non-DOS                  1803             47%
   4               Non-DOS                   181              5%

Total disk space is  3815 Mbytes (1 Mbyte = 1048576 bytes)


The Extended DOS Partition contains Logical DOS Drives.
Do you want to display the logical drive information (Y/N)......?[Y]




Press Esc to return to FDISK Options
```

Figure 2.7 *Your drive's partition table*

```
                 Display Logical DOS Drive Information

Drv Volume Label   Mbytes  System   Usage
D:                   803   FAT16    100%






Total Extended DOS Partition size is   803 Mbytes (1 MByte = 1048576 bytes)




Press Esc to continue
```

Figure 2.8 *Logical drives*

Deleting Partitions

To delete a partition using FDISK.EXE, follow these steps:

1. Start FDISK.EXE from a DOS prompt.

2. Type **3** in the FDISK Options menu.

3. Choose **1** from the Delete DOS Partition or Logical DOS Drive (see Figure 2.9) if your disk has only one partition. If it has more partitions, choose the appropriate option.

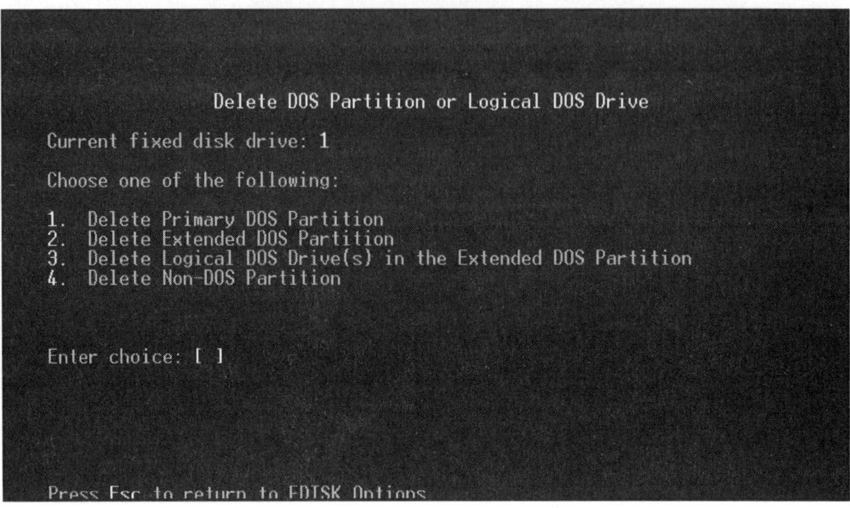

Figure 2.9 *The FDISK.EXE Delete DOS Partition or Logical DOS Drive*

4. Follow instructions displayed onscreen. You are asked to confirm changes to avoid the accidental removal of the selected partition.

5. Press Esc several times to return to the main menu and reboot your computer by pressing Ctrl+Alt+Del.

> If you notice that the changes you have made are incorrect, you might get out of FDISK.EXE by pressing the Reset button (do not press Ctrl+Alt+Del) located on your computer's case. All data ready to be written to the disk is lost and your disk is saved.

Creating Partitions

To create a partition using FDISK.EXE, follow these steps:

1. Start FDISK.EXE from a DOS prompt.

2. Choose **1** in the FDISK Options menu.

3. Choose **1** from the Create DOS Partition or Logical DOS Drive. FDISK.EXE asks you how much space you want to devote to the primary partition. If you want to use all space, just answer **Y** to the first question. If not, press **N** and then choose how much space you want to devote to the primary partition. You can specify that amount in megabytes, or you can use a percent value (for example, 50%).

4. Press the Enter key. The new partition is created.

5. Press Esc several times to return to the main menu and reboot your computer by pressing Ctrl+Alt+Del.

> If you are planning to use a dual-boot system, you must also make the primary MS-DOS/Microsoft Windows partition bootable. Press **2** in the FDISK Options menu to go the menu that allows you to choose which partition becomes active. You can change that later from Linux.

If all went well, you can now go straight to Chapter 3; the following sections about *fdisk* are to be read when you have started installing Slackware Linux 7 and need to repartition the space you freed on your hard drive.

Using fdisk to Partition a Hard Drive

The *fdisk* utility (and its more user-friendly, but entirely equivalent version, *cfdisk*) is used to modify the partition table under Linux. You can only start it from under Linux. To use it on IDE hard disks, use *fdisk* /dev/hda through /dev/hdd, and for SCSI disks use *fdisk* /dev/sda through /dev/sdh. Typically, *fdisk* /dev/hda or *fdisk* /dev/sda are sufficient if you only have one hard drive in your computer.

Linux *fdisk* does not have a fancy user interface; you need to use keystroke commands to call various functions and sometimes type numeric arguments. You can see the menu when you type the **M** key on the keyboard.

Displaying the Partition Table

To display the partition table for the selected partition, type **P**. You should see something similar to this:

```
Disk /dev/hda: 128 heads, 63 sectors, 969 cylinders
Units = cylinders of 8064 * 512 bytes

   Device Boot      Start       End     Blocks    Id    System
/dev/hda1    *          1       261   1052320+     6    FAT16
/dev/hda2             262       465    822528      5    Extended
/dev/hda3             466       923   1846656     83    Linux native
/dev/hda4             924       969    185472     82    Linux swap
```

Deleting Partitions

To delete a partition, follow these steps:

1. Start *fdisk*.
2. Type **P** to see the partition table.
3. Type **D** to call the delete function.
4. Type the number of the partition you wish to remove (use numbers printed next to the device names in the left-hand column).
5. Type **W** to write changes to disk, or type **Q** to quit without making changes permanent.

> When you want to resize a partition, you have to delete it and create it again (this is described in the next section). All data on the deleted partition is lost.

Creating Partitions

To create a partition, follow these steps:

1. Start *fdisk*.
2. Type **P** to see if there is any free space left in the partition table. You might have to delete another partition (after making proper backups first!).
3. Type **N** to add a new partition. *fdisk* suggests the start cylinder and the end cylinder; you can simply press Enter to use maximum available space for your partition, but it is better to leave some room for the swap and boot partitions. If you do not know what value to use, divide the capacity of your hard drive by the number of cylinders to get the number of megabytes per cylinder. You need approximately 10MB for the boot partition, and twice the amount of RAM for the swap partition. Subtract the number of the first free cylinder from the number of the last free cylinder, and multiply this by the number of megabytes per cylinder. From that result, subtract the number of megabytes needed for the boot and swap partitions, and divide the difference by the number of megabytes per cylinder. Add the integer part of the result to the number of the first free cylinder, and you have the number of the last cylinder to be typed as the argument of the N function. Repeat similar steps for the swap and boot partitions.
4. Press the Enter key.

5. Type **W** to write changes to disk, or type **Q** to quit without making changes permanent.

You can create only four primary partitions or three primary partitions and an unlimited number of logical partitions. Primary partitions can be bootable, which is why you should use them for MS-DOS/Microsoft Windows, if you want a dual-boot system, for the /boot partition, or for the Linux ext2 partition. Other filesystems can use logical partitions.

Creating Ext2 Partitions

Once you have created a new partition, you must specify its type:

1. Type **T** to call the partition ID change function.
2. Type the number of the partition you wish to set.
3. Type the partition ID number (**82** for Linux ext2, **83** for swap).
4. Press the Enter key.
5. Type **W** to write changes to disk, or type **Q** to quit without making changes permanent.

Creating Swap Partitions

Swap partitions are created just like other partitions. A good rule of thumb, however, is that they should be at least as large as the amount of physical RAM you have installed in your system. The largest swap partition you can have on an Intel-based computer is 2GB—although 100MB is usually plenty. It's also possible to have more than one swap partition.

Swap Partitions versus Swap Files

Swap partitions are much safer than swap files because they are hidden from you and your program's view. Only the Linux kernel can access them directly, which is a good thing. The only bad thing about swap partitions is their fixed size.

Other Filesystem Types

The Linux kernel can read and, in most cases, write to partitions formatted using many filesystems, such as msdos (MS-DOS with 8.3 character filenames), vfat

(Microsoft Windows with long filenames), minix, umsdos, nfs, iso9660, smbfs, coda, hfs, hpfs, ntfs, qnx4, sysv, xenix, and coherent. Their descriptions can be found in the *mount* man page (type **man mount** at the command-line prompt in Linux).

Troubleshooting

Assuming that you have made backup copies of your data, partitioning is safe. If things go wrong, you can always delete all partitions and start from scratch. But what if things go wrong and you have not made backup copies of data? If you used FIPS.EXE, Partition Magic, or other similar utilities, which save old data into a file on a floppy disk or another drive, you can probably recover your data without too much trouble. Remember to follow instructions for these packages, and you will be quite safe.

The FIPS.EXE utility gives you the option to create recovery files. You can recover from errors using the RESTORRB.EXE utility (part of the FIPS.ZIP archive). You can find detailed instructions in the FIPS.DOC file, but in essence, all you have to do is boot your system from the floppy disk I told you to create earlier in this chapter, run RESTORRB.EXE, and then tell it to use the most recent ROOTBOOT.00X drive structure recovery file.

If you are using Partition Magic or other such tools, follow the manufacturer's instructions.

In the worst scenario, when recovery of the old disk structure does not go as planned and you have not made backup copies of your data, you might need to use professional data recovery services. In such cases, do not format the drive or make any further changes to it, and call these people for help. They are expensive, but if your data is valuable, it might be worth using them. To find a data recovery service, type **data recovery** into your favorite search engine.

Summary

Slackware Linux 7, just like any other operating system on the face of the earth, needs a properly prepared drive to install it on. This is not hard if you remember to always make backup copies of your data, regardless of the drive partitioning strategy you choose. Once you do that, you are free to divide your drive as you please, remembering that you need between 500MB and 1GB for a reasonably useful Linux installation (that includes the space you need to set aside for swap).

Chapter 3: Installing Slackware

Brian Proffitt

Choosing Installation Media

Starting the Installation

Choosing Packages to Install

Continuing the Installation

By the end of this chapter, you should have Slackware Linux 7.0 installed on your PC.

Bold statement? Hardly. The plain fact is that installation is not that big of a deal anymore. *If* you did your preparation in Chapter 1, "Before You Install: Getting to Know Your Hardware," and *if* you correctly partitioned your hard drive as explained in Chapter 2, "Partitioning Your Hard Drive," you should be ready to go.

It is important that you gather all of the information specified in Chapter 1 because you are going to need it to double-check what the installation program does, entering the information yourself if need be.

Slackware offers a unique installation compared to other distributions. First, it's time consuming. This is not said to scare you off. You should be prepared to spend about an hour or two getting this OS up and running.

Three words of advice before you begin: do not panic. If you read the instructions carefully and have the right information, little can go wrong. You get some pointers as you go along to help you avoid some of the pitfalls you might see during installation.

Choosing Installation Media

Of course, when you start the installation, you need to ask yourself "Self, how will I install this OS?" Don't answer; that would be kind of odd. Here is the answer: install it the most efficient way you can.

The trick here is how you will boot your machine. The ultimate irony of installing any form of Linux is that you need some form of Linux running before you can run the setup program. This is done by loading just enough of the Linux operating system to get the setup program going.

When a computer starts, the BIOS software that permanently sits on every PC immediately goes through a certain set of steps. This is called the boot process. This process starts the various components of the machine in a certain order and looks for the operating system the PC will be running.

Does your floppy drive rattle a bit every time you start your PC? That's your BIOS looking for the operating system. On a typical PC, the BIOS looks for the OS on the floppy drive and then the hard drive. Once it finds the OS, it loads it and you are on your way.

When you install Slackware, you have to have either a boot disk in the floppy drive or an installation CD in your CD-ROM drive when you start your PC. Either way gets you a small Linux system started so you can run setup.

Booting from a CD-ROM

In the back of this book is a complete installation of Slackware 7 on CD-ROM. Everything you need is there. If you are fortunate enough to have a computer that supports booting from the CD-ROM drive, then you are good to go. Simply insert the CD-ROM and restart your computer. Linux boots from the CD and gets you started, as shown in Figure 3.1.

Although I am reasonably sure your bootable CD-ROM will start with the enclosed CD, different PCs and different configurations might not work the way mine do. Please be aware of this and be ready to follow the bootdisk and rootdisk procedures outlined in the "Booting from Floppies" section later in this chapter.

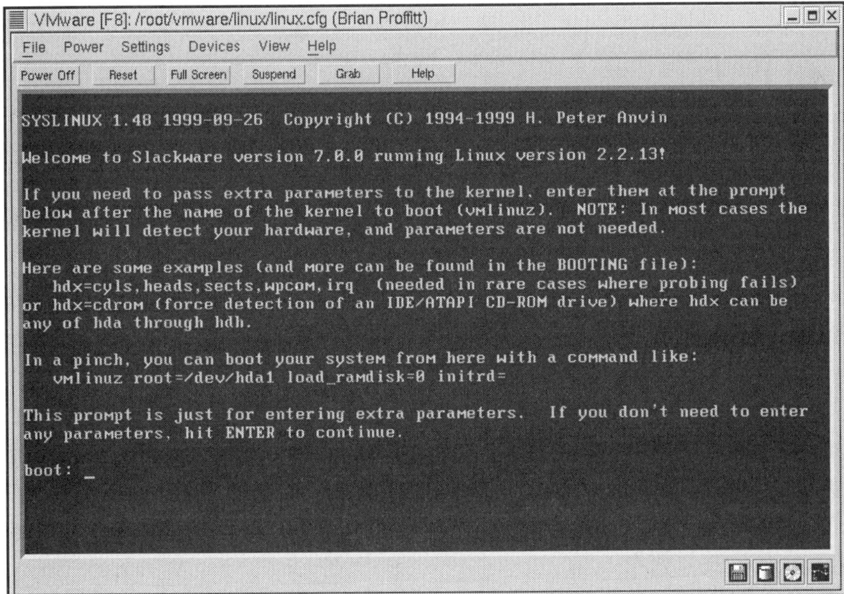

Figure 3.1 *A little bit of Linux to run setup*

If you do not think you have a bootable CD-ROM drive, check something first before you start making those floppies. Start your computer. Early in the boot process, you should see a message onscreen that says something like `Press Del to Setup` or `Press F2 to Setup`. Whatever the key, press it before your OS starts. This takes you to the hallowed BIOS setup screen.

Every BIOS is a little different, so I can't tell you exactly where to go. But in each BIOS setup there is a setting for what drives get booted. Typically you select this option and then cycle through the choices with arrow keys. See if there is a CD-ROM option. If there is, select it. Make sure you have the computer boot to your hard drive after the CD-ROM. Follow the BIOS instruction to save your changes and exit the BIOS setup. Your computer continues booting to the OS normally.

Now you can insert your Slackware CD and restart your computer. You can pick up the installation procedure in the "Starting the Installation" section later in this chapter.

Booting from Floppies

For those of you who have older PCs that cannot boot to the CD-ROM, you need to boot Linux from floppy disks. Actually, there is more to this going on. Not only are the boot floppies starting a mini-Linux, they are also starting a program that detects your CD-ROM drive and allows you to install Slackware within this mini-Linux.

These floppy disks are called the bootdisk and rootdisk floppies. You can make them yourself using information contained on the CD in the back of this book.

Making bootdisk and rootdisk Floppies

The first floppy you need to make is the bootdisk, which contains the actual Linux kernel that your PC will eventually use. It is also the disk that starts talking to your CD-ROM, so you should really get the proper kernel onto the bootdisk.

On the Slackware CD-ROM that came with this book, check the /README.TXT file in one of the two /bootdsks directories. The contents of each directory are the same, though the kernels are formatted a bit differently. Use the /bootdsks.144 directory if you have a 1.44MB floppy drive and the /bootdsks.12 directory if you have a 1.2MB floppy drive.

The README file should help you decide which kernel image to pick, based on the type of CD-ROM drive you have. For the most part (though this is not a hard and fast rule), IDE CD-ROM drives need the bare.i bootdisk and SCSI CD-ROM drives the scsi.s bootdisk.

You can't just copy these files to a floppy and go. You must transfer them to the floppy using a special application called *Rawrite*, which is also located on the CD-ROM. Copy *Rawrite* to your computer's hard drive, as well as the bootdisk image file you are using. If you are running Windows, restart Windows into MS-DOS mode, where *Rawrite* works best.

Once in the MS-DOS screen, insert a blank floppy disk into your floppy drive, and navigate to the directory where you saved RAWRITE and the image file. Then type **RAWRITE** *bootname* **a:** (where *bootname* is the name of the file you want *Rawrite* to transfer to the floppy). If I were making a bootdisk for a SCSI CD-ROM, I would enter

```
RAWRITE scsi.s a:
```

Once the bootdisk is made, you need to make a rootdisk. Rootdisks contain the Linux filesystem, in compressed form, as well as the setup application.

The rootdisk image files are stored on the CD-ROM in the /rootdsks directory. There is another README file in this directory to help you choose which one to use. The most common pick is the color.gz image, but your PC might need something different, so check first.

When you have selected the correct rootdisk image, copy it over to the hard drive directory where *Rawrite* is stored and go back to MS-DOS mode. Enter the following command to make the image on a blank floppy:

RAWRITE color.gz a:

That should do it. You now have the bootdisk and rootdisk, ready to use.

Using bootdisk and rootdisk Floppies

Once you have the two floppies, you are ready to install Slackware:

1. Insert the bootdisk into your floppy drive and restart the PC.
2. You are prompted to run the Linux kernel. Press Enter to continue this process.
3. After a whole bunch of diagnostic messages that Linux broadcasts while checking out your PC's hardware situation, you get this prompt:

   ```
   VFS: Insert root floppy disk to be loaded into ramdisk and press ENTER
   ```

   Swap out the bootdisk for the rootdisk, and press Enter. The rootdisk's contents are uncompressed, loaded into a virtual drive in your RAM, and mounted as your root filesystem.
4. This brings you to the Slackware login prompt, which is where the CD-ROM would have taken you had you been able to boot from it. The installation path merges back together at this point, and you are ready to start the setup program.

Starting the Installation

Okay, now the fun begins. You should have your Slackware CD in the CD-ROM drive (if it is not there already) and all the information you gathered in Chapter 1 right next to you. Kiss your significant other on the cheek; you will be too busy for a while.

The first thing you need to do is log in as root. Root, for those of you new to Linux, is essentially the superuser account you need to make major changes to the Linux operating system. Certainly installing the OS qualifies as a major change!

Figure 3.2 shows the initial screen where the login prompt appears. To begin, type **root** at the login prompt and press Enter. Don't worry about a password for root yet. You set that later on.

If you followed the instructions in Chapter 2, there should be room for Linux on your drive. The Slackware setup program assumes that you not only have room for your Linux partitions, but that you've already created them. So before you dive into installing Slackware, run the *fdisk* command to create your partitions. Even if you already created extra, empty partitions under Windows, you need to use *fdisk* now to mark these partitions as belonging to Linux.

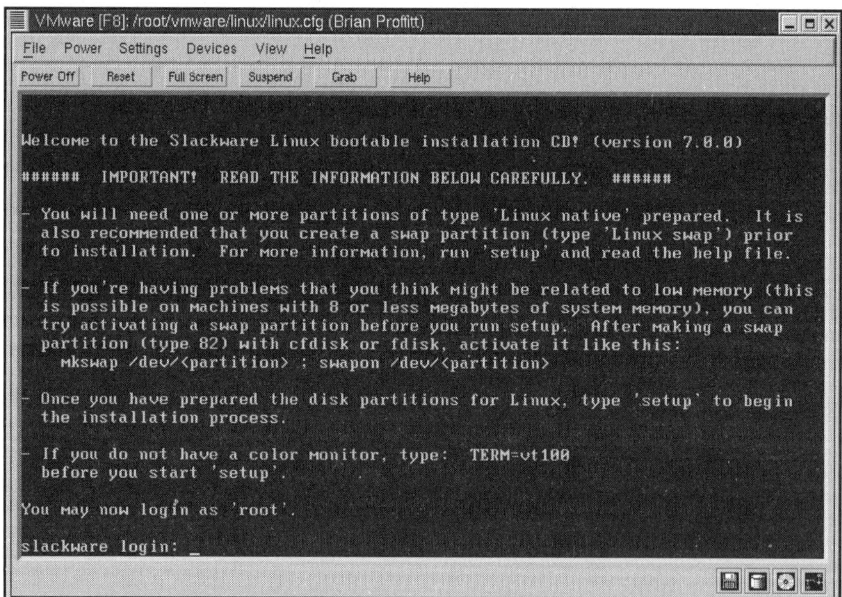

Figure 3.2 *Logging in to Linux before setup*

Launch *fdisk* with a command such as the one below, and refer back to Chapter 2 if you need a reminder how to navigate the program:

```
fdisk /dev/hda
```

Remember that you want at least one large partition of type "Linux native" for the main installation and a smaller one marked as "Linux swap" for the swap space. When you are done, write the changes to disk and exit. You shouldn't need to reboot for the changes to take effect.

Users with more than 8MB of RAM can configure the swap partition while in the setup program. If your machine has very little RAM (typically 8MB or less) you might not have enough memory to even run the setup program! Because of this, such users should manually configure their swap partitions before proceeding.

You need to run two commands on your swap partition to make it usable: *mkswap* and *swapon*. The first basically formats the swap space for use; the second tells Linux to start using it. So if your swap partition is /dev/hda2, for example, you type

```
mkswap /dev/hda2
swapon /dev/hda2
```

Now you can proceed with the installation.

Now that you have taken care of your partitions, the next step is to decide what form of the setup application you want to run. Unless you are a clear expert, just type **setup** to start the normal installation routine. This starts the initial setup screen, shown in Figure 3.3.

This screen is a bit confusing at first because there is no clear place to start. Indeed, it's possible to skip around among the choices, to some degree. But for now you should go through them pretty much in order.

A word about navigation within this application: There is no mouse support, so everything is done with the keyboard. Note the presence of red letters on the screen. To make navigating easier, you can just type the letter to move the cursor/selector to that option. If there is more than one instance of the letter, just type it again until you get to the right option.

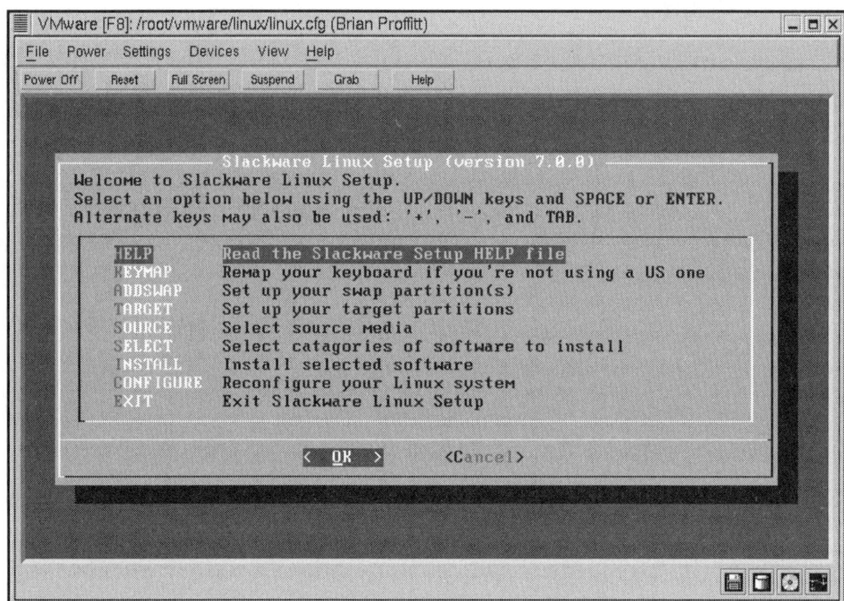

Figure 3.3 *The main setup menu screen*

There is no Back option in the setup, so make sure of your choices before selecting OK.

This said, let's start the setup program by selecting the Add Swap option and pressing Enter.

Adding the Swap Partition in Setup

The first thing you need to do is tell the setup program what swap partition to use. This setting is not just for now; this applies to your final installation of Linux too. After selecting Add Swap, you are presented with a list of swap partitions. You created these to be used, so answer yes to the question.

If you don't have much RAM in your computer and already manually enabled your swap partition, you now get a warning. Heed this warning and do not allow the setup program to run *mkswap* again. Once is enough!

The program then informs you that some lines have been added to your /etc/fstab file. These lines activate the swap partitions every time you boot.

Creating the Root Partition in Setup

After configuring your swap partitions, the setup program leads you to the next section, Target. The first thing you need to do is confirm the partitions you already have set up, which are listed in the first screen (see Figure 3.4).

If this looks correct to you, select the partition you want to be mounted as root (/). What strange words are these? Let me clue you in.

How Partitions Work in Linux

Linux manages its files in a completely different way than does Windows. Rather than using drive letters to refer to a partition and its corresponding filesystem, Linux merges all files and directories from any number of partitions into a single directory tree. In truth, this "single" directory is composed of separate directory trees that are seamlessly connected across partitions. Where these subtrees connect or break from the main directory tree are called mount points.

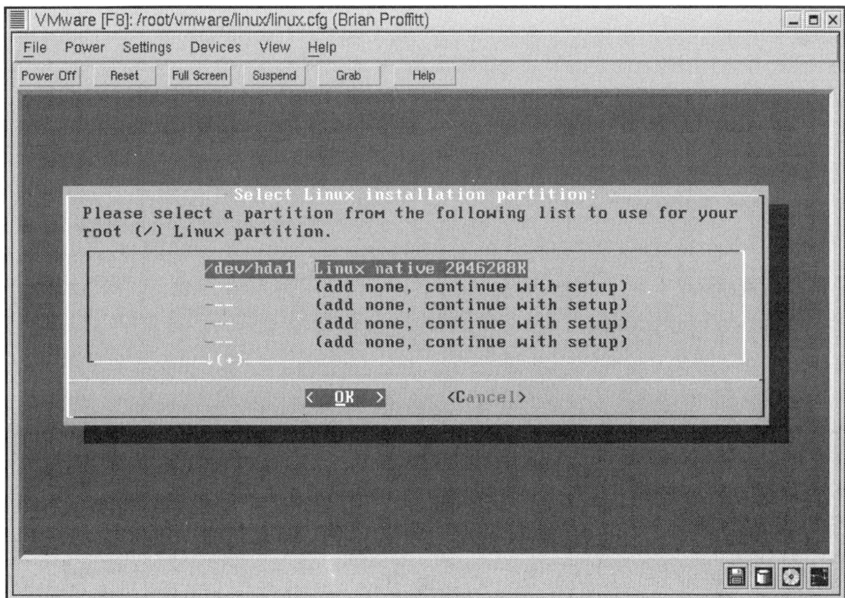

Figure 3.4 *Your Linux partitions are listed here.*

Rather than using drive letters to denote partitions, Linux uses a different naming convention:

/dev/[*Drive Type*][*Device Where Partition Resides*][*Partition Number*]

Table 3.1 explains the variables used in this naming convention.

Table 3.1 Partition Naming Convention

Variable	Definition
/dev/	All devices in Linux are managed in the /dev/ directory, including hard drives and their partitions.
[*Drive Type*]	Two-letter indicator of hard drive type. Possible values: hd (IDE disk), sd (SCSI disk).
[*Device Where Partition Resides*]	The device the partition is on. Possible values: /dev/sda (first SCSI disk), /dev/hdc (third IDE disk).
[*Partition Number*]	Denotes partition. Possible values: 1–4 (primary or extended partitions), 5+ (logical partitions).

Within Linux, this division of directories among partitions is seamless. But when installing Slackware Linux, you need to decide what partition should contain the root directory (/).

Once the right partition is selected and you press Enter, setup inquires whether you want this partition formatted (see Figure 3.5). The only time you don't want to format a partition is when it already contains a Linux filesystem with important data, and you want to mount it within the main directory tree as is. That's not the case here, so go ahead and format the partition. You probably can select Format; Check is slow and only useful for older hard drives you don't entirely trust. Press Enter to continue.

Once the root partition is set, setup informs you that the information has been added to the /etc/fstab file, which keeps track of these things. If it has detected a DOS/Windows partition on your hard drive, it also asks you if you want to have a permanent connection made from the Linux filesystem to your Windows filesystem. I recommend you take setup up on the offer and let it assist you in creating a folder in the Linux directory tree that opens up all the files in the Windows partition.

Once you have completed these steps, you are finished with the Target section. You are then prompted to continue to the Source section (see Figure 3.6). Select Yes and press Enter to continue.

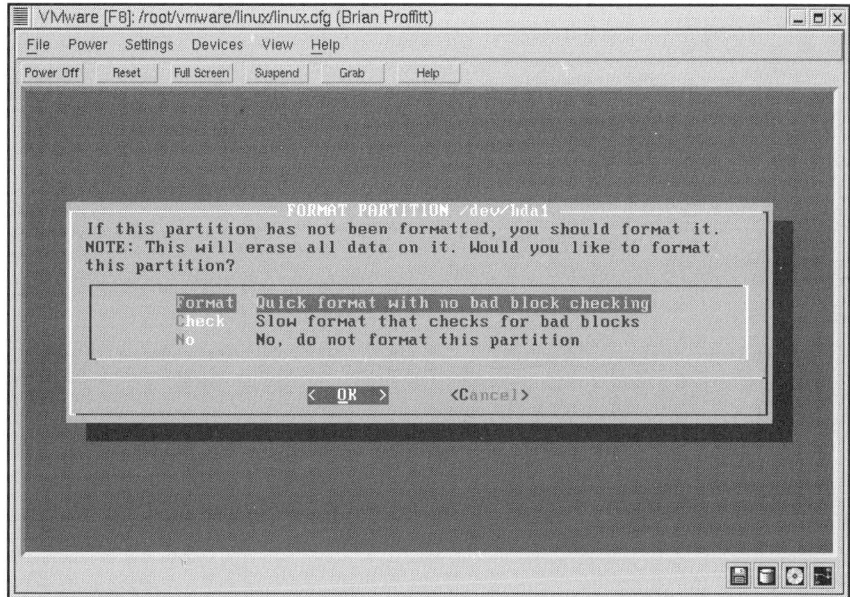

Figure 3.5 *You can format new partitions here if need be.*

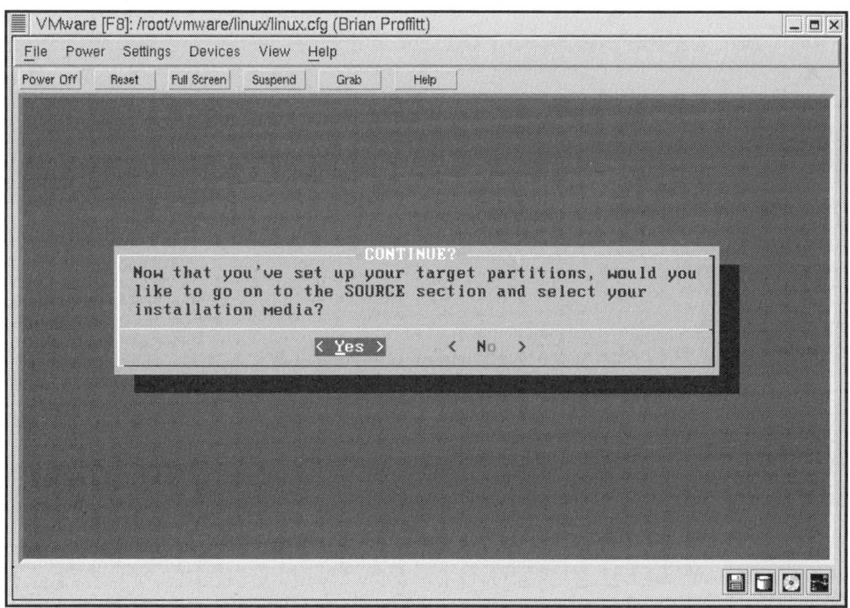

Figure 3.6 *Setup always asks before continuing on to a new section.*

Picking a Source

How you started the installation program determines your first choice in the Source section. As you can see in Figure 3.7, you can select a number of installation source options.

Of the five options listed, the Install from a Slackware CD-ROM choice is the most efficient way to go. But it's not the only path to Slackware. If you do not have a CD-ROM drive, you might have downloaded the Slackware files from the Internet and saved them on your hard drive. If that is the case, you can select option 2 or 4. These options are nearly the same, except option 4 expects that you have already mounted the partition. If you are going to access the files from another location on your network, you can choose Install via NFS.

The NFS installation selection can be problematic at times. You are encouraged to pull the installation files to your hard drive before starting setup so you can install the files locally.

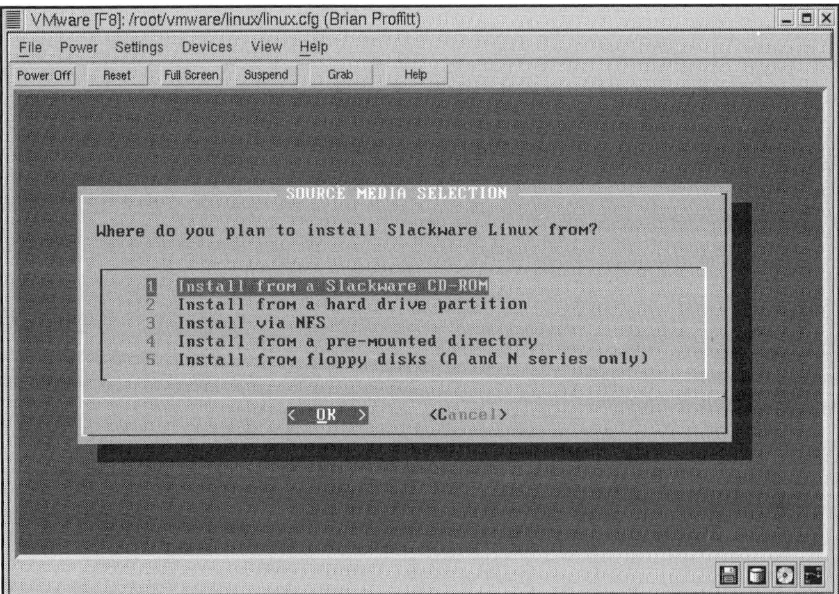

Figure 3.7 *Where will setup get the files it needs?*

You can even install from floppy disks, if you want. If you explore the installation CD-ROM, you can see in the /slakware directory a number of directories with a1, a2, and n1, n2, and so on. These folders each represent a single floppy disk's worth of data for the A and N package series. This is a minimum set of packages you need to get Linux up and running.

All you need to do is get 23 blank floppy disks (14 for A and 9 for N) and copy the contents of each folder to one floppy disk at a time. Then you use the floppies in sequential order during installation. Once Slackware is installed, you can install the other packages as needed.

For this installation, because you have the CD and a working drive, select Option 1 and press Enter to continue. There are a few options for what you want to install. You can install Slackware Linux in its entirety or, to save room, you can install the components needed to run the OS from your CD-ROM drive (see Figure 3.8).

Although you save some room on your hard drive using the CD-ROM method to run Slackware, I don't recommend it. You take a big performance hit if you do it this way. Stick with the Slackware option and press Enter to continue.

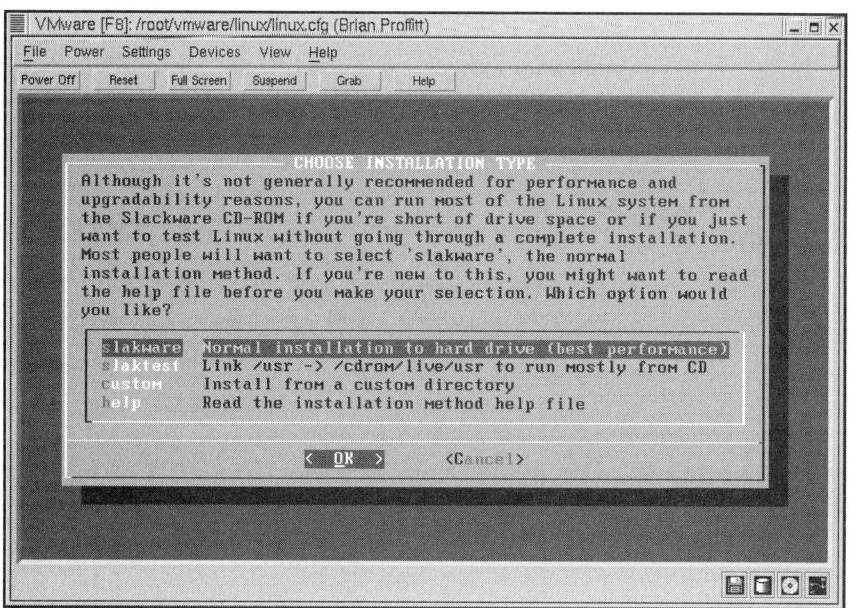

Figure 3.8 *Normal or CD-ROM install?*

At this point, you are asked if you want to proceed to the Select section. Choose Yes and press Enter to continue. Before the discussion of the setup application continues, however, a good look at the packages Slackware wants to install for you is warranted.

Choosing Packages to Install

In Slackware's setup, a package is a compressed file that contains any number of applications. There is usually one application per package, though that is not always the case. Some packages contain several applications and some have no apps at all—just documentation or support files.

Packages are arranged into series. Series are throwbacks to the days when Slackware Linux was always installed via floppy disk. You had an A series, an AP series, and so forth. Once CD-ROMs became more prolific, the Slackware designers held on to this series organization.

In this section, you take time to conduct a detailed examination of the package series—which packages in a series are required, which are recommended, and which are optional.

For more detailed information about applications in these packages, see the /PACKAGES.TXT file on the installation CD.

A Series: Base Linux System

The A series is the core series of packages that must be installed to run Slackware Linux. Without it, nothing could run. It contains the Linux kernel, which is the heart of any Linux distribution, and the components for the all-important Linux filesystem.

As you can see in Table 3.2, only a few packages are not required. There should be no hesitation here to install everything in this series, which takes up about 50MB if completely installed. This series is too important to take shortcuts.

Table 3.2 A Series Packages

Package	Application(s)	Requirement Status	Space Required (in Kb)
aaa_base	Basic Linux filesystem package	Required	90
aoutlibs	a.out (libc4) shared libraries	Required	1030
bash	GNU bash-2.03	Required	680
bash1	GNU bash-1.14.7	Recommended	450
bin	Binaries that go in /bin and /usr/bin	Required	1960
bzip2	bzip2	Required	260
cpio	GNU cpio backup and archiving utility v. 2.4.2	Required	200
cxxlibs	C++ shared libraries	Required	1250
devs	Device files	Required	1950
e2fsprog	e2fsprogs-1.15	Required	650
elflibs	Assorted ELF shared libraries	Required	1790
elvis	elvis-2.1_4	Required	1330
etc	/etc configuration files	Required	670
fileutls	fileutils-4.0	Required	1180
find	GNU findutils-4.1	Required	150
floppy	Floppy disk utilities	Required	680
fsmods	Filesystem modules for Linux 2.2.13	Required	1330
getty	getty_ps 2.0.7j	Optional	150
glibcso	glibc-2.1.2 runtime support	Required	1920
gpm	gpm-1.17.8	Recommended	500
grep	GNU grep 2.3	Required	340
gzip	GNU zip compression utilities. (v. 1.2.4a)	Required	100
hdsetup	Slackware setup/package maintenance system v. 7.0.0	Required	700
ibcs2	Intel Binary Compatibility Specification module	Optional	1290
ide	Linux kernel version 2.2.13, without SCSI support	Optional	990
infozip	Info-ZIP's zip 2.2 and unzip 5.40 utilities	Required	540

Table 3.2 A Series Packages (continued)

Package	Application(s)	Requirement Status	Space Required (in Kb)
isapnp	isapnptools-1.18	Optional	260
kbd	kbd-0.99	Recommended	1760
ldso	ld.so 1.9.9, the dynamic linker/loader	Required	470
less	less-340	Required	140
libc5	Linux libc5 ELF shared libraries	Required	2580
lilo	LILO 21	Required	530
loadlin	LOADLIN v1.6a	Recommended	100
lpr	lpr-0.35–6	Recommended	180
man	man-1.5g	Required	290
minicom	Minicom 1.82–3	Recommended	290
modules	Linux kernel modules for 2.2.13	Required	3110
modutils	modutils-2.1.121	Required	290
pciutils	pciutils-2.0 (Linux PCI utilities)	Optional	130
pcmcia	pcmcia-cs-3.0.14	Recommended	1320
procps	procps-2.0.2, psmisc-18, procinfo-16	Required	560
scsi	Linux kernel version 2.2.13, with SCSI support	Recommended	1300
scsimods	Linux SCSI, RAID, and CD-ROM kernel modules for Linux 2.2.13	Required	2190
sh_utils	GNU sh-utils-1.16	Required	620
shadow	Shadow password suite (shadow-19990607)	Required	930
sysklogd	Sysklogd 1.3–33	Required	130
sysvinit	sysvinit-2.76–4	Required	520
tar	GNU tar 1.13	Required	650
tcsh	tcsh 6.08	Recommended	480
txtutils	GNU textutils-1.22	Required	410
umsprogs	umsdos-0.9	Required	60
util	util-linux 2.9v	Required	1820
zoneinfo	time zone database	Required	1730

AP Series: Various Applications That Don't Require X

In Linux, there are two kinds of applications: those that run under the X Window System and those that don't need it at all. The AP series contains programs of the latter type.

A number of applications in this series are recommended and optional, so you can pick and choose what you need here. Table 3.3 lists the packages and their requirement status.

Table 3.3 AP Series Packages

Package	Application(s)	Requirement Status	Space Required (in Kb)
apsfilt	apsfilter-5.0.1	Recommended	600
ash	Kenneth Almquist's ash shell	Optional	100
bc	GNU bc 1.05a	Optional	210
cdutils	Tools for mastering and writing compact discs	Optional	1170
diff	GNU diffutils-2.7	Recommended	200
enscript	GNU enscript 1.6.1	Optional	1430
ghostscr	Ghostscript version 5.10	Recommended	3530
groff	GNU troff 1.11a document formatting system	Required	3200
gsfonts	Fonts for the Ghostscript interpreter/previewer	Recommended	3810
ispell	ispell-3.1.20	Optional	1030
jed	John E. Davis's JED 0.98–7 editor	Optional	1470
joe	Joe text editor v2.8	Optional	300
jove	Jonathan's Own Version of Emacs (4.14.10)	Optional	290
manpages	Man-pages 1.24	Recommended	1670
mc	mc-4.5.39	Optional	3250
mt_st	mt-st-0.4	Optional	30
quota	Linux disk quota utilities (1.70)	Optional	100
raidtool	raidtools-0.41	Optional	100
rpm	rpm-3.0.2	Optional	2640

Table 3.3 AP Series Packages (continued)

Package	Application(s)	Requirement Status	Space Required (in Kb)
sc	The sc spreadsheet (v. 6.21)	Optional	240
seejpeg	seejpeg-1.6.1	Recommended	120
sox	sox-12.15	Recommended	190
sudo	sudo-1.5.9p4-1	Recommended	210
texinfo	GNU texinfo-3.12	Recommended	770
vim	Version 5.5 of Vim: Vi Improved	Optional	3830
workbone	Workbone 2.31–5	Optional	30
zsh	zsh version 3.0.6	Optional	610

D Series: Programming Development

Now, if you are a programmer, this is the package series for you. You also need it if you plan to compile the kernel from time to time. Several compilers and other programming tools are contained within this series, as you can see in Table 3.4. If you do not wish to program in Linux, you can skip this package series altogether and save yourself about 180MB of drive space.

Table 3.4 D Series Packages

Package	Application(s)	Requirement Status	Space Required (in Kb)
autoconf	GNU autoconf 2.13	Optional	710
automake	GNU automake 1.4	Optional	750
bin86	bin86-0.4	Required	80
binutils	GNU binutils-2.9.1.0.25	Required	3200
bison	GNU bison-1.27	Required	220
byacc	Berkeley Yacc	Optional	70
egcs	GNU C and C++ compilers (egcs-1.1.2)	Required	7890
egcs_g77	GNU Fortran-77 compiler from the egcs-1.1.2 release	Optional	2260

Table 3.4 D Series Packages (continued)

Package	Application(s)	Requirement Status	Space Required (in Kb)
egcsobjc	GNU Objective-C compiler from the egcs-1.1.2 release	Optional	1640
flex	flex—fast lexical analyzer generator version 2.5.4a	Required	370
gcl	GNU Common LISP 2.2.2	Optional	3120
gdb	GNU debugger (v. 4.18)	Recommended	1520
gdbm	GNU gdbm-1.7.3	Required	150
gettext	GNU gettext-0.10.35	Required	1060
glibc	GNU glibc-2.1.2	Required	89880
gmake	GNU make-3.77	Required	470
jpeg6	Independent JPEG Group's JPEG software version 6b	Recommended	690
libgr	libgr-2.0.13	Recommended	2260
libpng	libpng-1.0.3	Recommended	650
libtiff	libtiff-3.4	Recommended	1200
libtool	GNU libtool 1.3	Optional	820
m4	GNU m4 1.4	Recommended	180
ncurses	ncurses-5.0-990918	Recommended	9430
p2c	p2c-1.21alpha2	Optional	730
perl	perl5.005_03	Recommended	9730
pmake	BSD pmake-4.4	Recommended	120
python	python-1.5.2	Optional	13630
rcs	GNU revision control system (v. 5.7)	Optional	490
readline	GNU readline-2.2.1	Optional	570
slang	slang-1.2.2	Recommended	1460
strace	strace-3.1.0.1	Recommended	160
svgalib	Svgalib Super-VGA Graphics Library 1.4.0	Recommended	2150
termcap	termcap-2.0.8	Recommended	100
zlib	zlib-1.1.3	Recommended	220

DES Series: Handling DES Encryption

Are you a security freak? Then this small series might be the thing you are looking for. In addition to adding backwards compatibility for older password files, this package (see Table 3.5) also allows users to compile programs that use DES encryption. If you don't really handle a lot of encrypted files, you can skip the installation of this series as well.

Table 3.5 DES Series Package

Package	Application(s)	Requirement Status	Space Required (in Kb)
descrypt	glibc-crypt-2.1	Required	320

E Series: GNU Emacs

Emacs is a very popular text editor for Linux. Many of my friends swear by it, extolling its virtues to the highest mountain.

Personally, I like it too, and I recommend that you install the entire series, including most of the optional and recommended packages detailed in Table 3.6. The one you might want to omit is elisp—it's only useful if you plan on modifying how Emacs works.

Table 3.6 E Series Packages

Package	Application(s)	Requirement Status	Space Required (in Kb)
elisp	Emacs lisp source files	Optional	18010
emac_nox	Emacs binary without X support	Optional	3580
emacinfo	Info files for emacs-20.4	Recommended	1190
emacmisc	Miscellaneous files for emacs-20.4	Recommended	3280
emacsbin	GNU Emacs 20.4	Required	17560

F Series: FAQ Lists, HOWTO Documentation

If you crave documentation for the OS you're about to install, you should definitely install this series, which contains HOWTOs, mini-HOWTOs, and FAQs for the Slackware distribution. As you can see in Table 3.7, everything in the series is installed for you, as they are all required.

Table 3.7 F Series Packages

Package	Application(s)	Requirement Status	Space Required (in Kb)
howto	HOWTOs from the Linux Documentation Project	Required	9830
manyfaqs	A collection of frequently asked questions and answers on many subjects	Required	1140
mini	Linux Mini-HOWTOs	Required	2470

GTK Series: GNOME

There are two big desktop environments out there: GNOME and KDE. This series contains the data needed to run the first one: GNOME. It also contains several other popular applications, including The GIMP. For this reason, and the others listed in Table 3.8, I recommend you install this series. Every package in the series is required and it takes up 135MB when installed, so be sure you want it.

Table 3.8 GTK Series Packages

Package	Application(s)	Requirement Status	Space Required (in Kb)
audiofil	audiofile-0.1.9	Required	350
control	control-center-1.0.51	Required	1730
econf	Enlightenment-conf-0.15	Required	430
enlight	enlightenment-0.15.5	Required	4310
esound	esound-0.2.15	Required	300

Table 3.8 GTK Series Packages (continued)

Package	Application(s)	Requirement Status	Space Required (in Kb)
eterm	Eterm-0.8.9	Required	1080
fnlib	fnlib-0.4	Required	590
freefont	freefonts-0.10	Required	2630
freetype	freetype-1.2	Required	1010
gdm	gdm-2.0beta4	Required	620
gedit	gedit-0.5.1	Required	540
gftp	gftp-2.0.5	Required	530
gimp	The GIMP—GNU Image Manipulation Program version 1.0.4	Required	16270
gmc	mc-4.5.39	Required	5560
gnoadmin	gnome-admin-1.0.3	Required	360
gnoaudio	gnome-audio-1.0.0	Required	7700
gnogames	gnome-games-1.0.51	Required	7360
gnoguide	users-guide-1.0.71	Required	2430
gnomcore	gnome-core-1.0.53	Required	4820
gnomedia	gnome-media-1.0.51	Required	400
gnomeicu	gnomeicu-0.65	Required	330
gnomenet	gnome-network-1.0.2	Required	490
gnomepim	gnome-pim-1.0.50	Required	990
gnomlibs	gnome-libs-1.0.53	Required	16000
gnomobjc	gnome-objc-1.0.40	Required	1660
gnoprint	gnome-print-0.9	Required	1280
gnotepad	gnotepad+-1.0.8	Required	220
gnoutils	gnome-utils-1.0.50	Required	1470
gnpython	gnome-python-1.0.50	Required	4940
gnumeric	gnumeric-0.38	Required	3670
gtkeng	gtk-engines-0.8	Required	690
gtkglib	gtk+-1.2.6, glib-1.2.6	Required	6020
guile	guile-1.3.2a	Required	2460

Table 3.8 GTK Series Packages (continued)

Package	Application(s)	Requirement Status	Space Required (in Kb)
imlib	imlib-1.9.7	Required	1370
libghttp	libghttp-1.0.4	Required	150
libglade	libglade-0.7	Required	600
libgtop	libgtop-1.0.5	Required	4920
libungif	libungif-4.1.0	Required	580
libxml	libxml-1.7.3	Required	1420
orbit	ORBit-0.5.0	Required	2390
wmaker	WindowMaker-0.60.0	Required	7720
xchat	xchat-1.2.1	Required	1020
xscrsave	xscreensaver-3.17	Required	4710

K Series: Linux Kernel Source

One of the unique things about Linux is that its raw source code is always distributed with it. This allows you to install the source code, make your own modifications, and then use them as you own. You could even sell the modified Linux to other people—provided you release your source code as well.

This series contains two packages that in turn contain the Linux source code, as listed in Table 3.9. If you do not plan to recompile your own kernel or play with the source code, you can skip this series and save about 72MB on your hard drive.

Table 3.9 K Series Packages

Package	Application(s)	Requirement Status	Space Required (in Kb)
linuxinc	Linux 2.2.13 kernel include files	Recommended	8150
lx2213	Linux kernel source version 2.2.13	Recommended	65090

KDE Series: K Desktop Environment

KDE is the other desktop environment that runs within Slackware. If you choose to run this instead of GNOME, then I suggest you install everything in the series, listed in Table 3.10.

Table 3.10 KDE Series Packages

Package	Application(s)	Requirement Status	Space Required (in Kb)
kadmin	kdeadmin-1.1.2	Optional	1700
kdebase	kdebase-1.1.2 (KDE base package)	Required	18260
kdegames	kdegames-1.1.2	Optional	6680
kdelibs	kdelibs-1.1.2	Required	5440
kdetoys	kdetoys-1.1.2	Optional	440
kdeutils	kdeutils-1.1.2	Recommended	4130
kgraphic	kdegraphics-1.1.2	Recommended	3290
kmedia	kdemultimedia-1.1.2	Optional	2740
knetwork	kdenetwork-1.1.2	Recommended	8420
korganiz	korganizer-1.1.2	Optional	1890
ksupport	ksupport-1.1.2 Support Libraries for the K Desktop Environment	Required	2650
qt_1_44	Qt-1.44	Required	16420

N Series: Networking

The N in N series stands for networking, as you might have guessed. If you have a standalone computer, you might be tempted to skip this series. You really shouldn't. As you can see in Table 3.11, several packages within this series contain Internet tools. So if you have any kind of connection to the Internet, even dial-up, you're going to need the packages in this series. You can be a bit selective here, however. If, for example, you do not plan to run your own Web server, then clearly you do not need apache. Use this table and the /PACKAGES.TXT file to choose your packages carefully.

Table 3.11 N Series Packages

Package	Application(s)	Requirement Status	Space Required (in Kb)
apache	Apache WWW server v 1.3.9	Optional	6930
bind	bind-8.2.2	Recommended	3680
dip	DIP—dial-up IP connection handler 3.3.7p	Optional	190
elm	Menu-driven user mail program (v. 2.5.1)	Optional	760
ftchmail	fetchmail-5.1.2	Optional	990
imapd	imapd-4.7-beta	Optional	1190
inn	INN-2.2.1	Optional	6060
lynx	Lynx 2.8.2rel.1	Optional	1530
mailx	BSD mailx 8.1.1-10	Recommended	180
metamail	metamail-2.7	Recommended	340
netatalk	netatalk-1.4b2+asun2.1.3	Optional	940
netmods	Network support modules for Linux-2.2.13	Required	3040
netpipes	netpipes 4.2	Optional	210
nn_nntp	nn-6.5.1 compiled to use NNTP	Optional	900
pine	Pine version 4.20	Optional	3760
ppp	PPP for Linux, version 2.3.10	Optional	490
procmail	The procmail mail processing program (v3.13.1 1999/04/05)	Optional	280
rdist	rdist-6.1.4	Optional	120
rsync	rsync-2.3.1	Optional	200
samba	Samba 2.0.5a	Optional	7030
sendmail	BSD sendmail 8.9.3	Recommended	1720
smailcfg	Configuration files for sendmail	Optional	580
tcpip1	TCP/IP networking programs and support files	Recommended	2190
tcpip2	Extra TCP/IP programs	Recommended	2560

Table 3.11 N Series Packages (continued)

Package	Application(s)	Requirement Status	Space Required (in Kb)
tin	The tin news reader (tinpre-1.4-19990805)	Optional	670
trn	A threaded newsreader for reading a remote NNTP server (v. 3.5)	Optional	340
uucp	Taylor UUCP version 1.06.1	Optional	1050
wget	wget-1.5.3	Optional	390
xntp	xntp3-5.93e	Optional	1550

T Series: TeX

TeX is a printing and document language tool that lets you do some remarkable things with documents. This series is big: about 125MB fully installed. Still, if you plan to do detailed documentation work, this application, shown in Table 3.12, might be a good fit for you.

Table 3.12 T Series Packages

Package	Application(s)	Requirement Status	Space Required (in Kb)
tetex	teTeX-1.0.6 base support files	Required	58520
tex_bin	teTeX-1.0.6 binaries	Required	6860
tex_doc	Documentation for teTeX-1.0.6	Recommended	40010
transfig	transfig 3.2.1	Optional	440
xfig	xfig 3.2.2	Optional	3920

TCL Series: Tcl/Tk Script Languages

The TCL series is another development series, this time focused on the Tcl/Tk scripting language that is popular in the Linux community. The components of this series are listed in Table 3.13. If you have no plans to develop anything, or to run any scripts someone else developed with Tcl, go ahead and skip this series.

Table 3.13 TCL Series Packages

Package	Application(s)	Requirement Status	Space Required (in Kb)
expect	expect-5.28	Optional	1020
hfsutils	hfsutils-3.2.6	Optional	480
tcl	The Tcl script language, version 8.0.5	Required	2170
tclx	Extended Tcl (TclX) 8.0.4	Recommended	4460
tix	Tix4.1.0.006	Optional	3820
tk	The Tk toolkit for Tcl, version 8.0.5	Recommended	3230

X Series: XFree86 X Window System

This series is the first of four series centered around the graphic interface that comes with Slackware: *XFree86*. Like A and N, this series is very important, as you can see by the packages listed in Table 3.14. I strongly recommend you install all of the tools within this series so you can have the most complete installation of the GUI.

Table 3.14 X Series Packages

Package	Application(s)	Requirement Status	Space Required (in Kb)
fvwm2	fvwm-2.2.2	Required	1970
fvwmicns	xpm3icons	Optional	210
lesstif	LessTif 0.89.0 (A Motif 1.2 alternative)	Recommended	8140
libc5x	ELF libc5 shared libraries from XFree86 3.3.3.1	Optional	2000
mesa	Mesa-3.0	Required	8710
oldlibs5	a.out (libc4) libraries from XFree86 2.1.1 (X11R5)	Optional	790
oldlibs6	a.out (libc4) libraries from XFree86 3.1.1 (X11R6)	Optional	1400
x3dl	An accelerated server for 3DLabs chipsets	Recommended	2170

Table 3.14 X Series Packages (continued)

Package	Application(s)	Requirement Status	Space Required (in Kb)
x8514	An accelerated server for cards using IBM8514 chips	Recommended	1680
xagx	An accelerated server for IIT AGX chipsets	Recommended	1870
xaw3d	Xaw3d-1.4	Required	690
xbin	Basic client binaries required for XFree86 3.3.5	Required	6950
xcfg	Configuration files for XFree86 3.3.5	Required	30
xdoc	Documentation and release notes for XFree86 3.3.5	Recommended	1090
xf100	100dpi screen fonts	Optional	1380
xfcyr	Cyrillic fonts for XFree86 3.3.5	Optional	360
xfnon	Some large X fonts	Optional	2450
xfnts	Fonts for the X Window system	Required	1520
xfscl	Scaled fonts	Optional	1630
xfsrv	xfs (X font server)	Optional	330
xhtml	Docs for XFree86 in HTML format	Optional	1630
xi128	A server for the Number Nine Imagine 128	Recommended	2140
xjdoc	Japanese documentation and release notes for XFree86 3.3.5	Optional	750
xjset	Japanese configuration utility for XFree86	Optional	1480
xlib	Various library files for XFree86 3.3.5	Required	1850
xlock	xlockmore-4.14	Required	2140
xma32	An accelerated server for cards using Mach32 chips	Recommended	1830
xma64	An accelerated server for cards using the Mach64 chipset	Recommended	1960

Table 3.14 X Series Packages (continued)

Package	Application(s)	Requirement Status	Space Required (in Kb)
xma8	An accelerated server for cards using Mach8 chips	Recommended	1690
xman	Man pages for XFree86 3.3.5	Recommended	2210
xmono	A Monochrome server	Recommended	2030
xnest	Xnest—a nested X server	Optional	1150
xp9k	An accelerated server for cards using the P9000 chipset	Recommended	1890
xpm	The Xpm shared and static libraries, v. 3.4k (with libXpm.so.4.11)	Required	240
xprog	Libraries, include files, and configuration files for X programming	Recommended	5690
xprt	Print-only server (Xprt) for XFree86 3.3.5	Optional	2730
xps	XFree86 documentation in PostScript format	Optional	2150
xs3	An accelerated server for cards using S3 chips	Recommended	2400
xs3v	An accelerated server for cards using S3 ViRGE chips	Recommended	2120
xset	Graphical configuration utility for XFree86	Recommended	1260
xsvga	A server for many SuperVGA video cards	Recommended	3040
xvfb	Virtual frame buffer X server	Optional	2700
xvg16	A server for 16-color EGA/VGA graphics modes	Recommended	1920
xw32	A server for chipsets in the ET4000/W32 series	Recommended	1730
xxfb	Frame buffer X server	Recommended	1990

XAP Series: X Applications

XAP, like the AP series counterpart, contains the applications that run well under X. There's a lot to play with in this series, as Table 3.15 demonstrates. You should load up everything in this series as well.

Table 3.15 XAP Series Packages

Package	Application(s)	Requirement Status	Space Required (in Kb)
fvwm95	fvwm95-2.0.43b	Recommended	2020
gnuchess	gnuchess-4.0.pl80 and xboard-4.0.2	Recommended	2370
gnuplot	gnuplot 3.7	Optional	2200
gs_x11	Replacement /usr/bin/gs with X11 options compiled in	Recommended	1300
gv	gv 3.5.8	Recommended	430
imagick	ImageMagick-4.2.2	Recommended	4500
netscape	Netscape Communicator 4.7 (v47.x86-unknown-linuxglibc2.0)	Recommended	33330
seyon	Seyon 2.14c	Optional	350
tkdesk	TkDesk 1.1	Optional	3370
x3270	x3270-3.1.1.6—IBM host access tool	Optional	760
xfm	xfm 1.3.2	Optional	840
xfract	xfractint-3.04	Recommended	1360
xgames	xgames collection	Recommended	150
xpaint	XPaint 2.4.9	Optional	510
xpdf	xpdf-0.7a	Optional	730
xspread	xspread-2.3	Optional	360
xv	John Bradley's XV 3.10a	Recommended	1900
xvim	X enabled version of vim-5.5	Recommended	3910
xxgdb	xxgdb-1.12	Recommended	110

XD Series: X Server Development Kit

This is the one X series that you might not want to install. Like the Linux kernel, the source code for X Window servers can be tweaked, developed, and recompiled (see Table 3.16). Again, unless you are a developer or hard-core Linux user, you likely can skip this small series.

Table 3.16 XD Series Package

Package	Application(s)	Requirement Status	Space Required (in Kb)
xlkit	XFree86 3.3.5 server link kit	Optional	16280

XV Series: XView

On Sun Microsystems PCs, typically XView is run instead of XFree86. If you have access to Xview applications, you can run them in XFree86 if you install the packages found in this series, listed in Table 3.17.

Table 3.17 XV Series Packages

Package	Application(s)	Requirement Status	Space Required (in Kb)
sspkg	SlingShot extensions 2.1	Optional	2850
workman	WorkMan-1.3a	Optional	420
xv32_a	Static libraries for xview3.2p1-X11R6.LinuxELF.4	Optional	1910
xv32exmp	Sample code for Xview	Optional	2090
xvinc32	Include files for xview3.2p1-X11R6.LinuxELF.4	Optional	1630
xvol32	Binaries for xview3.2p1-X11R6.LinuxELF.4	Optional	2660

Y Series: Games

Last, and certainly not least, is the Y series. Y? Because we all like to have fun! Table 3.18 lists this deceptively small package series. Go ahead, install it. We all need a break now and again!

Table 3.18 Y Series Package

Package	Application(s)	Requirement Status	Space Required (in Kb)
bsdgames	BSD games collection, version 2.7	Optional	5400

Continuing the Installation

Now that you have had a chance to analyze the package series, it's time to apply the stuff you have learned.

Package Selection and Installation

In the first and only screen of the Select section, you can see a list of all the available package series (see Figure 3.9).

To select or deselect series, simply move the selection cursor and toggle the selection with the space bar. Once you have finished, press Enter to move on. The next prompt asks you if you want to continue to the Install section. Select Yes and press Enter.

The Prompting Mode screen, shown in Figure 3.10, lets you choose how you want the package installation to proceed. If you just want setup to install *every* package in every series you selected in the previous screen (recommended and optional ones as well), select the Full option.

If you want a little more control over what gets in and what doesn't, select the Newbie option. This method auto-installs all the required packages in each series, but stops and asks you if you want to install a recommended or optional package. This one is time consuming, but it affords some control over the process. If you want full control, you can use the Expert or Menu options, which let you choose every package that gets installed from menus. This is also pretty time consuming, but you might find it worth it.

In this example, I selected Full and pressed Enter. The auto-installation starts and runs through every package in all the series you chose (see Figure 3.11).

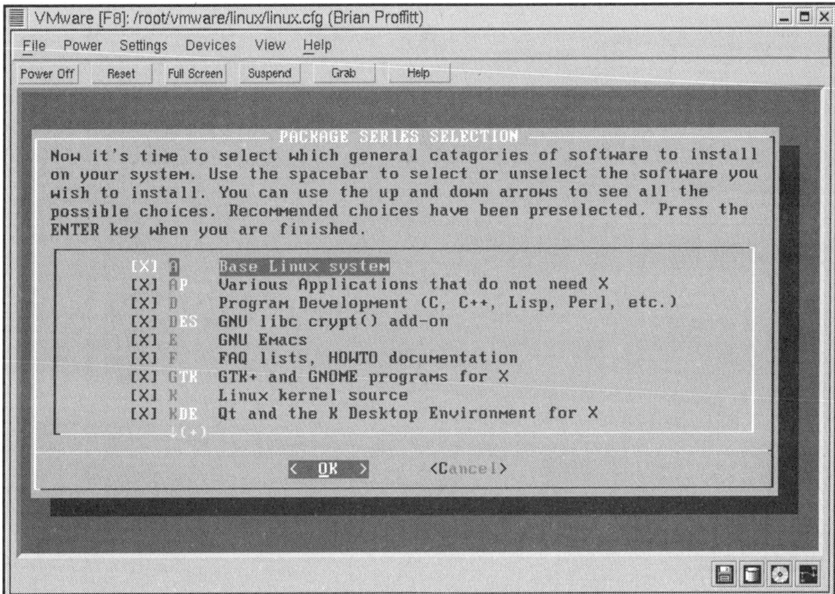

Figure 3.9 *Package series selection*

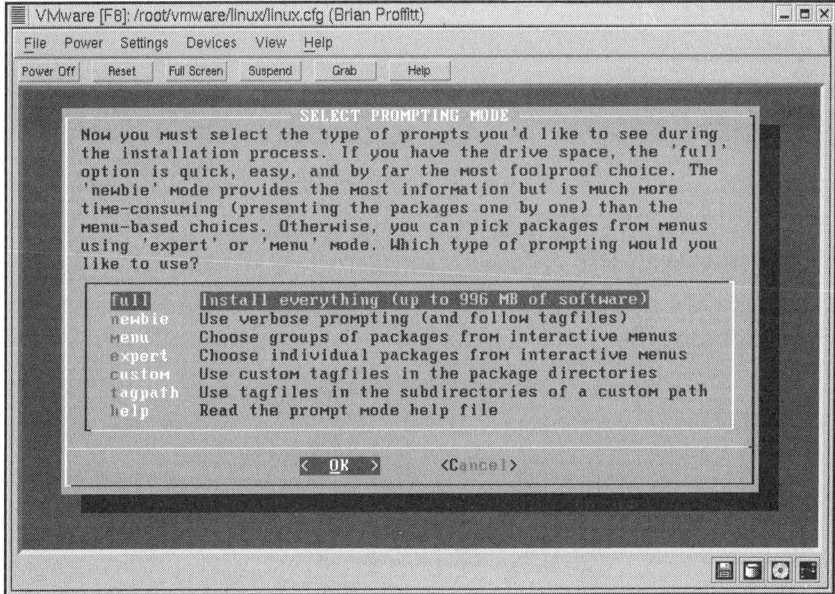

Figure 3.10 *Installation prompting*

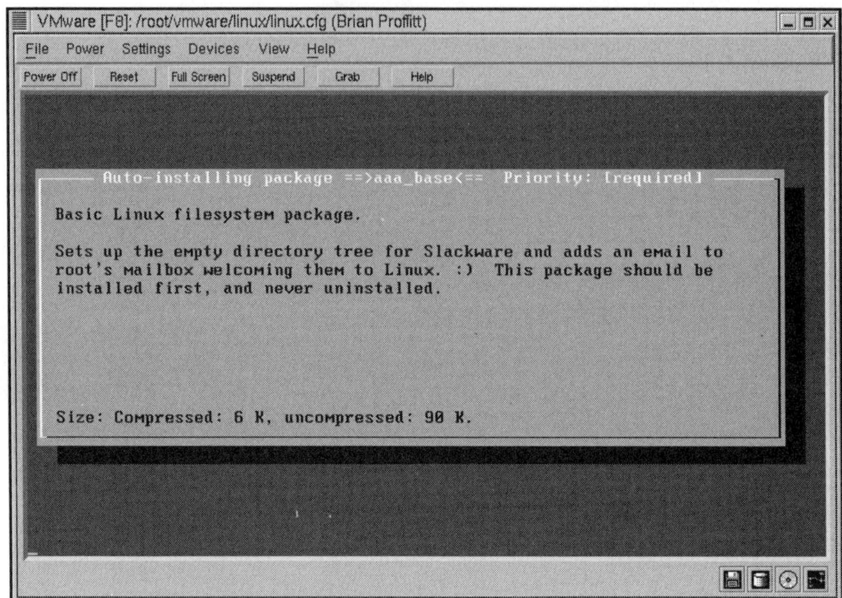

Figure 3.11 *Full-speed auto-installation in action*

Once the packages are installed, which can take a while, you move on to the rest of the setup program.

Making a Boot Disk

The next step immediately after installing packages is the creation of a boot disk. This is different from the bootdisk you made for the installation. This boot disk allows you to boot Linux if there are ever any problems with your PC.

As you can see in Figure 3.12, you have several options to choose from. I recommend you use the Format option to format a blank floppy disk and then use the LILO boot disk option.

If you choose to make a LILO boot disk, you are prompted at each step of the operation. Follow the instructions on the screen to complete the process.

Choosing a Modem and Screen Fonts

The next few screens are what I call housekeeping functions. After creating a boot disk, you are asked where your modem is connected to the PC. Match the /dev/tty setting to the COM port notation from Windows and press Enter to continue (see Figure 3.13).

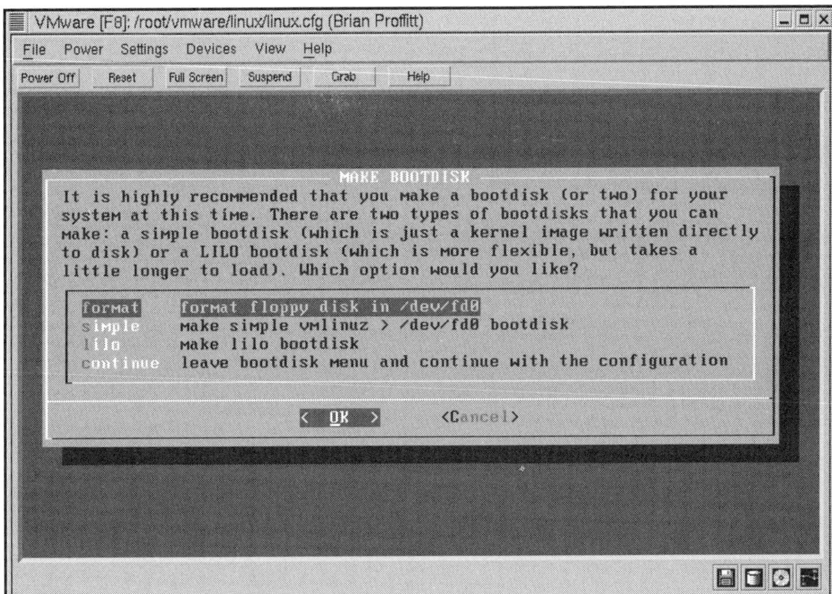

Figure 3.12 *Making a boot disk*

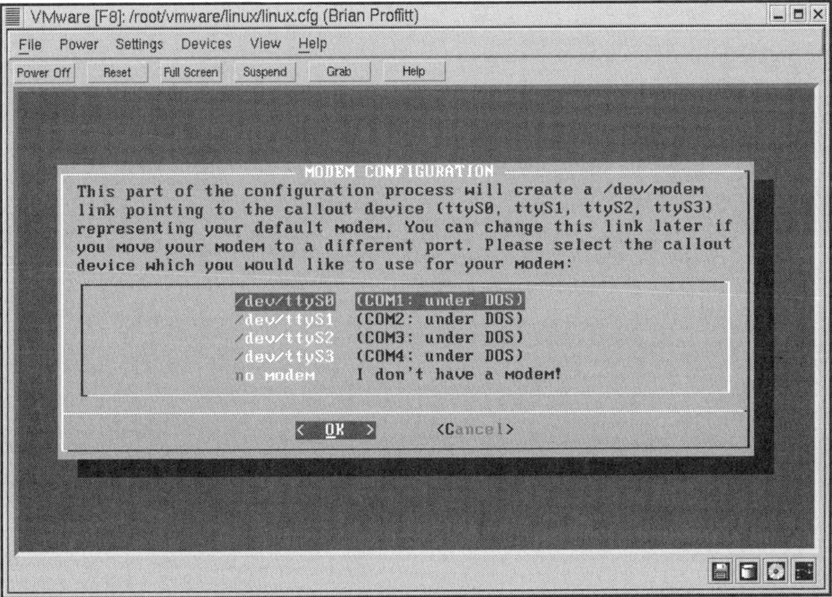

Figure 3.13 *Locating your modem*

After the modem, the setup installation asks you if you want to try out new screen fonts. Screen fonts are used whenever you run a text-based application, such as this setup app. If you say yes, you are shown a screen font selection screen (see Figure 3.14).

If you choose one of these fonts and press Enter, the next screen appears in the new font and asks you if you like it (see Figure 3.15). If you say no, you are taken back to the selection screen, and the cycle continues until you find one you do like. Once you select a font, you are taken to the LILO configuration portion of the program.

Configuring LILO

Remember when I told you how booting works? Well, when a PC with Linux boots, the BIOS doesn't call on Linux itself to start; it actually calls a program called LILO, which in turn starts Linux. The neat thing is this: LILO can also call up any other OS located on your PC.

When the LILO installation screens begin, you are prompted to start a simple or expert installation or skip LILO altogether (see Figure 3.16). LILO is pretty handy, so let's go with the simple install, pressing Enter to move ahead.

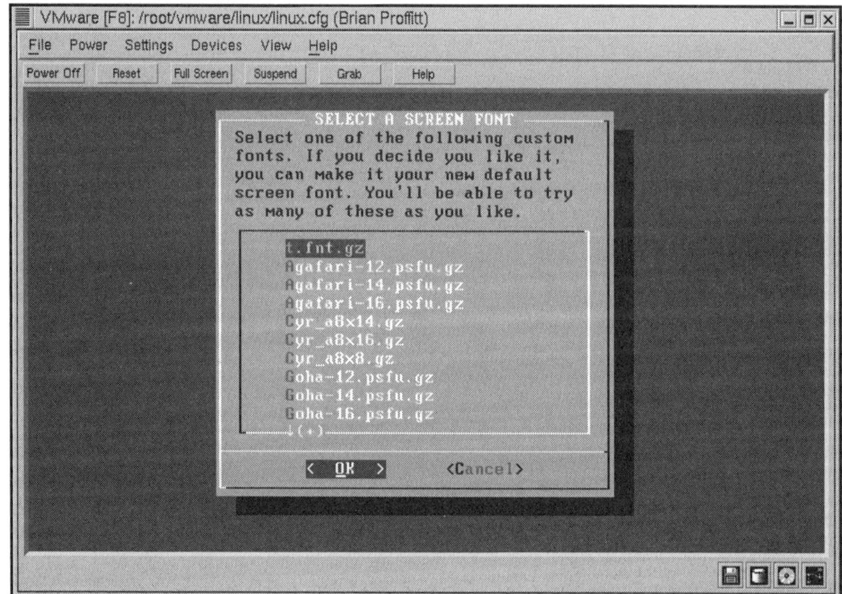

Figure 3.14 *Pick a font, any font....*

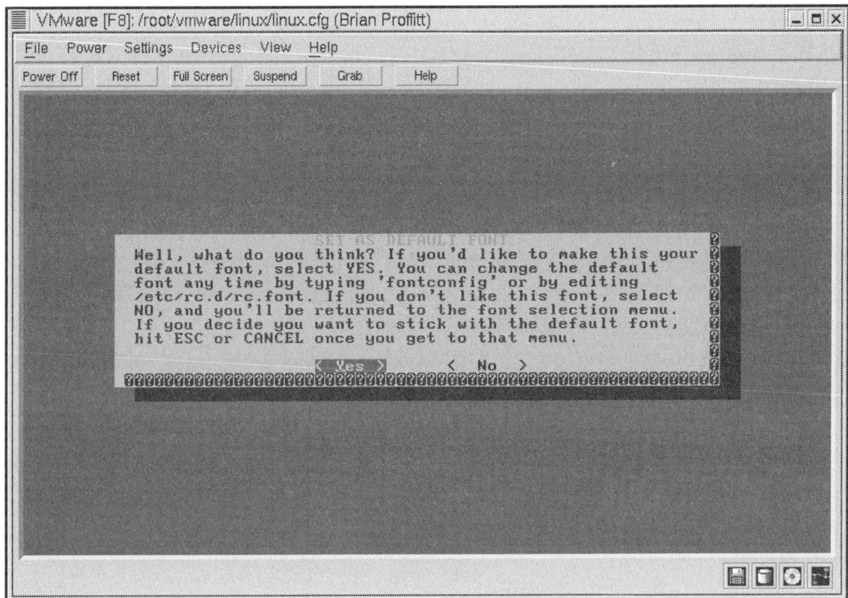

Figure 3.15 *New fonts can personalize every part of Linux.*

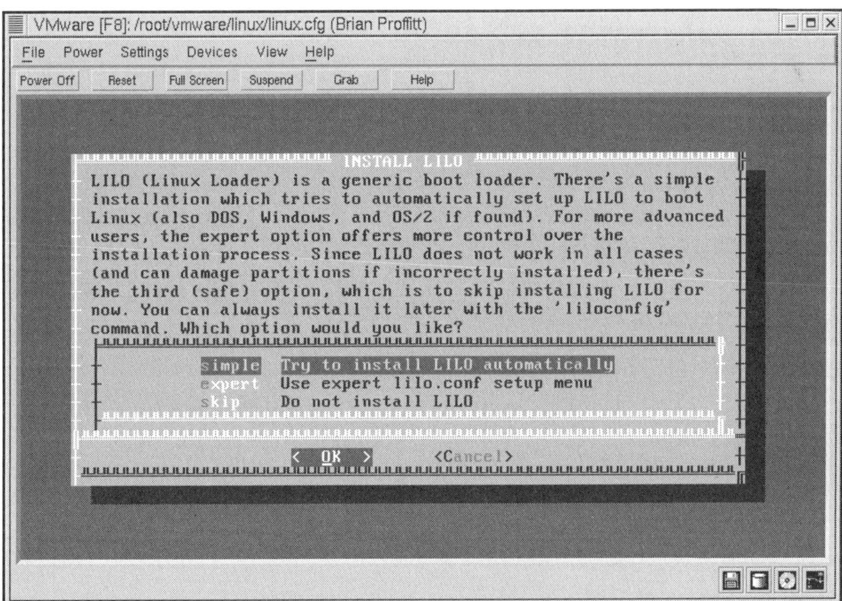

Figure 3.16 *LILO can be installed the easy way or the not-so-easy way.*

In the next screen, you can choose to install LILO on the root (/) partition, some other partition on your hard drive, or the master boot record, which is where the BIOS looks for operating systems to boot. If you have made the root partition bootable, then select the Root option. Otherwise, use the MBR option and press Enter to continue.

Do not select the Root option if you have another operating system installed (such as Windows) and left its partition marked as bootable while in *fdisk*. The master boot record (MBR) installed by Windows and many other operating systems simply looks for a bootable partition and boots that. If this is your setup and you select the Root option, Linux never gets a chance to boot!

It's safest to install LILO with the MBR option and let it boot your operating system(s). LILO is pretty good about booting other operating systems.

Finally, you can choose how the screen looks when LILO is booting Linux. There really isn't much here, just how big the characters are when Linux first starts. I recommend the Standard option. Press Enter to continue.

Configuring Networking: netconfig

If you installed network packages, you now have an opportunity to configure some of the network settings.

In the first *netconfig* screen, you are asked to enter your computer's host name. If you are already on a network, be sure to use the same one you had before so the network can see you (see Figure 3.17). If you're not on a network or only connect to a network via a modem, chances are you can call your computer whatever you like. The name **localhost** is the standard name to use in this case.

Next, you need to enter your network's domain name. This usually follows your host name in networking nomenclature. Enter the correct domain name and press Enter. For computers not connected to a network, **localdomain** suffices.

In the last *netconfig* screen, you need to set a network type (see Figure 3.18). If you're on a modem, choose loopback. Otherwise, you should be able to get the needed information from your network administrator. Choose the correct type and press Enter.

If you selected the Static IP option, a new screen appears and asks you about your network addressing information. Fill this in completely and press Enter. A message appears that indicates you are finished with the networking settings. Press Enter to move to the next portion of setup.

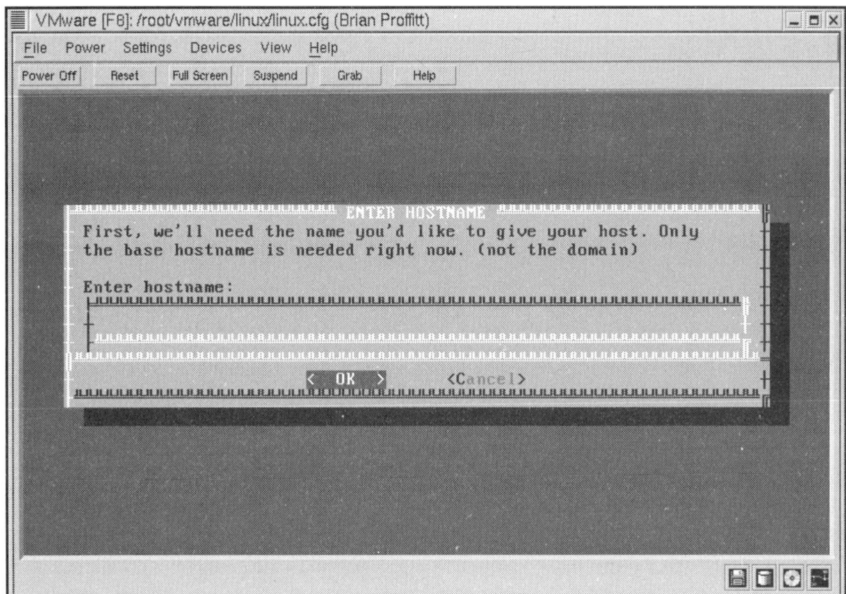

Figure 3.17 *Entering your computer's host name*

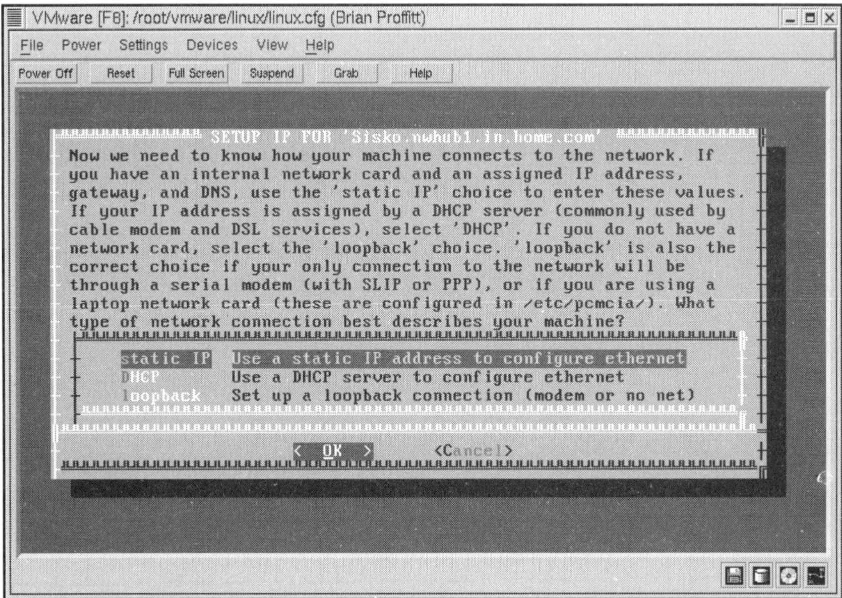

Figure 3.18 *What kind of connection do you have?*

Wrapping It Up

Now you need to zip through some fine-tuning configuration screens. Don't worry. You're almost done!

The first setting to configure is the mouse. The screen lists a fair number of mouse types for you, as shown in Figure 3.19. Select the correct mouse type for your system, and press Enter.

If you plan to use e-mail, you need to inform the *sendmail* application what type of protocol you are using. Figure 3.20 shows the two types to choose from: SMTP and UUCP. Most Internet providers use SMTP for their mail servers.

After dealing with the *sendmail* option, the next step is to tell your computer what time zone you are in. This helps the computer know when to change the time, if need be, for daylight savings time or when to ignore DST altogether.

Slackware lists all the U.S. time zones first, then the rest of the world (see Figure 3.21). Use the arrow keys to find your time zone and then press Enter.

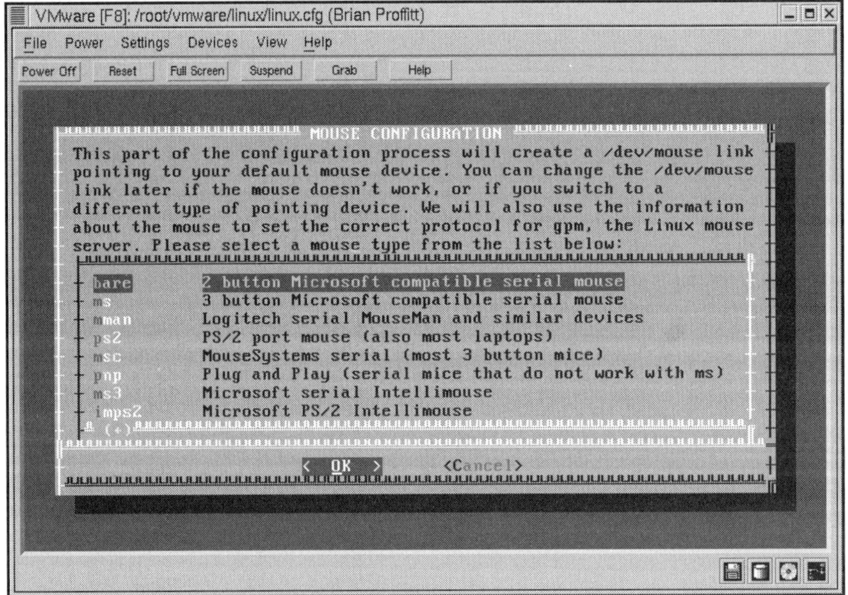

Figure 3.19 *A cat's dream: mice everywhere!*

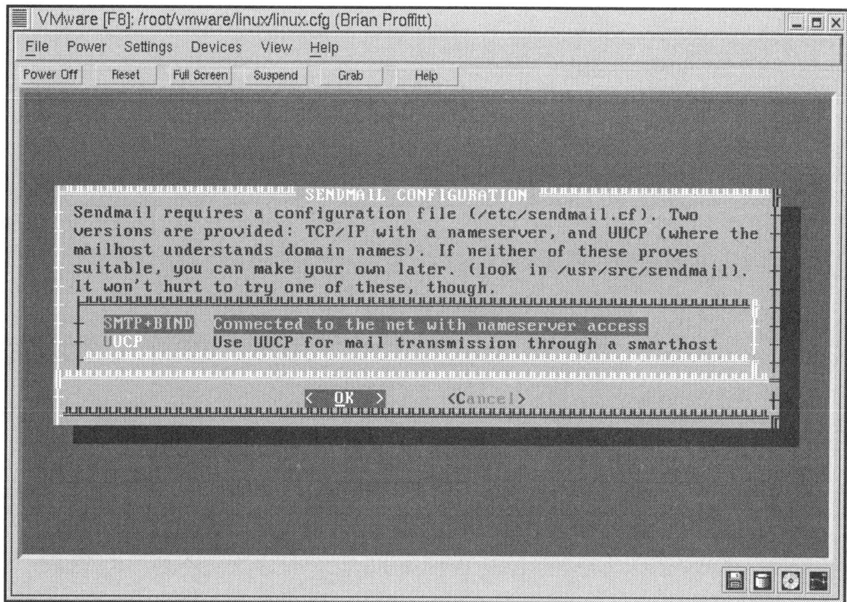

Figure 3.20 *Choosing the mail connection*

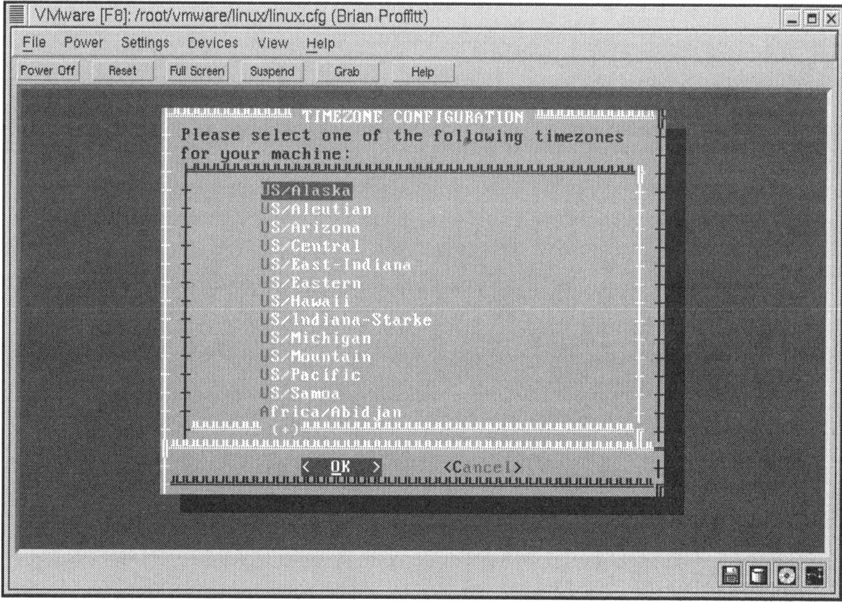

Figure 3.21 *Where in time is your PC?*

Now you get to choose something really important! Recall that there are two desktop environments included within Slackware 7: GNOME and KDE. Each has its own strengths and weaknesses, but KDE tends to be a bit more Windows-like, if that is your preference. Also, KDE includes its own window manager. With GNOME, you need to install the Enlightenment window manager to run underneath GNOME. In the Window Manager screen shown in Figure 3.22, use the arrow keys to choose the environment or window manager, and use the space bar to select. When finished, press Enter.

Way back at the beginning of the installation process, I told you that eventually you would have to set a password for the root account. Well, eventually has arrived, for in the next screen, you are reminded to set the password (see Figure 3.23).

It is a good idea to set this password as early as you can to eliminate a potentially huge security hole. Select Yes and press Enter. A command-line input appears below the colored screen, as shown in Figure 3.24.

When prompted, enter your password. If Slackware decides that this is a weak password—that is, it doesn't have enough mixed-case or numerical characters—it tells you and asks you to try again. Enter a password again as prompted. You then see the best screen of the whole program (see Figure 3.25).

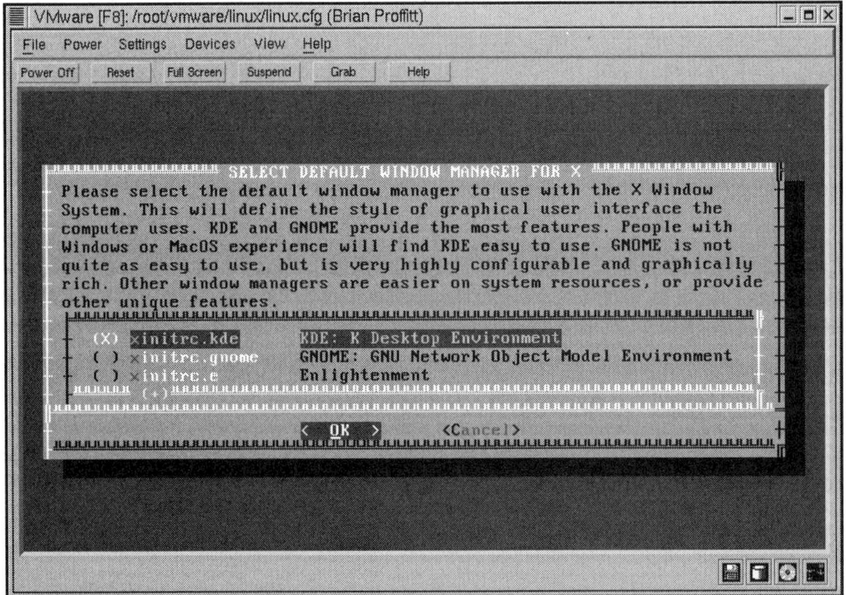

Figure 3.22 *KDE or GNOME? Decisions, decisions....*

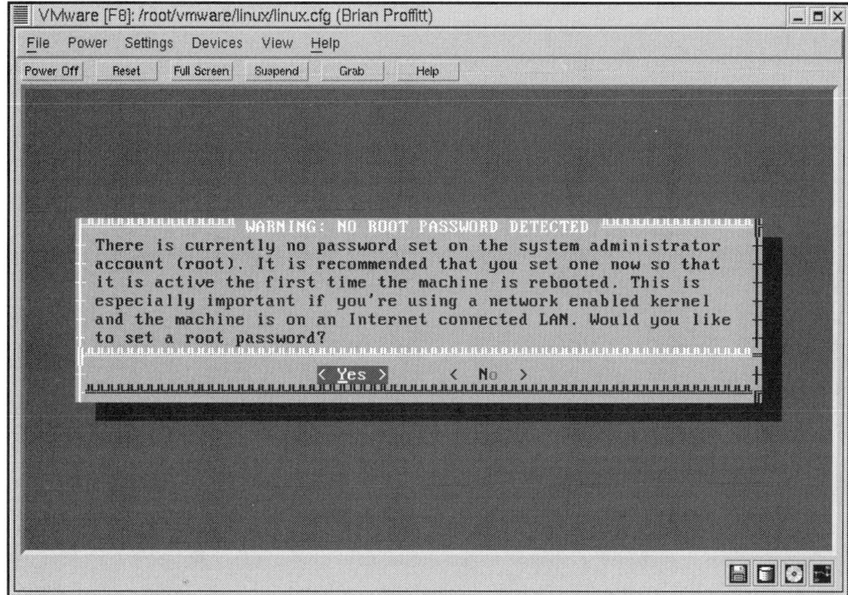

Figure 3.23 *Setup is no slouch when it comes to squaring things away.*

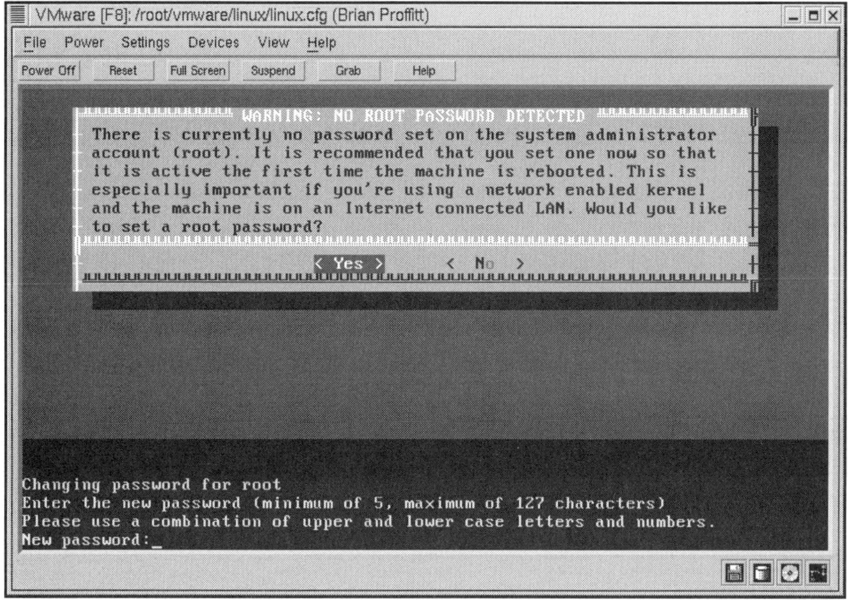

Figure 3.24 *Make sure your password is a good one.*

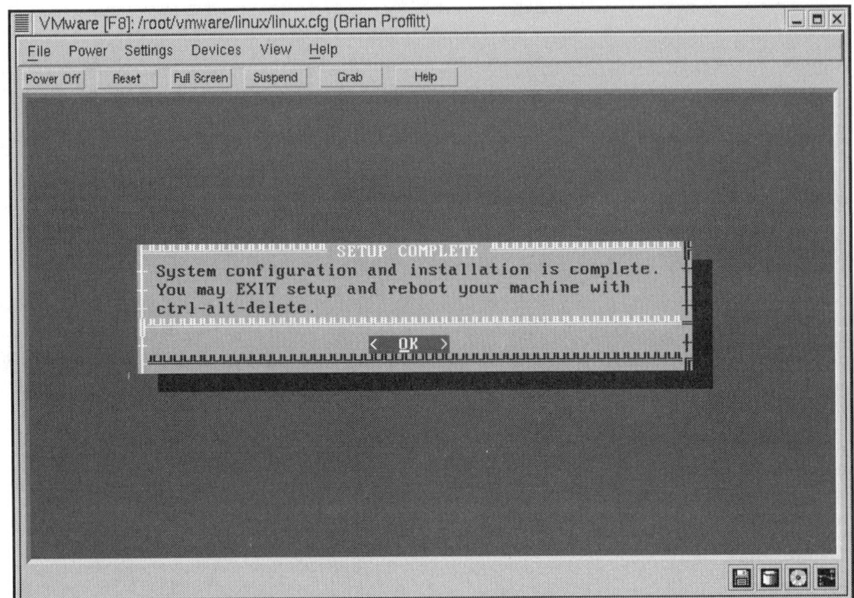

Figure 3.25 *Congratulations, you're done!*

Press Enter to close the completion screen and re-enter the main menu of setup. Type E and then press Enter to close the application down and reboot the system.

> If you have a bootable CD-ROM, be sure to remove the CD before the system completes the reboot process, or your computer boots to setup again!

Once the system reboots, it locates LILO and puts up a prompt. The prompt disappears in a few seconds and takes you to the default OS, which in this case is Slackware. If you want to load another OS, type its name at the LILO prompt and press Enter. (If you don't remember the possible names, press Tab at the prompt and LILO reminds you.) Finally, after the usual diagnostics, you arrive at the login prompt. Type **root**, then your password in the next prompt. You're done! When you want to use the GUI interface you chose, type **startx** at the command line.

Summary

In this chapter, you were guided through the lengthy yet relatively simple process of installing Slackware Linux 7 on your PC. Ideally, you can start up the OS now and start playing with all of its robust features. If things did not go according to plan, don't worry; hang on for some troubleshooting in Chapter 4, "After the Installation."

Chapter 4: After the Installation

Brian Proffitt

Troubleshooting the Installation

Making Other Users

Turning Off Linux

You've run through the setup application; you've got Slackware Linux running on your PC; and all is right with the world. Right? Well, in a perfect world, that would certainly be the case. Because we live on this planet, however, we have to contend with life's little mistakes. And, to be honest, you're not quite finished yet, even if Slackware is up and running normally. There are a few things you need to take care of before you can really start using the OS properly.

In this chapter, you look at two of the biggest problems that might happen after an installation and how you can go about fixing them. You also examine how to create new users for your Linux environment and how to properly shut down Linux.

Troubleshooting the Installation

If things did not go well during installation, the first thing you should do is examine the symptoms of the problem. For example, when I got X to run in my installation of Slackware, my mouse cursor was giving me fits. So, I ran the application that helped fix that particular problem.

Sometimes, the problem seems so big that you don't know where to start. Hopefully, this section of the book helps you surmount these huge issues.

What to Do If LILO Doesn't Boot

The first big problem you might face is a complete lack of Linux. After the installation, LILO might not start properly and thus prevent Slackware from even getting started. This happens more often than you might think; believe it or not, it's not as bad as it seems.

What has likely occurred is that you have a hardware conflict with your installed kernel of Linux. This is typically indicated by conflict messages flying down the screen. Take note of these messages; you need them later.

The reason this happens after installation is simple: The kernel you used to install Linux (either on the bootdisk or the CD) is not the same as the kernel that was actually installed.

If you recall from Chapter 3, "Installing Slackware," the kernel used was just a "mini-Linux" designed to let the setup program run, ideally off the CD-ROM. It did not present hardware conflicts, because it simply did not pay attention to much hardware.

Once the installation is done, the real kernel has to get along with all the hardware on your PC. And, in some unfortunate cases, it refuses to operate until the offending hardware is changed or removed or the kernel learns to get along with it.

The first thing to do is to try to get Linux running so you can make some changes. This may seem a classic catch-22, but you have a secret weapon: the original boot-disk you installed with. It contains the mini-kernel you need to get Linux at least partially going. This is called kickstarting Linux.

Restart the system and boot to the bootdisk. When the LILO prompt appears, you tell it to boot the root partition on your hard drive. By bypassing your kernel, you can get around the hardware conflicts. The proper command to type at the LILO prompt to do this is

```
mount root=/dev/<partition>
```

where `<partition>` is the location of the root partition, such as hda1 or hda5.

Once Linux is running, you should try to get the right support for the hardware giving you problems. A text editor such as VIM can be of use at this point. In the command line, navigate to the /etc/rc.d directory. Then, type **vi rc.modules**.

In this file are dozens of modules that Linux can load when started. These modules are designed to detect specific pieces of hardware. Many of them are commented out with the pound sign (#), but, using vi, you can remove those pound signs to activate the appropriate module.

If this is successful, the module detects the troublesome hardware and is able to accept it. If not, you might need to take the additional step of adding some new flags to the rc.modules file. These flags usually include information on the IRQ and the I/O port for a particular device, so using these parameters informs the driver exactly where to look for a device.

Different devices need different flags, so it's best to check the documentation in the rc.modules file to see what you need. If you need a flag for a SoundBlaster Pro CD, for example, then the parameters needed are just the I/O port address and the number 1, not the interrupt (IRQ).

So, in vi, you can open the /etc/rc.d/rc.modules file and change the existing Sound Blaster line from this:

```
#/sbin/modprobe sbpcd sbpcd=<I/O address>,1
```

to this:

```
/sbin/modprobe sbpcd sbpcd=0x300,1
```

Another way to accomplish the same general goal is to pass the parameters directly to the kernel when you boot. This might be useful if you need to configure a driver in the kernel—especially if the driver interacts with hardware before Linux has a chance to read any configuration files.

To pass these parameters, edit the /etc/lilo.conf file. You should add a line near the end of the file that contains your configuration settings. The line you type starts out with the word append because your parameters are appended to any others passed to the kernel. If you wanted to specify the type of your hard drive, the line might look like this:

```
append="hda=2100,255,63"
```

You can specify multiple settings. If, in addition to your hard drive setting, you also wanted to configure the Ethernet driver in your kernel, you would separate the settings with a space, as such:

```
append="hda=2100,255,63 ether=5,0x340,ne"
```

The best way to find out what parameters to pass to the kernel is to read the documentation in /usr/src/linux/Documentation. If documentation is sparse there for your particular piece of hardware, you can go to the source, literally, and look at the comments in the source code for the driver. The source is in /usr/src/linux/drivers.

> Every time you edit /etc/lilo.conf, you must reinstall LILO. To do so, simply type **lilo** while logged in as root.

The last thing you should do, because it is by far the most extreme solution, is open up your machine and start pulling out the hardware for which you have error messages. Once Linux boots, you can take steps to edit and recompile the kernel to make it fit your hardware needs. Chapter 8, "Compiling the Kernel," details how to perform this action.

Where Is X?

When I first started Slackware, I was surprised to see that it did not immediately go to X. Imagine my further surprise when I typed **startx** and nothing happened, save a slew of error messages concerning my video setup.

When you have video problems starting X, you should use *xf86Config* or *XF86Setup* to reconfigure X. You can use them to make the monitor and display setting changes that could be a big reason X might not start. In Chapter 5, "Configuring the X Window System," you learn how to use either program to make these changes.

Now about that graphical login. Whenever any Linux distribution gets started, it refers to a series of runlevels to decide how it will actually run for that session. Table 4.1 shows the runlevels and what they are supposed to do.

Table 4.1   INIT Runlevels in Slackware

Runlevel	Description
0	Halt system
1	Single-user mode
2	Unused (defaults to runlevel 3)
3	Multiuser mode
4	X11 with session managers (kdm, xdm, gdm)
5	Unused (defaults to runlevel 3)
6	Reboot

These runlevels are configured in the /etc/inittab file. The default runlevel for Slackware is 3, or multiuser mode. To get X11 to start automatically, you need to set the runlevel to 4.

While logged in as root, use vi or any other text editor to open the /etc/inittab file. Find the line that reads

```
id:3:initdefault:
```

and change it to

```
id:4:initdefault:
```

Never, I mean never, change the default runlevel to 0 or 6. This essentially renders your machine useless.

Save the file and restart your system. The Slackware login appears. This not only allows you to log in straight to X, but also lets you choose which window manager you want to use!

Making Other Users

When Slackware is running in anything but single-user mode, there should be more than just the root user. You might think this odd, especially when you are the sole user of the machine, but think about it this way: Absolute power over anything is not always a good thing.

The root account has the power to change anything on your system, good or bad. Recall the inittab edits you performed in the previous section. If someone is sharing your machine, do you want him to get a case of the clevers and try to fix your INIT sequence and end up sticking your machine in an endless loop? Certainly not! And if you are the sole user, why do you need absolute power on an everyday basis? Once Linux is configured the way you want, there should be no reason to log in as root.

For these reasons, you need to make at least one more regular user account, if only for yourself.

KDE User Manager

In the KDE environment, you can add users pretty easily with the KDE User Manager. To start the User Manager, click the Application Starter menu and then System, User Manager. The User Manager window appears (see Figure 4.1).

To add a user, click the Add button in the toolbar. In the Enter Username dialog box, type the desired user ID. Click OK to continue to the User Properties dialog box (see Figure 4.2).

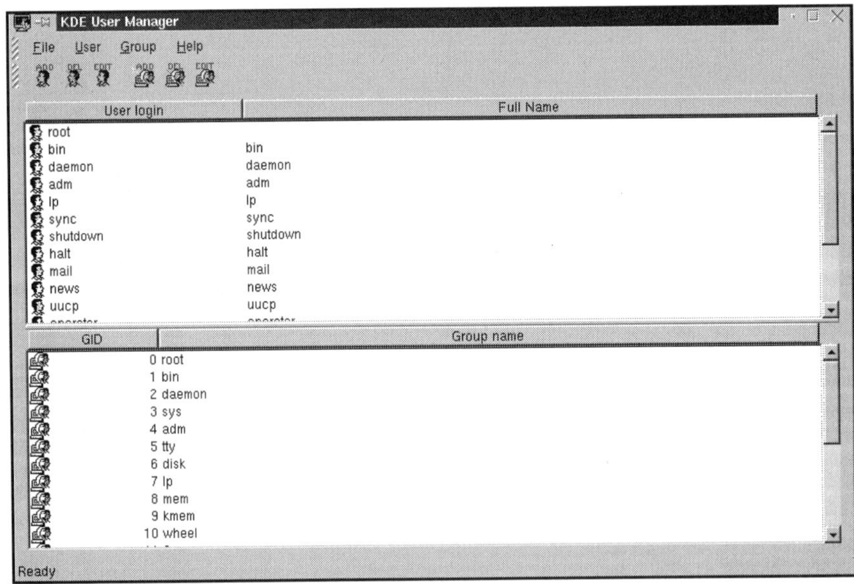

Figure 4.1 *The simple and functional User Manager*

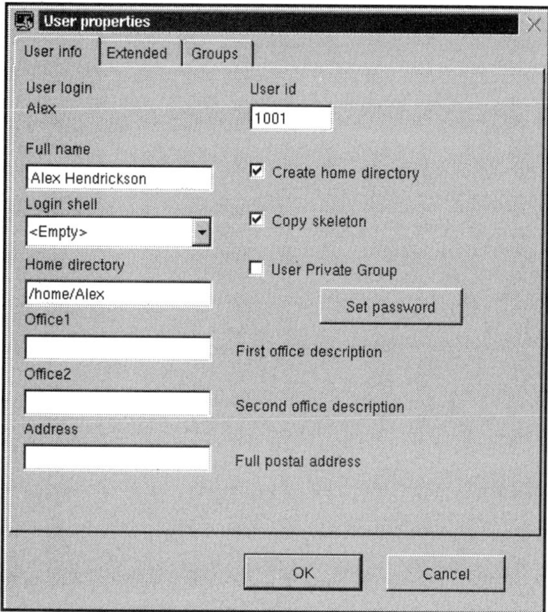

Figure 4.2 *Provide the user's information here.*

In this dialog box, you need to provide the user's full name. You can also select, from the following choices, which shell of Linux the user gets to use:

- ash
- bash
- csh
- sh
- tcsh
- zsh

Any of these shells is fine; it's really a matter of personal preference. The bash shell is the default for the root user.

If you do not like the default selection of the home directory, you can change it here. You can also set the user's password by clicking the appropriate button and entering it twice in the User Password dialog box.

If you'd like, you can enter office and address information, but it is not critical unless you are running a large network. Click the Extended tab to continue (see Figure 4.3).

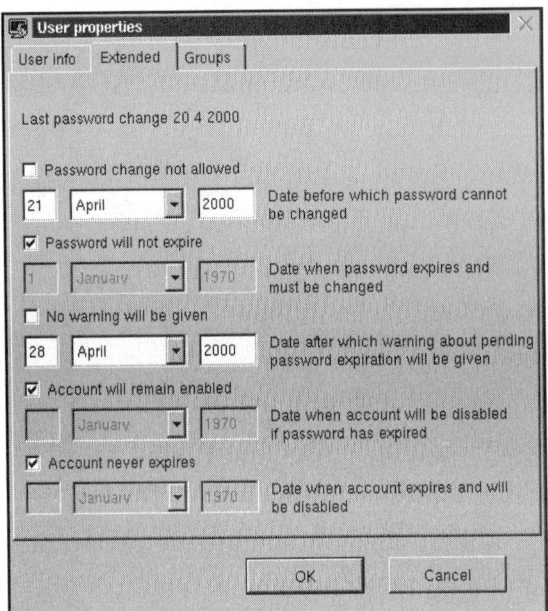

Figure 4.3 *The Extended pane controls password and account expiration times.*

If you are security-minded, it is a great idea to uncheck the Password Will Not Expire check box. This forces users to change their password every so often, which greatly enhances the security of their PCs and your network.

Of course, if you do this, it is also a good idea to set a warning date for the users so they know when to change their passwords. This should be about three days before the account is disabled with an expired password, a date you also need to set.

Once all the password settings are made, you can click on the Groups tab to set the permissions for the user.

Select a permission group on the left side of the screen and click the left arrow to assign a group to a user. I tend to give average users as many permissions as I can, except for root, adm, nobody, and nogroup.

Once complete, click OK to close the User Properties dialog box. The new user appears in the bottom of the top pane of the User Manager. Save the changes when you close the application so they apply the next time you start X.

adduser

For those of you who prefer a command-line approach to user management, there is the *adduser* application. Here's what you do:

1. In an xterm window or on the console itself, type **adduser** to begin.

2. The first prompt asks you for a username of eight characters or less. Type this in and press Enter.

3. *adduser* asks you for a numeric user ID for your user. Unless you have a special numbering scheme, just press Enter to use the next available default ID.

4. The next prompt wants to know what the group permissions are for this user. The default is users, so press Enter if you want that. If you want additional group permissions, you can add them in the next prompt, using just commas to separate the values.

5. The user's home directory is selected in the next prompt. Either type in a new directory or press Enter to accept the default value.

6. This brings you to the shell selection prompt. Unless you have serious objections to the default bash shell, press Enter to continue.

7. You then can enter the account's expiration date. Be sure to use the format outlined in the prompt.

8. Next, you are shown the selections you have made thus far and are given an opportunity to leave the application without saving the changes by typing Ctrl+C. If you accept the selections, press Enter.

9. Now you add information about the user, such as full name, office room number, and phone numbers. Enter all pertinent information.

10. After the personal information is entered, you need to add a password for the user. Enter this twice. You are finished with the *adduser* application and are returned to the command prompt.

Turning Off Linux

Windows and Mac users are accustomed to the fact that they simply can't just turn off their PCs. Instead, they must shut down first. Because most people are comfortable with this action, the steps necessary to leave X (and Linux) should feel familiar. Like its sister operating systems, Linux likes an orderly departure, not an abrupt power outage.

To leave X, you must first log out. Exactly how you do this depends on which desktop environment or window manager you are using, but typically you pull up a menu in the lower-left corner, or click on the background, and then select Logout.

If you have configured X to start when you turn on the computer, you are returned to the graphical login screen. You're now logged out and can leave the computer on for someone else to use. Or you could click on the Shutdown option to safely bring the computer down and shut it off.

If you're not using the graphical login screen, logging out of X returns you to the console's command line. You're still logged in at this point; it's just that X isn't running. If you are root you have the rights to type **shutdown -h now** to shut down and halt the computer. Linux closes all running processes as part of its halt sequence. If you're not root, you could, of course, become root to do this. But a faster way is to just press Ctrl+Alt+Del and turn the power off once the machine reboots.

Summary

The chapters in this part of the book got you where you wanted to be. You are the owner of a PC running Slackware Linux 7. Now that you have completed this task, it's time to move on to Part II, "Configuring and Customizing Slackware," to get your newly installed OS to meet your qualifications.

In Chapter 5, you learn about the underpinnings of the graphical interface: configuring the X Window System.

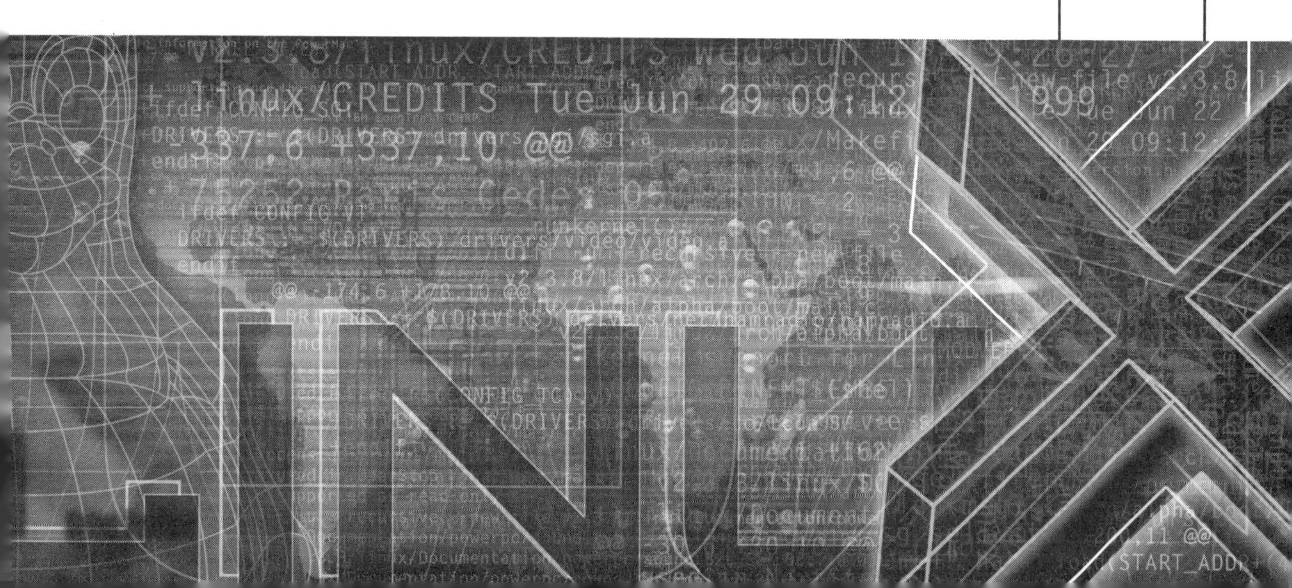

Chapter 5: Configuring the X Window System

Jacek Artymiak

Setting Up XFree86

*Understanding Desktop Environments
and Window Managers*

Almost all of today's operating systems have some sort of graphical user interface (GUI). Linux's X Window System is no exception; it's one of the most powerful GUIs available for any operating system, and you can use all of its power in Slackware Linux 7. Unlike Microsoft Windows or Mac OS GUIs, which you can get from only one source, there is more than one implementation of the X Window System, and you can choose between free and commercial versions. The most popular (and free) implementation, *XFree86*, comes with every decent Linux distribution and is of excellent quality.

What makes the X Window System different from other GUIs is its highly modular design; The basic services, window management, and desktop environment are separated and can be easily exchanged to suit the needs of the user. For example, currently more than two dozen window managers and two desktop environments are available for the X Window System. And more important, that abundant choice does not affect compatibility.

In this chapter I show you how to configure *XFree86 3.3.5* and customize it to your own needs.

Setting Up *XFree86*

The first rule for successful *XFree86* installation is similar to what you learned in Chapter 1, "Before You Install: Getting to Know Your Hardware"—start with the hardware that is compatible with *XFree86* and you can save yourself a lot of trouble. In general, the video card you want to use with *XFree86* should fulfill the following requirements:

- **Compatible system/video bus architecture.** Video cards connect to expansion slots on the computer's motherboard. These slots can be designed to use ISA, PCI, or AGP technology; the different technologies use different connectors to make sure you do not plug the card into the wrong type of slot. ISA is the oldest technology; you really should not use ISA video cards in computers fewer than five years old. PCI is better, and AGP is best in terms of speed.

- **Compatible chipset.** The chipset used by the card's manufacturer must be supported by *XFree86*; lists of supported chipsets can be found in the /etc/X11/doc directory (start with the README files). (Note that the same chipset can be used by different manufacturers.)

- **The card must use linear addressing.** Nonlinear addressing is one of the features of video cards that prevents them from working with *XFree86*, even if they work without problems with other operating systems.

If the card abides by these rules, it should work with *XFree86*, although that is by no means guaranteed. You can only be sure of that if you try it with *XFree86* yourself (make sure you can return the card in the event it does not work with *XFree86*). The best test of your card's compatibility is to run *XF86Setup*, a graphical configuration utility that makes the whole process of configuring *XFree86* quick and easy.

> In this chapter I assume that you installed the software necessary to configure and run *XFree86* (see Chapter 3, "Installing Slackware," for more information).

Using XF86Setup

To set up *XFree86* using *XF86Setup*, do the following:

1. Make sure that you are logged in as root, type **XF86Setup**, and press the Enter key to start the *XF86Setup* utility.

2. Answer yes (press the Enter key to do it) to questions about using existing configuration files and switching to graphics mode.

If all goes well, you should see a screen similar to the one shown in Figure 5.1. You can now start configuring *XFree86* using your mouse. If it is not working (which is quite likely), you can use your keyboard:

- Press the Tab key to switch between various options.

- Press the spacebar to select the chosen option.

- To select items from lists or change the values of sliders, use the Up and Down cursor keys.

- Instead of clicking the buttons on the top and bottom of the screen, simultaneously press the key corresponding to the underlined letter on the button and the Alt key.

The six buttons along the top edge of the screen are used to switch between different configuration modules. Make sure you take a look at all of them, and configure all the options that need to be set here. The three buttons along the bottom edge of the screen are used to abort the configuration process without modifying any files, to finish the configuration process and write the new setup to the disk, and to display help.

> If *XF86Setup* complains about a missing X server, make a note of which X server was missing and see Chapter 3 to learn how to install it. Should there be any more problems, try using the *XF86Config* script described in the "Using *XF86Config*" section later in this chapter.

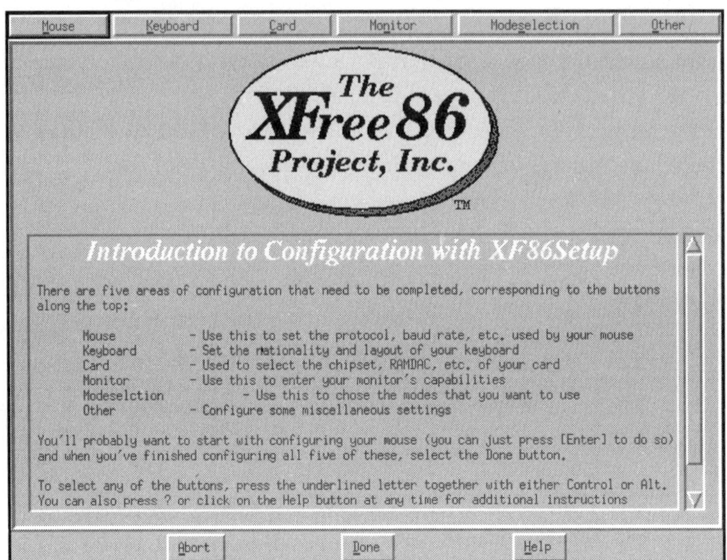

Figure 5.1 *Welcome to* XF86Setup.

The following options are available in the *XF86Setup* module:

- Mouse
- Keyboard
- Card
- Monitor
- Modeselection
- Other

The Mouse Setup Module

The Mouse setup module (see Figure 5.2), activated when you click the Mouse button or press Alt+M, is used to configure your mouse (trackball, glide pad, and so on) for *XFree86*. It is worth noting that the configuration files for *gpm* (the text-mode program that allows the user to cut and paste with the mouse) and *XFree86* are independent and not interchangeable.

Here is an explanation of each of the options on the Mouse configuration screen:

- **Mouse protocol.** Use the group of buttons near the top of the screen to select the type of mouse protocol used to communicate with the computer. Click the button for your mouse's manufacturer (note that those without the PS/2 suffix are used to communicate with mice that connect to the serial interface,

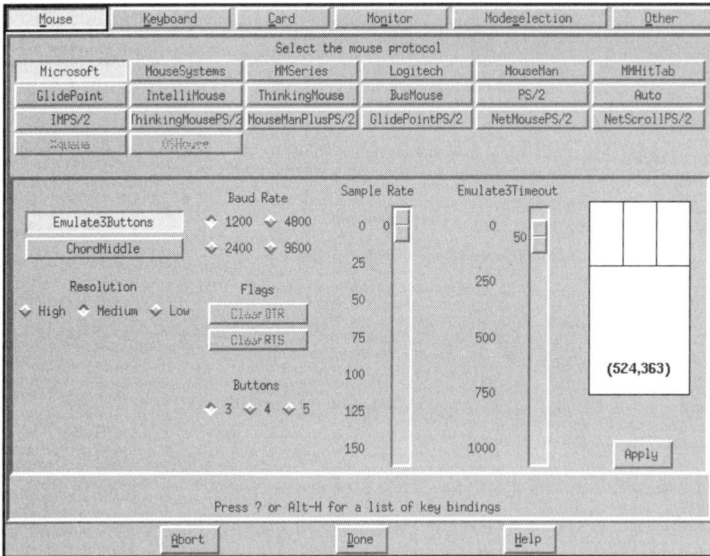

Figure 5.2 *The* XF86Setup *Mouse configuration module*

whereas those with the PS/2 suffix are used to communicate with mice that connect to the PS/2 interface).

If you're configuring a laptop, you probably have to look up this information in the manuals or data sheets for your computer. If no information is available, taking a quick look at the connectors on the back might help. If there are no PS/2 connectors, then the laptop's trackball (or other pointing device) is using a serial interface; otherwise, it quite possibly uses the PS/2 interface.

The so-called "no name" mice usually use the Microsoft protocol (some mice have a switch located at the bottom that allows them to emulate different types of protocols; you might need to switch off the computer to avoid damaging its circuits), so try clicking that first.

To test whether you chose the right protocol, click the Apply button located below the mouse diagram on the right side of the screen, and move the mouse around to see if the numbers representing the mouse coordinates change. If the mouse coordinates do not change, click the next protocol and repeat the test again.

- **Emulate3Buttons.** Although most PC mice have only two buttons, *XFree86* expects the mouse to have three. With two-button mice, the left button is knows as Button1, and the right one is known as Button3; the missing button (Button2) must be emulated in software. For all two-button mice other than those made by Logitech, the Emulate3Buttons option should be enabled (if your mouse is by Logitech, see the next paragraph). To make sure the mouse buttons operate correctly, click the Apply button and press each one in turn, and see if the left and right rectangles on the mouse diagram blink. To see whether Button2 emulation works, press and hold the left mouse button and press the right mouse button; the middle rectangle should blink to indicate that the emulation really works.

- **ChordMiddle.** This option has the same meaning as the Emulate3Buttons option, but it applies only to Logitech mice. If you enable ChordMiddle, you should disable Emulate3Buttons.

- **Resolution.** Use this option to specify how quickly the mouse cursor travels when you move the mouse. In most cases, the Medium setting is the best one to choose. If the cursor travels too slowly, choose the Low option; and if the cursor travels too quickly, choose the High option. (Again, you can click the Apply button to test the new settings.)

- **Baud Rate.** This option sets the speed at which the mouse is sending data to the computer. In most cases, 1200 is the right one to use. Setting a higher rate might lock the mouse.

- **Flags.** Use these options to force a three-button mouse to cooperate with *XFree86*. When you are having problems with such mice, click the ClearDTR and ClearRTS buttons to activate both functions.

- **Buttons.** For two- and three-button mice, set this option to 3. For four-button mice, click the 4 option; for mice with five or more buttons, click on the 5 option.

- **Sample Rate.** Use this slider to specify how often the computer polls the mouse for its position. In most cases you can leave it at 0, but you might want to adjust it if you have an older mouse.

- **Emulate3Timeout.** Use this slider to set the time delay (measured in milliseconds) used in the emulation of Button2. You can leave it set to 50 (its default value).

When you are finished with the mouse configuration, click the Apply button.

The Keyboard Setup Module

Click the Keyboard button to switch to the keyboard configuration module screen, shown in Figure 5.3.

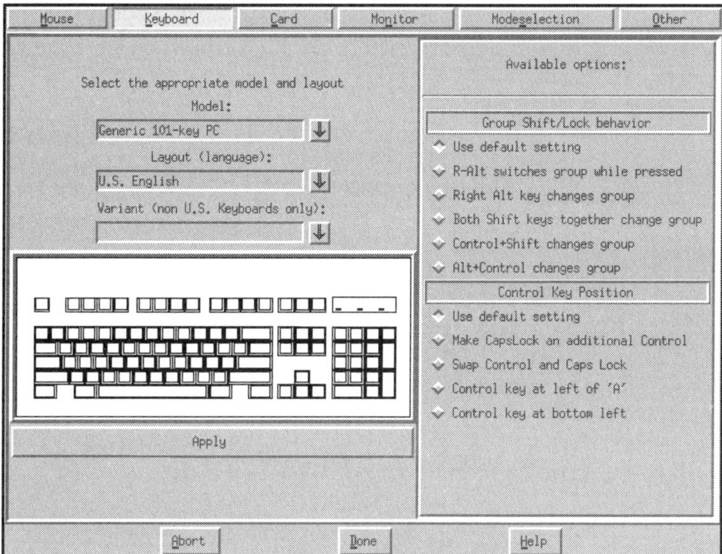

Figure 5.3 *The* XF86Setup *keyboard configuration module*

The keyboard configuration module contains three lists and two groups of options. Here is what they are used for:

- **Model.** In this area, you find all keyboard models known to *XFree86* (the list of predefined keyboards appears when you click the button with an arrow pointing down). The procedure is simple: If your keyboard's name appears on the list, select it. If not, choose one of the generic keyboards. (Note that the image of the keyboard changes as you select different keyboard models.)

- **Layout.** Use this list to select the language layout for your keyboard. English-speaking Americans should choose the standard U.S. English layout. If you speak a different language, choose the layout that matches the language in which you create documents.

- **Variant.** Use this list to choose the appropriate variant of the language layout chosen in the Layout list. (Note: This applies only to non-U.S. English layouts.)

- **Group Shift/Lock Behavior.** Select from the options listed in this group to specify which key combination allows you to enter characters not printed on the keys, such as accented letters or other symbols. If you use the U.S. English layout, click the Use Default Setting option.

- **Control Key Position.** Use the options listed in this group to specify which key should be interpreted as the Ctrl (Control on some keyboards) key. In most cases, it's best to choose the Use Default Setting option. (In reality, you could choose any key to be interpreted as the Ctrl key, but that requires understanding how the keyboard definitions work, which is well beyond the scope of this book.)

When you have finished configuring the keyboard, click the Apply button to accept the changes you have made.

The Card Setup Module

Click the Card button to switch to the card selection module screen, shown in Figure 5.4. You use this module to select the right *XFree86* server for your video card.

This screen contains the following options:

- **Card Selected.** Here you can choose the name of the card definition block (there may be more than one) you want to modify. In Figure 5.4, I named it Karta, but you can choose your own name, if you want.

- **Server.** Use the row of buttons near the top edge of the screen to select the *XFree86* server (the core program that controls the X Window System) for the video card installed inside your computer. The first three servers, Mono, VGA16, and SVGA, are known as generic servers and should work with almost any kind of a video card. The others are dedicated servers that work with cards using specific chipsets. For example, for cards using S3 chipsets, you should click the S3 button (or the S3V, if you have an S3 ViRGE chip instead of the old S3 chips). Similarly, the T128 server is meant to work with

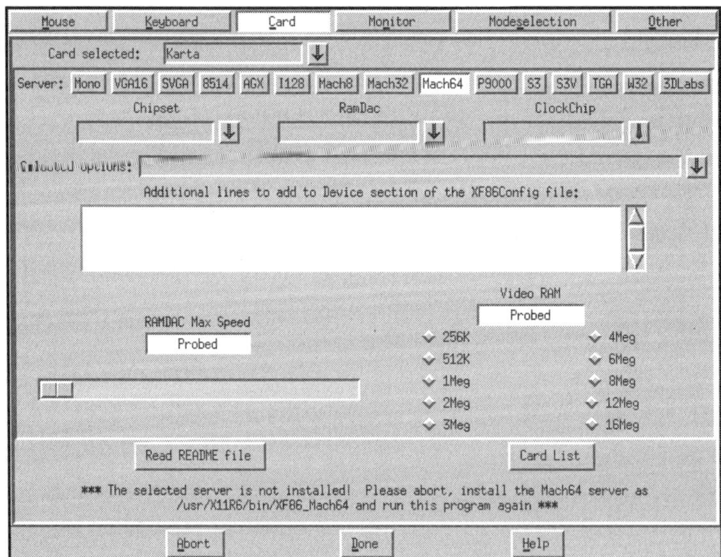

Figure 5.4 *The* XF86Setup *video card configuration module*

the video cards using the Tseng 128 chipset. You can find information about the chipset used in your card in the card's technical specifications, or you can read it off the (usually) largest chip on the card's printed circuit board. You should always try to use the dedicated *XFree86* server for the video card installed inside your computer; only when that fails should you try the SVGA, VGA16, or Mono server (in that order). If all of them fail, you can be quite sure that your card does not work under *XFree86*.

- **Chipset.** Use this list is to specify which chipset from a larger family of chipsets ought to be chosen by the dedicated server (this is necessary only when the server cannot make the right guess when it starts). In most cases you can leave this box empty or choose the Probed item from the list (the *XFree86* server determines the best setting).

- **RamDac.** More expensive video cards use special RAMDAC chips to boost the card's performance. Read the description of your card's technical parameters; if there is a mention of a RAMDAC chip, make a note of what it is and choose one from the RamDac list. Most cards do not have these chips, and it is usually safe to leave this field empty.

- **ClockChip.** Like RAMDAC chips, clock chips are usually found on more expensive cards. If yours has one, select it from the list; otherwise, leave this field empty.

- **Selected Options.** Some chipsets or video cards require you to set additional options; you can type them here. To see if you need to do this, click the Read README File button near the bottom of the screen—you are shown the README File for the selected *XFree86* server.

- **Additional Lines.** Use this text field to add lines to the Device section of the /etc/XF86Config file (the main configuration file for *XFree86*.) In most cases you can leave this field empty. See the appropriate README file for your card's chipset for more information about additional configuration options.

- **RAMDAC Max Speed.** If your video card has a RAMDAC chip, you can control its speed with this slider. If you do not want to set it manually, click the Probed button (the XFree86 server determines the best setting).

- **Video RAM.** This option is usually set to Probed, enabling the server to automatically determine the amount of available RAM. Should it fail, or should you want to limit the amount of RAM used, you can set one of the numeric options instead.

If you cannot find the name of the chipset used in your card, click the Card List button to view the list of all video cards whose configurations are known to *XFree86* (see Figure 5.5). Scroll down the list and select the entry that matches the name of your video card. (If you do not know the name of the chipset, and your card is not on the list, do not despair. You should be able to use it with one of the generic servers—

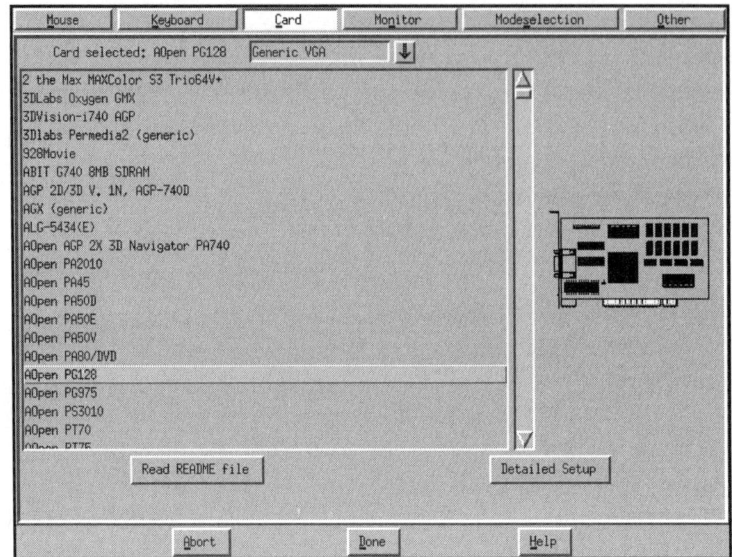

Figure 5.5 *The* XF86Setup *video card list*

SVGA, VGA16, or Mono). When you click on the appropriate entry, *XF86Setup* makes sure that the correct server for the selected card is installed on your system (it displays a warning if it cannot find the right server). To return to the card configuration module, click the Detailed Setup button.

The Monitor Setup Module

Click the Monitor button to switch to the monitor configuration module screen, shown in Figure 5.6. This module is used to define your monitor's basic parameters. These definitions are used by the *XFree86* server to decide how to display the contents of the video card's memory.

To properly configure your monitor, use these options:

- **Monitor Sync Rates.** Here you enter the horizontal and vertical synchronization rates of your monitor. You can find that data in your monitor's manual (look for technical specifications) or on the back of the monitor's case. Remember that you can enter multiple values (separate them with a comma) and ranges (marked with a minus sign). Make sure you do not confuse horizontal and vertical scan frequency!

- **Monitor List.** Many monitors' parameters fall into one of the monitor types listed inside the blue box on the screen. If your monitor has exactly the same parameters, simply select it from the list.

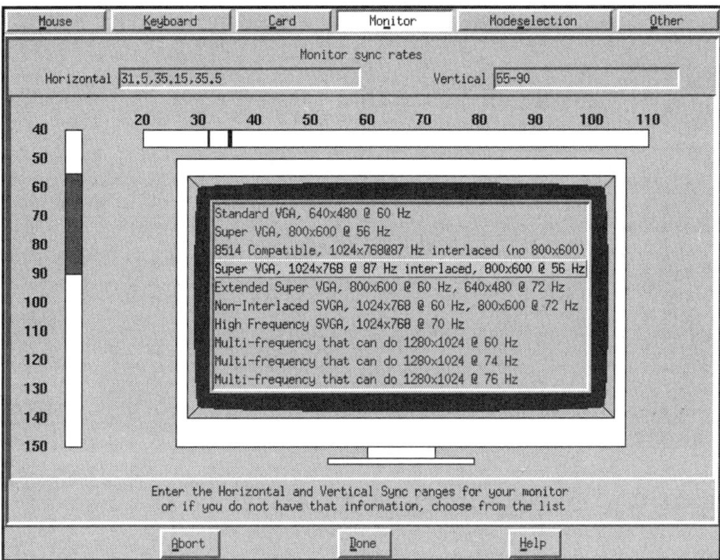

Figure 5.6 XF86Setup *monitor configuration module*

Make sure you select the right values for refresh rates because using the wrong ones can damage the monitor. Newer monitors tend to be more resistant to such damage, but still, be careful.

CAUTION

The Modeselection Setup Module

Click the Modeselection button to switch to the video modes configuration module screen, shown in Figure 5.7. On this screen, you can define the screen resolution and color depth.

Here is how you go about it:

1. Choose the screen resolutions. You can choose just one screen resolution, but it doesn't hurt if you choose more. Simply click on the maximum screen resolution supported by your card (this might vary with the amount of RAM that your card has installed) along with all smaller resolutions on the list. For example, if the maximum screen resolution that your card supports is 1024×768 pixels (screen points), then you can click on the following resolutions: 1024×768, 800×600, and 640×480.

2. Choose the default color depth, but make sure that the color depth you choose is supported at the maximum screen resolution you chose in step 1.

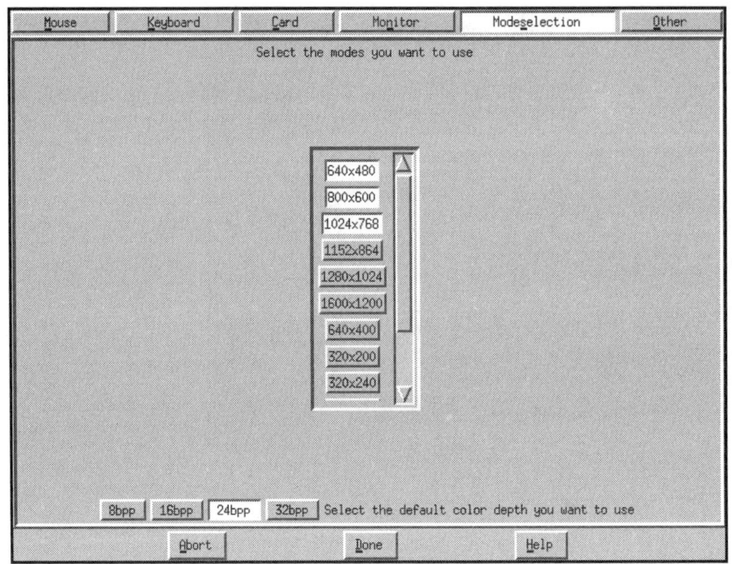

Figure 5.7 XF86Setup *video modes configuration module*

If your card has 4MB of RAM, then 1024×768 at 24bpp (that's millions of colors) is fine. If, however, your card has less memory, set the default color depth to 16bpp, or in extreme cases, to 8bpp. Otherwise, the *XFree86* server does not start, and it might give you the false impression that something is wrong with the video card. Remember that the more video RAM your card has, the greater color depths and screen resolutions it supports.

You can switch between various screen resolutions within the bounds of the same color depth by pressing Ctrl+Alt+<Numeric keypad +> and Ctrl+Alt+<Numeric keypad × >.

The Other Setup Module

To proceed to the last configuration module, click the Other button to view the screen shown in Figure 5.8. Here you can configure a few final options.

Optional server settings include the following:

- **Allow Server to Be Killed with Hotkey Sequence (Ctrl+Alt+Backspace).** Enable this option; sadly, it is sometimes necessary to kill the server and restart it again when it is not behaving properly. This is a particularly useful option if you discover (the hard way) that you defined your monitor's sync rates incorrectly.

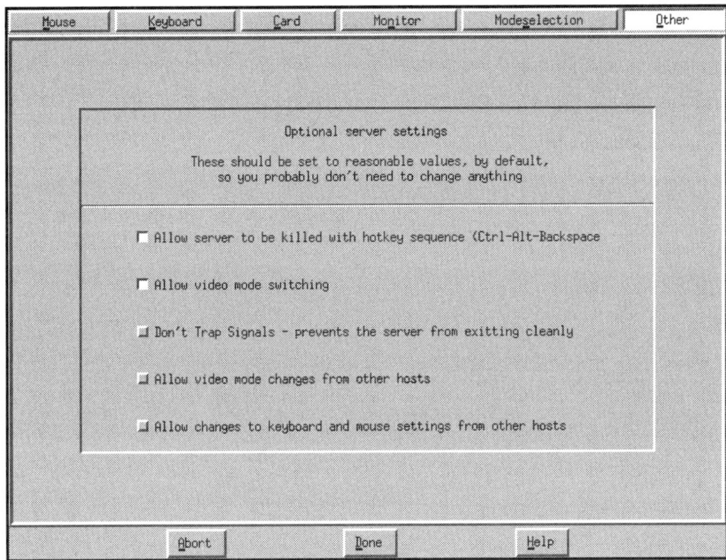

Figure 5.8 *The final options screen*

- **Allow Video Mode Switching.** Enable this option when you are testing various screen resolution/color depth combinations. Once you choose the one you like, you can turn it off.
- **Don't Trap Signals.** Disable this option.
- **Allow Video Mode Changes from Other Hosts.** Disable this option at all times, unless you are an administrator and want to be able to control screen resolution and color depth from another computer.
- **Allow Changes to Keyboard and Mouse Settings from Other Hosts.** Similar to the previous option, this one should be left disabled unless you are an administrator and you know what you want.

Last Screen

After you are finished with the general options configuration, proceed to the last *XF86Setup* screen, shown in Figure 5.9, which remains hidden until you click the Done button.

This screen can be used for the following purposes:

- **To specify the location of the new XF86Config configuration file.** It's a good idea to write it to your home directory first. In Figure 5.9, I'm telling *XF86Setup* to write it to /home/jacek/XF86Config, which prevents the existing configuration from being accidentally overwritten.

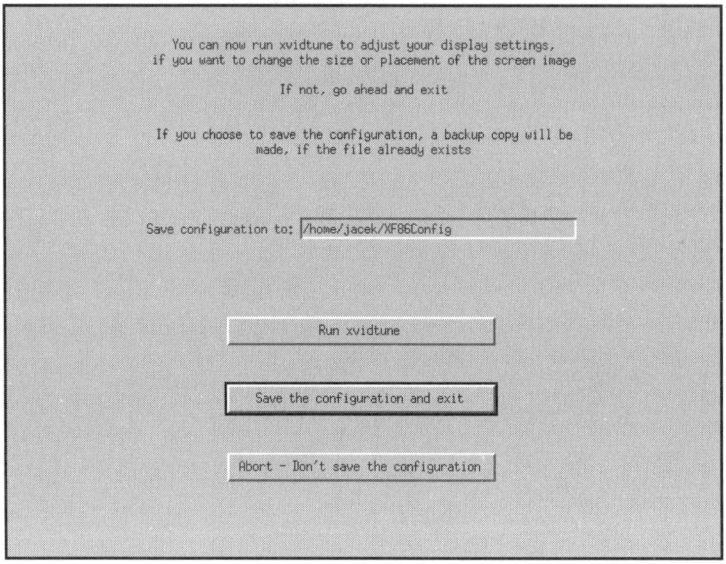

Figure 5.9 XF86Setup: *We're almost done.*

- **To run the *xvidtune* video mode tuner.** This piece of software allows you to fine-tune video mode configuration. It is particularly useful for making adjustments to the size and positioning of the display on the monitor's screen (you could use the monitor's own dials or onscreen menus for that purpose, but it could affect display positioning in text mode). To activate *xvidtune*, follow the instructions in the next section.

- **To save the new configuration and return back to the command line.** The new configuration is written to the file specified in the field located at the top of the screen; you should copy it to /etc/XF86Config. Make sure you make a backup copy of the previous XF86Config file first, for example, by renaming it with **mv /etc/XF86Config /etc/XF86Config.backup**.

- **To abort the configuration process.** If you select this option, all changes you have made so far are lost, and you are returned to the command line.

Activating *xvidtune*

To activate *xvidtune*, do the following:

1. Click the Run xvidtune button on the screen shown in Figure 5.9.

2. You see a dialog box, shown in Figure 5.10, that warns about possible monitor/video card damage that can be caused by the incorrect use of *xvidtune* (this happens very rarely, as all you really need in most cases is a small correction of the display size and position). Click the OK button after

```
WARNING     WARNING     WARNING     WARNING     WARNING     WARNING

THE INCORRECT USE OF THIS PROGRAM CAN DO PERMANENT DAMAGE TO YOUR MONITOR
AND/OR VIDEO CARD.  IF YOU ARE NOT SURE WHAT YOU ARE DOING, HIT CANCEL
NOW. OTHERWISE, HIT OK TO CONTINUE

THE SOFTWARE IS PROVIDED "AS IS", WITHOUT WARRANTY OF ANY KIND,
EXPRESS OR IMPLIED, INCLUDING BUT NOT LIMITED TO THE WARRANTIES OF
MERCHANTABILITY, FITNESS FOR A PARTICULAR PURPOSE AND NONINFRINGEMENT.
IN NO EVENT SHALL Kaleb S. KEITHLEY (or his employer) OR
The XFree86 Project Inc. BE LIABLE FOR ANY CLAIM, DAMAGES OR OTHER
LIABILITY, WHETHER IN AN ACTION OF CONTRACT, TORT OR OTHERWISE, ARISING
FROM, OUT OF OR IN CONNECTION WITH THE SOFTWARE OR THE USE OR OTHER
DEALINGS IN THE SOFTWARE.

[OK] [Cancel]
```

Figure 5.10 *Read this warning carefully.*

```
HDisplay:    800            VDisplay:     600
HSyncStart:     824         VSyncStart:    601
[          ▓                 ]  [  ▓                          ]
HSyncEnd:    896            VSyncEnd:     603
[       ▓                    ]  [  ▓                          ]
HTotal:   1024              VTotal:      625
[              ▓            ]  [          ▓                   ]
[Left] [Right] [Wider] [Narrower]   [Up] [Down] [Shorter] [Taller]

Flags (hex): [0000]          Pixel Clock (MHz):   36.00

[Quit] [Apply] [Auto] [Test] [Restore]   Horizontal Sync (kHz):   35.16

[Fetch] [Show] [Next] [Prev]             Vertical Sync (Hz):   56.25
```

Figure 5.11 *The* xvidtune *configuration dialog box*

reading the warning to proceed to the *xvidtune* configuration dialog box (you can click the Cancel button to abort *xvidtune*).

3. The *xvidtune* configuration dialog box opens; as you can see in Figure 5.11, it is quite crowded. Nonetheless, you should be able to quickly locate the buttons that control horizontal movement (Left and Right), horizontal scaling (Wider and Narrower), vertical movement (Up and Down), and vertical scaling (Shorter and Taller). Try altering these. Note that whenever you make a change, the sliders located in the upper part of the dialog move.

4. To see how the changes you have made affect the size and positioning of the display, click the Test button.

5. If you're not satisfied with the changes, click the Restore button to restore the original settings (or press the **R** key), and repeat steps 3 and 4.

6. To quit and save your changes, click the Apply button, and then on the Quit button. To exit from *xvidtune* without making changes permanent, click the Quit button only.

To find out more about *xvidtune*, read its man page (type **man xvidtune** on the command line and press the Enter key).

Troubleshooting the Setup

If everything goes well, you should be able to start the X Window System (to learn how to do it, skip to the "Understanding Desktop Environments and Window Managers" section later in this chapter).

When you get errors, they are most likely related to the missing *XFree86* server. Simply make a note of the name of the server, which always begins with XF86_ and ends with the name of the supported chipset, (e.g. XF86_S3 is the *XFree86* server for the whole family of S3 chipsets), install the missing server, and run *XF86Setup* again.

Another problem you might encounter is a missing or incorrectly configured link to the *XFree86* server. To check what it currently points to, type **ls -l /var/X11R6/bin/X** on the command line and press the Enter key. You should see something like this:

```
lrwxrwxrwx   1 root      root             22 Mar  19 14:57 /var/X11R6/bin/X ->
/usr/X11R6/bin/XF86_S3
```

The part after the arrow tells you what server is used as the default X Window System server. To change it to another server, type **ln -sf /var/X11R6/bin/XF86_nameofserver /usr/X11R6/bin/X** at the command prompt and press the Enter key.

If you are having further problems, try the *XF86Config* script described in the next section.

Using XF86Config

The *XF86Config* script is another *XFree86* configuration utility. It does not use a fancy graphical user interface, which is a plus when *XF86Setup* fails for some reason. Instead, the script asks you questions and you answer them; once you answer a question and confirm it by pressing the Enter key, it cannot be changed unless you press Ctrl+C and start the script again, so it is a good idea to make notes as you go along.

To use *XF86Config*, do the following:

1. Type **XF86Config** on the command line and press the Enter key (you ought to be root).

2. You see a message similar to the one shown in Figure 5.12. Press the Enter key to configure the mouse.

3. The *XF86Config* mouse configuration screen, shown in Figure 5.13, offers fewer options than the mouse configuration module in *XF86Setup*, but the rules are similar. If you have a serial two-button Microsoft-compatible mouse, type **1**. For a PS/2 mouse, type **4**. If your mouse is of another type, see if its

```
This program will create a basic XF86Config file, based on menu selections you
make.

The XF86Config file usually resides in /usr/X11R6/lib/X11 or /etc. A sample
XF86Config file is supplied with XFree86; it is configured for a standard
VGA card and monitor with 640x480 resolution. This program will ask for a
pathname when it is ready to write the file.

You can either take the sample XF86Config as a base and edit it for your
configuration, or let this program produce a base XF86Config file for your
configuration and fine-tune it. Refer to /usr/X11R6/lib/X11/doc/README.Config
for a detailed overview of the configuration process.

For accelerated servers (including accelerated drivers in the SVGA server),
there are many chipset and card-specific options and settings. This program
does not know about these. On some configurations some of these settings must
be specified. Refer to the server man pages and chipset-specific READMEs.

Before continuing with this program, make sure you know the chipset and
amount of video memory on your video card. SuperProbe can help with this.
It is also helpful if you know what server you want to run.

Press enter to continue, or ctrl-c to abort.
```

Figure 5.12 *Welcome to* XF86Config.

```
First specify a mouse protocol type. Choose one from the following list:

 1.   Microsoft compatible (2-button protocol)
 2.   Mouse Systems (3-button protocol)
 3.   Bus Mouse
 4.   PS/2 Mouse
 5.   Logitech Mouse (serial, old type, Logitech protocol)
 6.   Logitech MouseMan (Microsoft compatible)
 7.   MM Series
 8.   MM HitTablet
 9.   Microsoft IntelliMouse
10.   Acecad tablet

If you have a two-button mouse, it is most likely of type 1, and if you have
a three-button mouse, it can probably support both protocol 1 and 2. There are
two main varieties of the latter type: mice with a switch to select the
protocol, and mice that default to 1 and require a button to be held at
boot-time to select protocol 2. Some mice can be convinced to do 2 by sending
a special sequence to the serial port (see the ClearDTR/ClearRTS options).

Enter a protocol number:
```

Figure 5.13 *The mouse configuration screen*

manufacturer appears on the list and select it. When in doubt, type **1**. For
more information, see the section titled "The Mouse Setup Module" earlier in
this chapter.

4. Hit the Enter key to confirm your choice and configure additional mouse
   options.

5. If you choose mouse protocol 2 (a three-button mouse), the script asks you if
   you want to use the ClearDTR and ClearRTS options (see Figure 5.14).
   These help when a three-button mouse has problems communicating with
   the computer. Type **Y** and press the Enter key if you want to use this option.

   If you are configuring a two-button mouse, you're asked whether you want to
   use the Emulate3Buttons option. Alternatively, if your mouse was
   manufactured by Logitech, you're asked whether you want to use the

```
two main varieties of the latter type: mice with a switch to select the
protocol, and mice that default to 1 and require a button to be held at
boot-time to select protocol 2. Some mice can be convinced to do 2 by sending
a special sequence to the serial port (see the ClearDTR/ClearRTS options).

Enter a protocol number: 2

You have selected a Mouse Systems protocol mouse. If your mouse is normally
in Microsoft-compatible mode, enabling the ClearDTR and ClearRTS options
may cause it to switch to Mouse Systems mode when the server starts.

Please answer the following question with either 'y' or 'n'.
Do you want to enable ClearDTR and ClearRTS? n

You have selected a three-button mouse protocol. It is recommended that you
do not enable Emulate3Buttons, unless the third button doesn't work.

Please answer the following question with either 'y' or 'n'.
Do you want to enable Emulate3Buttons? y

Now give the full device name that the mouse is connected to, for example
/dev/tty00. Just pressing enter will use the default, /dev/mouse.

Mouse device: []
```

Figure 5.14 *Mouse configuration options*

ChordMiddle option instead. In either case, type **Y**. For more information, see the section titled "The Mouse Setup Module" earlier in this chapter.

6. Press the Enter key; you're asked about the mouse device—this is the interface to which the mouse is connected. In most cases, you can simply press the Enter key, but you may specify the full path to the device if you wish. For example, /dev/ttyS0 is the serial mouse port on most PCs, and /dev/psaux is the PS/2 connector. As a guideline for serial interfaces, remember that the PC port COM1 is /dev/ttyS0, COM2 is /dev/ttyS1, COM3 is /dev/ttyS2, and so on.

Mouse tablets and joysticks might connect to other interfaces; if these are serial interfaces, try one of the /dev/ttyS* devices. For joysticks, try either /dev/js0 or /dev/js1. Be warned, however, that you need to manually modify your *XF86Config* file (once you're done with *XF86Config*) if you want to use a tablet or joystick as your pointing device. For an example of how to configure these pointing devices, view the /usr/X11R6/lib/X11/XF86Config.eg file and search for this line:

```
Section "Xinput"
```

This section gives many examples for configuring tablets and joysticks. You want to copy the section for your device, paste it into your own XF86Config file, uncomment it, and finally, make any adjustments. You also might need to load a driver; search for this line in the XF86Config.eg file for an example:

```
Section "Module"
```

The XF86Config man page discusses these settings in great detail.

7. After you type the mouse device name and/or press Enter, you can begin configuring the keyboard. You're first asked your preferred method for managing keyboard layouts (see Figure 5.15). Just answer **Y** and press the Enter key, unless you have a good reason to use the old method (if you do not know what it means, then you do not need the old method).

8. The configuration script displays a list of all keyboard types it knows of (see Figure 5.16). In most cases, you need to use one of the first three types of preconfigured keymaps (typing **1** and pressing Enter ought to make *XFree86* work with all U.S. keyboards). For more information, see the section titled "The Keyboard Setup Module" earlier in this chapter. If your keyboard is not listed, and if it is nonstandard, you can try to assemble your own. Type **12** and

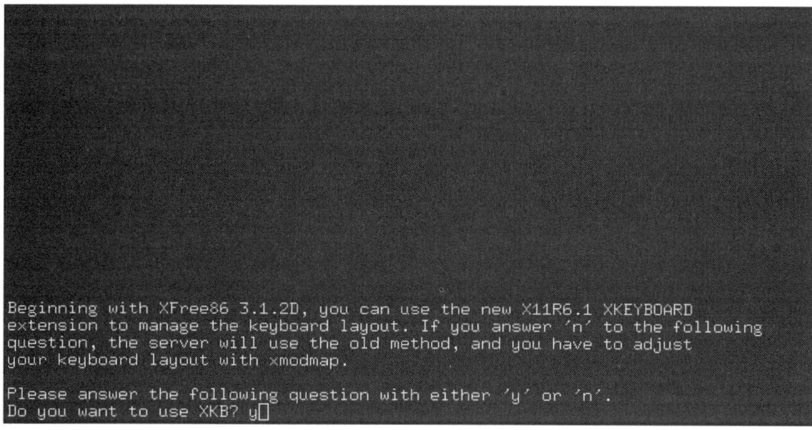

Figure 5.15 *The keyboard configuration screen*

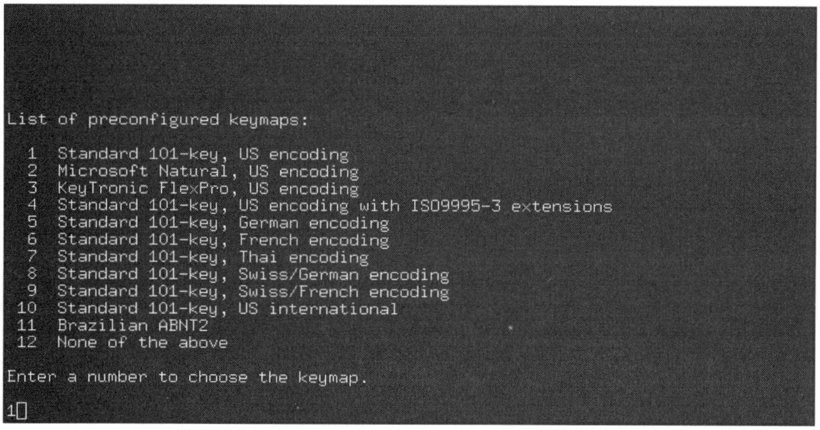

Figure 5.16 *Keyboard map configuration*

press the Enter key to enter a custom keyboard configuration menu. Here you can choose the kind of keyboard layout you prefer to use and language layout for the chosen keyboard.

9. After you've entered your keyboard type and pressed Enter, the monitor configuration screen appears. The first piece of information you must supply is the horizontal frequency of your monitor. It can be a single number, a series of numbers, or a range of numbers (or any mixture of the three). Try to find the range that your monitor supports, type its number (see Figure 5.17), and press the Enter key. If you cannot find the range that matches your monitor's parameters, type **11** and press the Enter key; then type the horizontal frequencies used by your monitor. Multiple ranges can be separated with a comma, and ranges are separated with the minus sign.

When your monitor's documentation does not specifically mention the supported range of horizontal frequencies, look for the numbers that end with kHz.

10. After you've entered your keyboard type and pressed Enter, you see the vertical frequency configuration menu, where you can specify the range of vertical frequencies supported by your monitor. Either select one from the list (see Figure 5.18) or type **5** to enter your own range (remember, multiple ranges can be separated with a comma, and ranges are separated with the minus sign). Press the Enter key.

```
You must indicate the horizontal sync range of your monitor. You can either
select one of the predefined ranges below that correspond to industry-
standard monitor types, or give a specific range.

It is VERY IMPORTANT that you do not specify a monitor type with a horizontal
sync range that is beyond the capabilities of your monitor. If in doubt,
choose a conservative setting.

    hsync in kHz; monitor type with characteristic modes
 1   31.5; Standard VGA, 640x480 @ 60 Hz
 2   31.5 - 35.1; Super VGA, 800x600 @ 56 Hz
 3   31.5, 35.5; 8514 Compatible, 1024x768 @ 87 Hz interlaced (no 800x600)
 4   31.5, 35.15, 35.5; Super VGA, 1024x768 @ 87 Hz interlaced, 800x600 @ 56 Hz
 5   31.5 - 37.9; Extended Super VGA, 800x600 @ 60 Hz, 640x480 @ 72 Hz
 6   31.5 - 48.5; Non-Interlaced SVGA, 1024x768 @ 60 Hz, 800x600 @ 72 Hz
 7   31.5 - 57.0; High Frequency SVGA, 1024x768 @ 70 Hz
 8   31.5 - 64.3; Monitor that can do 1280x1024 @ 60 Hz
 9   31.5 - 82.0; Monitor that can do 1280x1024 @ 76 Hz
10   31.5 - 95.0; Monitor that can do 1280x1024 @ 85 Hz
11   Enter your own horizontal sync range

Enter your choice (1-11): 
```

Figure 5.17　*The monitor configuration screen (horizontal frequency)*

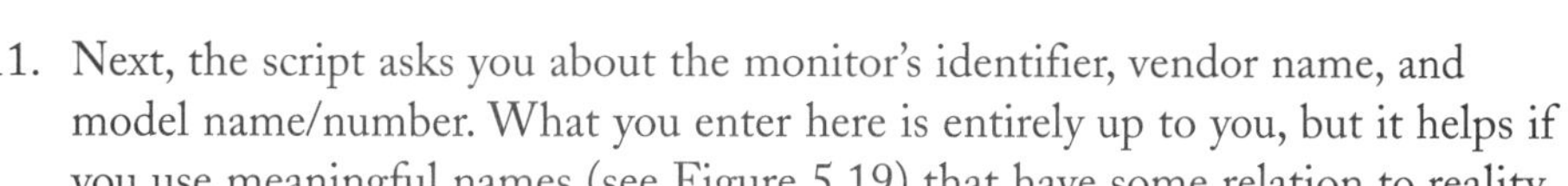

Figure 5.18 *The monitor configuration screen (vertical frequency)*

When your monitor's documentation does not specifically mention the supported range of vertical frequencies, look for the numbers that end with Hz (not kHz).

Make sure that you supply the right values or you might damage the monitor.

11. Next, the script asks you about the monitor's identifier, vendor name, and model name/number. What you enter here is entirely up to you, but it helps if you use meaningful names (see Figure 5.19) that have some relation to reality.

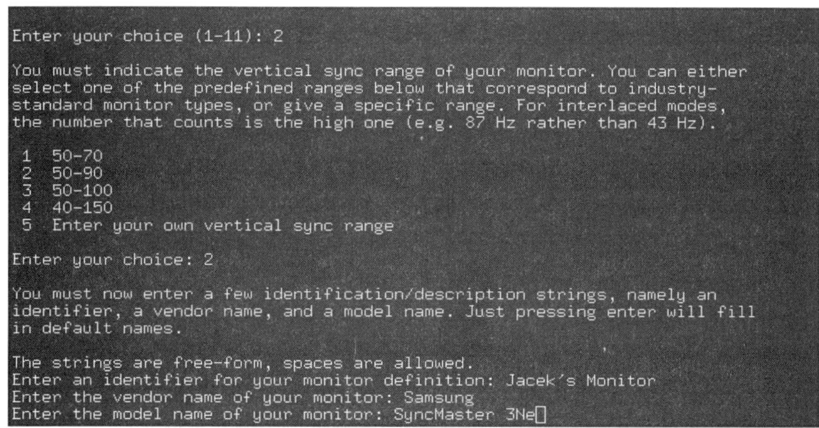

Figure 5.19 *Monitor identification information*

12. After you finish configuring the monitor, *XF86Config* asks for some information about your video card. To view the video card database, where your card is probably listed, type **Y** and press Enter at the first video card configuration screen (see Figure 5.20).

13. The list of video cards is divided into several screens; keep pressing the Enter key until you find your card or until you reach the end of the list. When you find your card, type its number and press the Enter key. The script lists some basic information about the selected card, the most important being the name of the *XFree86* server (see Figure 5.21). Press the Enter key to proceed. If you cannot find your card on the list, you should skip this section and use the *XFree86* server appropriate for the chipset used on your card (see next sections).

14. The next screen (see Figure 5.22) enables you to choose the *XFree86* server that is used to communicate with the video card you have chosen in previous steps. In most cases, typing **5** is a good idea, but if you later discover that the video card does not work, you should run the configuration script again and choose **3**, **2**, or **1** (listed in order from the highest to the lowest number of colors). Press the Enter key to proceed.

15. The script asks whether you want to set up a link to the server. Answer **Y** if you have the appropriate server installed; otherwise, answer **N** and install the server and link to it later using the command **ln -sf /var/X11R6/bin/XF86_***nameofserver* **/usr/X11R6/bin/X.**

16. Next, the script asks you to select the amount of memory installed on your video card (see Figure 5.23). Type the corresponding number, or type **6** to specify a custom amount of video RAM. This information is given in the card's documentation. If it is not available, you can start with 1024K, which is equal to 1MB, and increase this value later.

```
Now we must configure video card specific settings. At this point you can
choose to make a selection out of a database of video card definitions.
Because there can be variation in Ramdacs and clock generators even
between cards of the same model, it is not sensible to blindly copy
the settings (e.g. a Device section). For this reason, after you make a
selection, you will still be asked about the components of the card, with
the settings from the chosen database entry presented as a strong hint.

The database entries include information about the chipset, what server to
run, the Ramdac and ClockChip, and comments that will be included in the
Device section. However, a lot of definitions only hint about what server
to run (based on the chipset the card uses) and are untested.

If you can't find your card in the database, there's nothing to worry about.
You should only choose a database entry that is exactly the same model as
your card; choosing one that looks similar is just a bad idea (e.g. a
GemStone Snail 64 may be as different from a GemStone Snail 64+ in terms of
hardware as can be).

Do you want to look at the card database? y_
```

Figure 5.20 *The first video card configuration screen*

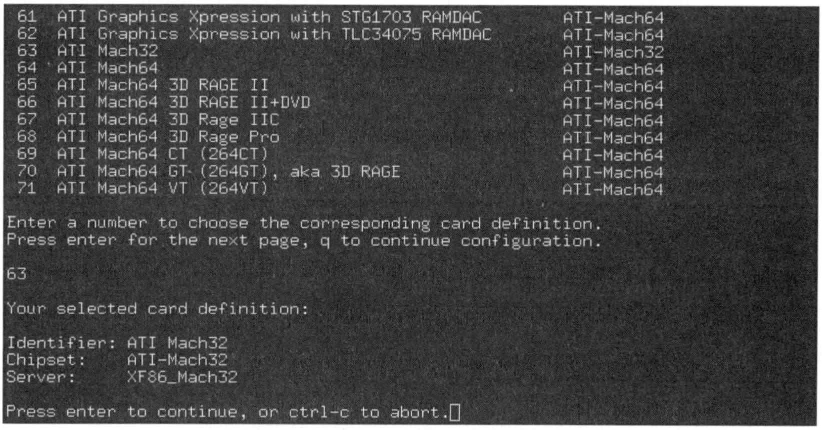

```
61  ATI Graphics Xpression with STG1703 RAMDAC          ATI-Mach64
62  ATI Graphics Xpression with TLC34075 RAMDAC         ATI-Mach64
63  ATI Mach32                                          ATI-Mach32
64  ATI Mach64                                          ATI-Mach64
65  ATI Mach64 3D RAGE II                               ATI-Mach64
66  ATI Mach64 3D RAGE II+DVD                           ATI-Mach64
67  ATI Mach64 3D Rage IIC                              ATI-Mach64
68  ATI Mach64 3D Rage Pro                              ATI-Mach64
69  ATI Mach64 CT (264CT)                               ATI-Mach64
70  ATI Mach64 GT- (264GT), aka 3D RAGE                 ATI-Mach64
71  ATI Mach64 VT (264VT)                               ATI-Mach64

Enter a number to choose the corresponding card definition.
Press enter for the next page, q to continue configuration.

63

Your selected card definition:

Identifier: ATI Mach32
Chipset:    ATI-Mach32
Server:     XF86_Mach32

Press enter to continue, or ctrl-c to abort.
```

Figure 5.21 *Choose your card from the list.*

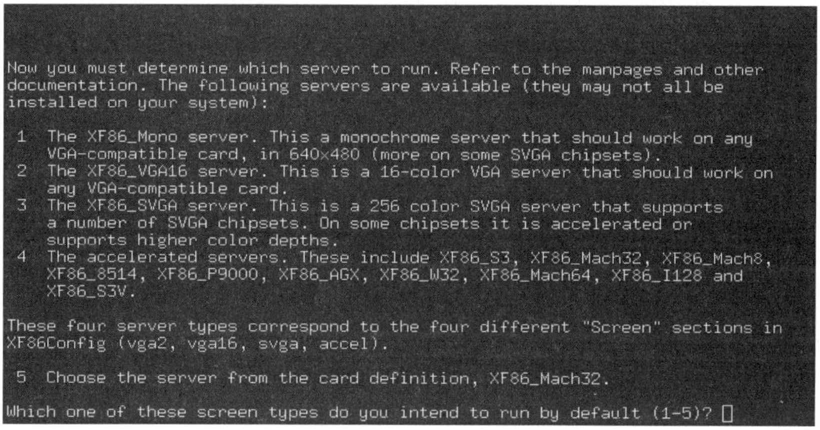

```
Now you must determine which server to run. Refer to the manpages and other
documentation. The following servers are available (they may not all be
installed on your system):

1   The XF86_Mono server. This a monochrome server that should work on any
    VGA-compatible card, in 640x480 (more on some SVGA chipsets).
2   The XF86_VGA16 server. This is a 16-color VGA server that should work on
    any VGA-compatible card.
3   The XF86_SVGA server. This is a 256 color SVGA server that supports
    a number of SVGA chipsets. On some chipsets it is accelerated or
    supports higher color depths.
4   The accelerated servers. These include XF86_S3, XF86_Mach32, XF86_Mach8,
    XF86_8514, XF86_P9000, XF86_AGX, XF86_W32, XF86_Mach64, XF86_I128 and
    XF86_S3V.

These four server types correspond to the four different "Screen" sections in
XF86Config (vga2, vga16, svga, accel).

5   Choose the server from the card definition, XF86_Mach32.

Which one of these screen types do you intend to run by default (1-5)?
```

Figure 5.22 *Choose the matching X server.*

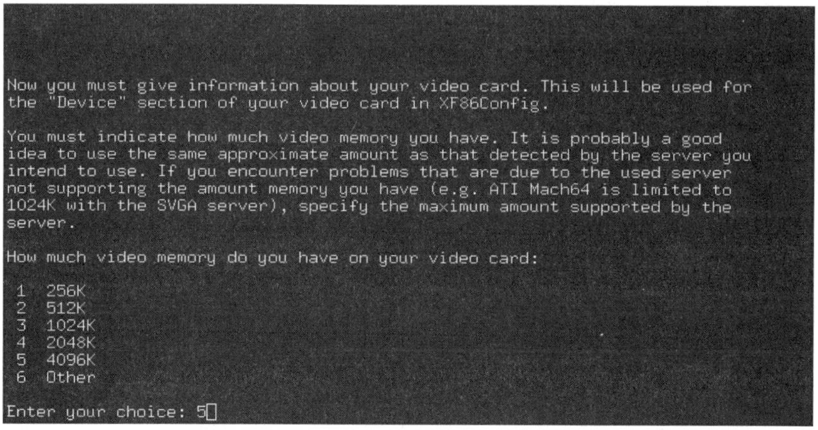

```
Now you must give information about your video card. This will be used for
the "Device" section of your video card in XF86Config.

You must indicate how much video memory you have. It is probably a good
idea to use the same approximate amount as that detected by the server you
intend to use. If you encounter problems that are due to the used server
not supporting the amount memory you have (e.g. ATI Mach64 is limited to
1024K with the SVGA server), specify the maximum amount supported by the
server.

How much video memory do you have on your video card:

1   256K
2   512K
3   1024K
4   2048K
5   4096K
6   Other

Enter your choice: 5
```

Figure 5.23 *Video memory configuration*

17. Next, the script asks about the card's identifier, vendor name, and model name/number. What you enter here is entirely up to you, but it helps if you use meaningful names (see Figure 5.24).

18. The next screen lists the RAMDAC chips known to *XFree86* (see Figure 5.25). These chips are found on more expensive cards; if your card has one, try to find it on the list, as selecting it improves your card's performance. Press the Enter key to scroll through the list, or type **Q** to quit without selecting any of the RAMDAC chips.

19. You're asked about the clock chip used in your card (see Figure 5.26). Either type the number next to the name of the clock chip your card uses or press the Enter key to skip this section (only more expensive cards have clock chips).

```
How much video memory do you have on your video card:

1   256K
2   512K
3   1024K
4   2048K
5   4096K
6   Other

Enter your choice: 5

You must now enter a few identification/description strings, namely an
identifier, a vendor name, and a model name. Just pressing enter will fill
in default names (possibly from a card definition).

Your card definition is ATI Mach32.

The strings are free-form, spaces are allowed.
Enter an identifier for your video card definition: Jacek's Video Card
You can simply press enter here if you have a generic card, or want to
describe your card with one string.
Enter the vendor name of your video card: ATI
Enter the model (board) name of your video card: Mach 64
```

Figure 5.24 *Card information identification*

```
The RAMDAC setting only applies to the S3, AGX, W32 servers, and some
drivers in the SVGA servers. Some RAMDAC's are auto-detected by the server.
The detection of a RAMDAC is forced by using a Ramdac "identifier" line in
the Device section. The identifiers are shown at the right of the following
table of RAMDAC types:

 1   AT&T 20C490 (S3 and AGX servers, ARK driver)            att20c490
 2   AT&T 20C498/21C498/22C498 (S3, autodetected)            att20c498
 3   AT&T 20C409/20C499 (S3, autodetected)                   att20c409
 4   AT&T 20C505 (S3)                                        att20c505
 5   BrookTree BT481 (AGX)                                   bt481
 6   BrookTree BT482 (AGX)                                   bt482
 7   BrookTree BT485/9485 (S3)                               bt485
 8   Sierra SC15025 (S3, AGX)                                sc15025
 9   S3 GenDAC (86C708) (autodetected)                       s3gendac
10   S3 SDAC (86C716) (autodetected)                         s3_sdac
11   STG-1700 (S3, autodetected)                             stg1700
12   STG-1703 (S3, autodetected)                             stg1703


Enter a number to choose the corresponding RAMDAC.
Press enter for the next page, q to quit without selection of a RAMDAC.
```

Figure 5.25 *RAMDAC setup*

```
A Clockchip line in the Device section forces the detection of a
programmable clock device. With a clockchip enabled, any required
clock can be programmed without requiring probing of clocks or a
Clocks line. Most cards don't have a programmable clock chip.
Choose from the following list:

 1  Chrontel 8391                                            ch8391
 2  ICD2061A and compatibles (ICS9161A, DCS2824)             icd2061a
 3  ICS2595                                                  ics2595
 4  ICS5342 (similar to SDAC, but not completely compatible) ics5342
 5  ICS5341                                                  ics5341
 6  S3 GenDAC (86C708) and ICS5300 (autodetected)            s3gendac
 7  S3 SDAC (86C716)                                         s3_sdac
 8  STG 1703 (autodetected)                                  stg1703
 9  Sierra SC11412                                           sc11412
10  TI 3025 (autodetected)                                   ti3025
11  TI 3026 (autodetected)                                   ti3026
12  IBM RGB 51x/52x (autodetected)                           ibm_rgb5xx

Just press enter if you don't want a Clockchip setting.
What Clockchip setting do you want (1-12)? []
```

Figure 5.26 *Clock chip settings*

20. The next section of the configuration script lists available screen resolutions
    at each supported color depth (see Figure 5.27). Using your card's technical
    specification list, check whether the video modes printed are correct. If they
    are not, use the commands listed in the lower half of the screen to modify the
    video modes. If you do not have details for your card, you can safely assume
    that it supports the following video modes:

    - 640×480, 800×600, 1024×768 for 8bpp

    - 640×480, 800×600 for 16bpp

    - 640×480 for 24bpp

    That is a very restrictive set, but should work with most video cards; you can
    change it later using *XF86Config* to see if your card supports better modes.

```
For each depth, a list of modes (resolutions) is defined. The default
resolution that the server will start-up with will be the first listed
mode that can be supported by the monitor and card.
Currently it is set to:

"640x480" "800x600" "1024x768" "1280x1024" for 8bpp
"640x480" "800x600" "1024x768" "1280x1024" for 16bpp
"640x480" "800x600" "1024x768" "1280x1024" for 24bpp
"640x480" "800x600" "1024x768" for 32bpp

Note that 16, 24 and 32bpp are only supported on a few configurations.
Modes that cannot be supported due to monitor or clock constraints will
be automatically skipped by the server.

 1  Change the modes for 8pp (256 colors)
 2  Change the modes for 16bpp (32K/64K colors)
 3  Change the modes for 24bpp (24-bit color, packed pixel)
 4  Change the modes for 32bpp (24-bit color)
 5  The modes are OK, continue.

Enter your choice: []
```

Figure 5.27 *Video modes configuration tables*

```
I am going to write the XF86Config file now. Make sure you don't accidently
overwrite a previously configured one.

Do you want it written to the current directory as 'XF86Config'? y

File has been written. Take a look at it before running 'startx'. Note that
the XF86Config file must be in one of the directories searched by the server
(e.g. /usr/X11R6/lib/X11) in order to be used. Within the server press
ctrl, alt and '+' simultaneously to cycle video resolutions. Pressing ctrl,
alt and backspace simultaneously immediately exits the server (use if
the monitor doesn't sync for a particular mode).

For further configuration, refer to /usr/X11R6/lib/X11/doc/README.Config.

bash-2.03$ []
```

Figure 5.28 *That's it!*

21. The configuration script now asks you if you want to write the new
    configuration to /etc/XF86Config (see Figure 5.28). Answer **Y** and you
    return to the command line.

If you have more questions about configuring *XFree86*, read the "Using *XF86Setup*"
section and the README documents for the *XFree86* located in the /var/X11R6/
lib/doc directory.

Commercial Servers

XFree86 is not the only X Window System implementation available for Linux; there
are commercial servers that often support chipsets unsupported by *XFree86*. They
can do this because their developers sign NDAs (nondisclosure agreements) with the
manufacturers of these chipsets that forbid them from releasing information about
the chipsets to the public. *XFree86* developers (and many other GPL/Open Source
developers) refuse to sign such agreements, which is why the only hardware supported by software distributed under the terms of the GPL or other Open Source
licenses is the hardware for which manufacturers have released information about its
inner workings.

The commercial X servers are often employed by the users of laptop computers
whose video chipsets are unsupported under *XFree86*. You can get more information
about these products at the following addresses:

- **Metro Link, Inc.** Metro-X (http://www.metrolink.com)
- **XiGraphics, Inc.** 3D Accelerated-X (http://www.xig.com)
- **The Linux laptop page.** http://www.cs.utexas.edu/users/kharker/linux-laptop/

Understanding Desktop Environments and Window Managers

Once the configuration of the basic X Window System services is finished, you can try starting one of many available user interfaces. (I assume that you installed at least one of the desktop environments and/or window managers mentioned in Chapter 3.)

Simply log in as an ordinary user (for example, as user or your own standard user account; see Chapter 4, "After the Installation," for more information) and create a new text file named /.xinitrc in the home directory (use a text editor, such as vi). This file contains instructions for the *xinit* program, which handles initialization of X and is called itself by the *startx* script. Once you have /.xinitrc configured for the display you like best, you can start *XFree86* with **startx -- -bpp 24** (the number at the end indicates the color depth to be used by the *XFree86* server; you can choose between 2, 8, 16, 24, and 32). I tell you about configuring the /.xinitrc file soon, but first I need to explain how desktop environments and window managers work.

> Each user can use a different desktop environment or window manager, as long as it is installed on the system. The /.xinitrc file controls which desktop environment or window manager is run when the user types the *startx* command.

The Difference between Window Managers and Desktop Environments

The *XFree86* server by itself does not provide any sort of user interface; that is the job of a desktop environment or a window manager. Window managers have limited functionality and generally control the appearance of the background and windows and allow windows to be moved, scaled, opened, and closed. Some window managers also offer a nice feature called virtual desktop, which enlarges the desktop size by stitching a few screens together in the form of a long tape or a large rectangular space. Desktop environments extend basic window manager functionality and add features such as drag and drop (which might not work in all applications), customized applications, international language support, a wide variety of customization options, and extensive help systems. Both window managers and desktop environments offer features such as cutting, copying, and pasting of text between applications (doing the same with graphics and other kinds of data is not always possible).

Popular Desktop Environments

Because developing desktop environments is much more complicated than writing a window manager, there are fewer full-blown desktop environments. Anyone who has been involved with a UNIX operating system in the past is likely familiar with the CDE environment. A simpler, yet similar, desktop environment is XFce. But by far, the two most popular desktop environments available for Linux at the moment are GNOME and KDE. Both are available as a part of Slackware Linux 7, and both have ardent supporters and critics.

GNOME

GNOME is the latest version of the desktop environment developed by the team led by Miguel de Icaza. Its appearance is highly customizable through many GNOME-compatible window managers (yes, the window managers used by GNOME can be used as standalone programs or from within GNOME). It comes with a wide range of personal-, system-, and network-management applications, along with productivity applications, all free and distributed under the terms of the GNU public license. Figure 5.29 shows a sample GNOME desktop. This is the default look when you run it for the first time; you can change it later by clicking on the toolbox icon.

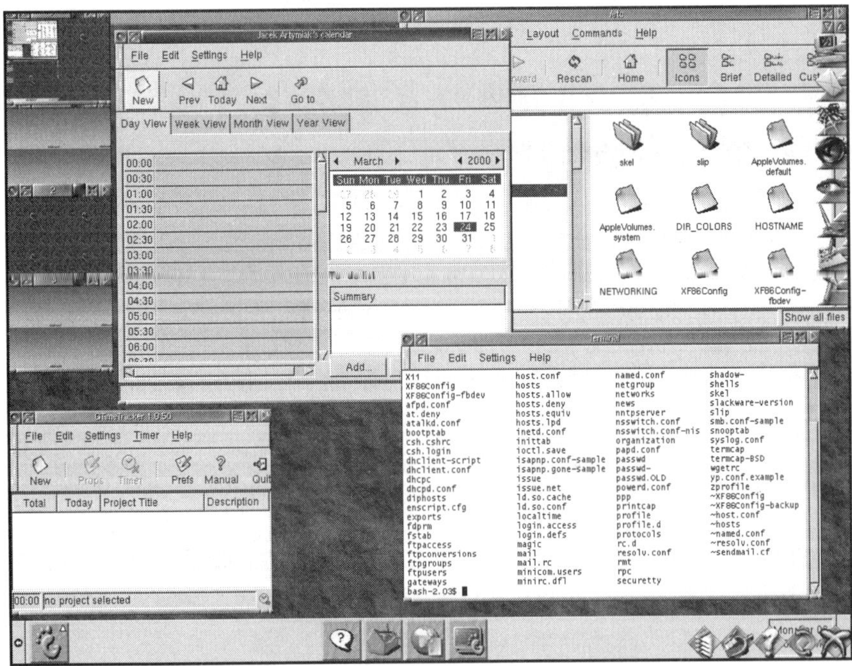

Figure 5.29 *GNOME running the Enlightenment window manager*

To run GNOME as your default desktop environment, make sure that you install at least the basic GNOME files (see Chapter 3). Also, you must create the /.xinitrc file in your home directory, making sure that it contains the following lines (you might want to simply copy this from /etc/X11/xinit/xinitrc.gnome):

```
!/bin/sh
userresources=$HOME/.Xresources
usermodmap=$HOME/.Xmodmap
sysresources=/usr/X11R6/lib/X11/xinit/.Xresources
sysmodmap=/usr/X11R6/lib/X11/xinit/.Xmodmap
if [ -f $sysresources ]; then
    xrdb -merge $sysresources
fi
if [ -f $sysmodmap ]; then
    xmodmap $sysmodmap
fi
if [ -f $userresources ]; then
    xrdb -merge $userresources
fi
if [ -f $usermodmap ]; then
    xmodmap $usermodmap
fi
Start GNOME
exec gnome-session
```

Save the /.xinitrc file to disk, exit from the editor, and type **startx -- -bpp 8**. This should start the X server in 8-bit-per-plane mode (256 colors). Once you get that working, you can later try changing 8 to 16, 24, and 32.

KDE

KDE was the first of the two main Linux desktop environments, but it got some bad press for initially using nonfree libraries. (The libraries were distributed for free, but not under the terms of the GNU public license. This has since changed, so KDE is now entirely free and open in the same sense as GNOME.) The current version of KDE does not offer as many appearance-customization options, but is still stabler and has a cleaner look than GNOME, although that might be only my own opinion. On the other hand, GNOME offers CORBA support and greater user interface customization options. You can expect KDE and GNOME to offer similar functionality soon.

Figure 5.30 shows a sample KDE desktop. To make KDE your default desktop environment, make sure you install at least the basic KDE files (see Chapter 3) and that

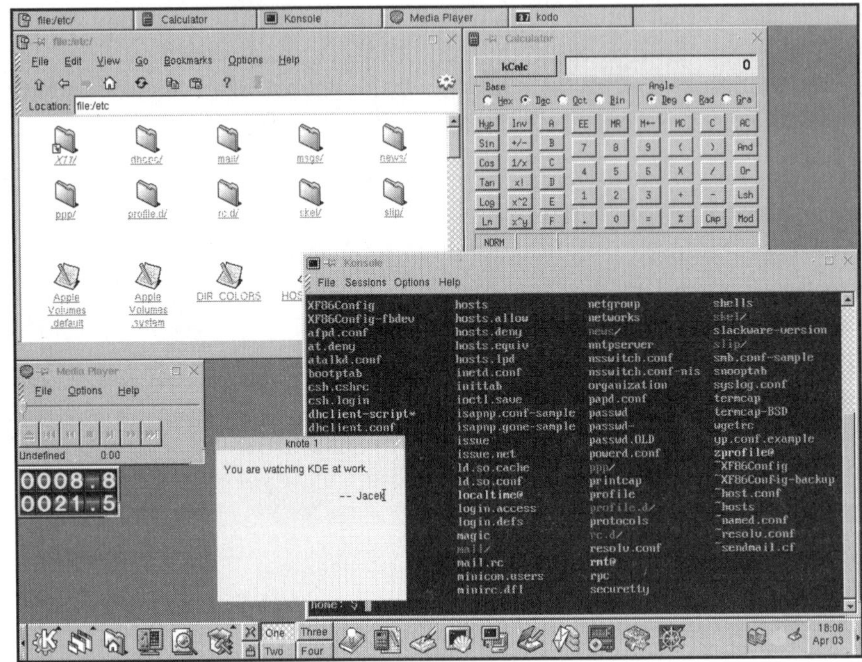

Figure 5.30 *A sample view of the KDE desktop*

the /.xinitrc file located in your home directory contains all of the lines listed in the section about GNOME, with the exception of the last two, which should be replaced with the following:

```
Start KDE
exec /opt/kde/bin/kde
```

Window Managers

Slackware Linux 7 is distributed with several window managers that you can choose to customize the look of your desktop when you do not want to use a full-blown desktop environment. Following, you find instructions for configuring the /.xinitrc file for a few popular window managers.

Fvwm95

The fvwm95 window manager is an extension of the old fvwm and fvwm2 window managers. It has a look similar to Windows 95 and adds a nice Windows-like toolbar at the bottom of the screen. A sample fvwm95 desktop is shown in Figure 5.31.

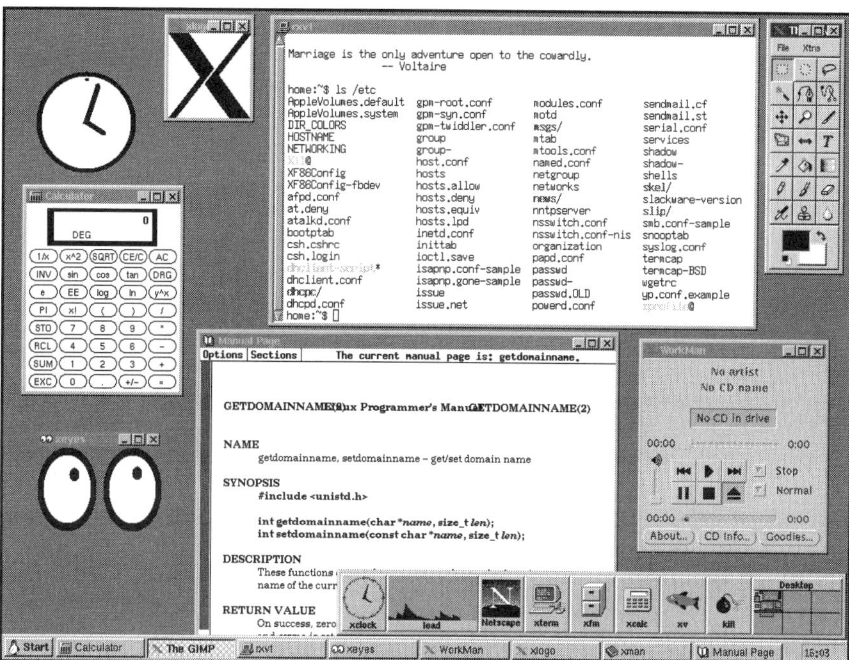

Figure 5.31 *The default look of the fvmw95 desktop*

This window manager implements virtual screens to allow the user to place windows on separate screens when the main screen becomes too crowded. Virtual screens are connected together. When a part of a window is placed outside the visible area of one screen, it is visible on an adjacent screen.

To use this window manager, make sure the /.xinitrc file contains exactly the same commands as those listed in the section about GNOME, but with the last two lines changed to the following:

```
Start fvwm95

exec /usr/X11R6/bin/fvwm95
```

Now you can use **startx -- -bpp 8** to start fvwm95 and see how it feels. Use the left, middle, and right mouse buttons to click the screen background; this displays application and system menus.

For more information about fvwm95, read files from the /usr/doc/fvwm95-2.0.43b directory or visit http://mitac11.uia.ac.be/html-test/fvwm95.html.

Fvwm2

The fvwm2 desktop environment is a close relative of the fvwm95 desktop environment, but it offers an attractive Motif-like look used by window managers developed by SGI, Hewlett-Packard, and Digital. Its functionality and configuration options are very similar to fvwm95. Figure 5.32 shows a sample fvwm2 desktop.

To use this window manager, make sure the /.xinitrc file contains exactly the same commands as those listed in the section about GNOME, but with the last two lines changed to the following:

```
Start fvwm2
exec /usr/X11R6/bin/fvwm2
```

After the changes to /.xinitrc have been saved, you can use **startx -- -bpp 8** to start fvwm2 and see how it feels. As with fvwm95, you can use the left, middle, and right mouse buttons to click the screen background to display the application and system menus.

For more information about fvwm2, type **man fvwm2** at the command line or visit the official FVWM site located at http://www.fvwm.org.

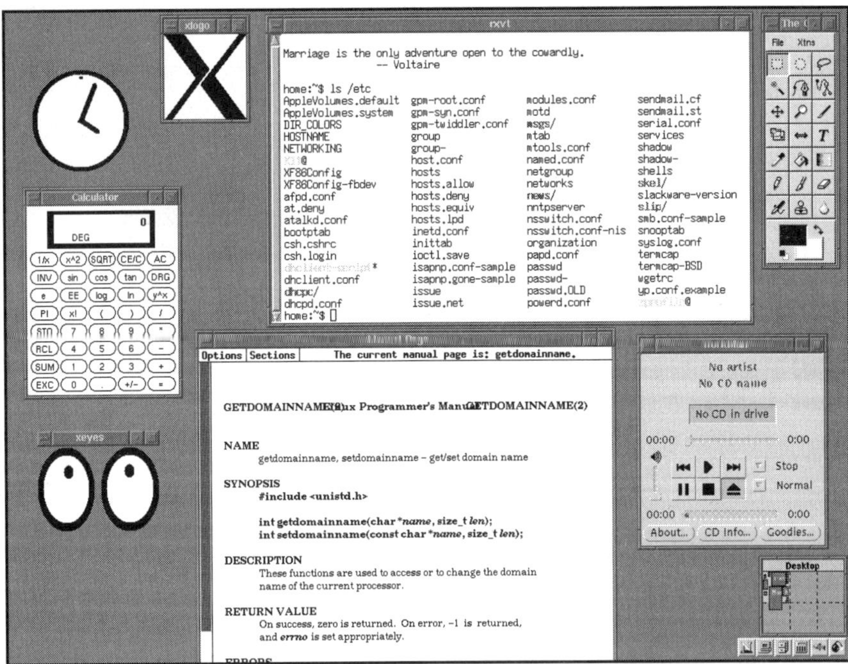

Figure 5.32 *The default look of the fvmw2 desktop*

Twm

For those users who prefer a minimalist approach, the twm window manager is one of the most basic you can find. It offers no advanced features, but works fast—and that is about all you can say in its favor. However, if you do not have a lot of RAM memory to spare, this is the window manager to use. It does not offer virtual screens, so you are limited to a single screen. Figure 5.33 shows a sample twm desktop.

To use this window manager, make sure the /.xinitrc file contains exactly the same commands as those listed in the section about GNOME, but with the last two lines changed to the following:

```
Start twm
xterm &
exec /usr/X11R6/bin/twm
```

After the changes to /.xinitrc have been saved, you can use **startx -- -bpp 8** to start twm and see how it feels. Click the desktop to display a basic system menu.

For more information about twm, type **man twm**. If you get bored using twm, press Ctrl+Alt+Backspace to kill the X server and return to the command line.

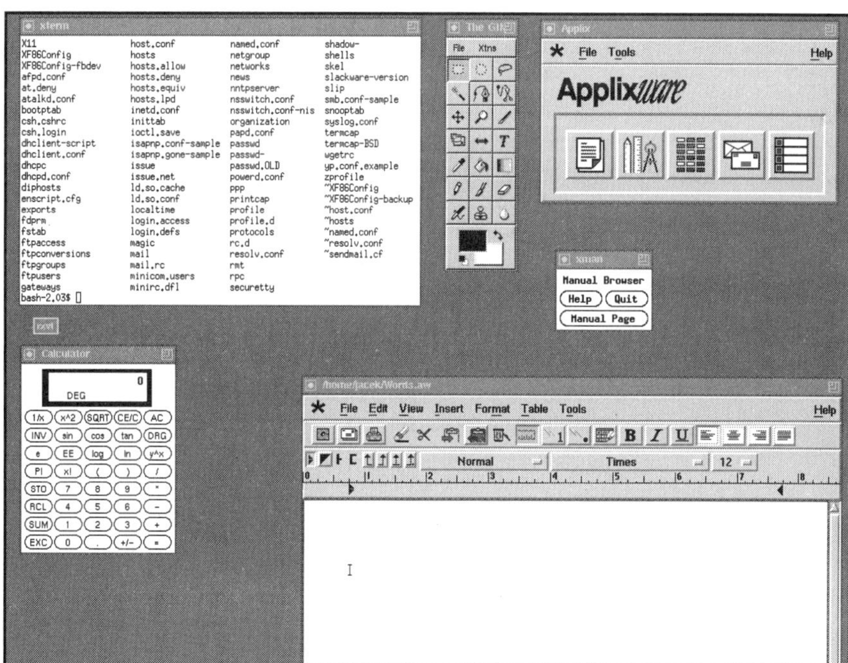

Figure 5.33 *The default look of the twm desktop*

Olwm

The olwm window manager implements the old Open Look style of windows, known particularly well to the users of computers made by Sun Microsystems, Inc. That particular window manager does not implement virtual screens (if you need them, use olvm). Figure 5.34 shows a sample olwm desktop.

To use this window manager, make sure the /.xinitrc file contains exactly the same commands as those listed in the section about GNOME, but with the last two lines changed to the following:

```
Start olwm
xterm &
exec /usr/X11R6/bin/olwm
```

After the changes to /.xinitrc have been saved you can use **startx -- -bpp 8** to start olwm and see how it feels. You can use the right mouse button to click the screen background, displaying application and system menus.

For more information about olwm, type **man olwm**.

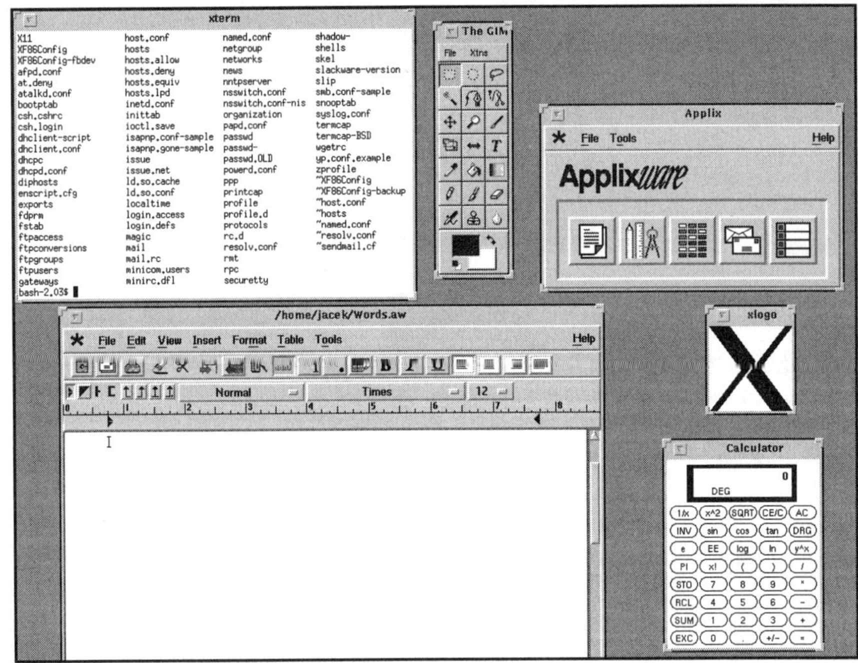

Figure 5.34 *The default look of the olwm desktop*

Mwm

Mwm is yet another implementation of a window manager with Motif looks. Motif is popular on many commercial versions of the UNIX systems, such as SGI Irix or HP HP-UX. Its functionality is similar to that of fvwm2, but it does not offer virtual screens. Figure 5.35 shows a sample mwm desktop.

To use this window manager, make sure the /.xinitrc file contains exactly the same commands as those listed in the section about GNOME, but with the last two lines changed to the following:

```
Start mwm
xterm &
exec /usr/X11R6/bin/mwm
```

After the changes to /.xinitrc have been saved, you can use **startx -- -bpp 8** to start mwm and see how it feels. You can use the left and right mouse buttons to click the screen background, displaying application and system menus. If you are interested in customizing mwm, type **man mwm** on the command line to display the mwm man

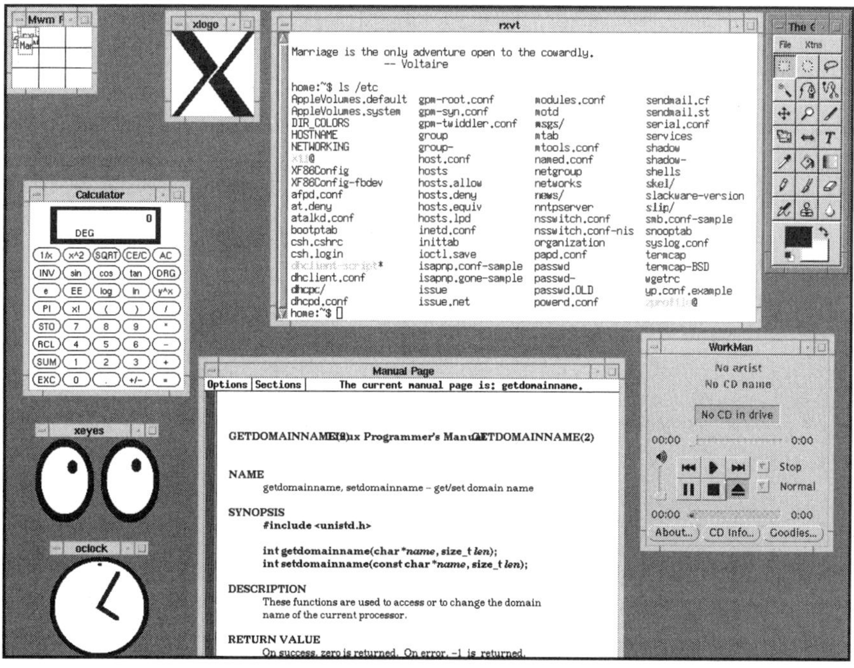

Figure 5-35 *The default look of the mwm desktop*

page. The look and behavior of mwm can be customized to a great extent by editing its resource files (all is explained on the mwm man page).

For more information about mwm, type **man mwm**.

Window Maker

This is a particularly interesting implementation of the NeXT Step window manager used on the NeXT computers. It is highly configurable, it has international language support, its looks are among the best, and it can be used with GNOME. It implements virtual screens, but each screen is a separate entity. Figure 5.36 shows a sample Window Maker desktop.

To use this window manager, make sure the /.xinitrc file contains exactly the same commands as those listed in the section about GNOME, but with the last two lines changed to the following:

```
Start wmaker
exec /usr/X11R6/bin/wmaker
```

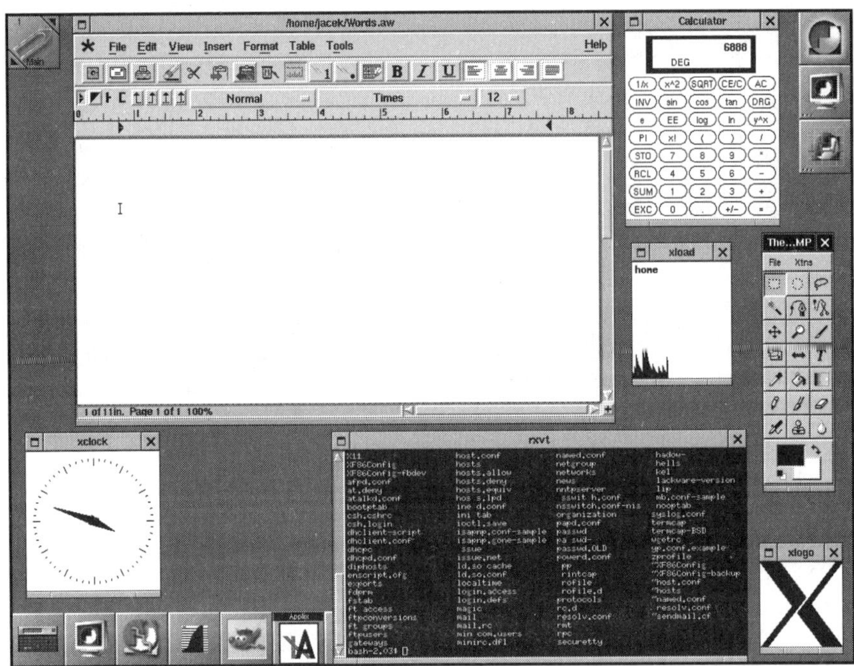

Figure 5.36 *The default look of the Window Maker desktop*

After the changes to /.xinitrc have been saved, you can use **startx -- -bpp 8** to start Window Maker and see how it feels. You can use the middle and right mouse buttons to click the screen background, displaying application and system menus.

For more information about Window Maker, type **man wmaker**.

Other X Window Managers

Other window managers worth mentioning are

- **Ctw.** An extension of twm
- **Wm2.** A very minimalistic window manager
- **Amiwm.** A window manager with Amiga-like looks and behavior
- **Scwm.** A highly configurable window manager using the Scheme language
- **Icewm.** A window manager with cool looks and GNOME-compatibility
- **Sawmill.** A highly configurable window manager using the Lisp language

For more information about window managers, visit the Window Managers for X page located at http://www.plig.org/xwinman/.

Summary

The *XFree86* implementation of the X Window System provides a framework for highly customizable graphical user interfaces for Linux. It supports a wide range of video cards, including the latest AGP cards. Configuration of *XFree86* can be performed using either a graphical configuration utility, *XF86Setup*, or a text mode script, *XF86Config*. Because the X Window System is highly modular, it is possible to choose the look and functionality that matches your preferences. There are two main desktop environments to choose from (GNOME and KDE) and well over a dozen different window managers.

Chapter 6: Configuring Your Computer to Work on a Network

Jacek Artymiak

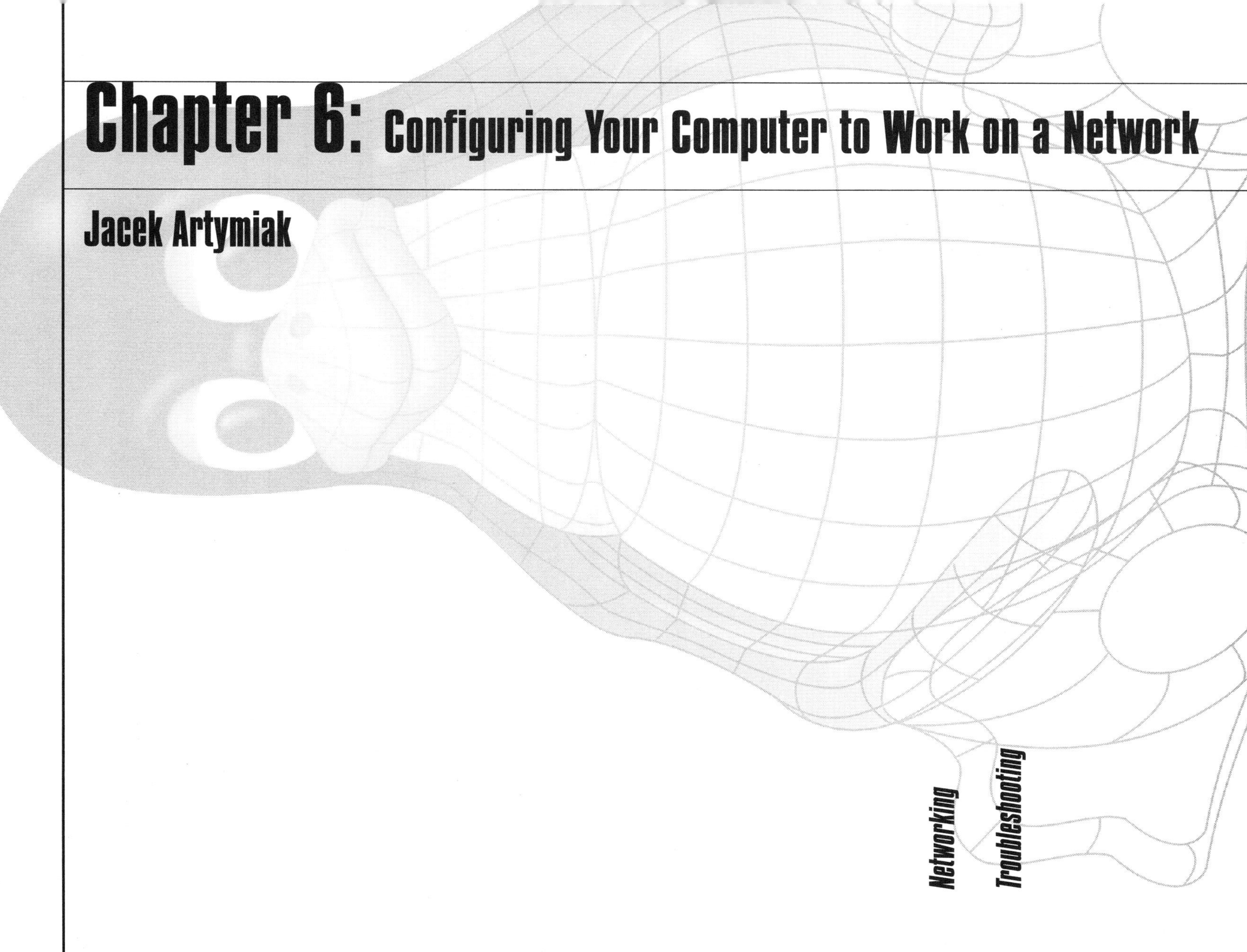

Today's personal computers are meant to communicate with each other, either via local networks or the global Internet. Slackware Linux 7 is one of the best operating systems for that purpose, because it offers quite possibly the widest choice of communication protocols and supports an enormous range of networking devices. You can use it to connect your computer to the rest of the world via phone lines, ethernet networks, packet radio modems, infrared communication ports, and so on. In this chapter I am going to talk about networking and guide you through the procedures necessary to set up dial-up and ethernet connections to other computers.

Networking

Networking is a huge topic and I could write about it at length, but it all boils down to connecting two or more computers and exchanging data between them. To accomplish that task, you need the following components:

- **Protocols.** Networking rules of the road that describe how computers communicate with each other
- **Network software.** Applications that implement protocols and talk to the network hardware and other applications
- **Network hardware.** Devices that send and receive data between computers and networks

The most popular networking protocol of today is TCP/IP, a time-tested set of rules for transmitting data between computers running different operating systems. It forms the foundation of the global Internet and is often used in intranets (local area networks that use TCP/IP and applications that support it).

Linux supports TCP/IP out of the box, in the kernel, and is distributed with a suite of software necessary for configuring, testing, and monitoring TCP/IP connections, as well as many applications that use TCP/IP (Web browsers, mailers, mail, FTP, IRC, Usenet news, and so on). In the case of hardware support, a majority of network interfaces (network cards, modems, ISDN adapters, and the like) are supported as well (check the Hardware-HOWTO for information about supported hardware).

How stable is TCP/IP support in Linux? Very stable. Because Linux inherits and borrows a lot of the best networking solutions (and adds some of its own) from versions of the UNIX and BSD families of operating systems, you can be sure that you have access to some of the best networking protocols and applications. In fact, many

ISPs (Internet service providers) and commercial users use Linux for their mission-critical applications.

Now I discuss two popular ways of connecting a computer to the external world: dial-up and Ethernet.

LAN versus Dial-Up

Out of many possible ways to connect your computer to other machines, two are most prevalent: local area networks (LANs) and dial-up connections. The former are most likely to be used by businesses, government agencies, and academic institutions. The latter are very popular with home users, although that is changing as more and more people build home networks or install faster, permanent connections to the Internet. Both methods can use the TCP/IP networking protocol, but they use different hardware interfaces to transmit data.

LANs

Computers on a local network use NICs (network interface cards), which are special plug-in cards that connect to your computer's motherboard. These cards can be made in either the ISA or PCI standard; to use them, your computer's motherboard must have a free expansion slot in the same standard. Computers made before year 2000 usually have two or three expansion slots in each standard, whereas the newer machines might not have ISA slots. In any case, always determine which expansion slots are free on your computer's motherboard, and then choose the card that fits into them.

Another thing to consider is the technology on which the network you want to connect to is based. In most cases it is ethernet, but there are other solutions, such as token ring or FDDI. Therefore, you should always make sure that your card (ISA or PCI) is compatible with the rest of the network.

If the network is ethernet, you must also determine the speed at which the network is transmitting data. There are three choices: 10Mb/s, 100Mb/s (sometimes called fast ethernet), and 1000Mb/s (or 1Gb/s, sometimes called gigabit ethernet). The NIC in your computer must work at the same speed or you have problems. Fortunately, there are many ethernet network cards that can work at both 10Mb/s and 100Mb/s; they are usually marked as 10/100.

The last thing to check is the cabling standard for ethernet, which can be either a coaxial cable (known as 10Base2) or a twisted pair cable (known as 10BaseT for 10Mb/s networks or 100BaseT for 100Mb/s networks). Check the Hardware-HOWTO and Ethernet-HOWTO for more information.

Once the networking software and hardware have been configured, connections to local area networks via permanent ethernet links are stable and very rarely cause problems.

Dial-Up Connections

Most home users neither need nor have local networks. (That doesn't necessarily apply to the authors of this book, but we have very understanding spouses.) Their preferred method of connecting to the Internet and other networks are analog modem connections via ordinary phone lines. This is one of the oldest methods of connecting to computer networks from home, and for some time it was the only inexpensive way to get on the Information Highway.

> The old analog technology cannot transfer data faster than 56Kb/s, and that is available only when mixed with some digital trickery. It's being slowly replaced by cable modems, ADSL, ISDN, and other similar solutions that make it possible for home users to surf the Information Highway without unnecessary delays. However, it will be a long time before these technologies become as ubiquitous as the good old analog phone lines.

Dial-up connections are good enough if all you want to do is send and receive mail, surf the Web, or read Usenet news, and you do not require a permanent and fast connection. They are ideal when you are a client of other servers. Ethernet connections, on the other hand, are essential when you want your machine to be the server for other machines.

There are many kinds of analog modems, both internal and external. External modems are generally better than internal ones. The main differences between them are the maximum speed of data transfer and the communication protocols they support. These protocols have nothing to do with TCP/IP; see Chapter 1, "Before You Install: Getting to Know Your Hardware," for details. One thing to watch for are the so-called "winmodems," very inexpensive devices designed to work exclusively with Microsoft Windows. Avoid them like the plague; they do not work under Linux. So, if you do not have a modem yet, get the fastest external model you can afford. Extra fax and voice functionality do not hurt either, because Linux does support them.

Some users wonder if it is possible to have a local ethernet network connecting to the outside world through a dial-up line. The answer is, yes, you can do that, and it is not overly difficult. Read this chapter and you have all the necessary information.

Modems and ethernet cards are not the only devices that can be used to connect computers. There are many other ways to do it, and you should always determine which connection method or device the computers to which you are trying to connect your machine use. For example, if the network you want to connect to uses IBM token ring protocol, you must use token ring hardware and enable support for that protocol in the kernel. The first place to look for information not included in this chapter is the NET-3-HOWTO, which offers a general introduction to Linux networking. Other HOWTOs worth mentioning here are AX25-HOWTO, Ethernet-HOWTO, IPX-HOWTO, IR-HOWTO, PCMCIA-HOWTO, and mini-HOWTOs like ADSL, Boca, Cable-Modem, and Token-Ring.

As you can see from this short introduction, there are many ways to connect your computer to others, and it is impossible to guess the hardware configuration on which you are going to run Slackware Linux 7. The enormous variety of devices makes it very difficult for the designers of any operating system to provide a simple network configuration procedure for all users. What Slackware Linux 7 offers is a preconfigured network skeleton, which you have to fill with only a few essential pieces of information. Let's see how it is done, starting with dial-up modem connections.

Modem

To establish a dial-up connection to another computer that speaks TCP/IP you need the following tools:

- **A PC working under Slackware Linux 7.** Chapters 1 through 3 describe how to get to that point.
- **A modem.** This is connected to your computer and the phone line.
- **An account at your ISP.** Make sure you have the following details handy: the phone number of customer/technical support at your ISP, ISP phone numbers for modem connections, your username, your password, and addresses of your ISP's DNS servers.

Once you have that, you can begin the dial-up networking configuration procedure. It consists of two separate steps. First you must set up basic TCP/IP networking services; once you get them working, you can configure the dial-up networking services.

Configuring Basic Networking

Before Linux networking software can show what it is capable of, you must give it a few essential pieces of information, such as the IP network address of your computer, its name on the network, and such. This information is stored inside a bunch of text files located in the /etc directory. You could edit these files yourself, but there is a better way—the *netconfig* script that painlessly guides you through the configuration process and automatically creates all necessary files. That method is the one I am going to use below (note that you can do this on the command line, outside of X):

1. Log in as root. If you are logged in as another user (you can check that with the *whoami* command), type **su root** and then type the correct password to become root.

2. Type **netconfig** and press the Enter key. You ought to see the screen shown in Figure 6.1. (I assume that you did install the networking software recommended in Chapter 3, "Installing Slackware.")

3. Press the Enter key again to begin network configuration. You can always stop configuration at any time by pressing Ctrl+C.

4. Type the name of the host into the box shown in Figure 6.2. The host name is the name of your computer on your local network. In the figure, the name of the host is home, which is a good name for a home system. It is a good habit to supply the host name even if your computer is not connecting to any other computer at your home, as you see later. After the network configuration is finished, the host name of your computer is displayed as a part of the login prompt.

5. Press the Enter key again to display the domain name dialog box.

6. Type the name of your network's domain. For dial-up networking systems, it can be anything you like, such as slackgeek.com, as shown in the example in Figure 6.3. For systems permanently connected to the Internet, it should be a proper Internet domain registered with one of domain registrars (see http://www.networksolutions.com or http://www.coronic.com for more information). For systems connecting to a LAN, it should be the same domain

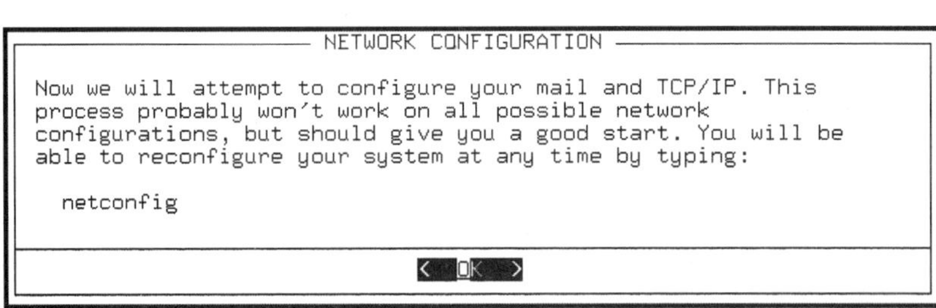

Figure 6.1 *Welcome to* netconfig.

```
┌───────────────────── ENTER HOSTNAME ─────────────────────┐
│ First, we'll need the name you'd like to give your host. Only │
│ the base hostname is needed right now. (not the domain)       │
│                                                               │
│ Enter hostname:                                               │
│ ┌───────────────────────────────────────────────────────────┐ │
│ │home█                                                        │ │
│ └───────────────────────────────────────────────────────────┘ │
│                                                               │
│           <  OK  >        <Cancel>                            │
└───────────────────────────────────────────────────────────────┘
```

Figure 6.2 *The host name is the name by which your computer is known to other computers.*

```
┌───────────── ENTER DOMAINNAME FOR 'home' ─────────────┐
│ Now, we need the domain name. Do not supply a leading '.' │
│                                                          │
│ Enter domain name for home:                              │
│ ┌──────────────────────────────────────────────────────┐ │
│ │slackgeek.com█                                          │ │
│ └──────────────────────────────────────────────────────┘ │
│                                                          │
│           <  OK  >        <Cancel>                       │
└──────────────────────────────────────────────────────────┘
```

Figure 6.3 *For modem users, your domain name can be anything you like.*

used by the network (there are exceptions to all of these rules). Remember not to type the leading dot (.) in the domain name; the *netconfig* script adds it automatically. Note that the full network address in human-readable form is now `home.slackgeek.com`, the combined host and domain name.

7. Press the Enter key again to display the IP address setup dialog box.

8. Press the down arrow key twice to choose `loopback`, as shown in Figure 6.4. This is the right choice for dial-up networking systems or those that do not connect to any other computer.

```
┌────────────── SETUP IP FOR 'home.slackgeek.com' ──────────────┐
│ Now we need to know how your machine connects to the network. If │
│ you have an internal network card and an assigned IP address,    │
│ gateway, and DNS, use the 'static IP' choice to enter these values.│
│ If your IP address is assigned by a DHCP server (commonly used by │
│ cable modem and DSL services), select 'DHCP'. If you do not have a │
│ network card, select the 'loopback' choice. 'loopback' is also the │
│ correct choice if your only connection to the network will be     │
│ through a serial modem (with SLIP or PPP), or if you are using a  │
│ laptop network card (these are configured in /etc/pcmcia/). What  │
│ type of network connection best describes your machine?          │
│ ┌──────────────────────────────────────────────────────────────┐ │
│ │ static IP  Use a static IP address to configure ethernet      │ │
│ │ DHCP       Use a DHCP server to configure ethernet            │ │
│ │ loopback   Set up a loopback connection (modem or no net)     │ │
│ └──────────────────────────────────────────────────────────────┘ │
│                                                                  │
│           <  OK  >        <Cancel>                               │
└──────────────────────────────────────────────────────────────────┘
```

Figure 6.4 *Select loopback.*

9. Press the Enter key again to finish configuration of the basic network services. You see the message shown in Figure 6.5.

10. Press the Enter key again to return to the command line.

Testing Network Operations

To test that your new configuration is working correctly, try the following:

1 Type **telnet 127.0.0.1** and press the Enter key. You should see a login prompt displaying the new name of your host.

2. Log in as an ordinary other user. If all goes well and you return to the command-line prompt, you can safely assume that basic TCP/IP services are operational. The *telnet 127.0.0.1* command is used to connect to the same computer.

3. Type **logout** and press Enter to return to the original state. The whole procedure is shown in Figure 6.6.

If there are problems, make sure that you installed the networking packages mentioned in Chapter 3 and repeat the whole procedure again (a system restart is also a good idea; type **reboot** and press Enter to restart Linux).

```
——————————————— NETWORK SETUP COMPLETE ———————————————
           Your networking software has now been configured.

                          <  OK  >
```

Figure 6.5 *You're all set! Congratulations!*

```
bash-2.03# telnet 127.0.0.1
Trying 127.0.0.1...
Connected to 127.0.0.1.
Escape character is '^]'.

home login: test
Password:
Linux 2.2.13.
No mail.

"It's men like him that give the Y chromosome a bad name."

home:~$ exit
logout
Connection closed by foreign host.
bash-2.03#
```

Figure 6.6 *This is how your network test session might look.*

Once you set up basic networking services, you can proceed to configure *pppd* (the Point-to-Point Protocol daemon). PPP is a protocol that makes analog phone lines a hospitable environment for TCP/IP and other communication protocols.

Configuring PPP

Here again you use a handy script that comes standard with Slackware Linux 7. Make sure that you are logged in as user root, and follow these steps:

1. Type **pppsetup** on the command line and press the Enter key. You should see the dialog box shown in Figure 6.7.

2. Press Enter again. You can always end the script without making changes permanent by pressing Ctrl+C.

3. Type four letters describing the dialing method to be used by the modem to connect to the phone exchange, followed by your ISP network access phone number (see Figure 6.8). In most cases, you need to type **atdt**, which tells the modem to use tone dialing. Some older phone exchanges use pulse dialing, in which case you need to type **atdp**.

```
PPPSETUP 1.98 on SLACKWARE.

Written by Robert S. Liesenfeld <xunil@bitstream.net> <IRC:Xunil>
Changes for 1.98 by Kent Robotti <robotti@erols.com>
Patched for Slackware by Patrick Volkerding <volkerdi@slackware.com>

You should get these docs if you don't already have them:

ftp://metalab.unc.edu/pub/Linux/docs/howto/PPP-HOWTO
ftp://metalab.unc.edu/pub/Linux/docs/faqs/PPP-FAQ

Press [Enter] to continue with pppsetup...
                                                        (100%)
                         < EXIT >
```

Figure 6.7 *Welcome to pppsetup.*

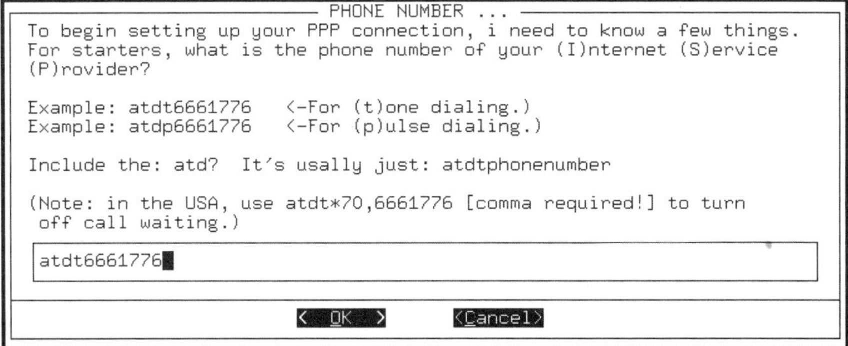
```
                        PHONE NUMBER ...
To begin setting up your PPP connection, i need to know a few things.
For starters, what is the phone number of your (I)nternet (S)ervice
(P)rovider?

Example: atdt6661776    <-For (t)one dialing.)
Example: atdp6661776    <-For (p)ulse dialing.)

Include the: atd?  It's usally just: atdtphonenumber

(Note: in the USA, use atdt*70,6661776 [comma required!] to turn
 off call waiting.)

atdt6661776

           <  OK  >          <Cancel>
```

Figure 6.8 *Let's start with the dialing method and the phone number.*

4. Press the Enter key to display the modem device dialog (see Figure 6.9). If you had your modem working under DOS or Windows and know what COM port it was using, you're in luck—select it from the list and press Enter. Otherwise, you need to do a little investigation. Go to another console or open another xterm and run this command:

```
dmesg ¦ grep ttyS0
```

In my case, I got back these two lines:

```
ttyS00 at 0x03f8 (irq = 4) is a 16550A
ttyS02 at 0x03e8 (irq = 4) is a 16550A
```

Each line represents a serial port. The modem could be on either—ttyS00 or ttyS02. Trial and error among these two is one way to find the modem, but if you have a serial mouse you can eliminate that possibility. I ran the command *ls -l /dev/mouse* and saw that it was linked to cua0. (As far as Linux devices are concerned, ttyS0 and cua are basically the same thing.) So if ttyS00 is my mouse, ttyS02 must be my modem.

5. Press Enter to display the modem baud rate dialog.

6. Look in your modem documentation for the baud rate of your modem. What you really want to know is the maximum transmission speed between your computer and modem, often called the DTR. This number is usually faster than the nominal speed of your modem—for example, most 56k modems have a DTR of 115200. (This larger number is due to compression of data by the modem before it is sent.) If you're unsure, follow the hints shown in Figure 6.10. Most analog modems are in the range 115200–9600.

7. Press Enter to display the callback service dialog box.

8. Decide whether you want to configure callback. You probably should answer No, as shown in Figure 6.11. ISPs almost never use callback, although some bulletin board systems do. If you later need to enable the callback function, simply make safety copies of all of the files in the /etc directory and run the

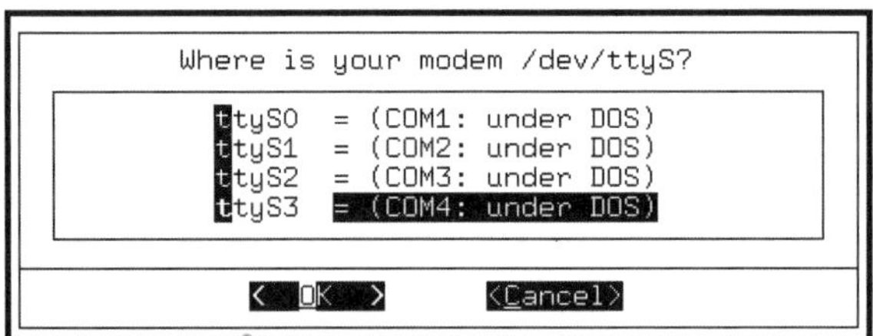

Figure 6.9 *Pick the serial interface your modem is connected to.*

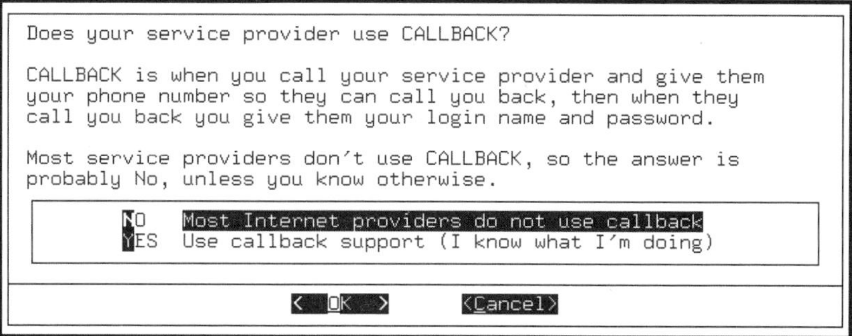

Figure 6.10 *Select the maximum speed that matches your modem's parameters here.*

```
Does your service provider use CALLBACK?

CALLBACK is when you call your service provider and give them
your phone number so they can call you back, then when they
call you back you give them your login name and password.

Most service providers don't use CALLBACK, so the answer is
probably No, unless you know otherwise.
    NO   Most Internet providers do not use callback
    YES  Use callback support (I know what I'm doing)

         <  OK  >       <Cancel>
```

Figure 6.11 *Do you use callback?*

pppsetup script again, following the onscreen instructions. (You have no problems understanding them after you finish the basic *pppd* configuration without callback.)

9. Press Enter to display the modem initialization string dialog.

10. The modem initialization string is used to pass additional commands to the modem before it begins dialing your ISP number; in most cases, you can leave this blank, as shown in Figure 6.12. If your modem needs any special commands or you want to turn down the modem's speaker, this is the place. (Read the Modem-HOWTO for more information). When this field is left blank, the script uses the default `init` string.

11. Press Enter to proceed to the ISP domain name box.

12. Type the name of the domain of your ISP, as shown in Figure 6.13. This must be the true name and not something you just make up; your ISP can tell you what it is.

13. Press Enter to proceed to the DNS server address dialog box.

```
The default modem init string will be: "AT&FH0" OK

If you want to change it, put your init string in the box below.

If you use \ in the init string, put it twice.
Example: "AT\&F\\K3\\N3H0" OK
M = No sound.  S95=46 = Show CARRIER speed: 28800 etc.
Put "" around each init string with "&" in it.
Put OK after each init string. Example: ATZ OK "AT\&F1MH0" OK

Just press [Enter] on a empty box to accept the default above.

█

              <  OK  >        <Cancel>
```

Figure 6.12 *Type the modem initialization string here.*

```
What is your (I)nternet (S)ervice (P)rovider's domain name?

This is usually something like...
Examples: something.edu something.net something.com something.org

slackisp.com█

              <  OK  >        <Cancel>
```

Figure 6.13 *Your ISP domain name goes here.*

14. Type the IP address of the DNS server used by your ISP, as shown in Figure 6.14. When you ask your ISP for this information, it might be called the DNS server or the nameserver. You also might have received several such IPs—pick any one.

15. Press Enter to proceed to the authentication setup dialog box where you can configure methods used by the ISP to recognize the users trying to log in.

```
What is the IP address of your Internet provider's nameserver?

It's important that these IP numbers be correct.
The IP numbers should not be: 0.0.0.0

Note: Your service provider's technical support can provide you
with this information.   Example: 207.132.116.5

█

              <  OK  >        <Cancel>
```

Figure 6.14 *Type the IP address of your DNS server here.*

16. Choose the authentication method used by your ISP. Your ISP can provide the necessary information about authentication protocol; if it does not mention PAP, CHAP, or MS-CHAP-80, then you can safely choose the last option, SCRIPT, as shown in Figure 6.15. Because most use script-based authentication, I walk you through that here.

17. Press Enter to begin creating the login script.

18. To connect to your ISP, you typically need to enter a username and a password at the ISP's prompts. It's possible to do this manually, but it's far easier to create a script that does this automatically every time you connect. The *pppsetup* program helps you create it. The script you are creating now is used by the *chat* program, which listens to the ISP server's prompts, compares them with the rules you define here, and sends an appropriate response. The first prompt is usually for your user name; the prompt might be Username, User, or Login. If your ISP told you what to expect, great; if not, the troubleshooting tips later help you fix it. Enter your string in the dialog box shown in Figure 6.16 and press Enter to continue.

19. In the dialog box shown in Figure 6.17, type the username you plan to use, and press Enter.

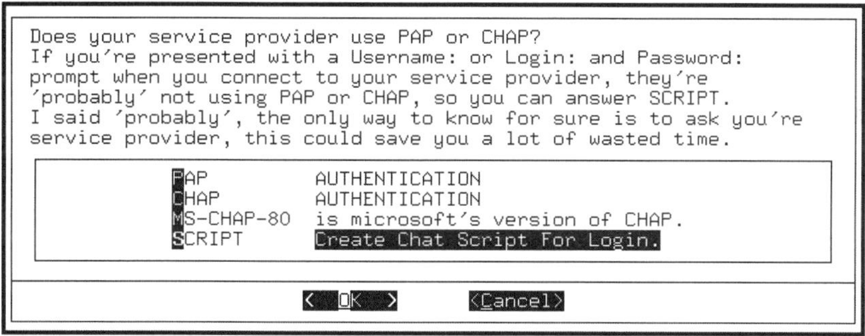

Figure 6.15 *It's time to select the right authentication method.*

Figure 6.16 *Here you tell* chat *what text to wait for after connecting…*

```
         And what text should I send?
 ┌──────────────────────────────────────────┐
 │ joe█                                      │
 └──────────────────────────────────────────┘

        <  OK  >           <Cancel>
```

Figure 6.17 *... then you tell* chat *what response it ought to send.*

20. Next, most ISPs prompt you for a password. The prompt string is usually `Password`, and that's what I told the script to expect in Figure 6.18. (By the way, these strings are case sensitive. If you don't know if the first letter is capitalized, you can leave it off. The script matches the end of the line, so it won't matter if it's capitalized or not.)

21. In the dialog box shown in Figure 6.19, type the password you plan to use, and press Enter.

22. To end the creation of the script, leave the text field in the next dialog box empty and press Enter. The *pppsetup* script displays the script you created.

23. Press the Enter key to end the configuration.

NOTE

If you do not know what words to type in the dialog boxes that appear in Figures 6.16–6.19, simply copy the texts shown in Figures 6.16–6.19 and read the next section to learn how you can find out the missing pieces of information.

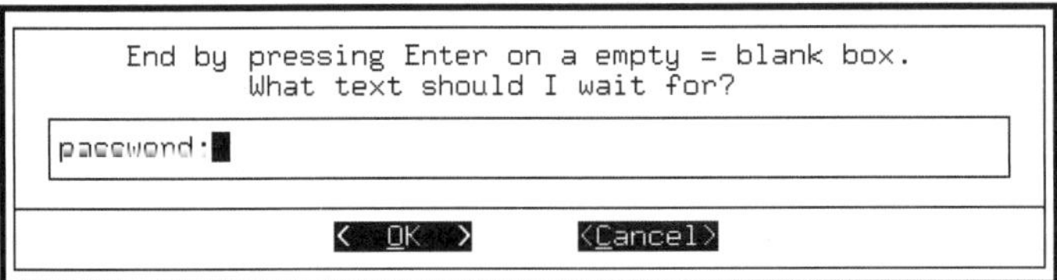

```
     End by pressing Enter on a empty = blank box.
          What text should I wait for?
 ┌──────────────────────────────────────────┐
 │ password·█                                │
 └──────────────────────────────────────────┘

        <  OK  >           <Cancel>
```

Figure 6.18 *Again, tell* chat *what text to expect...*

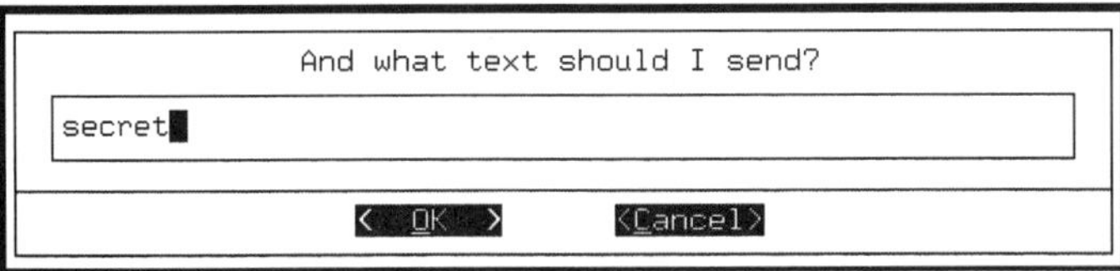

```
         And what text should I send?
 ┌──────────────────────────────────────────┐
 │ secret█                                   │
 └──────────────────────────────────────────┘

        <  OK  >           <Cancel>
```

Figure 6.19 *... then you tell* chat *what response it ought to respond with. Voila! Your script is ready.*

Testing Dial-Up Networking

Let's test the dial-up networking now. Follow these steps:

1. Type **ppp-go -d** on the command line and press Enter. The system should reply `Demand Dialing Started`, which tells you that *pppd* will dial your ISP number whenever any user on the system requests a connection to the Internet.

> You can always run **ppp-go -d** to restart *pppd* (only root can start and stop *pppd*).

2. Type **lynx http://www.slackware.com** and press Enter. You should observe some disk activity and hear the modem dialing the number of your ISP (make sure that all the cables are properly connected).

3. If you can see the text version of the Slackware page, you can safely assume that dial-up networking is working now (congratulations!).

4. Type **Q** to exit from *lynx*.

5. Type **ppp-off** to turn off dial-up networking. This breaks the connection to your ISP.

Troubleshooting Dial-Up Networking

What if things go wrong and you cannot get dial-up networking to work? First of all, make sure that you properly configured the basic networking services as described in the section titled "Configuring Basic Networking." Attempting *pppd* configuration only makes sense when you can telnet into your local system.

Second, did you hear your modem dial? If not, you might have selected the wrong device for your modem. Rerun the *pppsetup* script and try a different device.

A common problem with *pppd* and *chat* scripts is that they are missing bits of information that your ISP might have forgotten to give you. Fortunately, it is possible to discover most of the missing information from the messages sent by the ISP's server to your computer after your modem connects to the ISP's system.

You can find out what is being sent by monitoring the system log. To do so, do the following:

1. Switch to another virtual console (press Alt+F2 to switch to the second console and Alt+F1 to switch back to the first console). Or if you are in X, just open another xterm.

2. Log in as **root** (it is okay to be logged in at more than one console as the same user).

3. Type **tail -f /var/log/messages** and press Enter. You are now able to monitor all activity on the server.

4. Switch to the initial console (or xterm window).

5. Run *pppd* by typing the command **ppp-go –d**.

6. Run **ping www.slackware.com**.

7. Switch back to the second console to see what is happening during connection attempts.

Here are a few pointers on what to watch for:

- **Busy messages**. If you see busy messages, then the line is busy. You must keep on trying to connect until you see the connect message. On a positive note, at least you know your modem is working.

- **Messages received after the connection has been made.** Watch for the word `username` or something similar, copy it exactly as it appears onscreen, and then type it in when the *pppsetup* asks you for the first word to watch for (see step 18 in the section titled "Configuring PPP"). Similarly, watch for the word `password` or one of its variants.

- **Watch for text like DNS followed by IP addresses similar to 123.23.34.201.** This is the address of the DNS server necessary to configure dial-up networking. Not all ISPs print this information when you log on, so if you don't know this, at worst you need to call the technical support line again.

- **If you don't see any meaningful messages, watch for words such as PAP, CHAP, or MS-CHAP-80 in the system log**. These should give you a hint as to what authentication protocol your ISP is using.

As you can see, you can find out quite a lot about your ISP without asking. Once you have the missing information, run *pppsetup* again, type in the information you've found, and see if it works. If there are further problems, ask your ISP for help.

Ethernet

Configuring ethernet networking is very similar to configuring dial-up networking, only you do not have to set up *pppd*, as it is not needed in this case.

The first thing to configure is the network card. Linux supports numerous network cards in the kernel, and if you follow the recommendations in the Hardware-HOWTO and Ethernet-HOWTO, you should have no problems getting them to work. Some models might require kernel recompilation (see Chapter 3) or adding necessary modules to the kernel at system startup. The latter option, which I describe next, is more flexible.

If you want your computer to be connected to the local network via ethernet and use dial-up connections to the outside world, configure ethernet first, and then run *pppsetup*. (See the section titled "Configuring PPP" earlier in this chapter for information about running *pppsetup*.)

1. Log in as **root**.
2. Type **netconfig** and press the Enter key. You should see the same screen shown in Figure 6.1. (I assume that you did install the networking software recommended in Chapter 3.)
3. Press the Enter key again to begin network configuration. You can always stop configuration at any time by pressing Ctrl+C.
4. Type the name of the host; the host name is the name of your computer on your local network.

If you are connecting to an existing network, ask its system administrator for the proper host name. If your administrator says the network uses DHCP, you can probably make up a hostname.

5. Press the Enter key again to display the domain name dialog box.
6. Type the name of your network's domain. For systems connecting to a LAN, ask your system administrator for this. If the LAN is very small and not connected to the Internet (such as some home LANs), it might not have a host name. In such cases, you can use **localdomain**.

Remember not to type the leading dot (.) in the domain name. The *netconfig* script adds it automatically.

7. Press the Enter key again to display the IP address setup dialog.
8. Choose Static IP in the dialog box shown in Figure 6.20, unless your network support dynamic configuration with DHCP. For DHCP configurations, you won't have to enter an IP address.
9. Press the Enter key.
10. For static configurations, type the IP address of your computer in the dialog shown in Figure 6.21. If you plan to use your computer as the server for your local home network (not connected to the Internet), you probably don't have any IP assigned. In this case, type **192.168.0.1**. If you later add more computers to the network, pick their addresses from the range 192.168.0.0

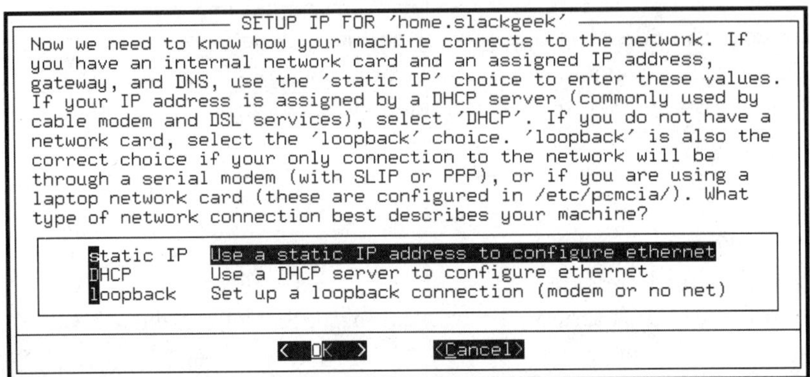

Figure 6.20 *Select* Static IP or DHCP for LANs.

Figure 6.21 *Your IP address, Sir....*

through 192.168.0.255. These addresses are reserved for use on private networks; they should never be used for connecting to the Internet.

11. Press the Enter key.

12. Type the netmask in the dialog box shown in Figure 6.22. Again, if you are a LAN, you should be able to obtain this from your system administrator. If this computer is on a private network such as a home LAN, use **255.255.255.0**.

13. Press the Enter key.

Figure 6.22 *What's your netmask, Zorro?*

14. Type the gateway IP address into the dialog box shown in Figure 6.23 and press Enter. For an Internet or intranet connection, your network administrator can tell you the right gateway to use. For LANs not connected to other networks, you don't need a gateway. Just press Enter without entering the gateway address.

15. Type the address of the DNS server in the dialog box shown in Figure 6.24. Your network administrator can help you here. Small, private LANs might not have a DNS server; computers on such a network might rely on static hosts to IP mappings defined in the /etc/hosts file.

16. Press the Enter key.

17. Decide whether you want the script to attempt to automatically detect the type of network card used in your computer. See Figure 6.25; I've chosen to probe. Press Enter.

```
──────────────── ENTER GATEWAY ADDRESS ────────────────
Enter the address for the gateway on your network,
such as 123.234.123.1

If you don't have a gateway on your network (or if this machine
is the gateway, such as if you'll be using it with a modem link
to the outside network as a router, firewall, or for IP
masquerading for a LAN), just hit ENTER without entering a
gateway IP address.

Enter gateway address (aaa.bbb.ccc.ddd):

 111.203.205.12█

        <   OK   >        <Cancel>
```

Figure 6.23 *The gateway address might be optional.*

```
──────────────── SELECT NAMESERVER ────────────────
Here is your current IP address, full hostname, and base hostname:
123.234.123.234        home.slackgeek      home

Please give the IP address of the name server to use,
such as 111.203.205.12.

You can add more Domain Name Servers by editing /etc/resolv.conf.

Name Server for domain slackgeek (aaa.bbb.ccc.ddd):

 119.2.45.100█

        <   OK   >        <Cancel>
```

Figure 6.24 *And the IP address of the DNS server is....*

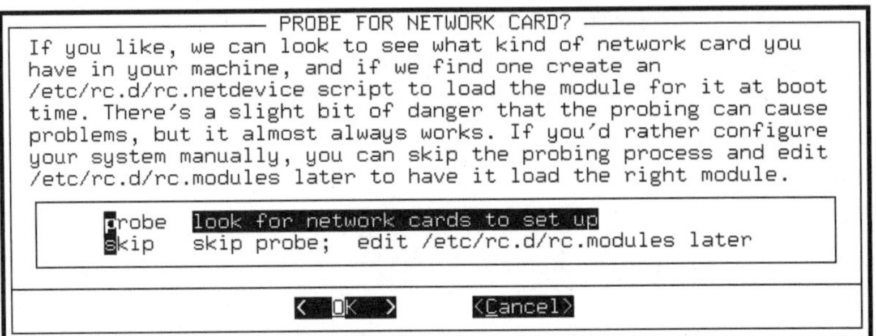

Figure 6.25 *To probe or not to probe?*

You can skip probing if you know what type of network card you have, but you later have to edit the /etc/rc.d/rc.modules file and uncomment the line that matches your network card by deleting the # character. For example, to enable support for the 3com 3c503 network cards, you would uncomment the `#/sbin/modprobe 3c503` line, save the file, and reboot the system.

Should probing for network cards fail, run *netconfig* again and skip this step. The configuration files are written to disk, and you have to find out by trial and error which module works best with your card. Gather as much information about your card (especially the chipset) as possible, and try uncommenting various modules to see if they work. Use the *telnet* test described in the "Testing Network Operations" section to determine if networking is functioning properly.

18. Once you have found the correct module for your network card and tried to telnet, you are all set!

Other Networking Devices

For an explanation of configuring other networking devices, read the following documents:

- AX.25: AX25-HOWTO
- Infrared: IR-HOWTO
- PCMCIA modems and network cards: PCMCIA-HOWTO

- ADSL and DSL: ADSL (mini-HOWTO)
- Cable modems: Cable-Modem (mini-HOWTO)
- Token ring: Token-Ring (mini-HOWTO)

Troubleshooting

There are many things that can go wrong with networking, but if you follow the instructions in this chapter and still have trouble getting everything to work, try the following:

- **Check connections.** Did you plug in all the cables and cards correctly?

- **Install network software (see Chapter 3).**

- **Make sure you are using hardware compatible with Linux.** Also make sure that the correct drivers are loaded. Either watch the messages while Linux is booting or run the command */sbin/lsmod* to find out what hardware Linux is recognizing.

- **Check for IRQ problems.** Older devices might need a unique IRQ (that's short for interrupt request number, often displayed at system boot). Make sure no two devices are using the same IRQ, or else one might not be recognized or might behave erratically. You can run the command *cat /proc/interrupts* to see which interrupts Linux is honoring.

- **Supply correct information to the *netconfig* and *pppsetup* scripts.** Read this chapter again and ask your ISP, network administrator, or someone experienced for help.

- **Do all configurations as root.**

- **Use ping *name of host on the network*.** For example, ping www.slackware.com. Ping several hosts. If you can ping hosts on your local network but not on the Internet, check your gateway setting. If they all fail, continue troubleshooting with the following *ping* tests to discover the problem.

- **Use ping *IP address of your nameserver*.** For example, ping 123.23.34.201. If you are unable to ping a hostname but can ping an IP, you most likely have DNS configured incorrectly.

- **Use ping 127.0.0.1.** If this last resort fails, then your networking software might not be installed or started. It's also possible that incorrectly configured hardware keeps the networking software from starting, so recheck your hardware.

Slackware Linux 7 includes excellent support for a wide range of networking hardware, and you can save yourself a lot of frustration if you read the following documents:

- Hardware-HOWTO
- NET-3-HOWTO
- Ethernet-HOWTO
- Config-HOWTO
- ISP-Hookup-HOWTO
- Networking-Overview-HOWTO

For more advanced users, the Network Administrators Guide is also a good choice.

Summary

Slackware Linux 7 networking is based on the TCP/IP protocol and software. It is preconfigured and can be used in the LAN or dial-up environment. All you have to do is supply some basic information needed by the *netconfig* and *pppsetup* scripts. Slackware Linux 7 can also be used in NetWare IPX and AppleTalk networks. It supports a wide range of networking hardware such as network cards, modem, ISDN adapters, IrDA ports, and even amateur shortwave radio. Additional information can be found in various HOWTO documents.

Chapter 7: Configuring Peripherals: Storage, Sound, and Printing

William Schaffer

Using Removable Storage

Tape Drives

Configuring for Sound

Printing

Using Removable Storage

You've gotten this far. Slackware Linux is installed on your hard drive, and it runs great now. But you would really like to use that CD drive somehow, and what about taking files to work on the Zip drive?

Everything UNIX has to fit into the filesystem somehow. The main filesystem that forms the base is called the root filesystem. The CD, Zip, Jaz, and even the venerable floppy drive all have a filesystem on them, in which files are stored. In order to access the filesystems on these devices, you need to graft them into your main filesystem.

So, how do you achieve this? There is a system utility called *mount*, which is used to perform this grafting. *mount* requires, at minimum, two parameters. The first is the device file in the /dev directory, which identifies the device you are looking to mount; the second is the location in your filesystem where you want the grafting to be done. This is called the mount point, and its location is entirely up to you. However, there are certain practical constraints. For one, the mount point must exist as a directory within your filesystem. It need not be an empty directory, but when you perform the mount, anything in the previous mount point directory remains hidden until you unmount it. Because of this trait, make sure you do not mount over anything important to system operation, such as /dev or /bin! Your system isn't of much use that way. Table 7.1 shows some common devices and their mount points.

Table 7.1 Mount Points of Common Devices

Device	Dev Entry	Mount Point
1st hard drive, 1st partition	/dev/hda1	/
CD-ROM	/dev/cdrom	/cdrom
Floppy	/dev/fd0	/mnt
External Zip drive	/dev/sda4	/zip

mount has a counterpart utility called *umount* (notice that it is *u-mount*, not *un-mount!*). This is used to get the device out of your filesystem and should be used before any mounted medium is removed from your system, including CD-ROMs, Zip disks, and floppy disks. Some of these devices do not eject the medium while it is mounted.

Using a Data CD

Let's mount the CD that was supplied with the text as an example. If you have an IDE- or SCSI-based CD, you probably already have support for it loaded with the default installation, so skip ahead to the "Loading the CD" section. If you have a parallel port CD drive, you need to do some work now.

Parallel Port CD Drives

If you have a parallel port CD-ROM drive, you need to load the parallel IDE device support, the appropriate protocol driver for your unit, and the parallel CD device support. Take a look at the file /usr/src/linux/Documentation/paride.txt (installed as part of the kernel source package) to find a reference to the type of CD unit you possess. See what protocol the document references for your drive. Table 7.2 shows some of the name-brand CD options and their module names available as of this printing.

Table 7.2 External CD Options and Their Module Names

Manufacturer	Model	Protocol
MicroSolutions	BackPack CD-ROM	bpck
FreeCom	Power CD-ROM	frpw
Hewlett-Packard	7200e(CD)	epat

The documentation does say that if you have something else, you can load all the protocol modules and let the system try them. The choices are aten, bpck, comm, dstr, epat, epia, fit2, fit3, friq, frpw, kbic, ktti, on20, and on26. So, load these modules:

```
modprobe            paride
modprobe            (protocol driver, e.g., epat)
modprobe            pcd
```

If this is a mostly permanent attachment, you probably want these modules to load during system start. Edit the file /etc/rc.d/rc.modules, and add these entries to the end of it. Now you are ready to go.

Loading the CD

Put the CD in your CD drive, and log in as the root user. Before you perform the mount, take a look at the /cdrom directory on your system by running the following command:

```
ls -la /cdrom
```

It is empty, except for the . and .. entries. The device file for the CD is usually /dev/cdrom, which is a soft link to the true device. Mount it by issuing this command:

```
mount /dev/cdrom /cdrom
```

If that does not work, it is possible that the link is to the wrong device. Try one of the devices listed in Table 7.3 instead.

Table 7.3 CD Drive Types and Their Device Filenames

Device Type	Dev Entry
SCSI CD	/dev/sr0
IDE CD on primary slave	/dev/hdb
IDE CD on secondary master	/dev/hdc
IDE CD on secondary slave	/dev/hdd
Parallel port CD	/dev/pcd0

If it still doesn't work, check to see if the kernel even knows the device exists. Use the *dmesg* command, and pipe it through the pager *less* so it doesn't scroll past you:

```
dmesg | less
```

If you have a SCSI CD, page up and down looking for a message like the following one:

```
(scsi0:0:4:0) Synchronous at 8.0 Mbyte/sec, offset 15.
 Vendor: YAMAHA  Model: CRW4416S     Rev: 1.0f
 Type:  CD-ROM               ANSI SCSI revision: 02
Detected scsi CD-ROM sr0 at scsi0, channel 0, id 4, lun 0
```

If you have an IDE CD, look for the following sample output:

```
hdc: ATAPI 8X CD-ROM drive, 128kB Cache
Uniform CDROM driver Revision: 2.55
```

These messages tell you that the driver is loaded and where to find the CD drive; the SCSI drive is at sr0 and the IDE is at hdc. If you do not see anything about the CD, check the cabling. Also, check the BIOS settings on the motherboard and controller cards. Otherwise, read Chapter 8, "Compiling the Kernel," because you might need to compile the correct device driver.

Assuming the CD has been mounted, use the same *ls* command as above to look at the directory, and you should see a lot more entries. Also notice how you cannot eject the CD by pushing the button on the front of the unit. Some devices, such as CD drives, allow the device to be locked while the system has it mounted. In order to remove the CD, you must *umount* the device, like this:

```
umount /cdrom
```

Now, it can be removed. Observe the output of the *ls –la /cdrom* command again; it's empty once more.

This mounting/unmounting procedure can be scripted for convenience. That way, instead of having to remember the *mount* command, you can just call this script. You might want to place this script in a directory referenced by your path, such as ~/bin or /usr/local/bin.

```
#!/bin/bash

# Define what device your CD drive shows up as
DEV="/dev/cdrom"

# Now, find out if we are mounting or unmounting
grep cdrom /etc/mtab > /dev/null 2>&1
RESULT=$?

# Act appropriately
if [ $RESULT -eq 1 ]
then
    # Mounting
    echo "Mounting "$DEV"..."
    mount ${DEV} /cdrom > /dev/null 2>&1
    RESULT=$?
    if [ $RESULT -eq 0 ]
    then
        echo "Success, "$DEV" was mounted on /cdrom"
        exit 0
    fi
    echo "Failure."
else
    # Un-mounting
    umount /cdrom > /dev/null 2>&1
    echo "CDROM has been unmounted"
fi
```

This first checks to see if the CD is already mounted. If so, it assumes you want to unmount. If it isn't, then it mounts it. No more, no less.

Using a Floppy Disk

A floppy disk can be used in a similar fashion, and it can be mounted into the filesystem just like the CD. Files can then be copied to it using the *cp* command. For example, the floppy formerly known as A has a device entry of /dev/fd0, so mount it as such:

```
mount /dev/fd0 /mnt
```

This mounts a formatted floppy under the /mnt directory, so the following command shows you the contents of that disk:

```
ls -la /mnt
```

Most PC floppy drives have no locking mechanism to prevent premature removal of the disk, so you must make certain that you leave the disk in the drive while it is mounted. To remove it, run the following command and wait for the drive light to go out:

```
umount /mnt
```

This might take a while, as the system is writing cached data from disk operations. After the light goes out, you can safely remove the disk.

Formatting Removable Media

Most removable disks these days are already formatted when you buy them. You can just put these disks in, mount them, and use them. But occasionally you need to format a disk. Maybe you have an unformatted floppy, or perhaps you want to scrub it clean of any previous information.

Floppies actually need to be formatted twice—a low-level format and a high-level format. (Everything else, including hard drives, LS-120 disks, Zip disks, and Jaz disks, shouldn't be low-level formatted.) A low-level format only needs to be done once on a floppy, but you might repeat it later if you want to check for bad blocks on the disk. The best way to perform a low-level format is to use the program *superformat*, which is part of the fdutils package. It supports many options, but in the simplest usage you only need to specify the device to be low-level formatted:

```
superformat /dev/fd0
```

After it's formatted, you can put a filesystem on it. This step is the high-level format and applies to all removable media. Most are formatted for MS-DOS, which is adequate for simply moving small files from one place to another. But because MS-DOS does not support user ownership and full permissions like UNIX does, backing up to an MS-DOS formatted disk isn't recommended. You could, of course, use the *tar* utility, which preserves ownership and permissions within the archive itself, regardless of the filesystem on which you save the archive. But if you want to use your disks without the extra step of an archiving program and without worrying about lost attributes, you should format the floppy with the native Linux filesystem, Ext2.

To reformat a floppy with the Ext2 filesystem, run the following command:

```
mke2fs /dev/fd0
```

When it is finished, the disk is ready for use in Linux systems. Windows and DOS machines, however, no longer recognize it, making it useless for transporting data between machines running these operating systems.

If you want to use the MS-DOS filesystem, run this command instead:

```
mkdosfs /dev/fd0
```

mtools

If the idea of mounting and unmounting floppy disks seems a little cumbersome, there is an alternative: the mtools suite of utilities, included in the Slackware distribution. These tools allow you to perform operations only on MS-DOS formatted floppies, but without the burden of mounting the filesystem.

Because the mtools suite bypasses the Linux kernel's filesystem implementation entirely and directly reads and writes to the floppy, you must give the users of these tools permission to read and write to the floppy device. If only you use your computer, and you don't care much about security, you can let everyone read and write the floppy with this command:

```
chmod 0666 /dev/fd0
```

Otherwise, you need to add the usernames of those allowed to use the floppy to the floppy group in /etc/group.

Using the utilities should be relatively intuitive to anyone who has used MS-DOS. To list the files on a disk, run this command:

```
mdir a:
```

To copy a file to a disk, run

```
mcopy filename a:
```

Table 7.4 shows the mtools and their MS-DOS counterparts.

Table 7.4 mtools and DOS Counterparts

mtool	MS-DOS	Function
mattrib	attrib	change a file's attributes
mcd	cd	change the working directory
mcopy	copy	copy a file
mdel	del	delete a file
mdeltree	deltree	delete a subdirectory and its files
mdir	dir	display a directory or directory entry
mformat	format	format a disk, similar to mkdosfs
mlabel	label	change the label of a disk
mmd	md	make a subdirectory
mmove	move	move a file
mrd	rd	remove a subdirectory
mren	ren	rename a file
mtype	type	display the contents of a file

I think you get the idea.

LS-120 Floppy Drives

If you have an LS-120 ATAPI floppy drive, you need to load a kernel module to use it. The ide-floppy module tells the kernel how to access this type of drive. So, as the root user, type the following:

```
modprobe ide-floppy
```

Remember to add this line to your /etc/rc.d/rc.modules file so it is done automatically on system startup. Edit the file /etc/rc.d/rc.modules and search for the line containing `ide-floppy`. Delete the # character from the beginning of the line, then save and exit the file. The floppy drive now shows up as another IDE hard drive. So for example, if the drive is the primary slave, it is accessed through /dev/hdb (see Table 7.5.)

Table 7.5 LS-120 Drives and Their Device Filenames

Device Type	Dev Entry
LS-120 on primary slave	/dev/hdb
LS-120 on secondary master	/dev/hdc
LS-120 on secondary slave	/dev/hdd

Now you can mount and unmount the LS-120 floppy. Just like regular floppies, LS-120 floppies come from the factory without partitions. Because of this, you mount it without a partition number, like this:

```
mount /dev/hdb /mnt
```

Using a Zip or Jaz Drive

Iomega Zip drives come in a few varieties of interface types. There are normal external parallel port Zip drives, external Zip Plus drives, internal IDE Zip drives, internal ATAPI Zip drives, and internal and external SCSI Zip drives. The Zip 250 drives use the same configurations as their 100MB counterparts. USB-based Zip drives are coming, but USB support in Linux is still being developed. Jaz drives come in SCSI and parallel port versions. For these versions, the directions are the same as for their Zip counterparts. If you don't know exactly what type of Zip or Jaz drive you have, check the following sites:

- http://www.iomega.com/zip
- http://www.iomega.com/jaz

One thing to note is that preformatted Iomega Zip disks are set up to use partition 4. That means that a disk in a drive that shows up as /dev/sda is accessed as /dev/sda4.

IDE Zip Drives

If you are lucky enough to have an internal IDE Zip drive, things are basically plug and go. The kernel sees it as another hard drive. So, if it is connected as the primary slave, it is found at /dev/hdb, the secondary master at /dev/hdc, and the secondary slave at /dev/hdd. If you are daring, you can make it your primary master and find it at /dev/hda.

SCSI Zip Drives

The SCSI Zip drives are almost as simple to configure as the internal ones. If your system is already configured for SCSI, then find an unused SCSI ID, plug it in, set the termination on the chain, and you are set. If you are installing the adapter as well, you should probably read the manufacturer's literature about selecting SCSI ID numbers and termination. The drive shows up following the normal rules for SCSI disks that is, /dev/sda if it is the first SCSI disk found in the system, /dev/sdb if it is the second, and so on.

ATAPI Zip Drives

If you have an ATAPI Zip drive, a newer version of the IDE Zip drive, it still gets plugged in to your system like an IDE Zip drive. However, you must configure for an ATAPI floppy drive in order to use it. To do this, you load the ide-floppy module. You can do this manually by using the following command:

```
modprobe ide-floppy
```

This needs to be done automatically during system startup. Edit the file /etc/rc.d/rc.modules and search for the line containing `ide-floppy`. Delete the # character from the beginning of the line, then save and exit the file. This Zip drive now shows up as /dev/hdb, /dev/hdc, or /dev/hdd, similar to the internal IDE Zip drive.

Newer External Zip, Zip Plus, and External Zip 250 Drives

These drives plug in to the parallel port on the back of your system. If your PC's BIOS has settings for ECP/EPP, you get the best performance by using these settings over the standard parallel port protocol. To use them with Linux, you need to have the imm module loaded. You can do this manually by issuing the following command:

```
modprobe imm
```

But if the lp module is already loaded, you might not succeed. You want it done at system startup anyway, so edit the file /etc/rc.d/rc.modules and search for the line containing `modprobe imm`. Delete the # character from the beginning of the line, then save and exit the file. This Zip drive now shows up according to the SCSI drive rules, such as /dev/sda, similar to the SCSI Zip drive.

If the imm module does not work for you, try the ppa module, described in the next section.

Older External Zip Drives

These drives also plug in to the parallel port on the back of your system. Again, if your PC's BIOS has settings for ECP/EPP, you get the best performance by using these settings over the standard parallel port protocol. These drives require the ppa module to be loaded. You can do this manually by issuing the following command:

```
modprobe ppa
```

But again, if the lp module is already loaded, you might have problems. You want it done at system startup anyway, so edit the file /etc/rc.d/rc.modules and search for the line containing `modprobe ppa`. Delete the # character from the beginning of the line, then save and exit the file. This Zip drive now shows up according to the SCSI drive rules, such as /dev/sda, similar to the SCSI Zip drive.

Using the Drive

If you did get the manual modprobes to work, you should see a message like the following. If not, reboot, and while the boot messages are going by, look for a notice about the device being found. If you have a parallel port or SCSI version, you see something like this:

```
scsi3 : Iomega VPIO (ppa) interface
scsi : 4 hosts.
    Vendor:    IOMEGA    Model: ZIP 100    Rev: D.09
    Type:    Direct-Access    ANSI SCSI revision: 02
Detected scsi removable disk sdc at scsi3, channel 0, id 6, lun 0
SCSI device sdc: hdwr sector= 512 bytes. Sectors= 196608 [96 MB] [0.1 GB]
sdc: Write Protect is off
    sdc: sdc4
```

If you have an IDE or ATAPI version, look for something like

```
hdb: IOMEGA ZIP 100, ATAPI FLOPPY drive
...
Partition check:
 hdb: hdb4
```

If you have a Jaz drive, it says Jaz instead of Zip. Notice that these messages not only tell you that the device was found, but what its device name is in the /dev directory. In the first example, the Zip drive is located at /dev/sdc, and the disk that was inserted is partitioned to use partition number 4. So, to access the contents of the Zip disk as the root user, type the following:

```
mount -t vfat /dev/sdc4 /zip
```

This mounts the filesystem on the Zip disk into the root filesystem under the directory /zip. If you don't have a directory called /zip, you can make one by typing

```
mkdir /zip
```

In the second example, the Zip drive is located at /dev/hdb, again using partition number 4. To mount that one, run

```
mount -t vfat /dev/hdb4 /zip
```

While the disk is mounted, you can copy files to and from it using the directory /zip. Observe that while the Zip disk is mounted, you are unable to eject the disk. In order to eject, you need to unmount the disk:

```
umount /zip
```

A note on filesystems: The preformatted Zip disks are set up to use the MS-DOS filesystem. This is perfectly usable by Linux and necessary if you are transferring data between Linux and Windows-based systems. However, as with floppy disks, you might wish to use the Ext2 filesystem instead. This allows you to use the disk under Linux without worrying about losing file attributes, such as ownership and permissions.

Ziptool and Jaztool

Ziptool and Jaztool are utilities to set the write-protect status of the disk. You must have read and write access to the device, and the Zip or Jaz disk must not be mounted into the filesystem in order for this command to work. The first parameter is the main device entry for the disk, such as /dev/sda. The second parameter is the action you want to take, either *eject*, *ro*, *rw*, or *status*. *eject* simply pops the disk out. The *ro* command sets the disk to read-only and prevents writing. The *rw* command does the opposite, and sets for read-write to allow writing. *status* simply returns the current write protect state. Here's an example:

```
ziptool /dev/sdc ro
ziptool: /dev/sdc is write-protected
```

A Convenience Script for Zip Drives

Here is a convenience script to automate the mounting and unmounting of a Zip disk. You can type it in and save it to the /usr/local/bin directory. The script attempts to find your Zip drive automatically. Run it once to mount your Zip disk; run it again to unmount. With slight modifications you could use this same script to mount other types of removable drives.

```
#!/bin/bash

# Define what raw device your Zip drive shows up as
```

```
# /dev/sda, /dev/sdb, /dev/hdb, and so on
# Mine uses /dev/sdf ...sometimes.
DEV="/dev/sdf"


# Now, find out if we are mounting or unmounting
grep zip /etc/mtab > /dev/null 2>&1
RESULT=$?


# Act appropriately
if [ $RESULT -eq 1 ]
then
    # Mounting

    # Check the four most likely partitions
    for I in 1 2 3 4
    do
        echo "Trying "$DEV$I"..."
        mount -t vfat ${DEV}${I} /zip > /dev/null 2>&1
        RESULT=$?
        if [ $RESULT -eq 0 ]
        then
            echo -n "Success, "$DEV$I" was mounted "
            grep zip /proc/mounts | grep ro > /dev/null
            RESULT=$?
            if [ $RESULT -eq 0 ]
            then
                echo -n "READ ONLY "
            fi
            echo "on /zip"
            exit 0
        fi
    done
    echo "Failure."
else
    # Un-mounting
    umount /zip > /dev/null 2>&1
    /sbin/ziptool $DEV eject
    echo "Zip disk has been unmounted"
fi
```

Because it is feasible that each Zip disk might be partitioned differently, this script scans through and mounts the first configured partition on the disk. Iomega likes to use partition 4. I make mine use partition 1 when I reformat them.

Writing Data CDs

In order to write CD-R and CD-RWs, you need to go through a few hoops. First of all, go to the /usr/doc/Linux-HOWTOs directory and view the file CD-Writing-HOWTO. Page down to section 1.5, titled "Supported CD-Writers." Make sure that your CD writer is in the list. Assuming that it is, proceed to modify the kernel to support CD writing. This requires that several modules be loaded.

If you have a SCSI CD writer, and have already configured your SCSI adapter, you need the generic SCSI support:

```
modprobe sg
```

If you have an IDE CD writer, you need to load the SCSI host adapter emulation and generic SCSI support.

```
modprobe ide-scsi
modprobe sg
```

You also need to make sure that the kernel doesn't grab the device as a read-only CD device before the SCSI emulation is loaded. This can be accomplished with a LILO parameter. If the CD is the primary slave on the IDE bus, you use this line in the image section of your /etc/lilo.conf file:

```
append="hdb=ide-scsi"
```

Then reinstall LILO and reboot.

If you have a parallel port writer, you need to load the parallel IDE device support, the parallel CD device support, the associated generic device support, paride, pcd, pg, and the appropriate low-level driver for your unit. In the kernel documentation file /usr/src/linux/Documentation/paride.txt, the only brand-name IDE CD writer that is mentioned is the Hewlett-Packard 7200e, which uses the Shuttle EPAT driver. The documentation does say that if you have something else, you can load all the protocol modules and let the system try them, the choices being aten, bpck, comm, dstr, epat, epia, fit2, fit3, friq, frpw, kbic, ktti, on20, and on26. So, load these modules:

```
modprobe          paride
modprobe          (low lever driver. For example, epat for HP 7200e)
modprobe          pcd
modprobe          pg
```

For all of the CD writers, you need to load the loop-back and ISO9660 filesystem support modules:

```
modprobe loop
modprobe isofs
```

Once you have all of these drivers loaded, issue the command

```
cdrecord -scanbus
```

If you see your CD drive in the list, you have a collection of drivers that works. Add the drivers to the end of your /etc/rc.d/rc.modules file, so they are loaded upon system startup.

Now the kernel is configured for CD writing. The next step is to build a CD image. First, collect all the files that are to be on the new CD in one directory that, for this example, I call cdsource/. A 74-minute CD holds 650MB of data, but some is required for the filesystem itself, so figure around 620MB of files at most. You also need an extra 650MB free on your disk, because you need to create a temporary CD image with copies of the files. Once you have everything collected in the directory, make the CD image with *mkisofs*.

```
mkisofs -r -o newcdimage cdsource/
```

When this is finished, you can verify the new CD image using *mount* and the loop-back device.

```
mount -o ro,loop=/dev/loop0 newcdimage /mnt
```

Now, if you change to the /mnt directory, you should see the files that you collected in the cdsource directory. If you see mistakes, you need to edit the files in the cdsource/ directory and rerun *mkisofs*. When you are satisfied, change back to your source directory and *umount /mnt*.

You are almost ready to burn a new CD. Because writing a CD requires that a constant stream of data be fed to the writer, it is best to make sure that nothing else is going on in the system during the burn, especially if your system is older and slower or if you are trying burn through the parallel port. If the burn gets interrupted, you wind up making a coaster.

You need to find the device identification of your CD writer. This is done with the command *cdrecord*:

```
cdrecord -scanbus
```

If everything is working, you should see output similar to what is shown in Figure 7.1.

```
kitzbuhel:~>cdrecord -scanbus
Cdrecord release 1.8a29 Copyright (C) 1995-1999 Jörg Schilling
scsibus0:
        0,0,0     0) 'QUANTUM ' 'FIREBALL SE2.1S ' 'PJ09' Disk
        0,1,0     1) 'QUANTUM ' 'FIREBALL ST3.2S ' 'OFOC' Disk
        0,2,0     2) *
        0,3,0     3) *
        0,4,0     4) 'YAMAHA  ' 'CRW4416S        ' '1.0f' Removable CD-ROM
        0,5,0     5) 'SONY    ' 'SDT-5200        ' '3.30' Removable Tape
        0,6,0     6) *
        0,7,0     7) *
kitzbuhel:~>
```

Figure 7.1 *The output of the* cdrecord -scanbus *command*

From this listing, find your CD writer, and note the three first numbers on the line, which are separated by commas. In this example, the drive is located at device number 0,4,0.

The command to burn the disk is also *cdrecord*. It takes many parameters, so run the following to read them all:

```
man cdrecord
```

You are just going to use a few here. For one, you need to set the speed of the burn. This rating should be on the drive somewhere, listed as 2x or 4x or something similar. CD-R drives usually have two numbers, so use the lower (the higher is the readback speed). CD-RW drives have three numbers; for safety's sake, use the lowest of the three. You also need to specify the device number from the *scanbus* command:

```
cdrecord -v speed=2 dev=0,4,0 -data newcdimage
```

If you have a CD-RW, and want to erase it first, add *blank=all* to the preceding command before the *speed* parameter. This should chug along and eventually produce the CD.

There are utilities out there that can be used as a front end to *mkisofs* and *cdrecord*. An example of a graphical front end is X-CD-Roast, found at http://www.xcdroast.org.

Tape Drives

Tape drives are a little different from the other removable media discussed in this chapter. They are sequential access devices and do not get mounted into the filesystem.

SCSI Tape Drives

If you have a SCSI tape device, you need to have SCSI tape support loaded. It uses the device /dev/st0.

```
modprobe st
```

These tapes do not need user formatting. Pretty simple.

Floppy-Based Tape Drives

If you have a floppy controller–based tape drive, you need to load the ftape and zftape modules. It uses the device /dev/ftape.

```
modprobe ftape
modprobe zftape
```

These tapes might require formatting before first use. In order to format, you need a package called ftape-tools. The latest can be obtained from ftp://metalab.unc.edu/pub/Linux/kernel/tapes.

Get the file named /ftape-tools-*x.xx*.tar.gz into a working directory. The *x.xx* is the version number of the package; get the highest number in this format. Then unpack the archive by running

```
tar -xzvf ftape-tools-x.xx.tar.gz
```

This creates a directory called ftape-tools-x.xx. Change to it and, as the root user, of course, run these commands:

```
./configure
make
make install
```

Now you have several useful utilities, including *ftformat*, which you can use to format the tapes. This command takes a lot of different parameters based on your tape drive type; use the following command to view them:

```
man ftformat
```

Note, however, that the software can attempt to autodetect your tape type, using this command:

```
ftformat —mode=auto
```

Getting Data to and from the Tape

Regardless of which type of tape drive you have, you can use *dd*, *tar*, or *cpio* to get data to and from the tapes. There are other more advanced utilities available, but these are the ones in the Slackware distribution. For example, suppose you want to back up your user directories, located in /home, and the system configurations, located in /etc. Using the *tar* command, the root user would do this for a floppy-based tape:

```
tar -czvf /dev/ftape /home /etc
```

And this if for a SCSI-based tape:

```
tar -czvf /dev/st0 /home /etc
```

The collection of options, *-czvf*, tell the *tar* command to create a new archive (the *c*), use compression (the *z*), give lots of information to the user (the *v*), and to create this archive on the device /dev/st0 (the *f /dev/st0*). Everything after these parameters describes what is to be archived: the /home and /etc directories.

To view the contents of the tape, you replace the *c* option with a *t*, and drop the source info (the /home and /etc). For floppy tape, run

```
tar -tzvf /dev/ftape
```

For SCSI tape, run

```
tar -tzvf /dev/st0
```

To extract your data off of a floppy tape, you could use this command:

```
tar -xzvf /dev/ftape
```

To extract your data off of a SCSI tape, run

```
tar -xzvf /dev/st0
```

These commands extract (the *x*) all data from the said devices and dump it into the current directory. That is an important thing to remember! Make sure you are in a safe directory, such as /tmp, when you extract, or you might overwrite something vital. To extract something specific from the archive, you could add it as another parameter after the device specification. For example,

```
tar -xzvf /dev/st0 home/snowman/
```

This would only extract the home/snowman portion of the archive. As you see, *tar* drops the leading slash, so all stored filenames are relative. If you specify the leading slash, *tar* doesn't find your file.

Configuring for Sound

The first step to getting your sound system working is to make sure you have a sound card that is supported under Linux. Change to the /usr/doc/Linux-HOWTOs directory. View the file Sound-HOWTO, and page down to section 3.1, Sound Cards. Make sure your sound card is listed here. If it isn't, check the literature on the card to see if it claims compatibility with a card that is in the list. If so, consider the card to be the listed type for the rest of this section. If you still don't find a match, the card does not work; either buy a new card, wait for your old card to be supported, or go turn on the radio.

Setting Up the Hardware

Let's start from the hardware and work up to the applications. Assuming that your sound card is either a jumper-configurable card or an ISA-based Plug and Play card, you need to read this section. If it is a PCI-based card, install the card in your system according to the manufacturer's directions and proceed to the section titled "Setting Up the Device Driver Module."

This sound card is going to need to be configured for use. It needs to have its interrupt number (IRQ), its input/output address (I/O), and a direct memory access channel (DMA) selected. Interrupts are used by a peripheral device to tell the system there is data to be processed. The I/O address is where the system controls and transfers data to and from the peripheral. The DMA channel is used to get information from the system's memory to the peripheral without CPU intervention.

Note that if your sound card is a jumper-configurable device, is already installed, and is working properly with that other operating system you might have on your computer, then you need to find out how it is configured. There are two ways to do this. You can turn off the computer, open it up, and look at the jumper settings. Alternatively, you can reboot into the other operating system and check the configuration settings there. Then proceed to the section titled "Setting Up the Device Driver Module," because the following information is irrelevant to you.

Now, assuming that you either have your sound card in your hand, or it is a Plug and Play configurable device, you need to decide how that device should be configured. To begin, log in as root and issue the command **cat /proc/interrupts**. This produces a listing that looks something like Figure 7.2.

This is a list of interrupts that are already in use within your system. The column on the far left is the interrupt number, and the column all the way to the right is the device using that interrupt. The numbers range from zero to 15. Any number not listed in the leftmost column is available for use by your sound card.

Almost.

```
kitzbuhel:~>cat /proc/interrupts
           CPU0
   0:    1267618        XT-PIC  timer
   1:       8986        XT-PIC  keyboard
   2:          0        XT-PIC  cascade
   5:     187063        XT-PIC  soundblaster
   7:          0        XT-PIC  parport0
   8:          1        XT-PIC  rtc
  10:      72545        XT-PIC  aic7xxx, aic7xxx
  12:     556797        XT-PIC  PS/2 Mouse
  13:          1        XT-PIC  fpu
  14:        207        XT-PIC  ide0
  15:      80759        XT-PIC  aic7xxx
 NMI:          0
kitzbuhel:~>
```

Figure 7.2 *Output of* cat /proc/interrupts

It is important to know that there might be other devices in your system that are not presently in use, and may not show up here. The most likely are any inactive serial and parallel ports, as well as an inactive modem. Typically, these devices use IRQs 3, 4, and 7. If you have any of these devices, you need to check their configurations to find out exactly what IRQ numbers are used by them. A conflict could cause you problems. If you have a Plug and Play modem, check how you have it configured. The serial ports are either jumper configurable (meaning you have to check by opening the case), or they are configurable in your BIOS settings.

Another pitfall to avoid is the main board's BIOS settings regarding Plug and Play and interrupts. Available interrupts are used for the automatic PCI Plug and Play configuration. The BIOS should have a setting to reserve an interrupt for ISA Plug and Play, or a legacy setting. If you encounter problems, check this setting.

With all that in mind, select an unused IRQ for your sound card. It must be an IRQ that is not used by any other device and must be an IRQ that your sound card can be set to use. I use IRQ 5. For instance:

```
5:                187063        XT-PIC  soundblaster
```

Make a note of what your selection is. Next, you need to select the I/O port address. Issuing the command **cat /proc/ioports** produces a listing that looks something like Figure 7.3.

The leftmost column contains the I/O ranges that are currently in use by the system. The right column lists what devices are using those ports. Again, it must be mentioned that a device that is not currently in use might not show up in this list, just as

```
kitzbuhel:~>cat /proc/ioports
0000-001f : dma1
0020-003f : pic1
0040-005f : timer
0060-006f : keyboard
0070-007f : rtc
0080-008f : dma page reg
00a0-00bf : pic2
00c0-00df : dma2
00f0-00ff : fpu
01f0-01f7 : ide0
0220-022f : soundblaster
02f8-02ff : serial(set)
0330-0333 : MPU-401 UART
0378-037f : parport0
03c0-03df : vga+
03f6-03f6 : ide0
03f8-03ff : serial(auto)
d800-d8be : aic7xxx
dc00-dcbe : aic7xxx
ec00-ecbe : aic7xxx
ffa0-ffa7 : ide0
kitzbuhel:~>
```

Figure 7.3 *Output of the cat /proc/ioports command*

with the list of interrupts. I have a SoundBlaster, which is set up via jumpers to use

```
0220-022f    :    soundblaster
0330-0333    :    MPU-401 UART
```

Note here that one card might use more than one I/O range. Check with the literature for your card. Your mileage might vary. Select an applicable I/O range that your card can use, and make a note of it.

The last thing you need to check is available DMA channels. The command is **cat /proc/dma**, and yields the following list:

```
cat /proc/dma
   4:    cascade
```

Most devices allocate and deallocate DMA channels as needed, but an ISA sound card does not. DMA channels number 0 through 3 are the 8-bit channels, whereas channels 4 through 7 are 16-bit channels. The 16-bit channels can transfer more data in one session than the 8-bit channels and thus require less CPU intervention for large amounts of data. Check the literature for your sound card for which channels it is capable of using. Many cards, such as the SoundBlaster 16, support both an 8-bit channel and a 16-bit channel. Pick an unused DMA channel that your card can use, and make a note of it. My setup is this:

1: SoundBlaster8

5: SoundBlaster16

Now, if your sound card is not yet installed, you need to shut down the system and open it up. Logged in as the root user, issue the command **shutdown -h now.**

Wait until you have a message on your screen that says

```
Power down.
```

Now you can power off your system. You now need to physically install the sound card into your computer system. If your sound card is jumper configurable, now is a good time to do so. Please follow the manufacturer's directions for installing the card, and observe proper electrostatic discharge (ESD) procedures. Static electricity can ruin computer components.

When you have the card installed and your computer sealed up again, power on the system. If your card is jumper configurable, proceed to the section titled "Setting Up the Device Driver Module". Otherwise, if you have an ISA-based Plug and Play card, read on.

To configure your ISA-based Plug and Play card, you need to query the card for its allowable settings, and then create a file to be used at system startup to configure that card. You might have already done this for configuring a Plug and Play modem. To create this file, you need to log in as root again. Then issue the command **pnpdump > newisapnp.conf.**

This queries all the ISA-based Plug and Play cards in your system and creates a file called /newisapnp.conf in your current directory. Depending on how many such cards you have, this file could get large. Not only does every card get listed, but all of its supported configurations are there as well. So, now that you've created the file, you need to edit it. Type

```
vi newisapnp.conf
```

Page up and down to take a look around this file. You are looking for blocks of lines that contain the phrases `serial identifier` and `ANSI string`. The lines with these phrases should be a few lines from each other and form a documentation header block for each card. Look for an ANSI string line that describes the type of sound card that you have something like what is shown in Figure 7.4.

Everything between this header and the next such header (`Card 2` or whatever card number is next) is pertinent to this sound card. They are instructions to the system on how to configure your sound card's IRQ number, I/O address, and DMA channels. Moving down from here, you will see a line containing `CONFIGURE`. This marks the beginning of the configuration choices for this card, which continues until the next `Card` line. There might be multiple sets of configurations to choose from, and they begin with a comment line like this:

```
Start dependent functions: priority preferred
```

```
(READPORT 0x020b)
(ISOLATE PRESERVE)
(IDENTIFY *)
(VERBOSITY 2)
(CONFLICT (IO FATAL)(IRQ FATAL)(DMA FATAL)(MEM FATAL)) # or WARNING

# Card 1: (serial identifier 87 13 33 db 7f 2c 00 8c 0e)
# Vendor Id CTL002c, Serial Number 322165631, checksum 0x87.
# Version 1.0, Vendor version 1.0
# ANSI string -->Creative SB16 PnP<--
#
# Logical device id CTL0031
#     Device supports vendor reserved register @ 0x38
#     Device supports vendor reserved register @ 0x39
#     Device supports vendor reserved register @ 0x3c
#     Device supports vendor reserved register @ 0x3f
#
# Edit the entries below to uncomment out the configuration required.
# Note that only the first value of any range is given, this may be changed if r
# Don't forget to uncomment the activate (ACT Y) when happy

(CONFIGURE CTL002c/322165631 (LD 0
#     ANSI string -->Audio<--
```

Figure 7.4 *This is the start of a card definition block in the Plug and Play configuration file.*

The first set of choices is the set that is recommended by the card manufacturer. As long as these values do not conflict with anything in your system, stay with these values.

You need to select a configuration set and uncomment the INT, DMA, and IO lines. By uncomment, I mean that you should remove the leading # from the line. (The # character tells the system to ignore the line, which is counter to what you want to achieve.) Before continuing, you need to check to see what function each uncommented line performs.

If this line is the INT line, then you need to edit the number to the right of the word `IRQ`. This is where you need to put your interrupt number. If the number already on the line was available in the /proc/interrupts listing, it is probably best to leave it as is, but you can put your selected interrupt number here. Figure 7.5 shows a condensed sample of a modified configuration file.

If this line is an IO line, you need to edit the number to the right of the word `BASE`. This is the first number describing the range of I/O addresses for your card. Note that there may be several of these in the group, depending on your sound card. You need to uncomment the entire group. If the preferred I/O addresses are not conflicting with anything, leave them. Otherwise, put your selected values here.

The other line you might need to edit is the DMA line. You might have multiple instances of this line as well. Find the number to the right of the word `CHANNEL`. This is the DMA channel that the card uses. Edit appropriately.

Proceed down the page with the arrow key, uncommenting and editing the # (lines, until you get to the next `#__Start dependent function` line, the next `Card` line, or the end of the file.

There are two more lines that are important. You should not need to edit their values; just make sure they are uncommented. There should be a line called NAME, which is a descriptor line for the card. This already is uncommented. Following that line, one finds a line that contains the string ACT Y. This line makes the configuration active and needs to be uncommented.

Now that you are finished editing, you need to save and exit the file. Figure 7.5 shows the sound card section of my configuration file, with the nonfunctional comments removed.

I have my sound card using interrupt 5. The 8-bit DMA is using channel 1, and the 16-bit DMA is using channel 5. The I/O ranges used are 0x0220 through 0x022f, 0x0330 through 0x0333, and 0x0388.

Now that you have the hardware configuration file set up, try it out. As root, issue the command:

isapnp newisapnp.conf

If all goes well, you get your command prompt back with no error messages. You see a success report like this:

```
Board 1 has Identity 87 13 33 db 7f 2c 00 8c 0e: CTL002c Serial No322165631
[checksum 87]
```

```
# Card 1: (serial identifier 87 13 33 db 7f 2c 00 8c 0e)
# Vendor Id CTL002c, Serial Number 322165631, checksum 0x87.
# Version 1.0, Vendor version 1.0
# ANSI string -->Creative SB16 PnP<--
#
# Logical device id CTL0031
#     Device supports vendor reserved register @ 0x38
#     Device supports vendor reserved register @ 0x39
#     Device supports vendor reserved register @ 0x3c
#     Device supports vendor reserved register @ 0x3d
#     Device supports vendor reserved register @ 0x3e
#
# Edit the entries below to uncomment out the configuration required.
# Note that only the first value of any range is given, this may be changed if
# Don't forget to uncomment the activate (ACT Y) when happy .

(CONFIGURE CTL002c/322165631 (LD 0
#     ANSI string -->Audio<--
(INT 0 (IRQ 5 (MODE +E)))
(DMA 0 (CHANNEL 1))
(DMA 1 (CHANNEL 5))
(IO 0 (SIZE 16) (BASE 0x0220))
(IO 1 (SIZE 2) (BASE 0x0330))
(IO 2 (SIZE 4) (BASE 0x0388))
(NAME "CTL002c/322165631[0]{Audio                    }")
(ACT Y)
))
# End tag... Checksum 0x00 (OK)
```

Figure 7.5 *This is a sample of a modified card configuration block in the Plug and Play configuration file.*

If you do get errors, they might contain the words `warning`, `fatal`, or `not permitted`. The `not permitted` error means you aren't logged in as root. The other errors are allocation or conflict errors. Re-edit the /newisapnp.conf file, and make sure you saved your changes. Make sure there are no strange characters on the uncommented lines. Finally, check that the selected IRQ, IO, and DMA values are not conflicting with other peripherals, and that they are valid choices for the card.

If everything is good, you need to make these changes effective on system startup. First of all, check to see if you already have a file called /isapnp.conf in your /etc directory. If you do, you need to add the contents of the new one to it; otherwise, you destroy the configuration for your other devices. Issue the command

```
ls -l /etc/isapnp.conf
```

If you get a message that says `No such file or directory`, then you can simply copy the new file to the proper place. Issue the command

```
cp newisapnp.conf /etc/isapnp.conf
```

If you instead get a directory listing for a file, you have a tricky issue to deal with. You need to re-edit your new configuration file and delete all the lines that are not part of your sound card configuration. That is, you want only the lines between and including the `CONFIGURE` line for the sound card and the `)` line after the following `ACT Y` entry. Everything else must go. You may keep comment lines if you wish, but I delete them to remove the clutter. Once you have something that looks like my sample configuration above, save and exit the file.

Now, you need to edit the existing /isapnp.conf file. So, enter the following command:

```
vi /etc/isapnp.conf
```

Go to the bottom of the file by pressing Shift+G. Next, up-arrow to the blank line above the `WAITFORKEY` line. Now, you load in your new file. Enter the command

```
:r newisapnp.conf
```

This should copy your newly created configuration file into this file, starting at the line below the cursor. Now, save and exit to finish with that file.

The last thing you need to do is plug the speakers into your sound card, and you're ready to move on to the device driver!

Setting Up the Device Driver Module

Now, let's move on to setting up the device driver. The device driver tells the kernel how to talk to the sound card.

I assume that you are using the loadable kernel modules included in the standard Slackware distribution. The sound modules need to be loaded during startup, and they need to have the correct parameters passed to them. If you are instead using a device driver that is permanently linked into the kernel, it needs to be configured as part of the kernel compilation, which is covered in Chapter 8.

So, log in as root again. Change to the /etc/rc.d directory. Now, edit the rc.modules file:

```
vi rc.modules
```

Search for the section on sound support. You should find a section that looks like Figure 7.6.

This section lists the most common sound card configurations. If you are lucky enough to have one of these cards, you can simply uncomment the appropriate /sbin/modprobe line and edit the IO, IRQ, and DMA values to match your card settings. (If you've already configured a PnP card, you can ommit the IO, IRQ, and DMA settings here.) If your sound card is not one these, check the literature to see if it claims compatibility with one of them. Many cards are nominally SoundBlaster compatible. This means they use the SoundBlaster device driver, so you could uncomment that line for your card. If you still have no choices here, take a look at the files in the directory /usr/src/linux/Documentation/sound. There you find tips on which sound module to use.

```
/sbin/modprobe hsd comp

### Sound support ###
# Sound Blaster Pro/16 support:
/sbin/modprobe sb io=0x220 irq=5 dma=1 dma16=5 mpu_io=0x330
# MAD16 support:
#/sbin/modprobe mad16 io=0x530 irq=7 dma=0 dma16=1
# AD1816(A) sound driver:
#/sbin/modprobe modprobe ad1816 io=0x530 irq=5 dma=1 dma2=3 ad1816_clockfreq=330
# ES1370 support, such as Sound Blaster 128PCI:
#/sbin/modprobe es1370
# (For information on configuring other sound cards with Linux,
# see the documentation in /usr/src/linux/Documentation/sound/)

### Joystick support ###
# The core joystick support module, needed by all of the
# joystick devices below:
#/sbin/modprobe joystick

### Drivers for various joystick devices ###
# Analog joysticks and gamepads:
#/sbin/modprobe joy-analog.o
# FPGaming Assasin 3D, MadCatz Panther or MadCatz Panther XL:
```

Figure 7.6 *The sound module section from /etc/rc.d/rc.modules*

Assuming you have found a suitable driver, uncomment or enter it in this file. Then save and exit the file. Now, to test it, you can either reboot your system or enter that `modprobe` line manually. You should see a message like

```
Soundblaster audio driver Copyright (C) by Hannu Savolainen 1993-1996
SB 4.12 detected OK (220)
```

So what does this module do? It activates entries in the filesystem that are connected to the sound card, through the device driver. Any utility or program that is intent on making music is going to need to send that data through these device entries. These entries are listed in Table 7.6.

Table 7.6 Audio Device Entries and Their Functions

Dev Entry	Function
/dev/audio	device for au files
/dev/dsp	device for wav files
/dev/midi	device for midi files

You might discover that normal users are not able to play sounds due to permission problems on the device entries. Because you are setting up the device driver, you might as well address this now. Take a look at the device entries in Figure 7.7.

```
kitzbuhel:~>ls -l /dev/audio* /dev/dsp* /dev/mixer* /dev/midi* /dev/sequ*
crw-rw-r--   1 root      sys       14,    4 Jul 18  1994 /dev/audio
crw-rw-rw-   1 root      sys       14,   20 Jul 18  1994 /dev/audio1
crw-rw-rw-   1 root      sys       14,    3 Jul 18  1994 /dev/dsp
crw-rw-rw-   1 root      sys       14,   19 Jul 18  1994 /dev/dsp1
crw-rw-rw-   1 root      sys       14,    2 Jul 18  1994 /dev/midi
crw-rw-rw-   1 root      sys       14,    0 Jul 18  1994 /dev/mixer
crw-rw-rw-   1 root      sys       14,   16 Jul 18  1994 /dev/mixer1
crw-rw-rw-   1 root      sys       14,    1 Jul 18  1994 /dev/sequencer
kitzbuhel:~>
```

Figure 7.7 *Checking the permissions of the audio devices*

The left column shows the permissions of who might use these devices. Make sure that they show `crw-rw-rw`. If not, only the root user can use the sound card. To change this, issue the command

```
chmod 0666 /dev/audio* /dev/dsp* /dev/mixer* /dev/midi*
```

This allows anyone logged on to the system to use the sound card. Although this should not pose a problem to the standalone system, it might to the networked workstation. Others can log in to your system remotely and start playing or recording sound through your sound card. One way to limit who has use of the sound card would be to issue these commands:

```
chown (your_prefered_userid) /dev/audio* /dev/dsp* /dev/mixer* /dev/midi*
chmod 0600 /dev/audio* /dev/dsp* /dev/mixer* /dev/midi*
```

This first command sets ownership of the device file entries to your specified user account. The second command sets them such that only your user has access to them.

Actually Using the Sound Card

Now that the sound card is configured, it would be nice to use it. Luckily, the Slackware distribution includes some tools for playing sound files. These include everything from a generic file-manipulation utility to command-line programs. Fancy graphic interface programs are available as well.

First, let's verify that you can play audio CDs simply to test that the speakers and other cables are connected. In this mode of operation, the music data does not really pass through your computer's CPU. It just passes through that cable from your CD drive to the sound card and then out the speakers. Make sure there is no data CD mounted. As the root user, issue the command

```
umount /cdrom
```

Remove the data CD from the drive, and insert your favorite audio CD. The program to play audio CDs is called *workbone*. It should present you with a control screen that approximates the numeric keypad. Key number **9** is play; press it. In a moment, you should see the light on your CD drive flashing, and music should be playing. Type the **7** key to stop playing, and **0** to exit workbone.

You also want to play music that originates from your computer. On the CD supplied with the book, there are several sound files. Remember how you mounted the CD into the filesystem, earlier in the chapter? Mount the CD under /cdrom.

```
mount /dev/cdrom /cdrom
```

Let's start at the most basic way of playing music originating from your computer. This uses the handy UNIX utility called *cat*, which reads the contents of a file and outputs that data to what is called the standard output. When executing *cat* from the command line, the standard output is simply your display. So, if you were to *cat* your /etc/isapnp.conf file, you would see the contents of this file fly by on your screen. One nifty thing about UNIX is that this standard output can be redirected elsewhere. So let's use this utility to read the contents of an audio file and redirect the output to one of the sound-related device-driver entries in the /dev directory. Note that if the volume is too loud, or you are greeted with a horrible cacophony, you can press Ctrl+C to stop it.

```
cat /cdrom/sounds/soundfile.au > /dev/audio0
```

At this point you should hear a recognizable sound. If not, double check the easy stuff first, your wiring connections and volume knobs on the speakers. Then, check that the interrupts are set up. If you *cat /proc/interrupts* once, dump a file to the sound device, and then *cat /proc/interrupts* again, you should see the number increase in the second column on the line for your sound card. If not, you have to recheck your interrupt and IO port settings and possibly pick different ones.

You have now successfully set up the sound system. There are better ways of playing music than dumping the file to the device entry. A utility that is included with Slackware to play sound files is called, originally enough, *play*. Other available command-line utilities include *wavplay* and *mpg123*. Sound utilities for X include *XMMS* and *RealPlayer*.

Printing

Printing under Linux can vary from simple to complex. At its simplest, ASCII text files are dumped out the parallel port to the printer. At its most complex, rendered graphics are queued from multiple networked systems and run through a filter from one description language to another. Here, you concentrate on a basic printing setup for a standalone system. Slackware Linux includes with it a service called *lpd*, which has its origin in the BSD world.

Physical Issues

When printing under Linux, you must first determine whether your printer is supported. Sadly, there are printers that were made without a brain to save a few pennies; these require special device drivers running in the OS to operate. The information on how to manipulate these printers is proprietary, so they are not likely to be supported under Linux. Also, USB printers require USB support in Linux, which is still under development, so I don't discuss them here.

A collection of HOWTO documents is provided with your Slackware distribution. If you did a full installation, they are located under /usr/doc/Linux-HOWTOs. If they are not located there, they are on the Slackware CD, under docs/Linux-HOW-TOs. Log in, change to that directory, and view the Printing-HOWTO file as such:

```
cd /usr/doc/Linux-HOWTOs
less Printing-HOWTO
```

Now, page down to the section marked "Printer Compatibility List." Read the notes on the categories: perfectly, mostly, partially, and paperweight. Using the up and down arrow keys, hope for the best, and locate your printer in this list. If your printer is listed as printing perfectly or mostly, great! Continue on. If it is listed as partially, you can continue, but you might not be able to use the full capabilities of the printer yet. As Linux continues to grow, support for more devices is growing, so keep a check on the online version of this HOWTO at http://www.linuxdoc.org/HOWTO/ Printing-HOWTO.html. If your printer is listed as a paperweight, sadly, you can skip the rest of this chapter.

Assuming you have a workable printer, plug it in to an available port on your system.

Generic Print Setup

There are two paths for getting data to the physical port. The most straightforward is to directly dump the data out of the device, for example:

```
cat datafile > /dev/lp0
```

This requires your application to produce data that is already formatted for the printer.

The other method is to use software to spool the data first and possibly filter and manipulate it. Slackware includes a package called *lpr*, which performs this spooling function. It does not contain any filters, but it does send the print data through any filtering software that is defined. It is set up by default to just spool data and send print jobs to the parallel port. If you edit and look at the /etc/printcap file, you see an entry for Generic Printer; it looks like this:

```
lp:lp=/dev/lp0:sd=/var/spool/lpd:sh
```

This defines the system printer device called *lp*, sets the physical device to /dev/lp0, and spools the print jobs in the directory /var/spool/lpd. It defines no filter.

Filtering

Why filter? Some applications produce PostScript data for printing, others produce PCL data for printing, and yet others produce ASCII text. All viable printers accept ASCII text, but for the other types, they tend to fall into two other categories: Either they accept PostScript or they don't and use a different control language such as PCL. Some printers accept both, but these tend to cost more. If your printer accepts both, you could probably stop here and skip to the section on using the printer, but read on anyway.

If you send plain ASCII text to the printer, you are likely to see a staircase effect with the printed lines. This is due to an old UNIX/MS-DOS difference in interpreting the end of a line. In the DOS world, text files tend to end their lines with a carriage return and a line feed. In the UNIX world, just a line feed is used. The staircase arises because most printers do not perform a carriage return when they encounter just a line feed. So, a simple filter is used to insert a carriage return after every line feed.

As an example, this line could be used in the /etc/printcap file:

```
lp-crlf:lp=/dev/lp0:sd=/var/spool/lpd:if=/var/spool/lpd/filter:sh:
```

This adds a new printer definition with an input filter. This input filter is a script located in /var/spool/lpd and called, rather unoriginally, *filter*. Add this to the line after the original lp definition line. Save and exit the file. In order for this change to take effect, you need to restart the lpd process. Using *ps*, find the process ID for /usr/sbin/lpd or [lpd]. Then kill it with *kill [pid]*, and restart it with /usr/sbin/lpd. Now, if you query the printer status using lpc status, you see something like this:

```
kitzbuhel:~>lpc status
lp:
        queuing is enabled
        printing is enabled
        no entries
        no daemon is present

lp-crlf:
        queuing is enabled
        printing is enabled
        no entries
        no daemon is present
kitzbuhel:~>
```

This is good and means that you have successfully added another printer definition to your lpd setup. Now, to add the filter itself. Here is the sample filter from the Printing-HOWTO:

```perl
#!/usr/bin/perl
while (<STDIN>) {
    chop $_;
    print "$_\r\n";
    };
```

To enter this filter, change directories to /var/spool/lpd, and type in **vi filter**. When you are done typing it in, save and exit. Then, you need to change the file permission on the filter, so it can be executed by *lpd*.

```
chmod 0755 filter
```

Now, whenever you want to send ASCII text files to your printer, you can use

```
lpr -P lp-crlf filename
```

Ghostscript and apsfilter

There is a better way, though. Slackware ships with two packages called *Ghostscript* and *apsfilter*, located in the AP1 disk set. These are useful for printing mixed Post-Script, non-PostScript, and ASCII text jobs to the same printer. The *apsfilter* gets configured into the /etc/printcap entries as a filter, and when it receives a print job, it uses *Ghostscript* to convert PostScript or ASCII into the appropriate format for your printer. This even takes care of that annoying little staircase effect with the ASCII print jobs.

Setup of the *apsfilter* is rather straightforward (see Figure 7.8). The setup program asks you a series of questions concerning your printer and print setup. As the root user, change to the /usr/lib/apsfilter directory and run the setup program.

```
cd /usr/lib/apsfilter
./SETUP
```

Press Enter until you get to the main menu. From here, press **1** to select your printer type. You are presented with a category selection (as in Apple, Canon, HP LaserJets, and so on). Pick the appropriate category. Then you are shown the list of supported printers. You might find your exact printer listed or hopefully something close. Consult your printer documentation to see if you can determine whether your printer is

```
================================================================
  A P S F I L T E R   S E T U P                -- MAIN MENUE --
================================================================

                                              currently selected
----------------------------------------------------------------
  (D)      Available Device Drivers in your gs binary   (gs -h)
  (R)      Read ghostscript's docu about device drivers (devices.txt)
  (1)      Printer Driver Selection            [laserjet]
  (2)      Interface Setup                     [parallel]

  For printing the test page:
  (3)      Print Resolution in "dots per inch"  [default]
  (4)      Toggle Monochrom/Color (1bpp=b&w)    [default]
  (5)      Paper Format                        [letter]
  (T)      Print Test Page (after step 1-5)

  (C)      ==> Continue printer setup with values shown above

  (Q)      Quit Setup

  Your choice ? █
```

Figure 7.8 *The main menu for the apsfilter configuration utility*

similar to one listed. If you cannot determine this, you can use the trial and error method. Select a printer, and continue. If it doesn't work, come back and pick the next one.

Once you've picked a printer, go back to the main menu. Now, press **2** to set up the physical interface, and answer the questions. You are asked whether you have a parallel or serial printer. Then you need to supply the path to the print device. This is the /dev directory entry for it, as in /dev/lp0 for the first parallel port (LPT1 under DOS), /dev/lp1 for a second parallel port (LPT2), /dev/ttyS0 for the first serial port (COM1), /dev/ttyS1 for the second (COM2). The serial printer configuration also asks for the serial communication parameters, baud rate, handshaking, stop bits, and parity. Consult your printer manual to determine how it is configured, and make these parameters match.

You see the main menu again. You need to select the paper format, option **5**. If you are a U.S-based reader, select letter size. The rest of the world uses the other two sizes. Back to the main menu.

Time to try it. Type **T** to print a test page. This might take a little while, but, hopefully, you are presented with a printed page of a tiger. This started out as a PostScript file and was converted to print on your printer. If this does not work, you might get a few pages of garbage. Press Ctrl+C to abort the setup program, and power off your printer to clear the buffer. Turn the printer back on, run the SETUP program, and try a different printer selection.

When you have good output, select C from the main menu to finish this process. It asks a few more questions. If it finds previous *apsfilter* entries, select override, because it means you have had a problem and were running SETUP again. It might ask if you have a color or mono printer; answer appropriately for what you have. Then it verifies your spool directory ownerships. It should show root for the owner, and lp for the group. Then you get several screens of information. Press Enter until you get a command prompt back.

The *apsfilter* is now set up. It creates a couple of system printer devices. The default device is defined as `lp`. It is an automatic device that tries to guess the format of the data. If you send it PostScript, it converts it to print. If you send it ASCII, it inserts the carriage returns if needed. If you send it data native to your printer, the filter ignores it and passes it through. Most likely, printing to this produces the desired output.

The other printer devices created allow the user to specify how the data should be treated. The device defined as `raw` passes the data through untouched. The device known as `ascii` treats it as ASCII data and adds the carriage returns only if they are warranted.

Using the Printer

The printer is hooked up to your system, and the system knows how to talk to the printer. Filtering is configured as needed. Now you need to know how to print.

Printing from the command line is fairly straightforward. To do this, use the *lpr* command. If called with no parameters, *lpr* attempts to send anything on the standard input to the default printer. This is useful if you are redirecting output from elsewhere to the printer, for example, the output of a *ps* command:

```
ps -aux | lpr
```

The *lpr* command has some other parameters. Adding a filename after the *lpr* command causes *lpr* to print that file. If you have multiple system printer devices defined, for filtering as an example, the one used can be specified with the –*P* option.

```
lpr -P ascii myprogram.c
```

This prints the source code file myprogram.c to the ascii print device defined by the *apsfilter* setup.

Printing from within applications is fairly application specific, but one thing they all have in common is that you must specify the print device. It is possible that you have to specify this as part of the print command. For example, printing from Netscape presents the user with a dialog box that includes the line `print command`. It defaults to the value lpr. Leaving this as is sends the output to the default system print device. Netscape produces PostScript output, so if you have a PostScript-capable printer, or are using *apsfilter*, this is probably okay. But, for the purpose of an example, assume the default device doesn't know PostScript, but that a different device called *postscript* is set up to filter it. You can change the print command line and add the *-P* option:

```
lpr -P postscript
```

Some applications give you a list of defined printers on the system from which to choose. Just select the appropriate choice and go.

Queue Management

Whenever something is printed, it is put into the print queue. This usually resides on the disk under /var/spool/lpd. If your printer has problems and goes offline, your print jobs accumulate there. You can check the status of the print queue using the command *lpq*. This command also accepts the *-P printername* parameter. Suppose you had printed a few jobs to the printer ascii; the *lpq* output would look like:

```
kitzbuhel:~>lpq -P ascii
Rank     Owner     Job     Files                     Total Size
1st      prgrmr    4       mud.c                        50 bytes
2nd      jsmith    5       notes                        79 bytes
3rd      snowman   6       eastboundanddown.txt      1522 bytes
kitzbuhel:~>
```

This shows the order of printing for the jobs, who owns the job, the job number, what file is being printed (if known), and the job size. Certain printer-related information also shows up here, for example, if printing is disabled. If you want to delete a job, look at the queue, and find the job number you want to delete. Then, issue the *lprm* command with the printer name and job number. If you are the owner of the job, or the root user, you should see something like this:

```
kitzbuhel:~>lprm -P ascii 5
dfA005AMLTzUo dequeued
cdA005AMLTzUo dequeued
kitzbuhel:~>
```

This looks like garbage, but it indicates that the command worked. The dequeued message contains the filename that the printing system used for the spooled files. If you don't own the job, you see a `permission denied` message, indicating that the delete did not work.

The printer and print queue can be manipulated with the *lpc* command. This has several parameters to it and even can be used interactively. The parameter most likely used in a standalone system is the *status* command, used to view the current printers and their states. Figure 7.9 shows the output of the *lpc status* command.

Notice how the printer ascii is showing that printing is disabled. It also shows that there are two print jobs waiting. This printer had been stopped earlier during paper reloading to prevent partial printing, via the command *lpc stop ascii*. The *lpc* command can be used to start printing again:

```
kitzbuhel:~>lpc start ascii
ascii:
    printing enabled
    daemon started
kitzbuhel:~>
```

Your printer should happily print away now. Other nifty things you can do with *lpc* include moving jobs to the top of the queue, enabling and disabling job queuing, and the bulk deletion of jobs from a queue. Here are the *lpc* commands that you might find useful (see Table 7.7 also). *printer* refers to which print queue you wish to manipulate and can be replaced with the word *all* to operate on all printers.

```
kitzbuhel:~>lpc status
ascii:
        queuing is enabled
        printing is disabled
        2 entries in spool area
        no daemon present
lp:
        queuing is enabled
        printing is enabled
        no entries
        no daemon present
raw:
        queuing is enabled
        printing is enabled
        no entries
        no daemon present
kitzbuhel:~>
```

Figure 7.9 *Output of the* lpc status *command*

Table 7.7 Common *lpc* Commands and Their Results

Command	Result
clean printer	removes all incomplete print jobs
disable printer	prevents new print jobs from being queued
down printer msg	disables queuing, stops printer, msg is a text field displayed when the printer status is queried
enable printer	allows new print jobs to be queued
restart printer	stops and restarts the printer and service
start printer	allows the printer to print jobs from the queue
status printer	reports the status of printer and service
stop printer	prevents printer from printing jobs in the queue
topq printer jobnum	moves the print job specified by jobnum to top of queue
up printer	enables printer and printing

Networked Printers

Just a few notes on networked printing. If you need to have your Linux system print to another UNIX system that is running the BSD flavor of *lpd*, you can simply add another entry to your /etc/printcap file:

```
# A remote Unix printer
lp-remote:\
    :sd=/var/spool/lpd/lp-remote:\
    :rm=printerhost.company.com:\
    :rp=printername:\
    :lp=/dev/null:\
    :sh:
```

Where the *rm* entry defines the hostname of the UNIX server running the *lpd* service for the printer in question. The *rp* entry is the name of the target printer on that server. The *sd* option still defines a local spool directory, and you must make sure this directory exists, that the permissions are 0755, owned by root, and the group is set to *lp*. Remember to stop and restart the *lpd* process.

Printing to other servers, such as NetWare and NT servers, or accepting print jobs from clients of those operating systems, requires the configuration of additional software that is outside the scope of this chapter. To get printing support between NetWare and Linux, you need to use the ncpfs package. This can be obtained from ftp://metalab.unc.edu/pub/Linux/system/remotefs/ncpfs.

To print between Linux and those Windows-based systems, refer to these fine resources:

- /usr/doc/Linux-HOWTOs/Printing-HOWTO
- /usr/doc/Linux-HOWTOs/SMB-HOWTO

Summary

The topic of printing alone can fill a book. This chapter is an attempt to guide you through some basic configurations. It is also intended to point you to some other sources of information and teach you how to use them. Stay tuned for Chapter 8, where I discuss how to compile the kernel on your own.

Chapter 8: Compiling the Kernel

William Schaffer

What Is the Kernel?

Technically, the name Linux refers only to the kernel. Everything else in your system is a utility, library, or application that has been written or ported to work with the Linux kernel. The kernel is the heart of the system, providing the tasking mechanisms and determining which process is to run next. It also maintains the network connections between other computers. It is the entity that manages the hardware and interfaces to the applications. The kernel manages memory, gets data to and from the hard drive, and controls your sound card. It knows how to do this via special pieces of software called device drivers.

One of the biggest advantages to the Linux kernel over other systems is that you can recompile it to suit your specific needs. You can decide what device drivers are necessary for your setup. They can be hard-compiled into the kernel, or they can be compiled as loadable modules. It is your choice.

Reasons for hard-compiling the device drivers into the kernel include necessity and simplicity. The BIOS and LILO know how to load the kernel off the boot device, but the kernel is on its own after that. Device drivers necessary for booting, such as the SCSI or IDE controller drivers, need to be present in the kernel before the kernel can load anything else off the hard drive. For simplicity's sake, any hard-compiled device drivers are always loaded and available for use and don't need to be loaded via /etc/rc.d/rc.modules.

Reasons for compiling device driver code as loadable modules include memory space savings and on-the-fly reconfiguration. Machines short on memory can regain some memory by using loadable modules. These modules can be automatically unloaded when not needed, freeing RAM for other uses. Another reason for using loadable modules is to resolve driver conflicts. Some devices share resources and only one can be active at a time. So, loading and unloading the device driver module are necessary. A system administrator can also use loadable modules to protect parts of the system from users or intruders, by unloading modules for hardware not in immediate use. Finally, unloading and reloading a module make it possible for some newly attached devices to be recognized without rebooting.

Why Recompile?

Your Slackware Linux system came loaded with a plethora of device drivers compiled as loadable modules, so why bother to recompile anything? Here are a few reasons, in no particular order:

- If space on your hard drive is tight, you might want to create the smallest kernel possible. By compiling the kernel yourself, you create only those parts you need.

- You might recompile the kernel to remove hard-compiled device-driver code for equipment that is no longer present in your system. For example, if you recently removed a floppy controller-based tape backup, you don't need the code taking up space in memory. Driver code probing for nonexistent hardware might cause problems for your other peripherals. Further suppose you replaced that tape backup with a SCSI DAT drive. You need to add device driver code to support it. Granted, if you are using kernel modules, you could just modify /etc/rc.d/rc.modules to load the correct one.

- The biggest reason to recompile the kernel is to upgrade to a new one. Slackware 7 ships with kernel version 2.2.13, but Linux is always progressing. The next version of the kernel always has bug fixes, security enhancements, and support for even more types of hardware. It is always a good idea to watch for the new kernel releases to see what has changed. A list of current changes can be found at http://www.kernelnotes.org.

Why You Might Not Want to Recompile

I realize this chapter is about recompiling the Linux kernel, but here is a quick note to the contrary. Sometimes it might not be in your best interest to recompile. If the system is running well, and the list of bug fixes and security enhancements does not affect your operations, then it is best to just leave things alone. It might not be worth the downtime, especially when things go wrong, if you are not going to gain anything from it.

Getting the Current Kernel Sources

The latest and greatest version of the Linux kernel can be obtained, in source-code form, from http://www.kernel.org. Maintained here are the current kernels and the past versions. The very latest version of the kernel might be one from the development track. Such a kernel is bleeding edge and includes experimental code. So, unless you are interested in helping to test it and iron out bugs, you are advised to pass on this one. Also archived here are all the older versions of the kernel, going all the way back to its humble beginnings. If you have an interest in Linux history, you can peruse them. However, in most cases, you want the latest stable version of the kernel. The stable kernels have been tested and proven to be reliable.

How do you tell stable from developmental kernels? This is all in the version numbering. The kernels use three number fields for their version information. The first number is the major version number. The second is the minor version number, which differentiates between stable and development kernels. If this number is even, it is stable. If it is odd, it is a developmental version. The third number represents a level of bug fixes and security enhancements within this version. Slackware 7 comes with the 2.2.13 version, but, for example, take the source archive named linux-2.2.14.tar.gz. This is the fourteenth revision of the stable 2.2 kernel version

You need to download the latest stable source file and save it in the /usr/src directory. If you have an older version of the kernel code, which was probably installed with your system, it is also in this directory, and you need to remove or move it. As the root user, you can use the following command:

```
mv linux linux.oldversion
```

to relocate it, or

```
rm -rf linux
```

to remove it. Then, you need to unpack the new version. The following command uncompresses and untars this file into its constituent parts:

```
tar -xzvf linux-2.2.14.tar.gz
```

Now, you can skip ahead to the section titled "Other Requirements." However, if you have a slow Internet connection, read on for an alternative to downloading the complete kernel source.

Patching an Existing Kernel Source Tree

Notice that the 2.2.14 source file is 15MB. This might take quite a while to download, especially over a 33.6Kbps modem. If you obtained your kernel from one of the FTP sites, you might have noticed files such as /patch-2.2.14.gz. These are patch files for the kernel. They are used to bring the previous version's source code up to date with the current source code. These are useful if you do not have the bandwidth to download the 15MB of the full source code. This patch file is 1.6MB. Most others are a lot smaller.

So, if you want to go the patching route, follow along. Otherwise, skip ahead to the next section. For the sake of this discussion, I am assuming that you have version 2.2.13 of the kernel and are patching up to 2.2.14. If you are using other versions, change the numbers accordingly. Obtain the patch file, and put it in the /usr/src directory. Before you apply the patch, it is best to make sure you have a backup of the previous source tree. Follow these steps to clean up all remnant files from previous compilations. Type

```
cd /usr/src/linux
make clean
```

Then, make the backup file:

```
cd /usr/src
tar -czvhf linux-2.2.13.tar.gz linux/
```

This creates a big file called /linux-2.2.13.tar.gz in your /usr/src directory. You only need to keep this long enough to find out that the patch works correctly. After that, you can delete it if you desire. Now, on to the patch. If your patch file ends in a .gz, issue this command:

```
cat patch-2.2.14.gz ¦ gunzip - ¦ patch -p0
```

Note that the - character after the *gunzip* command is significant. It tells *gunzip* to use standard input for its source, which in this case is the output of the *cat* command.

Sometimes, gzipped files get uncompressed by the downloading client. If so, your patch file does not end in .gz, and you should use this command:

```
cat patch-2.2.14 ¦ patch -p0
```

These commands run the contents of the patch file into the *patch* command, uncompressing it along the way in the first case. They both produce output that should end with something like what's shown in Figure 8.1.

Note that a patch only updates the previous version of the kernel source to the version embedded in the patch's name. If you want to upgrade your Slackware's 2.2.13 source to version 2.2.15, you need to get and apply the patches for 2.2.14 as well as 2.2.15.

```
patching file linux/net/ipv4/syncookies.c
patching file linux/net/ipv4/tcp.c
patching file linux/net/ipv4/tcp_input.c
patching file linux/net/ipv4/tcp_ipv4.c
patching file linux/net/ipv4/tcp_timer.c
patching file linux/net/ipv6/README
patching file linux/net/ipv6/addrconf.c
patching file linux/net/ipv6/tcp_ipv6.c
patching file linux/net/irda/irda_device.c
patching file linux/net/irda/irlan/irlan_eth.c
patching file linux/net/irda/irmod.c
patching file linux/net/netsyms.c
patching file linux/net/packet/af_packet.c
patching file linux/net/sunrpc/clnt.c
patching file linux/net/sunrpc/svc.c
patching file linux/net/sunrpc/svcsock.c
patching file linux/net/sunrpc/xprt.c
patching file linux/net/unix/sysctl_net_unix.c
patching file linux/net/wanrouter/wanmain.c
patching file linux/net/wanrouter/wanproc.c
patching file linux/scripts/Menuconfig
patching file linux/scripts/ver_linux
kitzbuhel:/usr/src>
```

Figure 8.1 *Output from a successful* patch *command*

What Are Those .sign Files?

The other important things to notice while downloading the kernel sources are those .sign files. These are used to verify that you have the real thing and not a possibly altered file from a questionable source. To use these, you need to install GPG or PGP 5.0 or newer. Unfortunately, these packages are not included in Slackware 7. For more information about the .sign files from kernel.org, refer to http://www.kernel.org/signature.html. Basically, these .sign files contain encrypted file signatures for those kernel sources. When you run the *key-validation* program against a kernel source file you downloaded, it produces an encrypted signature for that file. This is then compared to the signature in the .sign file to make sure that it matches. These topics are outside the scope of this chapter; for more about GPG and PGP, check out http://www.gnupg.org and http://www.pgp.com.

If you plan to use the .sign files, you need to download and install the public key from http://www.kernel.org/signature.html. So long as you are sure you got the public key from kernel.org (instead of someone tricking you into accepting a fake one), you can prove to yourself whether or not the kernel sources you download are authentic, regardless of what mirror you downloaded them from.

Other Requirements

There are a few other things needed for a successful kernel compile. You need to make sure that you have at least 32MB of combined RAM and swap space available for the compile. You also need a fair amount of disk space available; the previously mentioned 2.2.14 kernel sources are 15MB compressed, but uncompress to 75 MB, and when the kernel is compiled, could fluff to over 100MB!

To recompile the latest kernel, not only do you need to have the latest kernel source code, you also need to have the compiler, linker, and other build tools installed. Table 8.1 shows the needed tools and the packages that contain them.

Table 8.1 Required Utilities to Compile a Linux Kernel

Utility	Purpose	Package
egcs	Compiler	d1/egcs.tgz
as86	Assembler	d1/bin86.tgz
ld	Linker	d1/binutils.tgz
gmake	Coordinates the *make*	d1/gmake.tgz
ncurses	Needed for *make menuconfig*	d1/ncurses.tgz
tk	Needed for *make xconfig*	tcl1/tk.tgz

Slackware ships with the 2.2.13 kernel. If you attempt to upgrade to a much newer kernel, such as one of the 2.4 series, you might need to update some parts of your system. For example, how the kernel supports *PPP* has changed slightly, so you want a newer version of *PPP* than what came with Slackware. To discover the minimum required versions of some packages, read the /changes file in the /usr/src/linux/ Documentation directory. If you stick with just the 2.2 series, you don't need to update any packages.

Deciding What to Recompile

Now that everything is in place, let's go a step closer to recompiling. Make sure you are logged in as the root user, and change to the /usr/src/linux directory. You must now decide what is to be hard-compiled as part of the kernel, what is to be compiled as a loadable module, and what is to be left out altogether. There are two easy ways to do this. If you are running X, you can use *make xconfig*. If you are not running X or prefer to stay in an Xterm window, you can use *make menuconfig*. There is also a question and answer format in *make config*, but that can be difficult to maneuver and might not be supported much longer.

make xconfig

The graphical front end to configuring the kernel compilation is via the *make xconfig* command. Enter it from an Xterm prompt; this starts a flurry of messages in the window and produces a new window (see Figure 8.2). This screen shows all the categories for kernel configuration and device drivers.

Linux Kernel Configuration		
Code maturity level options	Ethernet (1000 Mbit)	Ftape, the floppy tape device driver
Processor type and features	Appletalk devices	Filesystems
Loadable module support	Token ring devices	Network File Systems
General setup	Wan interfaces	Partition Types
Plug and Play support	Amateur Radio support	Native Language Support
Block devices	IrDA subsystem support	Console drivers
Networking options	Infrared-port device drivers	Sound
QoS and/or fair queueing	ISDN subsystem	Additional low level sound drivers
Telephony Support	Old CD-ROM drivers (not SCSI, not IDE)	Kernel hacking
SCSI support	Character devices	
SCSI low-level drivers	Mice	Save and Exit
Network device support	Joysticks	Quit Without Saving
ARCnet devices	Watchdog Cards	Load Configuration from File
Ethernet (10 or 100Mbit)	Video For Linux	Store Configuration to File

Figure 8.2 *The main window of* make xconfig

Processor Type and Features

Select the Processor Type and Features box (second down on the left) to open the dialog box shown in Figure 8.3.

Move your mouse over this window; any selectable field changes to a lighter shade as the mouse passes over it. Click the Processor Family area to view the processor selections. Selecting the appropriate choice for your system produces a kernel performance optimized for your processor. Selecting the wrong choice might result in a slower kernel or a kernel that doesn't run at all. If you are unsure about this selection, click the Help button to the right of the Processor Family area to view some helpful information about this configuration topic (see Table 8.2).

Table 8.2 The x86 Processor Family Selections

Selection	Covers These Processor Types
386	AMD/Cyrix/Intel 386DX/DXL/SL/SLC/SX
	Cyrix/TI 486DLC/DLC2
	UMC 486SX-S
486	AMD/Cyrix/IBM/Intel DX4 or 486DX/DX2/SL/SX/SX2
	AMD/Cyrix 5x86
	NexGen Nx586
	UMC U5D or U5S.
586	Generic Pentium CPUs
Pentium	Intel Pentium/Pentium MMX
	AMD K5, K6, and K6-3D
PPro	Intel Pentium II/Pentium Pro
	Cyrix/IBM/National Semiconductor 6x86MX, MII

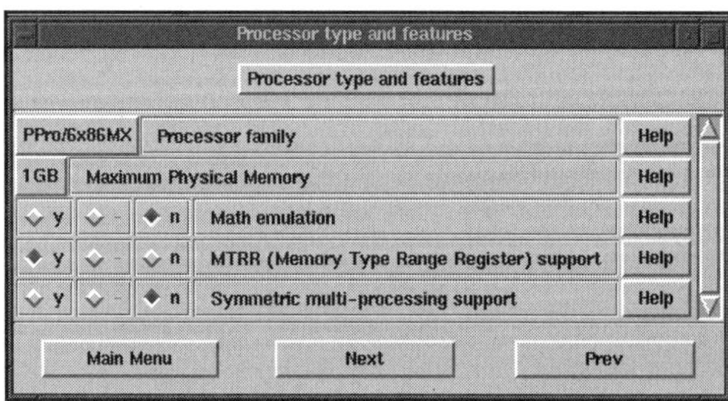

Figure 8.3 *The Processor Type and Features dialog box*

Notice that, in most cases, the help windows are actually helpful. Find the best match for your processor and close this window. Then, go back to the processor selection box and select appropriately.

The help window for the next option line, Maximum Physical Memory, is not so helpful. This entry has to do with sizing internal kernel tables pertaining to memory management. Unless you have more than 1GB of RAM, select 1GB.

The remaining three configuration options do not have pull-down menus for their selections. Instead, they have three areas to the left of the title. Looking at the Math Emulation option, notice that only two of the three areas highlight, and those are labeled `y` and `n`. The middle option is for compiling as a module, which is not selectable when it is not relevant. From the help information on this parameter, you find out that if you have a processor with no math coprocessor, such as a 386 or a 486SX, you need to select `y`. This compiles the kernel with code to emulate the math functions. Otherwise, you can select `n`.

You can get pretty far just by reading the help information. Even if you've read it and have no idea what it is talking about, it usually makes a recommendation. For example, look at the help for the next parameter, the MTRR option. It discusses memory type range registers, address range registers, and something about buggy SMP BIOSes. This has to do with performance improvements in PCI systems. However, if all that meant nothing to you, they do make a recommendation at the bottom: `You can safely say Y even if your machine doesn't have MTRRs, you'll just add about 3k to your kernel`. So, you can answer y here and be oblivious to the meaning; it doesn't hurt your system, but it does take up a small amount of memory. In this case, though, they did list the processors that support this feature: Intel Pentium Pro, Pentium II and III, Cyrix 6x86, 6x86MX and M II, and the AMD K6-2 and K6-3. If you've got one of those, select y. Otherwise, select n.

The last option here is Symmetric Multiprocessing Support. Do you have more than one CPU in your system? Probably not, so select n. If you are so lucky, you should select y, but make sure to read the help information. It refers you to several other references pertaining to this configuration (they are outside the scope of this chapter).

Loadable Module Support

Click the Next button to close the processor dialog box and open a new one, the Loadable Module Support dialog box. This has three configuration entities. The first is to enable loadable module support. As mentioned earlier in this chapter, the use of modules can make the system very flexible and is highly recommended. Saying yes to this option allows you to select other drivers to be compiled as modules. If you say no, you do not have that option.

The Set Version Information option enables you to use modules from other kernel versions with this one. It requires additional support and could be tricky. The Kernel

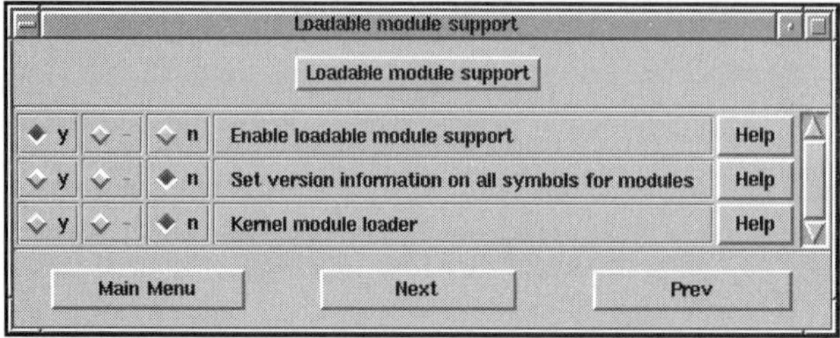

Figure 8.4 *The Loadable Module Support window of* make xconfig

Module Loader option provides for a mechanism by which the kernel automatically decides which modules to load and unload. These two options are more advanced and are probably best left set to no for now.

General Setup

Click the Next button to proceed to the General Setup dialog box, which covers a mix of topics. It is the first section to have the module option available (that's the area between y and n). Selecting that compiles the device driver code as a loadable module. Remember, any code so compiled needs to be configured in /etc/rc.d/rc.modules.

The first option in this section is Networking Support. Leave this set to yes, even if you don't have a network adapter card in your system. Some applications (such as *PPP*, which is used to connect to your Internet service provider) use networking features anyway, and removing this breaks them.

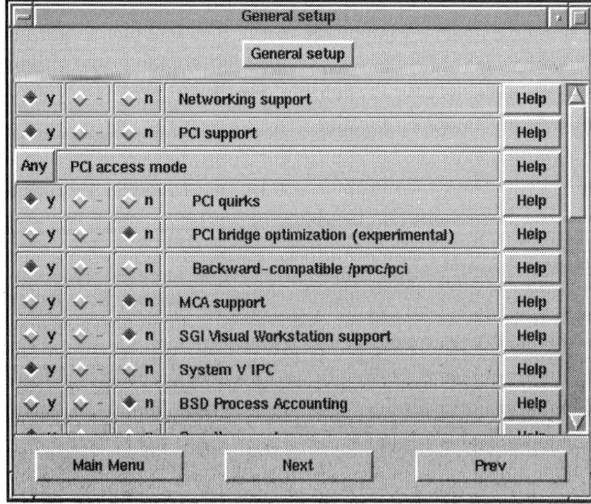

Figure 8.5 *The General Setup window of* make xconfig

The next option is PCI Support. If you have PCI expansion cards in your system, say yes. If you don't, say no. If you are unsure, say yes.

The rest of the options in this section are probably best left at their defaults. If you have any parallel port devices, such as a Zip drive or a printer, make sure that Parallel Port Support is set to m or y (the default is m, which is probably a good choice). Click Next to continue.

Plug and Play Support

The next section is Plug and Play support. There's not much to choose from here; if you have a plug-and-play parallel device, you can use these options. It's probably best to leave them at their defaults.

Figure 8.6 *The Plug and Play Support window of* make xconfig

Block Devices

Click the Next button to view the Block Devices dialog box. Block devices include hard drives, floppy drives, and CD-ROM drives. Also included here are RAM disks, RAID modes, and various IDE controller boards, along with the parallel port IDE devices. Scroll through the list and check out the options. If you have any of these in your system, this is where you select them. Remember, if your system boots off an IDE hard drive, the device driver needs to be compiled into the kernel and not as a module, so select y.

Networking Options

The next section is Networking Options. This does not specify what specific networking hardware you have in your system, but rather what types of networks will be in use. Most likely, the defaults here are fine, which include TCP/IP networking. However, if you are going to talk to other types of networks, such as AppleTalk or IPX, you'd better investigate the whole list.

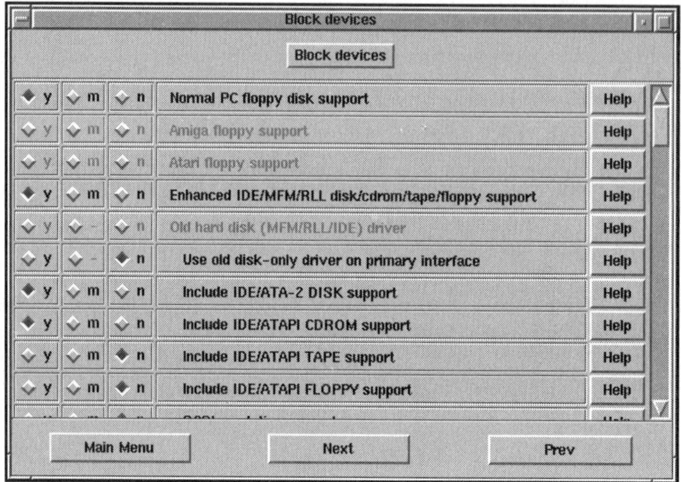

Figure 8.7 *The Block Devices window of* make xconfig

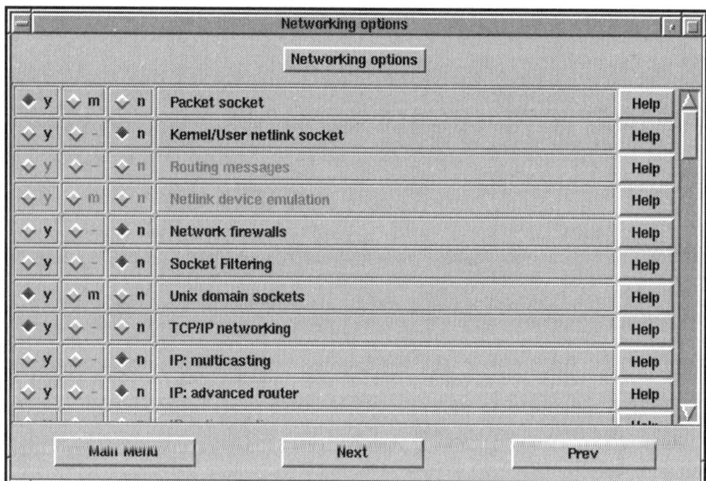

Figure 8.8 *The Networking Options window of* make xconfig

Click Next three times to skip over QoS (Quality of Service) and Telephony Support to get to SCSI Support. QoS and Telephony deal with situations that are not found on a typical desktop installation.

SCSI Support

The next section that is commonly used is SCSI Support. This is where you select what types of SCSI devices are to be supported, for example, disk, tape, CD-ROM, and so on.

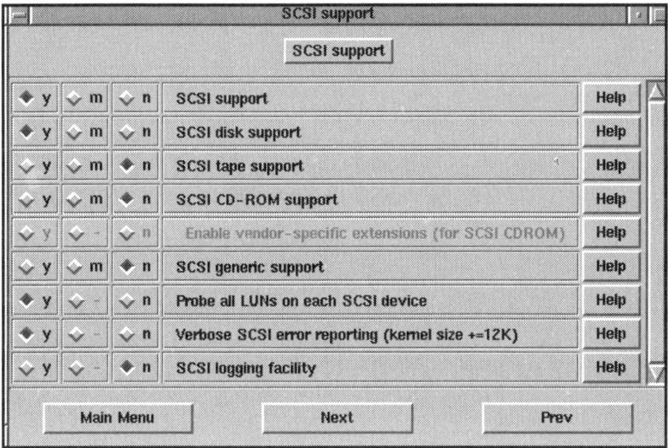

Figure 8.9 *The SCSI Support window of* make xconfig

After clicking Next, you see the SCSI low-level drivers selection, where you pick the type of SCSI controller card that you have. Note that the Iomega parallel port Zip drives are here, but if you have not selected parallel-port support in the General setup dialog box, the driver for the Iomega devices is not selectable.

Network Device Support

This and the next several sections define the network devices. This is where the drivers specific to the type of networking hardware in your computer are selected. Also, if you are going to use this system to dial in to an ISP, you need to select PPP under Network Device Support. If you have an Ethernet card, find it under the Ethernet sections.

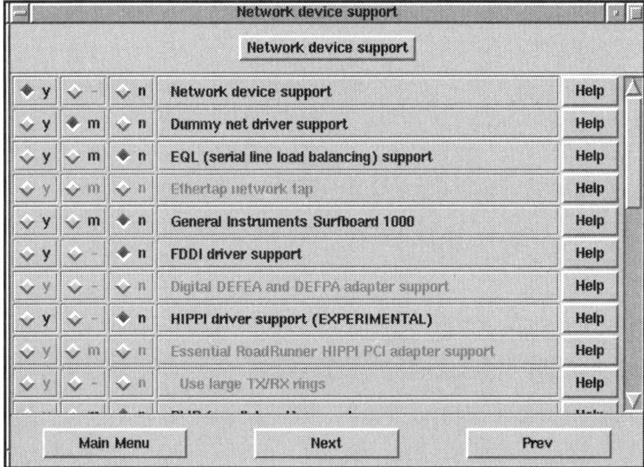

Figure 8.10 *The Network Device Support window of* make xconfig

Character Devices

Now skip ahead to the Character Devices section. This is where you opt to have parallel printer and serial device support. If you plan to use a modem, you need to say *y* or *m* to the standard serial support. Also, if you have a PS/2 or bus mouse, you need to select the mouse support option and proceed to the next screen, entitled Mice, where you select the type of mouse that you have. Next!

Filesystems

Skip ahead to the Filesystems section, where you specify what filesystems the kernel can read. This applies to any hard drives in your system and any removables, such as CDs, floppies, and Zip disks. You definitely want to say y to the second extended fs support option! This is the native Linux filesystem and needs to be in the kernel. Other options that are good to include are /proc, used for system information reporting, ISO9660, used for reading CD-ROMs, and the DOS FAT and VFAT support options.

Network Filesystems

Proceed to the next section, Network File Systems. If you are going to be mounting any volumes from another system, such as another UNIX system or Windows NT, you need to select the drivers here. The drivers for those are NFS and SMB, respectively.

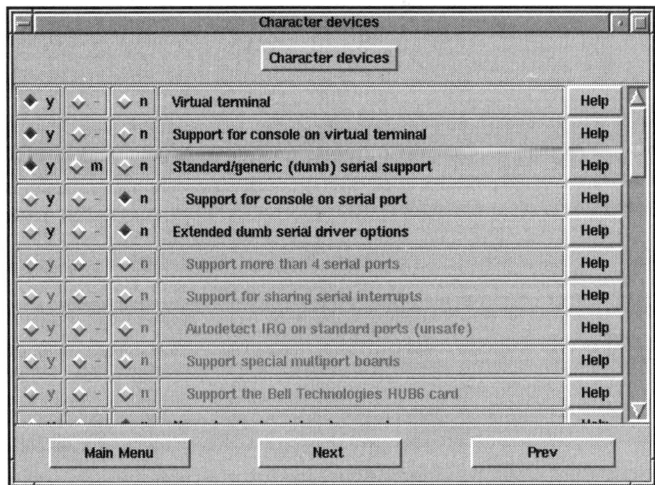

Figure 8.11 *The Character Devices window of* make xconfig

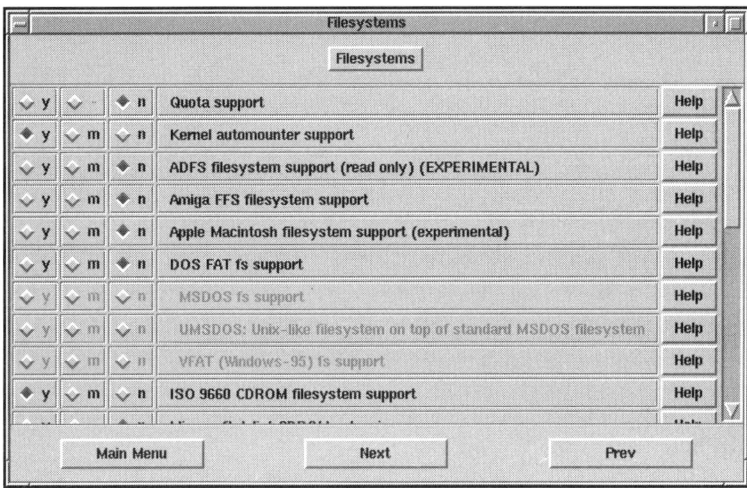

Figure 8.12 *The Filesystems window of* make xconfig

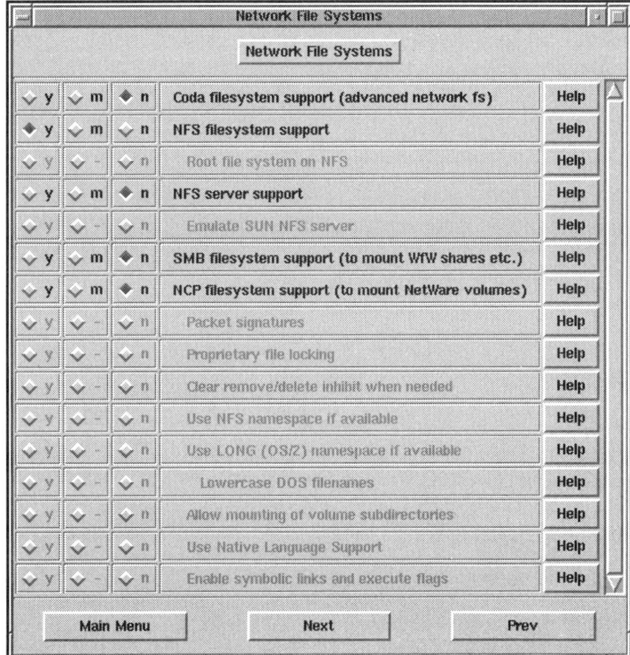

Figure 8.13 *The Network Filesystems window of* make xconfig

Sound

The last sections that are probably of interest are the Sound section and the Additional Low Level Sound Drivers section. It is probably best to compile these as modules. That way, you can tweak the settings without rebooting when you are trying to make it work. Find your sound card, or one that it claims compatibility with, and select m. If your card is shaded out so you cannot select it, scroll back up to the next selectable option, and select it. This should enable the options that follow it. For example, to select the SoundBlaster driver, you must select the Open Sound System driver. If you choose to compile the driver into the kernel instead of a module, you need to supply the configuration settings now.

If your sound card doesn't seem to have a driver listed in the Sound section, try the next section, Additional Low Level Sound Drivers.

Finishing Up

Once you have made all the configuration changes that you plan to make, you need to save them and exit the utility. In the lower right corner of the main configuration window, there are two important options. If you like what you've chosen, choose Save and Exit. Proceed to the section of this chapter entitled "Actually Recompiling." If you do not want to save your changes, choose Quit without Saving, and start over.

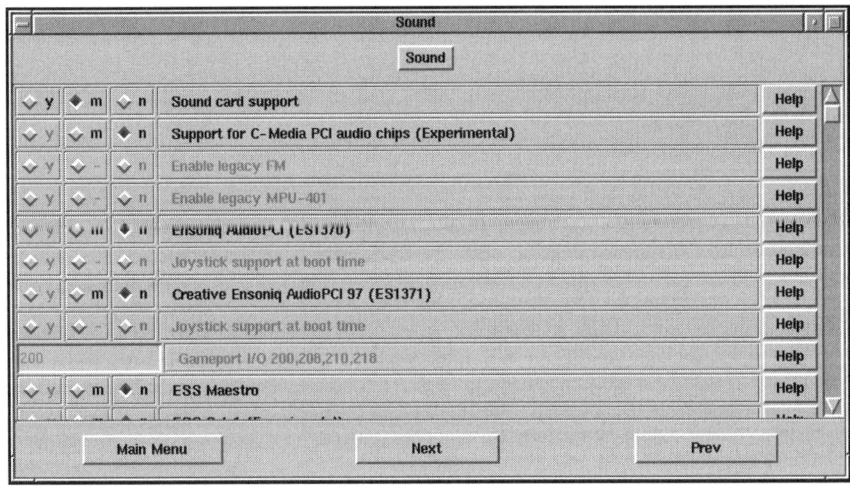

Figure 8.14 *The Sound support window of* make xconfig

make menuconfig

If you need to go with the text window route for configuring and compiling, you use the *make menuconfig* command. This presents you with a screen like the one shown in Figure 8.15.

You can use the up and down arrows to move the selection bar amongst the options. If your arrow keys do not work properly here, you can use the plus and minus keys. Use the ones on the main section of your keyboard, as the numeric keypad keys might be defined differently. When you have the category you want highlighted, press Enter to select it and proceed to that submenu.

The configuration choices here are the same as those in the *make xconfig* section; they are just presented slightly differently:

- An entry that begins with something in parentheses or ends with an arrow means you can press Enter to see a further submenu.

- An entry that begins with square brackets means you can select this option to be included with a y or not included with an n.

- If the entry begins with angle brackets, then you can also select it as a module with an m, in addition to the y and n choices.

- Typing ? at any time brings up the help screen for that option.

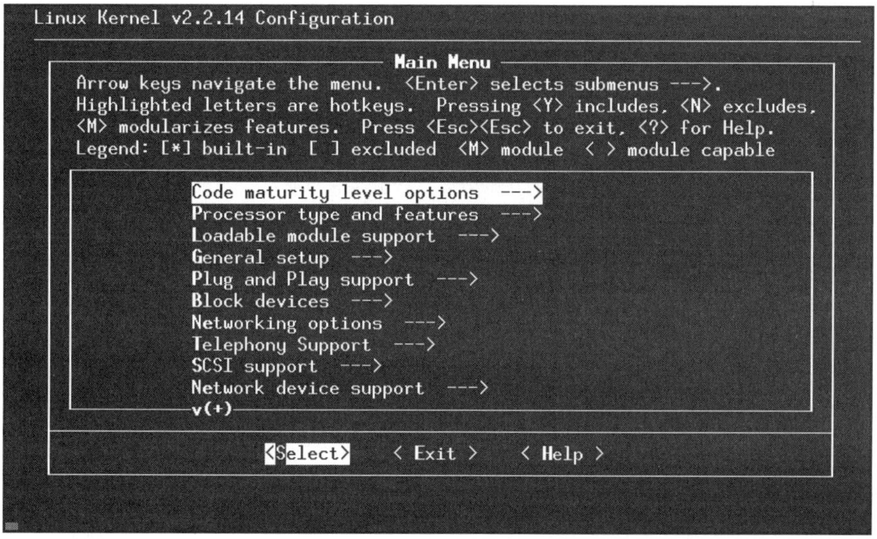

Figure 8.15 *The* make menuconfig *screen*

When you are finished in a submenu, or finished altogether, press the right-arrow or the Tab key to move the highlight at the bottom of the screen to Exit. Then press Enter to exit one level. If you are at the top menu and do this, you are prompted with the question: `Do you wish to save your new kernel configuration?` If you want the changes to be used, you have to answer yes. If you have decided that your choices weren't so good, pick no. Use the Tab key to highlight the correct answer and press Enter. You now are at the command prompt again and ready to start the compile.

Actually Recompiling

Now that you have selected what options you want to be part of your kernel, it is time to start the compile itself. Depending on how fast your computer is, this could take a few minutes, or it could take hours.

Linux is about choice, and there are a couple of choices to make here, too. The basic command is *make zImage*, which produces a compressed kernel image. You might have to precede that with a *make dep* to build the dependencies needed. As a user, you don't really need to know what the dependencies are. I cover what to do with the compiled image a little later. For now, issue the *make dep* and *make zImage* commands and go watch TV for a while. When it finishes, you should see the screen shown in Figure 8.5.

If the image you made is too large, the compilation process tells you (see Figure 8.17).

```
as86 -0 -a -o setup.o setup.s
ld86 -0 -s -o setup setup.o
make[2]: Entering directory `/usr/src/linux-2.2.13/arch/i386/boot/compressed'
tmppiggy=_tmp_$$piggy; \
rm -f $tmppiggy $tmppiggy.gz $tmppiggy.lnk; \
objcopy -O binary -R .note -R .comment -S /usr/src/linux/vmlinux $tmppiggy; \
gzip -f -9 < $tmppiggy > $tmppiggy.gz; \
echo "SECTIONS { .data : { input_len = .; LONG(input_data_end - input_data) inpu
t_data = .; *(.data) input_data_end = .; }}" > $tmppiggy.lnk; \
ld -m elf_i386 -m elf_i386 -r -o piggy.o -b binary $tmppiggy.gz -b elf32-i386 -T
 $tmppiggy.lnk; \
rm -f $tmppiggy $tmppiggy.gz $tmppiggy.lnk
ld -m elf_i386 -Ttext 0x1000 -e startup_32 -o vmlinux head.o misc.o piggy.o
make[2]: Leaving directory `/usr/src/linux-2.2.13/arch/i386/boot/compressed'
objcopy -O binary -R .note -R .comment -S compressed/vmlinux compressed/vmlinux.
out
tools/build bootsect setup compressed/vmlinux.out CURRENT > zImage
Root device is (8, 1)
Boot sector 512 bytes.
Setup is 1292 bytes.
System is 505 kB
make[1]: Leaving directory `/usr/src/linux-2.2.13/arch/i386/boot'
kitzbuhel:/usr/src/linux>
```

Figure 8.16 *Output of successful compilation*

```
t_data = .: *(.data) input_data_end = .: }}" > $tmppiggy.lnk: \
ld -m elf_i386 -m elf_i386 -r -o piggy.o -b binary $tmppiggy.gz -b elf32-i386 -T
 $tmppiggy.lnk: \
rm -f $tmppiggy $tmppiggy.gz $tmppiggy.lnk
gcc -D__KERNEL__ -I/usr/src/linux/include  -traditional -c head.S
gcc -D__KERNEL__ -I/usr/src/linux/include -O2 -DSTDC_HEADERS    -c misc.c -o misc
.o
ld -m elf_i386 -Ttext 0x1000 -e startup_32 -o vmlinux head.o misc.o piggy.o
make[2]: Leaving directory `/usr/src/linux-2.2.13/arch/i386/boot/compressed'
gcc -Wall -Wstrict-prototypes -O2 -fomit-frame-pointer -o tools/build tools/buil
d.c -I/usr/src/linux/include
objcopy -O binary -R .note -R .comment -S compressed/vmlinux compressed/vmlinux.
out
tools/build bootsect setup compressed/vmlinux.out CURRENT > zImage
Root device is (8, 1)
Boot sector 512 bytes.
Setup is 3420 bytes.
System is 848 kB
System is too big. Try using bzImage or modules.
make[1]: *** [zImage] Error 1
make[1]: Leaving directory `/usr/src/linux-2.2.13/arch/i386/boot'
make: *** [zImage] Error 2
kitzbuhel:/usr/src/linux>
```

Figure 8.17 *Oops. This kernel is too big. Use* make bzImage.

You need to use the *make bzImage* command. This structures the kernel differently, so that a large kernel can still find a good place to load itself into memory when booting. With the explosion of Linux support, the need to use this command is becoming more and more common.

If you are planning to boot from a floppy disk, you can use *make zdisk* instead of *zImage* or *bzImage*. Make sure there is a blank floppy in the /dev/fd0 (A) drive. This command compiles the kernel and then dumps it to that disk. This is useful for testing the new kernel to make sure it works before putting it into duty, should something go wrong. Don't forget to write-protect this disk afterwards!

Modules

If you opted back in the *make xconfig* or *make menuconfig* sections to compile any device drivers as loadable modules, you now need to build them. The magic incantation is:

```
make modules
```

Easy enough. Once that is finished, the following command sees that the new modules get placed where the kernel and module loader utilities can find them:

```
make modules_install
```

They are placed in the /lib/modules/*x.x.x* directory, where the *x.x.x* represents the kernel version numbers (in this case, /lib/modules/2.2.14). The startup scripts and *modprobe* look for them here. If you have added new modules, you need to update your /etc/rc.d/rc.modules script file to reflect the new equipment.

Using the New Kernel

In order to use the spiffy new kernel, it needs to be placed in the appropriate place. If you built it with *make zdisk,* then this part is finished. Just make sure that the floppy is in the drive and your BIOS boot order starts with A. Note that once the kernel is loaded, you can remove the disk and use the drive for other purposes.

If you used *make zImage* or *make bzImage,* then you still have some work to do. The newly compiled kernel is located in the /usr/src/linux/arch/i386/boot directory and is called *zImage.* This file must be copied elsewhere for use, just in case you want to recompile again or something—you don't want to overwrite it. The kernel installed as part of Slackware is in your root directory and is called *vmlinuz.* You are going to copy this new kernel image to the root directory. But, you don't want to overwrite the original, so you are going to rename the new one to something different, but similar. I use the convention of adding the date to the filename, as in /vmlinuz.2000.04.04. You are free to create your own convention; just don't overwrite the previous version of /vmlinuz! You might need it to recover from a problem. So, let's copy the new image to the root directory as:

```
cp zImage /vmlinuz.2000.04.04
```

Good. Now you need to configure LILO to use this new kernel. Change to the /etc directory and edit the /lilo.conf file. There are a couple of changes you need to make here. First of all, make sure that the line with the word `delay` is uncommented and is set to some reasonable value. The number is in tenths of a second, so a value of 50 is equal to five seconds. This allows you time at the LILO boot prompt to select a kernel image that is not the default to use for booting.

The second thing you need to add is another image section. This should be toward the bottom of your file and begins with the line containing the word `image`. The following indented lines are part of this section and are likely to begin with the words `root`, `label`, `read-only`, `append`, and possibly others. It should end with a comment line stating `Linux bootable partition config ends`. This whole section needs to be duplicated. Note that you might have other image sections pertaining to some other operating system. Leave these intact, especially if you plan to continue to use that other OS. Use the screen shown in Figure 8.18 as an example.

```
# LILO configuration file
# generated by 'liloconfig'
#
# Start LILO global section
boot = /dev/sda
append="mem=192M"
#compact            # faster, but won't work on all systems.
delay = 50
# Normal VGA console
vga = normal
# VESA framebuffer console @ 1024x768x64k
# vga=791
# VESA framebuffer console @ 640x480x256
# vga=769
# ramdisk = 0       # paranoia setting
# End LILO global section
# Linux bootable partition config begins
image = /vmlinuz.2000.04.04
  root = /dev/sda1
  label = linux.20000404
  read-only
# Linux bootable partition config ends
image = /vmlinuz
  root = /dev/sda1
  label = linux
  read-only # Non-UMSDOS filesystems should be mounted read-only for checking
# Linux bootable partition config ends
```

Figure 8.18 *Example of modified LILO config file*

Once you have made a copy of the original image section, you need to modify the first of the two sections. It is the first section that is used as the default image by LILO, unless otherwise specified. So, change the first `image` line to reflect the file name of the new kernel, in this case /vmlinuz.2000.04.04. The `root` line should not need changing. The `label` line needs to be changed, as it allows image selection from the LILO boot prompt. I choose to add the date to this label, just as was done with the kernel filename. Notice that I dropped the periods from the label. LILO has a 15-character limit on the length of labels.

When you are done making these changes, save and exit the file. The last step is to install this new LILO configuration. Issue the command **/sbin/lilo -C /etc/lilo.conf**, and you should see output similar to that shown in Figure 8.19.

Now the new kernel is successfully installed. If you don't see anything similar to this, you've had a problem. Double-check everything.

Does the new kernel work? It is time to reboot and find out. If everything was done correctly, you are in business.

```
# End LILO global section
# Linux bootable partition config begins
image = /vmlinuz.2000.04.04
  root = /dev/sda1
  label = linux.20000404
  read-only
# Linux bootable partition config ends
image = /vmlinuz
  root = /dev/sda1
  label = linux
  read-only # Non-UMSDOS filesystems should be mounted read-only for checking
# Linux bootable partition config ends




kitzbuhel:/etc>/sbin/lilo -C /etc/lilo.conf
Added linux.20000404 *
Added linux
kitzbuhel:/etc>
```

Figure 8.19 *Sample output from the LILO command*

Troubleshooting

What could go wrong? Well, lots, actually. Perhaps there is a driver conflict, or an important device driver is simply missing from the new kernel, or the code for that newly supported board isn't reacting well with something else in your system. You could be getting nasty messages from the kernel; your system might be continually rebooting; or your system might just lock up. But don't fear. Instead of having to reinstall the OS, there are some ways back into it that can help you correct the problem.

When you install the new kernel, you can take the easy way out and just copy it over the old one. However, this eliminates one of your escape routes. If something goes wrong with the compile, you'll probably be glad you took the extra steps.

When you reboot, you see the word LILO show up on your screen. Because of the delay line in your /lilo.conf file, you have a specified amount of time to activate the LILO prompt. You do this by pressing the Shift key during the delay period. This adds a colon to the end of the word LILO. Now, if you press the Tab key, you see an entry for every image section in your /lilo.conf file, including the original kernel image. You can now type the label for the original and press Enter. The system should now boot using the original kernel image. You are back where you started.

However, should the LILO installation have failed, you have one more fallback. The boot disk images on your Slackware CD can be used to recover. If you don't already have one from the installation, you need to make it. This might require taking your CD to another operable computer to make the disk. Reread the section entitled "Making bootdisk and rootdisk Floppies" in Chapter 3, "Installing Slackware."

Now that you have the boot disk, put it in your system and reboot. Make sure that your BIOS boot order starts with A. Wait until you see the screen that looks like the one shown in Figure 8.20.

Then, you need to enter a special command at the LILO prompt. Note that you need to know the device where your root filesystem is located. Enter this command, with the appropriate value:

`mount root=/dev/sda1`

Change the `/dev/sda1` part to reflect your setup. An IDE system would use /dev/hda and the partition number of your root filesystem. Your system should now boot using the kernel from the installation disk and the root filesystem from your hard drive. Once it is booted, you can log in and fix the LILO installation. Edit the /lilo.conf file, and be sure that the kernel is named what you think it should be. Then, reissue the `/sbin/lilo -C /etc/lilo.conf` command.

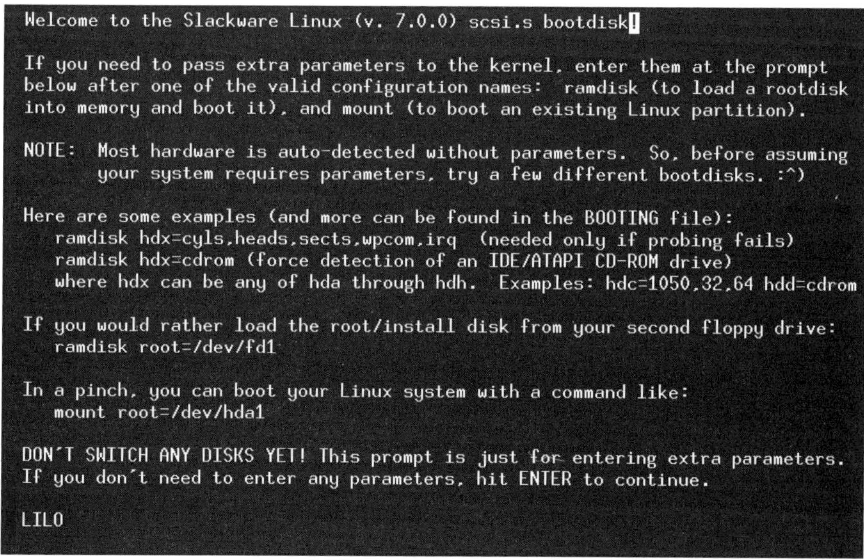

Figure 8.20 *Slackware boot messages*

Summary

By now, you should have successfully recompiled and installed a new Linux kernel. Perhaps there were some bumps in the road along the way, but consider those learning experiences. Think of your parents saying "It builds character." Some further suggested reading on your way to Linux mastery:

- http://www.linuxdoc.org/HOWTO/Kernel-HOWTO.html
- http://www.linuxdoc.org/LDP/tlk/

Good luck.

Chapter 9: System Upkeep: Administering Your System

Keith Pettit and Charles Coffing

Keeping Your System Secure

Frequently Used root Commands

Editing Config Files

Doing Backups and Disaster Recovery

Installing Software Binaries

Installing Software from Source

Administering a system can be a daunting task, but if you know the tools that are available it can be a snap. Most of the commands that I talk about in this chapter have to be issued when you are the root user. So if you haven't already, log in as root and let's get things set up.

Keeping Your System Secure

One of the main concerns with any system—especially networked systems—is security. Even if you do not feel that you have important data on your computer, it's vital that you keep your networked computer secure from break-ins because compromised machines can be controlled remotely to attack other machines. Although it's almost impossible to prove that your system is secure (after all, it's far easier to learn the hard way that it is *not* secure), there are a number of steps you can take to reduce your chances of having your machine compromised.

Passwords

Your first line of defense is to have good passwords. Having weak, easily guessed passwords leaves the doors to your machine wide open. Even having passwords that aren't easily guessed by humans but that are still common words isn't very good. Attackers sometimes use programs to automatically generate and test passwords. This is called a dictionary attack.

Using randomly generated passwords is a great defense against dictionary attacks, but passwords are only good if you can remember them. When you come up with a password, at least don't use common words, your name, family member's names, birthdays, anniversaries, and the like. It's best to use a combination of letters, numbers, and special charters, and to make them longer than five characters.

Groups and Permissions

By default, Slackware has reasonable file permissions and group settings. To keep your system secure, don't blindly loosen these restrictions. A user should only have access to a device if there is a need for access. For example, if you added a new CD writer to your system and want to burn CDs as a regular user, don't do something like this to give yourself permission:

```
chmod 0666 /dev/sr0
```

That opens up the drive to the whole world. Instead, create a group, add yourself to that group, make the device owned by that group, and finally, give that group read and write permission to the device:

```
vi /etc/group
chgrp cdwriter /dev/sr0
chmod g+rw /dev/sr0
```

If you're not in the group, you can't touch the device. That's how it should be.

Daemons

Daemons are wonderful creations, serving files and requests in the background without your needing to know. But just like their supernatural counterparts, you had better keep an eye out for them. Running old, forgotten, or unnecessary daemons on your computer can provide a perfect entrance for someone wishing to break in.

You should periodically browse through your /etc/inet.conf file and comment out any daemons that you really don't need. If your machine doesn't offer FTP or POP3 services, comment these out. Even if you allow people to log in remotely, you might want to comment out *telnet* and use *ssh* instead because it uses encryption. *IMAP*, *ntalk*, and *finger* are some others that you might not need to have enabled.

Blocking and Allowing Hosts

If your machine should only be accessible to a specific set of other computers over the network, you can prevent unauthorized users from even connecting to your machine by editing your /etc/hosts.allow and /etc/hosts.deny files. This way, even if there is a bug in a daemon that could allow an attacker to gain access, the attacker simply can't get to it.

Any daemon listed in /etc/inet.conf which uses /usr/sbin/tcpd can have its access controlled through these hosts.allow and hosts.deny files. When a request comes in, *tcpd* first checks hosts.allow. If the host is explicitly listed, access is granted. Otherwise, hosts.deny is checked. If a match is found, the connection is immediately dropped. If no matches are found, the connection is allowed to proceed.

A simple configuration might list the domain of the local network in the hosts.allow file and a wildcard in the hosts.deny file. This protects against many external attacks, while still giving your machine free access to the Internet. You should read the tcpd man page for an overview of this process and the hosts_options man page for the format of the allow and deny files.

Frequently Used root Commands

All basic Linux administration tasks can be run and controlled from the command line. There are additional tools you can use that apply a neat graphical interface to these tools, but using the command line is the most reliable way to administer your system. In this section I cover some of the most commonly used root commands:

- *adduser*. Use this little script to add a user to your system.
- *chmod*. This command changes permissions.
- *chgrp*. This command changes the group of a file.
- *chown*. This command changes the owner of a file.
- *su*. This command lets you log in as root (super user).
- *shutdown*. This command shuts down the system.
- *kill*. Use this command to kill a particular process.

Most commands used to manage the system are stored in /sbin and /usr/sbin. If you want to learn how to use these commands in more detail, type **man *commandname*** (where *commandname* is the name of the command about which you want more information).

adduser

This is a great little script that helps you set up a new user on your Linux system. To use it, make sure you're logged in as root, and then type **adduser**.

The script then asks you for the following:

- **Login name**. This is the name the user uses to log on to the system.
- **User ID**. This is usually an autogenerated number. Just press Enter to have it automatically assigned.
- **Initial group**. This is the user's group. You can accept the default or type in a different one.
- **Additional groups**. If you want the user to have access to additional groups, use a comma to separate them.
- **User's home directory**. The default is a directory named after the user within the /home directory, but you can assign another location.
- **User's shell**. The default is /bin/bash; if you don't want the user to have telnet or other system access, use /bin/false. (The user retains mail and FTP access.)

- **User's account expiration date.** If this is a permanent account, press Enter. Otherwise, type the date on which you want the account to expire.

After you've completed the above information, you see all your selected options. Press Enter to create the account or Ctrl+C to exit. If you pressed Enter, you are asked for some miscellaneous information, such as the user's full name, room number, work phone, home phone, and any additional information you want to provide. You can leave this blank or fill it in. Finally, you are asked to provide a password for the user. As I mentioned earlier, passwords should be a combination of letters and numbers and should consist of more than five characters.

To test the account you just created, type **su - *username*** (where *username* is the user's username). Type the password if prompted and explore the account you created. When you are done, type **exit** to return to being root.

chmod

You can use the *chmod* command to change the permission(s) on a particular file or directory. When using the *chmod* command, you must also include a number or letters that represent the permissions you want to assign. Table 9.1 illustrates what numbers and letters represent the various permissions.

Table 9.1 Permission Numbers and Their Assignments

Number	Letters	Permission
1	x	Execute only
2	w	Write only
3	wx	Write and execute (1+2)
4	r	Read only
5	rx	Read and execute (4+1)
6	rw	Read and write (4+2)
7	rwx	Read, write, and execute (4+2+1)

The command *chmod 644 test* (in this case, *test* is the name of the file) specifies that the user has read-write access to the file *(6)*; that the group has read-only access to the file *(4)*; and that others have read-only access to the file *(4)*. You can also specify just what permissions to change. The command *chmod g-w test*, for example, denies the group associated with the file the ability to write.

You can also change the permissions for a directory and all its contents by using the recursive command *–R,* like this:

```
chmod -R u+rw directory
```

Be careful using this command recursively. It might make sense to recursively change file modes within your home directory, but doing it as root on system files could open big security holes.

chgrp

You can use the *chgrp* command to change what group has access to a particular file or files. In the following example, `jsmith` is the owner of the file named *test*, and `users` is the group.

```
drw-r-r-   1 jsmith  users         9 Mar 24 10:25 test
```

If you want to change the group to root, then you type the command *chown root test* (where *test* is the name of the file). The result looks like this:

```
drw-r-r-   1 jsmith  root          9 Mar 24 10:25 test
```

chown

You use the *chown,* or *change owner,* command to change the owner of a file, with a syntax almost identical to the *chgrp* command. In the following example, `jsmith` is the owner of the file named *test*:

```
drw-r-r-   1 jsmith  users         9 Mar 24 10:25 test
```

To change the owner to `john`, you use the command *chown john test* (where *test* is the name of the file). The result looks like this:

```
drw-r-r-   1 john  users           9 Mar 24 10:25 test
```

To change both the owner and the group at the same time, use the *chown* command like this:

```
chown jsmith:users test
```

This changes the owner to `jsmith` and the group to `users` on the file named *test*.

su

su is the *switch user* command. You might hear people refer to this as the *super user* command, but that is a misnomer. It really stands for *switch user*—you can use it to become any user, not just root. If you are already root, you can switch to another user (perhaps to test a change you did to the user's account) without needing a password. If you are a regular user, you, of course, need to type a password.

The usual form of this command is *su username*, where username is the user you want to become. (If you don't specify a user, the system assumes you want to become root.) When you become another user this way, you just assume their identity; you don't actually run through their login scripts. If instead you want to fully log in as the user (again, this is quite useful to test changes to an account or if you need all the user's environment variables), use a dash: *su - username*.

You need to use *su* if you are trying to telnet into your machine from a remote location and need to have root privileges. You cannot simply log in as root for security reasons. First you have to log in as a regular user and then use the *su* command to change to the root user.

shutdown

You can use *shutdown* to delay a shutdown for a certain amount of time, to reboot or halt your system, and more. It also notifies users that the system is going down. Here are a couple common commands:

- *shutdown –h now*   This halts (and perhaps turns off) your system without rebooting or waiting.
- *shutdown –r now*   This shuts down and reboots your machine without waiting. You can also use the *reboot* command.
- *shutdown –r 2*   This tells your system to wait two minutes, then shutdown and reboot.

If you are the only user on your system, *shutdown –h now* and *shutdown –r now* might be the only forms of this command you need. If others use your computer, too, over the network, it's good to give *shutdown* a time delay before rebooting so the users have a chance to save their work.

kill

This is a very useful command if you need to terminate a process or service that has locked up or is not working correctly. To use this command, you first need to know the process ID—that is, the ID of the process or service giving you trouble. You can figure this out by finding out what processes are running. To do so, type the following command:

```
ps -aux
```

Find the process that's giving you trouble in the list that is displayed. If this list is too long to search through, you can narrow it down. Suppose Netscape is frozen. You type something like this:

```
ps -aux | grep netscape
```

To kill the process and restart it, issue the command *kill PID*, where PID is the number you found in the second column.

Scheduling Commands with cron

Say you want to erase some old logs, and you want to do it once every few weeks. Or suppose you want a certain batch process to run every 10 minutes. If so, *cron*, a daemon that lets you schedule commands, is the program for you.

For example, I like to use a little program called *Webalizer*. It analyzes my Web traffic and puts it into a useful Web-page format with graphs and charts. But to get it to work, I have to type *webalizer* every time I want the page updated. This is a pain! Instead, I set up a *cron* job to run that file for me once a day.

If you want to schedule a program to run at an assigned time, do the following:

1. Type the command **crontab –e**. This opens your /var/cron/tabs/root file. If this is the first time you've scheduled a program, your file is probably blank.

> If you don't want to use vi, you can edit the crontab file by going into /var/cron/tabs/username and editing the file with your editor of choice.

2. Suppose you, like me, want to schedule the *Webalizer* program to run once a day at 12:05 a.m. (0005 for you military folk). Add this line to your crontab file:

```
05       0       *       *       *        webalizer
```

So you want to schedule a program other than *Webalizer*? Simple. The line you added in step 2 consists of six parts:

```
minutes  hours  days  months  weekdays  command to run
```

Simply substitute your own time (use military time to figure out your minutes and hours), day of the month, month (1 – 12), weekdays (0-6, with 0 being Sunday, 6 Saturday), and command. If you don't want to specify a particular field, like days or months, just enter an asterisk (*) as I did in step 2 to make it happen for all possible values. If you want to enter more than one value in a field—say, for instance, you want to run a command on Mondays, Wednesdays, and Fridays—simply separate the values with commas.

Editing Config Files

Configuration files tell your system what to run and how to run it. They are usually located somewhere in the /etc directory. To edit your files, all you need is some sort of text editor such as vi, Emacs, or pico. In this section, I cover some of the most common configuration files.

Some configuration files are self-documenting to help walk you through their setup. Any text line in a configuration file that is preceded by a # symbol is considered a comment. Read all commented sections of a configuration file before you make any changes. I also suggest adding your own comments to these files so you can keep track of what you've done.

Following is a list of some of the most common files and their uses:

- **fstab**. This file tells your system what filesystems to mount and how to mount them.
- **hosts**. This file defines manual mappings between hostnames and IP addresses.
- **inetd.conf**. This file defines what program to invoke when a request comes in on a particular port.
- **resolv.conf**. This file lists your DNS server(s) used.

fstab

The file /etc/fstab defines what partitions your system mounts automatically when it boots. It also can define where to mount removable media, such as your floppy drive.

You need to edit this file if you add a new hard drive, or a new removable drive, or if you rearrange your partitions after running out of space. Appendix A "A Linux Primer" reviews the format of this file in detail.

hosts

Your /etc/hosts file describes the local host IP address and name and your main IP address and name. This is an example of a /etc/hosts file:

```
127.0.0.1       localhost
127.150.10.6          name.domain.com name
```

The first line is for the local host. Your machine is assigned a local IP address, which is almost always 127.0.0.1, and is known as *localhost*. You can only get this address and name from the actual machine; if you're at your machine and ping *localhost*, you are pinging yourself.

The next line is your machine's IP address with your full domain name, optionally followed by a nickname such as the name of your machine without the domain name.

Most machines don't need any more changes to this file. If you are running a very small network, however, you can assign names to IPs in this file. Even if a little is good, a lot needn't be better—don't get carried away here. If the network gets larger than just a few hosts, it is easier to run a dedicated name server rather than keep track of things by hand in this file.

inetd.conf

This file tells your machine what program to run when network requests are received on certain ports. For example, if someone tries to connect to your FTP port, your inted.conf starts an FTP server to deal with the request. Your FTP line should look something like this:

```
ftp     stream    tcp    nowait    root    /usr/sbin/tcpd    wu.ftpd -l -i -a
```

The first column defines the service. (For possible services and their common port numbers, look at the /etc/services file.) The sixth column is the program to run, followed by any options. The *tcpd* program is actually a security wrapper. Once it determines that the request really should be answered, it starts the FTP program (wu.ftpd, which was passed as an argument) to handle it.

If you don't want to use FTP, just put a comment mark (#) in front of the `ftp` line. You should go through this file and turn off everything that you don't want to use. For example, if your server is used only for mail, you probably want to comment out the `ftp`, `finger`, and other lines that you're not using.

resolv.conf

This file lists your domain name servers. By default, when you set up Slackware, it lists only one name server. It's a good idea to add a second and maybe a third name server if you have them, in case one is not available. The file should look something like this:

```
search domain.com
nameserver 192.233.80.1
```

The first line needs to be your fully qualified hostname, but with the hostname cut off. For example, if your computer's name is penguin.provo.novell.com, the domain you need to specify is provo.novell.com. The next line is the IP address of your primary name server. If you want to add a second and a third name server it should look something like this:

```
search domain.com
nameserver 192.233.80.1
nameserver 192.233.80.2
nameserver 192.233.80.3
```

Doing Backups

Setting up a basic backup system is a fairly simple process. There are some free tools you can grab off the Net, or you can just set up a *cron* job to schedule a backup using the *tar* and *gzip* commands.

For a basic nightly backup, you could add a line to your crontab file that looks something like this:

```
0 1 * * * tar -zcf /var/backup/backup.tar.gz /home
```

This backs up your entire /home directory every day at 1:00 a.m.

First and foremost, you should back up your data and any customized portions of the system. This means that /home, /etc, and /usr/local should probably be on your list. Depending on your setup, the rest of the system might just as easily be restored from the Slackware CD as from a backup.

You also need to keep in mind what you expect your backups to protect you from. The above example would only protect you against deleting an important file if you realize it before the next backup is made. This simple system can't help you if you want a file you deleted a week ago or if your hard drive crashes. To handle these scenarios you need to keep a set of previous backups offline (perhaps one from a month ago, one from a week ago, and last night's).

You can get pretty tricky when creating these backups. Just make sure you test whatever system you're going to use to see how easy it is to restore.

Disaster Recovery

The best way to prepare for a disaster is to practice for one. Create a backup of some test directories using whatever scheme you developed above. Then corrupt the files and try to restore them from the backup. You can use *tar* and *gzip* or you can get one of the many other software packages out there, but the important thing is to prepare for a disaster. It's not a matter of if it will happen but when.

In this section I cover how to create and restore files with *tar* and *gzip*.

tar

A tar file is a file that contains the contents of many other files. It also keeps the permissions, dates, and structures the same. Tar files were originally developed to back up files onto tapes (*t*ape *ar*chiver), but can be used on all media and even over the network.

To create a tar file (or tarball), type the following command from the command line, where *filename.tar* is what you want the tar file to be named, and *file1*, *file2*, and *file3* are files that you want in the tarball:

```
tar -cvf filename.tar file1 file2 file3
```

The *c* option means you want to create an archive and add things to it. The *v* causes tar to be verbose, listing the files as they are added. The last option, *f*, specifies what file to create as the archive.

You can also specify entire directories to include. Here is a sample command that grabs an entire directory:

```
tar -cvf /tmp/httpd.tar /var/lib/apache/htdocs
```

This creates a backup of your files in the /htdocs directory and saves it as /tmp/httpd.tar.

By default, *tar* does not keep the leading / on the pathnames while adding them to the tar file. Because of this, you can easily extract the files into the current directory. This lets you restore individual files by hand. If you prefer that *tar* use absolute pathnames (which makes files always extract to their proper location, regardless what your current directory is when you extract), include the *P* option when creating the backup:

```
tar -cvPf /tmp/httpd.tar /var/lib/apache/htdocs
```

If you are not sure what's in the archive and you want to check before extracting and potentially clobbering files (always a good idea), use the *t* option. *t* means lis*t*:

```
tar -tvf /tmp/httpd.tar
```

Restoring files is very similar. (Be warned that *tar* overwrites files without prompting.) Change the *t* option to *x* to extract. If you did not create the archive with absolute pathnames (the *P* option), then you need to be in the directory to which you want to extract the files. Change there and then extract:

```
cd /
tar -xvf /tmp/httpd.tar
```

There are a lot of different things you can do with the *tar* command, and it can get pretty tricky when you start backing up files that are in use or that are so big you have to do it in pieces. To find out more about the *tar* command try these resources.

- **tar —help**. This lists the different options you can use.
- **info tar**. This lets you view more help for the *tar* command. This has more extensive documentation than the man page.
- **http://www.gnu.org/software/tar/**. This is the Web version of the info help page, in case you prefer to view it with your browser.

gzip

gzip is the command used to compress and uncompress a file. Unlike the zip format often used under Windows, *gzip* only compresses one file at a time. If you want to archive and compress multiple files, you need to use *tar* and *gzip* together.

To compress a file, simply type

```
gzip filename
```

The file is compressed as `filename.gz` and the original is removed.

To uncompress a file, type

```
gzip -d filename.gz
```

or

```
gunzip filename.gz
```

You can view the various options to *gzip* by typing **gzip—help**. You should also be aware that there is a program similar to *gzip*, called *bzip2*, which often achieves better compression. The *bzip2* program is used almost identically to *gzip*. Files that end in .gz have been compressed with *gzip*; those ending in .bz2 were compressed with *bzip2*.

To create an archive and compress it all in one step, similar to using *zip* under other operating systems, you merely need to pass *tar* the -z option. If you are creating a tar file, *tar* is smart enough to compress as it goes. If you are extracting a tar file, the -z option causes *tar* to automatically uncompress. Here is how you create a backup of your Web documents, using both *tar* and *gzip*:

```
tar -zcvf /tmp/httpd.tar.gz /var/lib/apache/htdocs
```

The -z option assumes you want to use *gzip*. If you instead want to use *bzip2*, you need to say so. Here is the same command using *bzip2*:

```
tar --use=bzip2 -cvf /tmp/httpd.tar.bz2 /var/lib/apache/htdocs
```

Installing Software Binaries

There are a couple different ways that you can install any given program, and opinions are very strong on which way is the best. My suggestion is to use what you're most comfortable with but keep track of how you install your programs. You don't want to install a program from a tarball and then try to update it with an RPM file—it doesn't work.

installpkg

One way to install a program is via a Slackware tgz package. This sort of package is basically a tar file with a specific installation script that integrates the files into the system. The *installpkg* utility is the simplest way to install such packages onto your system. When the *installpkg* tool is run, it extracts the tar file and then runs the configuration script.

Do not use the *installpkg* tool on a tar.gz or .tgz file that is not Slackware specific. If you're not sure, don't do it. Extract the file using the *tar –zxvf* command and read the INSTALL and README files.

To install using the *installpkg* tool, simply type

```
installpkg packagename.tgz
```

Depending on the program that was installed, you might see some configuration options run by.

If you want to see, from the command line, which packages are installed on your system, look in the /var/log/packages directory:

```
ls /var/log/packages
```

To remove a package, type

```
removepkg packagename
```

pkgtool

This is a utility that helps you install, remove, or view a package. *Pkgtool* is essentially a single interface for the *installpkg* and *removepkg* tools. To start up the utility, type

```
pkgtool
```

This opens a little menu with some basic functions, including

- **Current**. Use this to look in your current directory for any package files.
- **Other**. Use this to define where you want *pkgtool* to look for your package files.
- **Floppy**. Select this to install from a floppy.
- **Remove**. When you select this option, you see a list of packages currently installed. You can select as many packages as you want to remove.
- **View**. Select this to view a list of all your packages. When a particular package is selected, you see the package details (size, name, location) and a list of all the files and where they are installed.

rpm2tgz

RPM stands for Red Hat Package Manager. RPMs are a package format similar to Slackware's package management tool, but they have a very extensive feature set. One thing the rpm tool can do which Slackware's own package tools cannot, is enforce dependencies between packages.

If all you can find is a .rpm for a particular file, the *rpm2tgz* tool converts your .rpm to a .tgz file that *pkgtool* can use. After you convert it, install it as you would any other tgz package.

> When you convert an RPM file, it does not change the directories where the files are installed. If the directories were specific to some other distribution of Linux, they remain that way. That could mean that your program might not function correctly.

Using RPM

If you want to install many RPMs, you might want to actually use the *rpm* tool rather than convert the RPMs to Slackware's native format. Here are some of the more common RPM commands:

- *rpm –i file-1-0-1.rpm*   Install.
- *rpm –e file*   Uninstall.
- *rpm –Uvh file-1-0-2.rpm*   Upgrade a package.
- *rpm –qpi file-1-0-1.rpm*   View the description of a package that is not installed.
- *rpm –qi file*   View the description of a package that is installed.
- *rpm –qpl file-1-0-1.rpm*   List files in an RPM that is not installed.
- *rpm –ql file*   List files that the RPM installed.

Installing Software from Source

If you have the time and patience, installing software from the source is often a better choice than installing it as a precompiled binary. One reason for this is that source code tends to not be dependent on what Linux distribution you are running, but binaries often are distribution specific. By compiling a program yourself, it is just about guaranteed to work on your system. Not only that, but you have a lot more control over how the software works. You can enable options you want and disable those you don't.

Unpacking the Source

Usually you get the source as a compressed tarfile. You need to uncompress it somewhere—the directories /usr/src, /usr/local/src, and your home directory are all reasonable places to put it. These tar files tend to have the directory structure in them already, so you don't have to make a directory yourself—just uncompress it:

```
tar -zxvf program-1.0.tar.gz
```

Now change into the new directory, and look around:

```
cd program
```

Often source code tar files include helpful files such as /README and /INSTALL. The /README might give useful general information; the /INSTALL file might tell about any installation oddities of which you should be aware. It's a good idea to skim these files before beginning the compilation.

configure

Before compiling the sources, you need to acquaint them with any peculiarities of your system. Usually, the source can compile on all distributions of Linux and even on UNIX platforms other than Linux. The *configure* command examines your system and figures out a number of settings so that the program compiles, regardless of what type of system you have.

The *configure* command also might give you options to enable or disable features of the program. To see what options you have for installing a particular program, type

```
./configure --help
```

This should give you a list of all the options you can use. Simple programs might not have any features listed. Occasionally you might find a program that doesn't even have a *configure* script; in this case you certainly need to read any /README or /INSTALL files. For example, when installing MySQL from source, you can choose what directory you want to install it in by using this option with the *configure* command:

```
./configure --prefix=/usr/local/mysql
```

If you want to add multiple options, it looks something like this:

```
./configure --prefix=/usr/local/mysql --sbindir=/usr/sbin – binddir=/usr/bin
```

You don't need to choose an option for everything listed in ./configure -–help, just the ones that are different from the default. Again, make sure to look over the /README or /INSTALL files to learn more about installing your particular program.

make

After you have selected your configure options, *make* compiles the program. All you need to do is type **make**.

Compiling can take some time, depending on the program and your machine. If you get an error message saying an include file or a library was not found, you probably need to install other libraries. Try finding and installing the needed dependencies, or change your configuration options so that they are not needed. Then try running *make* again.

make install

This is the part that actually installs the program. If you made it though the ./configure and *make* steps without any error, running the *make install* command is your last step. For this step, just type **make install**. Usually you need to be root to do this step.

This should be fairly quick. All the system needs to do is copy all the files it just created to the appropriate directories.

Summary

Using various tools, I've covered how painless administering your system can be. Keeping your system secure, using various methods to install software, and creating backups are some of the basics necessary for maintaining a system. The most important thing is to not be intimidated by Slackware, but to be patient in learning how to properly use it.

Chapter 10: Getting Started with KDE

Joe "Zonker" Brockmeier

Beginning to Use KDE

Using KDE Applications

ow that you've got Linux installed and XFree86 configured, you probably want to get into a graphical user interface (GUI) to get some real work done. This chapter covers the K Desktop Environment (KDE), which is the most common of several available Linux GUIs.

Unlike Microsoft Windows or the Mac OS, Linux is not limited to one GUI. KDE is one of the most popular Linux GUIs and ships as the default for most Linux distributions. KDE is not a commercial product; it is developed completely by volunteers who want to contribute a world-class GUI for Linux and other UNIX-style operating systems. Currently, KDE runs on FreeBSD, Solaris, IRIX, and HP-UX, as well as Linux. The KDE project began in 1996, initiated by Matthias Ettrich. The goal of the KDE project is to bring UNIX to the desktop, or the desktop to UNIX—whichever you prefer. You can find KDE on the Web at http://www.kde.org.

If KDE doesn't suit your needs, you can try several other alternatives, including GNOME (covered in Chapter 11, "Getting Started with GNOME") and other window managers and desktop environments.

You can get a lot done at the command line, but many people are much more comfortable using a GUI these days.

KDE is a full desktop environment, meaning it comes with the whole shebang—a file manager, configuration system, help system, and tons of utilities and applications. The idea behind KDE is to provide Linux users with a GUI environment that more than rivals Windows or the Mac OS. KDE is not a window manager, but it does include its own—the K Window Manager.

Okay, the KDE team might not come up with the most original names, but the names are descriptive.

If you're new to Linux, the KDE is probably familiar to you right away. Anyone who's been using Microsoft Windows or the Mac OS takes to KDE like a duck to water.

Beginning to Use KDE

After you configure *XFree86* (see Chapter 5, "Configuring the X Window System," if you haven't set everything up already) you're ready to rock and roll. At your shell prompt, type **startx**, and you're brought into KDE. (This is assuming you haven't changed the default for Slackware.)

The KDE Control Center

The KDE Control Center, shown in Figure 10.1, allows you to manage features in KDE and gather information about your Linux system. The Control Center allows you to configure sounds for events in the system, the wallpaper on your desktop, and even gives you information about your hardware and what processes are running on your Linux box. KDE makes life a lot easier than it used to be on the Linux desktop. The first window managers for Linux required configuration through text files only, meaning that nongurus were in for a hard time if they wanted to make changes to the way that the window manager operated. By using the KDE Control Center (see Figure 10.1) you should be able to configure the look and feel of KDE to behave exactly as you like so that you'll be able to enjoy a very comfortable desktop environment, without learning an obscure scripting language.

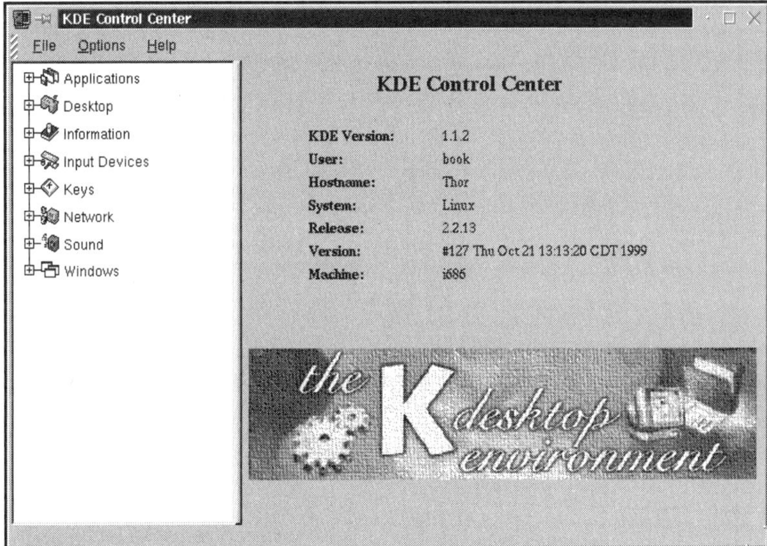

Figure 10.1 *The KDE Control Center*

You can start the KDE Control Center from the KDE Panel by using the K Menu and selecting the KDE Control Center (see Figure 10.2), or by single-clicking the Control Center icon. (Unlike Windows or the Mac OS, you start applications under KDE by single-clicking rather than double-clicking on icons. This might take a little getting used to, especially if you have an itchy mouse finger like I do.)

When the KDE Control Center is started, it shows the eight categories available for you to choose as a list of small icons with the name of each category next to it. If you click on the plus sign next to the icon, another list of options will drop down to display the individual items that you can configure.

The Applications Category

The first category in the KDE Control Center is Applications (see Figure 10.3). You can use this category to configure the Login Manager, K File Manager, Konqueror (the KDE Web browser), and the KDE Panel. You can select the number of workspaces you'd like to use under the panel configuration, how Konqueror handles cookies under the Web browser tab, and the look and feel of the Login Manager and K File Manager.

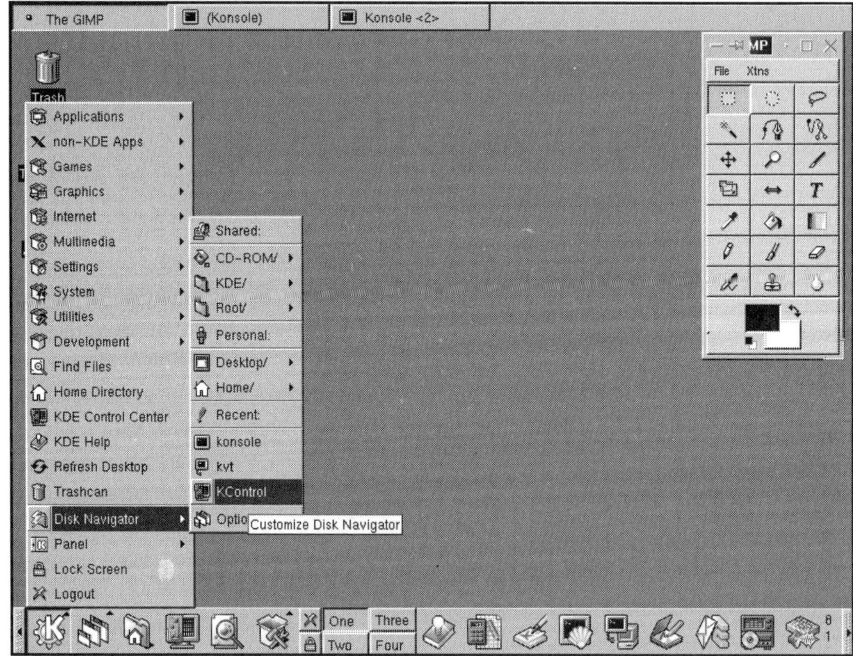

Figure 10.2 *Starting the Control Center*

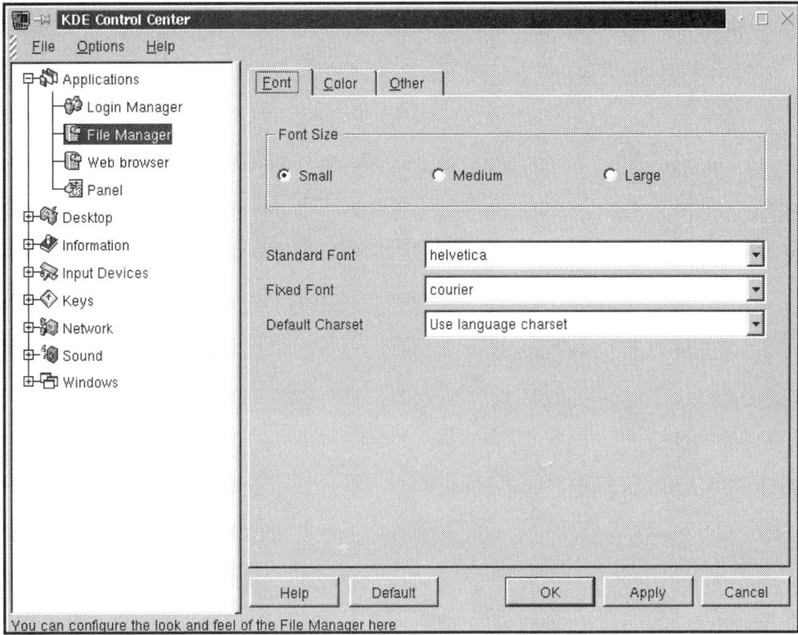

Figure 10.3 *The Control Center Applications category*

The Desktop Category

The second category is the Desktop category (see Figure 10.4). You can control the look and feel of your K Desktop Environment here, making KDE look simply marvelous or plain as can be—depending on your taste. You can select screen savers, themes, background images or colors, window styles, and much more.

The Information Category

The third category, Information (see Figure 10.5), doesn't actually allow you to configure anything, but it does display important system information. You can use this to easily see what devices are attached to the system, your memory usage, X-Server information, and what type of processor you have—if you don't know already. This category in KDE's Control Center also displays the status of Samba, if you happen to have it running, and your partition information as well. This is very handy for users who are new to Linux and need to find out this sort of information quickly without having to look up the commands.

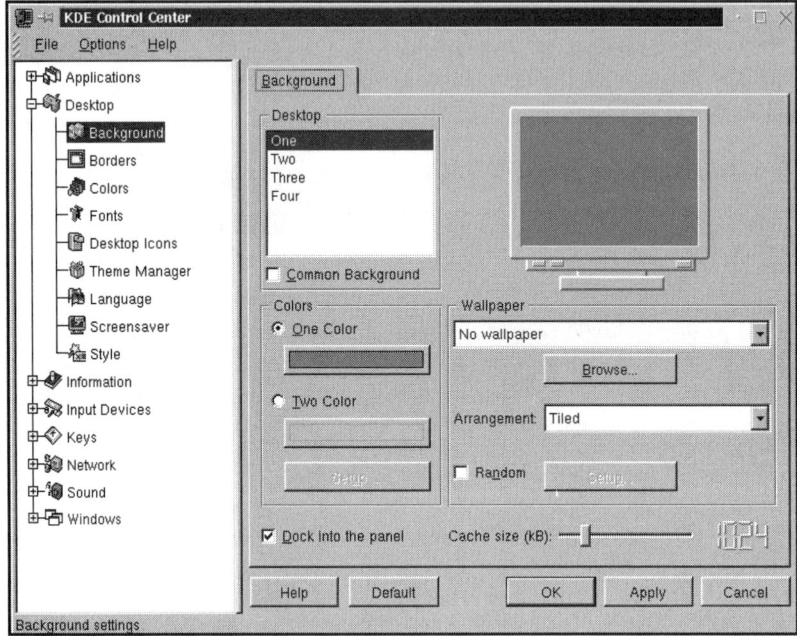

Figure 10.4 *The Control Center Desktop category*

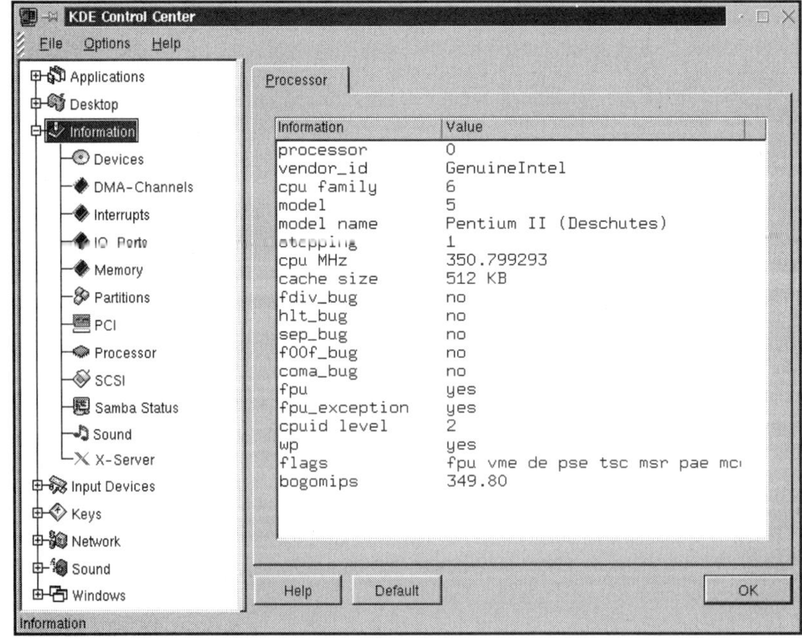

Figure 10.5 *The Control Center Information category*

The next set of goodies under the KDE Control Center are Input Devices (see Figure 10.6). You can select an international keyboard layout or simply configure some of the mouse and keyboard behavior under KDE. The international keyboard layout selection is particularly useful for students taking foreign-language classes (if only I had been able to use this feature while I was taking Spanish in college!) or multilingual Linux users who want to switch between languages quickly while using KDE.

Most power users are familiar with hot keys, or key combinations that are equivalent to commands or actions. KDE allows you to create new hot key combinations or modify existing ones using the Keys category in the Control Center. There are two types of hot key selections: Global and Standard (see Figure 10.7). Global keys are key combinations that allow you to perform window-management functions without using the mouse, such as switching between windows or workspaces. The Standard keys are actions such as cut, paste, copy, and quite a few others. You can practically train KDE to sit up and beg using these keys!

The next selection, Network, is somewhat misleading. The only tab available under Network is Talk Configuration (see Figure 10.8), which allows you to chat with other users who are on the same network as you. Not very useful for standalone workstations, but quite handy in office environments.

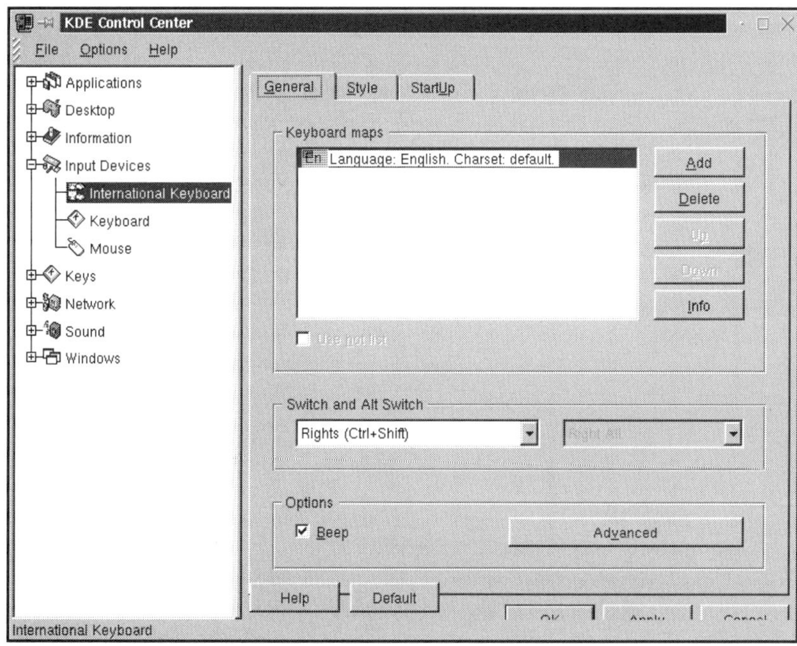

Figure 10.6 *International keyboard layouts*

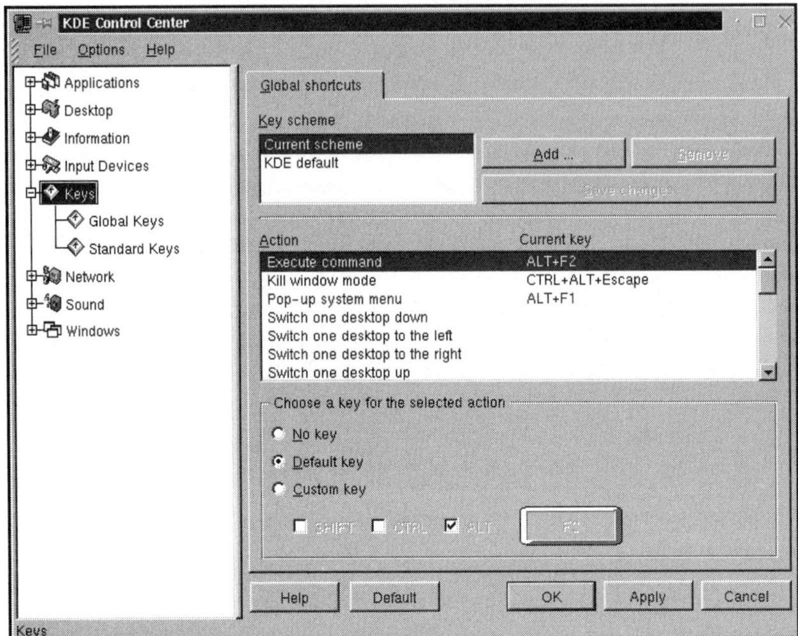

Figure 10.7 *Use the Global Shortcuts tab to change or add hot key functions to KDE.*

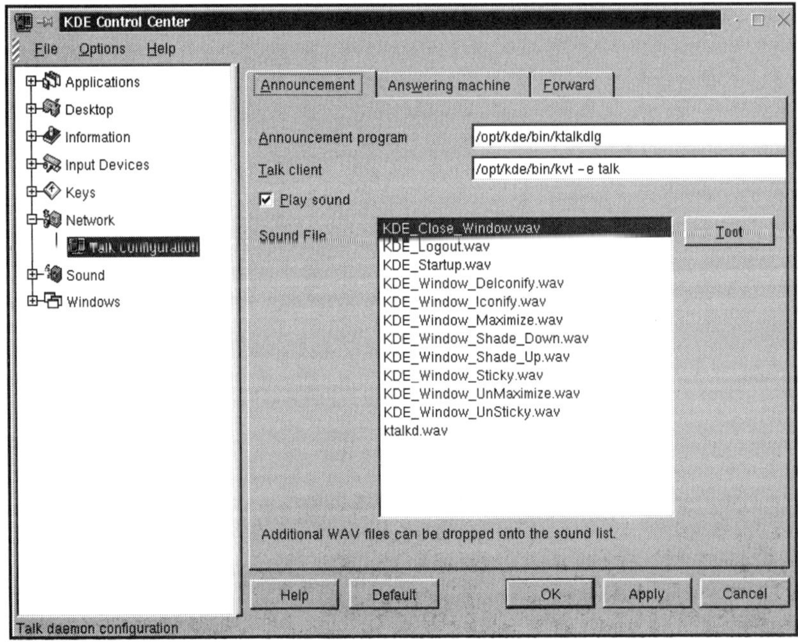

Figure 10.8 *The Control Center Network category*

If you've gotten your sound card configured successfully under Linux, you can assign sounds to events under the Sound tab in the KDE Control Center (see Figure 10.9). You can assign default sounds or even use your own. I personally like to download *South Park* or *Simpsons* sound files and assign them to error events. It never fails to startle people using my computers. They don't expect to have audio feedback to their errors. You can also configure the system bell that operates using the PC speaker.

Finally, the KDE Control Center provides the Windows category (see Figure 10.10) for setting the behavior of windows under KDE. You can assign behavior to the mouse buttons, the focus policy of the K Window Manager, and other handy features.

KDE Features

KDE is a very advanced GUI. It has a number of features that make it an attractive alternative to the Windows and Mac OS GUIs.

Under X, windows behave slightly differently than under Windows or the Mac OS. Under many X window managers you need only hover your mouse over a window that is under another window to get it to pop to the forefront and let you type. This is generally called giving a window the focus. In other words, the window that is currently accepting your keystrokes has the focus. Because the Linux way is to provide options rather than decide how resources should act, the KDE team allows the user to choose his or her focus behavior. This way, Unix gurus and Linux newbies alike should be happy with KDE.

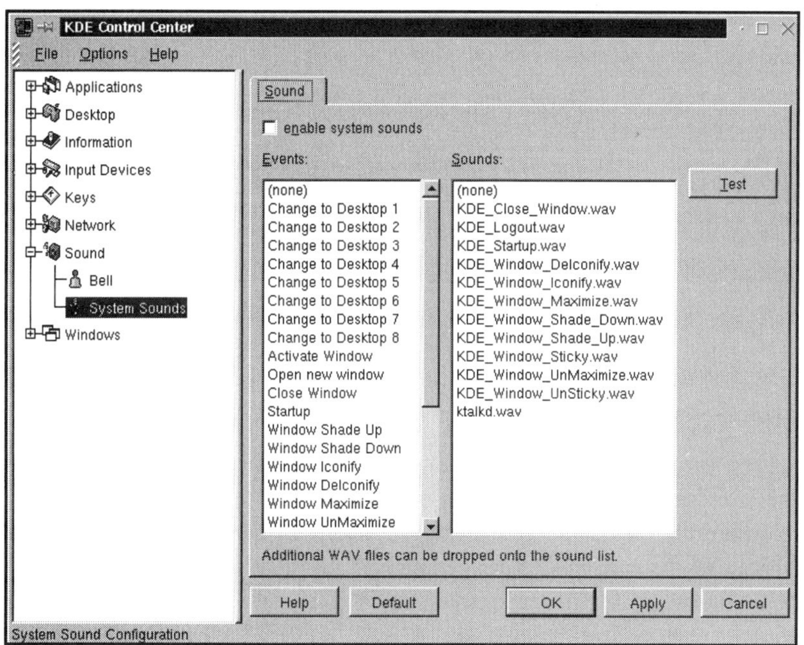

Figure 10.9 *Use the Control Center Sound category to change or add sounds to events in KDE.*

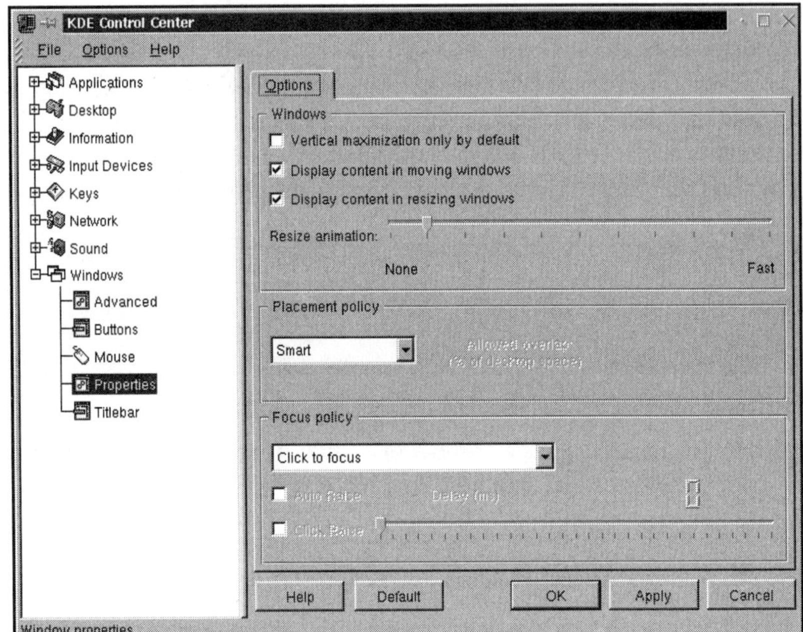

Figure 10.10 *The handy Control Center Windows category*

Workspaces

KDE also makes use of features that you might not be used to: UNIX-style workspaces. Basically, the idea is to give the user a bunch of desktops, rather than just one. On the KDE panel you find four numbered buttons. Each one of these buttons corresponds to a workspace. The workspace is the equivalent of the desktop in Windows or the Mac OS, but you can have multiple under KDE. This allows you to work on several things simultaneously without having overlapping windows.

Figure 10.11 shows a typical KDE Panel including the workspace buttons. By default they're simply numbered one through four, but you can change the names of your workspaces to whatever you'd like. To change the names of the workspaces, click on the active workspace's button; a blinking cursor will appear, allowing you to edit the text that is in the button.

Figure 10.11 *KDE workspace buttons*

By default, the KDE panel has four workspaces. I'm usually pretty happy with four, but if you're a hard-core window freak you can have as many as eight workspaces. Note that background images do use system resources, so you might want to go with a common image among all your workspaces, or none at all, if you've got a lower-end system that doesn't have much memory.

Window Behavior in KDE

Windows behave slightly differently under KDE than they do under some other operating systems or window managers. You have a few extra options under KDE that you don't have with Windows or the Mac. For instance, Windows doesn't have the windowshade feature that KDE has; nor can you decide how windows react to mouse input or customize the title bar operations buttons.

By default, the title bar contains five buttons: the menu button, a sticky button, a minimize button, a maximize button, and the close button. You can use the KDE Control Center to rearrange or remove these buttons if you wish (see Figure 10.12). The sticky button is particularly useful because it allows you to tell a window to appear in all of your workspaces. It also allows you to tell a window not to appear in all of your workspaces.

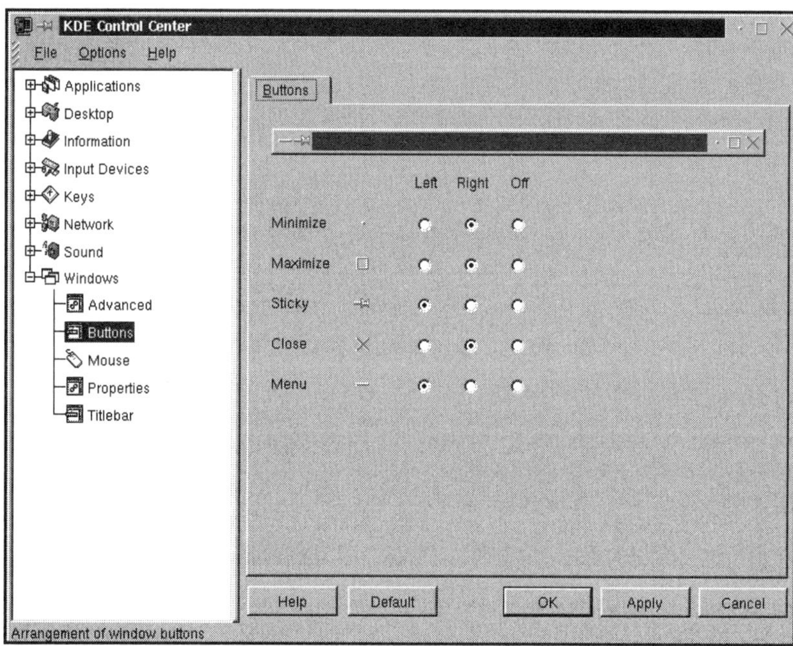

Figure 10.12 *KDE title bar buttons*

Other window behavior under KDE is fairly straightforward. Most windows are resizable, and the scrollbars behave as you'd expect under any other GUI.

Cutting 'n Pasting

KDE allows you to copy and paste text between programs in several ways:

- By selecting text with your mouse and putting it onto your Clipboard by choosing Edit, Copy; then pasting the text to another window or area by choosing Edit, Paste.
- By using the hot keys for copy (Ctrl+C) and paste (Ctrl+V).
- By selecting the text and clicking the middle mouse button (or both buttons together if you have a two-button mouse) to paste the text in the desired area. This third option is specific to UNIX environments. It usually works both in X and at the command prompt.

The middle-button method is a much faster and more convenient way to cut and paste text, compared to using hot keys or menu items. Unfortunately, some programs don't recognize this key binding. For instance, Star Office doesn't seem to recognize this type of cut-and-paste operation. Most native Linux or UNIX programs allow you to do this, but programs ported to Linux sometimes do not, and programs running under emulators like DOSEmu or Wine might have problems with pasting this way.

If you do a lot of writing or text editing, you find that this method of cutting and pasting greatly enhances your speed once you get in the habit of using it. Unfortunately, if you switch between Linux and Windows or another OS, you get greatly annoyed that you can't use this shortcut when cutting and pasting in those operating systems!

The KDE Disk Navigator

The KDE Disk Navigator is kind of the Swiss Army knife of GUI menus. It allows you to quickly access files in your home directory, start a frequently used program or one of the KDE utilities, and access the desktop from a menu so you don't have to minimize windows to get to the desktop icons. You can find the Disk Navigator under the main KDE Panel menu (see Figure 10.13).

Using the Disk Navigator, you can launch the most recently used applications, browse your home directory files, launch applications on your desktop without having to get to the desktop itself, or choose to start one of the utilities available under the Disk Navigator.

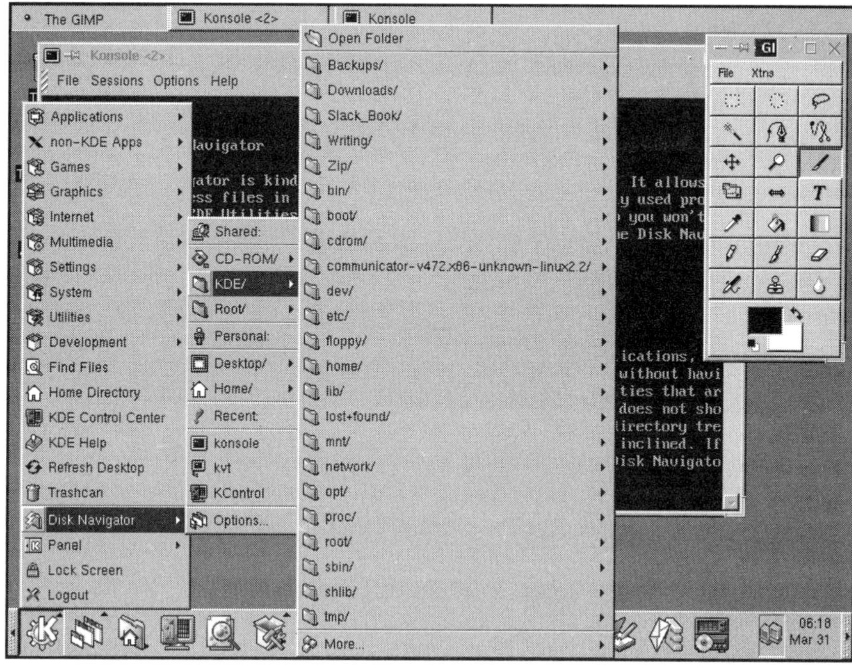

Figure 10.13 *The KDE Disk Navigator*

By default the Disk Navigator does not show hidden dot files. I generally like to see all the files in my directory tree. Happily, this is one of the options you can change if you are so inclined. If you want to configure the Disk Navigator, select Options from the Disk Navigator menu. You see the dialog box shown in Figure 10.14.

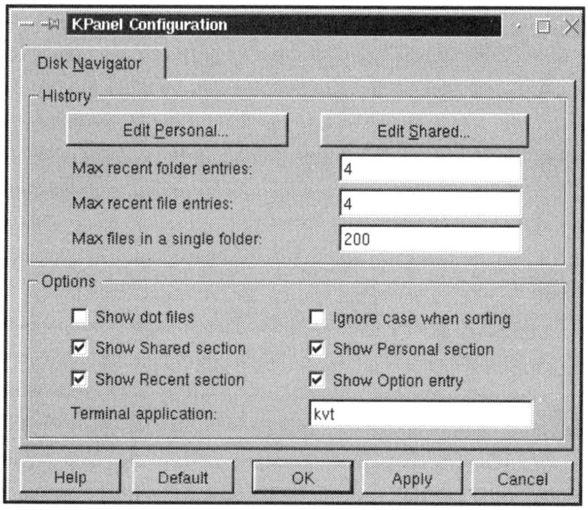

Figure 10.14 *The Disk Navigator Options panel*

This allows you to edit the behavior of the Disk Navigator, including what applications are shared and how many recent folders or files are displayed. Like many Linux utilities, the Disk Navigator is somewhat different from what you're probably used to and takes a little while to become proficient with. However, once you use it for a while it can be very useful and can allow you to be more productive while using Linux—even if it is just being more productive in launching your favorite game.

Making New Icons on the KDE Desktop

You can create new icons on your KDE desktop or on the KDE Panel to launch applications. You can also make shortcuts to Web pages or FTP sites on your desktop if you have frequently used URLs you want to be able to get to quickly.

To add an application to the KDE Panel, open the main KDE Panel menu and select Panel, Add Application, and the application that you want to add to the main menu (see Figure 10.15).

If the application you want to add is not available under the current menu, you can add it under the main menu by choosing Panel, Edit Menus, as shown in Figure 10.16.

This opens the menu editor, which allows you to add an application by right-clicking on the menu section under which you wish to put the application (see Figure 10.17).

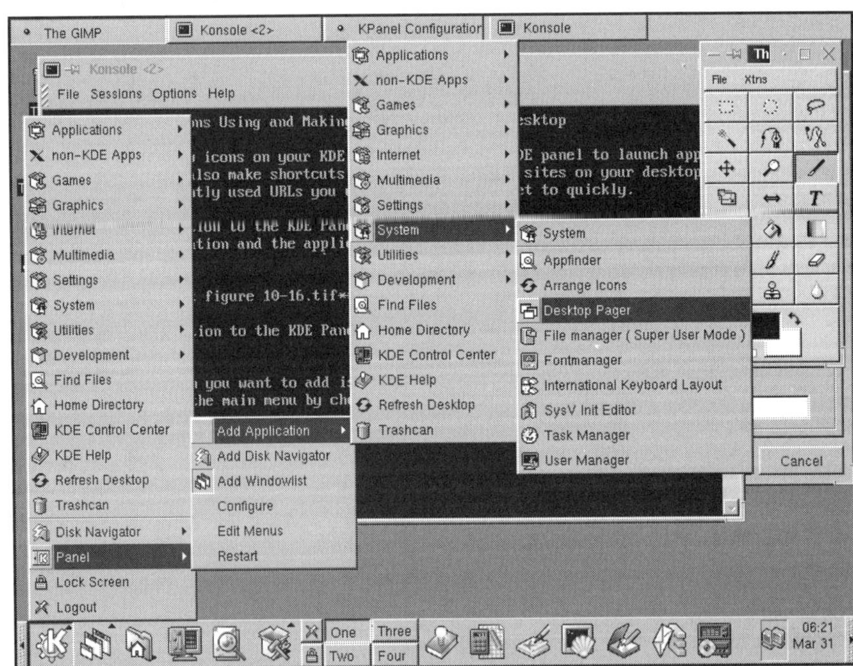

Figure 10.15 *Adding an application to the KDE Panel*

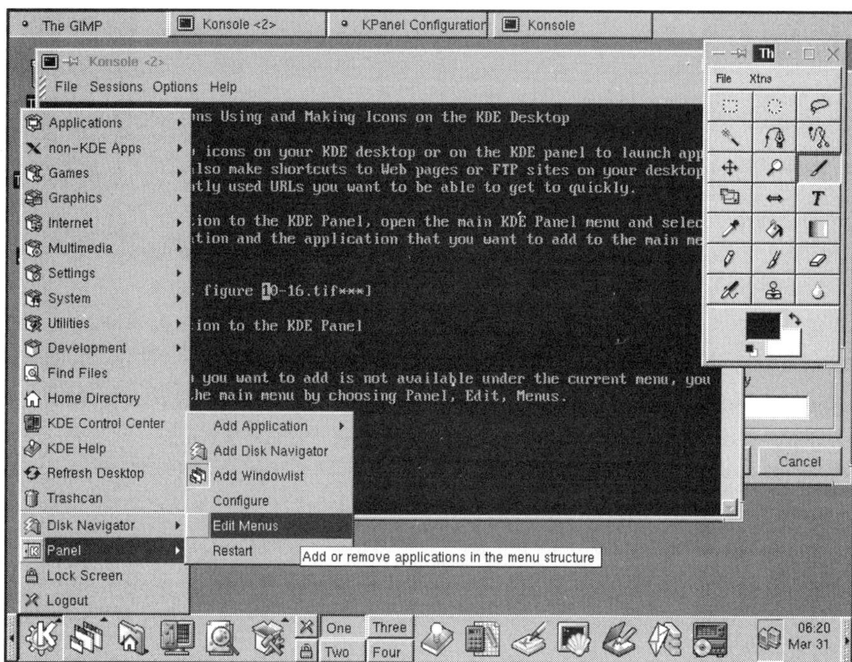

Figure 10.16 *Opening the menu editor*

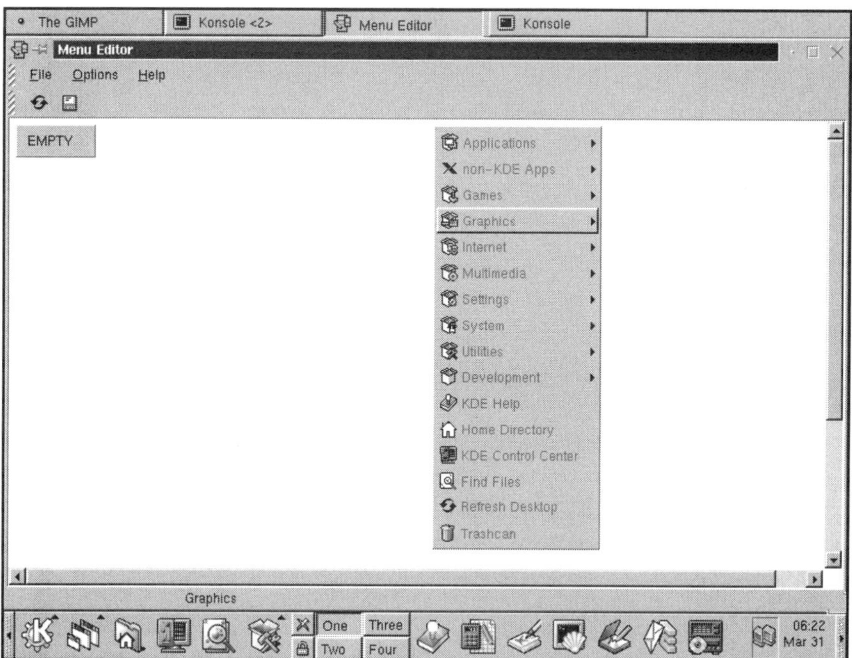

Figure 10.17. *Menu editor*

The KDE Taskbar

The KDE taskbar is very handy. If you're used to other operating systems, you've probably used a taskbar before. It allows you to quickly switch between running programs by choosing the proper icon on the taskbar (see Figure 10.18). If you're like me, your taskbar is probably full at all times.

By default, the KDE taskbar is located at the top of the screen. If you'd prefer it somewhere else on your desktop, right-click on the KDE Panel and select Configure. This is somewhat counter-intuitive because you'd probably expect to be able to right-click on the taskbar itself.

Once the KPanel Configuration dialog box is open, you can choose to locate the taskbar at the bottom or the top left-hand corner of the desktop (see Figure 10.19). You can also hide the taskbar if you don't find it useful.

Figure 10.18 *KDE taskbar*

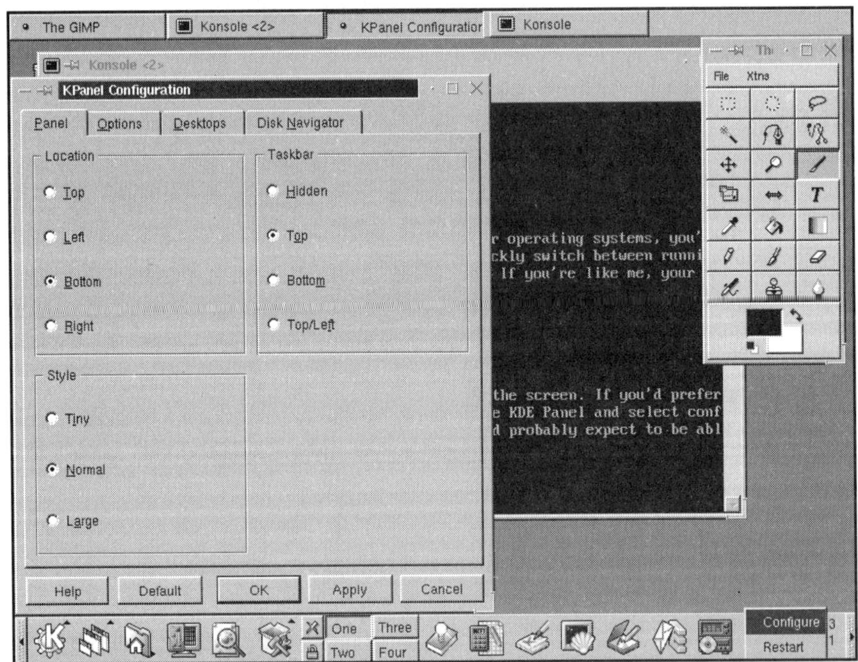

Figure 10.19 *Configuring the taskbar*

Adding Shortcuts to the KDE Desktop

You can add icons to your KDE desktop by right-clicking on the desktop, which brings up the desktop context menu. At this point, you can choose to add a new folder (directory), application, URL, or filesystem device (see Figure 10.20).

Adding an Application Shortcut

If you want to add an application to your desktop for quick launching, follow these steps:

1. Right-click the desktop, and select New, Application in the context menu.
2. You see the dialog box shown in Figure 10.21, which asks you the name of the application. By default, it says Program.kdelnk. Change the first part to whatever name you'd like the icon on the desktop to have.

A context menu is a menu that pops up when you right-click the mouse in a certain area. Depending on where you right-click, you might get different menus—or possibly no menu at all if the place you click has no menu function associated with it. If you've used any version of Windows since Windows 95, or the Mac OS 8.5 or later, you're probably already familiar with context menus—even if you didn't know what they were called.

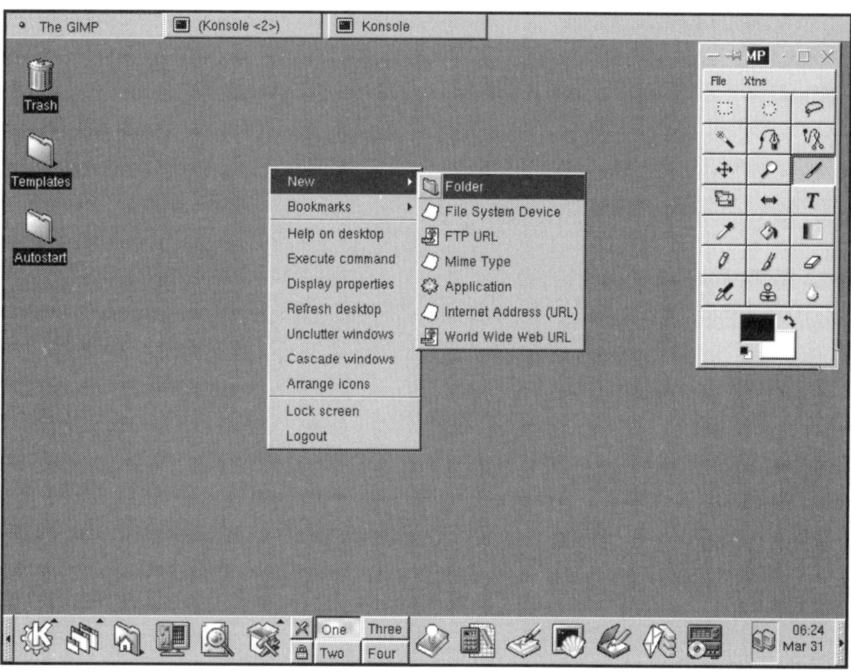

Figure 10.20 *The desktop context menu*

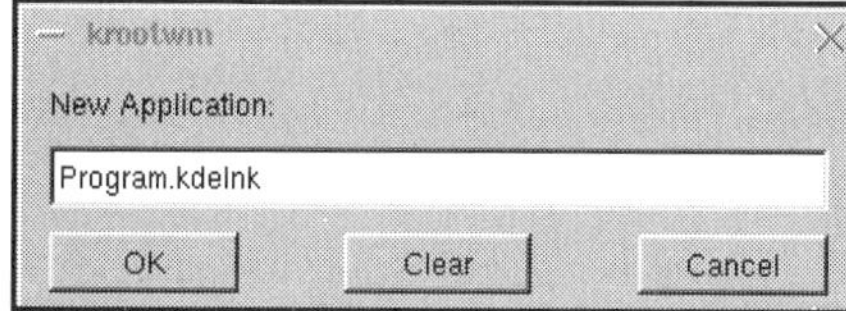

Figure 10.21 *The Add Application dialog box*

3. Once you've chosen the name of your application, you see the configuration dialog box that allows you to set permissions and choose the executable that the shortcut will run, as shown in Figure 10.22. If you're using a console program, select the Run in terminal check box under the Execute tab. Alternatively, you can select the program icon by clicking on the icon shaped like a gear, which brings up a select dialog box displaying all the icons available to KDE.

Adding a Folder to Your Desktop

To add a new folder to store stuff on your desktop, right-click the desktop to bring up the context menu. Choose New, Folder. You are prompted by a dialog box to type in the name you'd like to give the folder (see Figure 10.23).

That's all there is to creating the folder. If you want to change the default permissions or the icon associated with the folder, right-click directly on the folder to bring up a context menu that allows you to select Properties. By selecting Properties, you bring up the Permissions dialog box, shown in Figure 10.24.

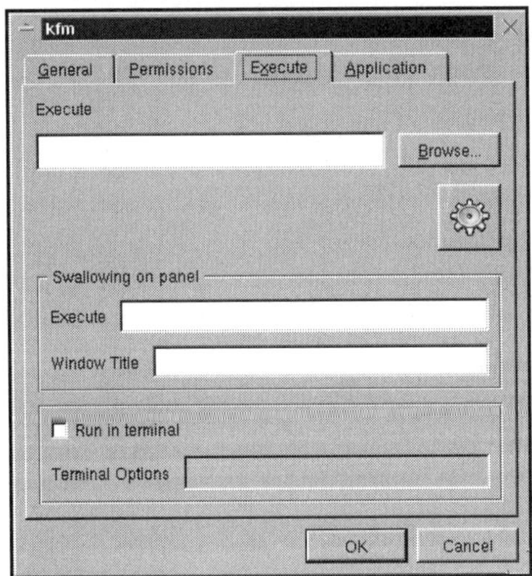

Figure 10.22 *Choosing an executable for the shortcut*

Figure 10.23 *Adding a folder to your desktop*

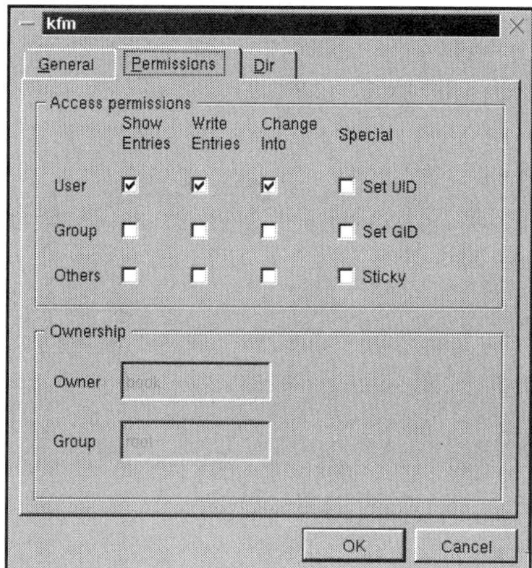

Figure 10.24 *Changing or setting folder properties*

Adding a Filesystem Device

To add a filesystem device, such as your floppy drive or CD-ROM drive, right-click to bring up the context menu, and choose New, File System Device. You type in the name of the device the same way that you did with the application icon (see Figure 10.25).

You are presented with File System Device Properties dialog box, where you can select permissions, the device, and the directory under which it should be mounted.

Figure 10.26 is an example of a CD-ROM shortcut. The device is /dev/hdc. The directory under which it is mounted is /cdrom. I chose to go ahead and enter the proper filesystem type for CD-ROMs, iso9660, rather than auto or default.

You can also choose to have two different icons to display whether the device is currently mounted or not.

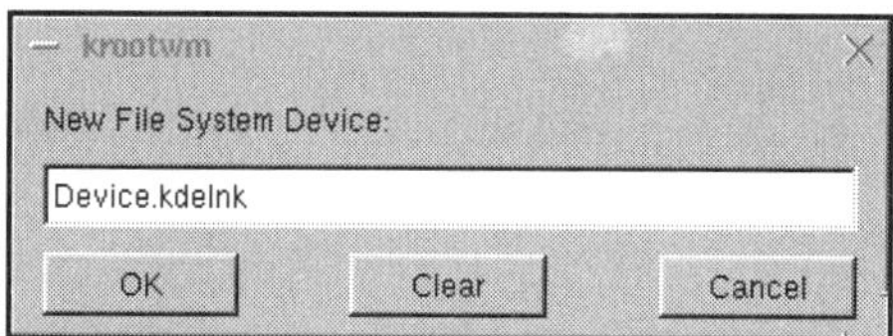

Figure 10.25 *Name the new filesystem device in this dialog box.*

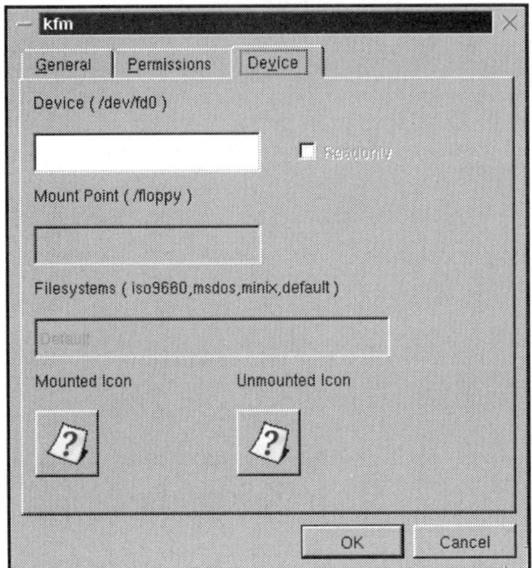

Figure 10.26 *KDE CD-ROM shortcut*

Finding Files and Applications

If you want to quickly find a file or application that you know the name of, you can use the KFind utility. You can launch KFind directly from the KDE Panel by clicking on the magnifying glass icon (see Figure 10.27).

If you don't know the file's name, you can also search for files by date or size or use wildcard expressions if you know only part of the filename (see Figure 10.28). Check Appendix A, "A Linux Primer," for more on using wildcards in Linux.

To find a file by name, type in the name of the file in the Named field and then select the folder(s) that you want checked in the Look in dialog box. Click Browse when you've set your search criteria.

Figure 10.27 *The KFind icon*

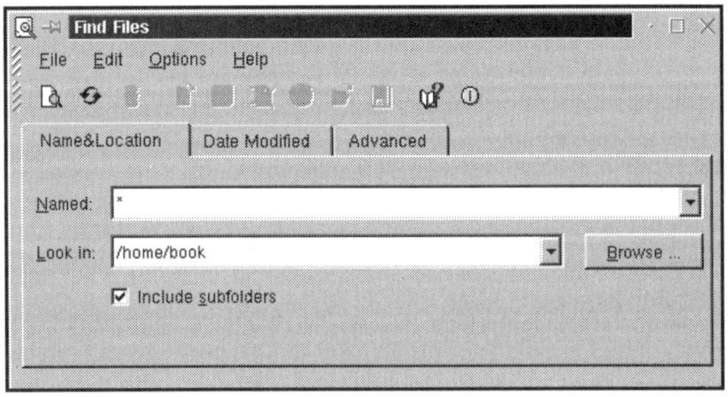

Figure 10.28 *Using KFind*

Exiting KDE

To exit KDE, do the following:

1. You can exit KDE by clicking on the X icon next to the workspace icons on the KDE Panel, or by selecting Logout from the main KDE menu (see Figure 10.29).

2. You are prompted before KDE exits. Click Cancel if you clicked the Logout button in error; otherwise, click OK. KDE warns you if you have applications still open before exiting, so that you don't lose anything you're currently working on.

In the rare event that KDE or another program locks up and you need to exit KDE but you can't select one of the Logout icons, you can kill the X Server by using the Ctrl+Alt+Backspace key combination.

The Ctrl+Alt+Backspace key combination should be used only as a last resort! Also, under Windows, the Ctrl+Alt+Del key combination brings up the task manager, allowing you to kill a hung application. The same does not work within X. You need to go to a command prompt to kill off the application or use Ctrl+Alt+Backspace to kill all of X.

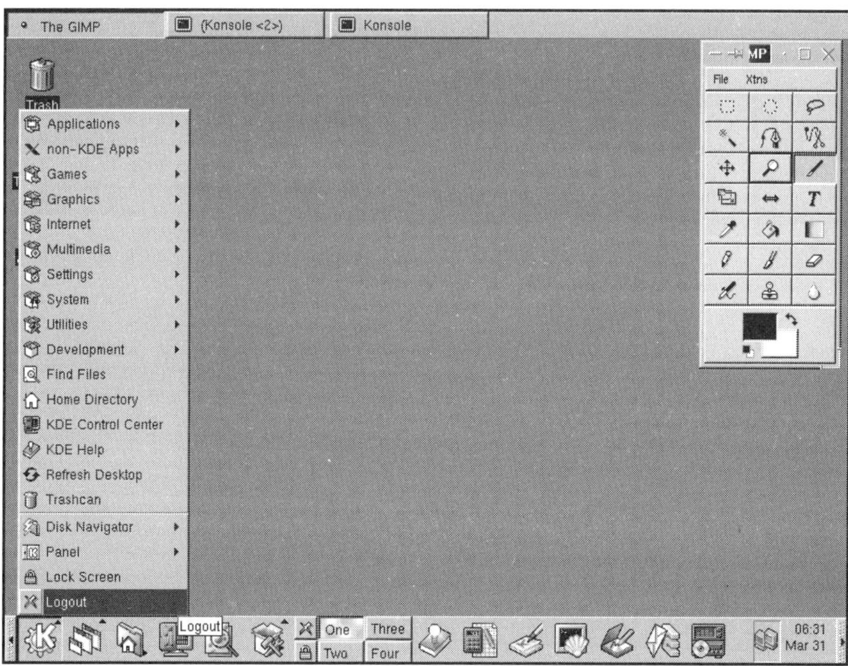

Figure 10.29 *Exiting KDE*

Using KDE Applications

There are entirely too many applications under KDE to explain all of them in a book of this size. However, I wanted to detail a few of them because they come in quite handy. You can experiment with other applications under KDE or browse KDE's help system to find out more about various KDE applications that aren't explained here. There are also a few good books on the market that focus solely on KDE, though they might be behind by a few versions.

KDE Help

To start KDE help, either select the Help option from the menu of one of the applications you're interested in learning more about, or select the Help icon from the KDE taskbar. Figure 10.30 shows the KDE Help window.

Unfortunately, there might be some help sections that are incomplete. Remember, KDE is created by a volunteer organization. If someone hasn't gotten around to writing documentation, it won't exist. They're also always looking for help in that area if you'd like to pitch in and help an Open Source project, but aren't a coder.

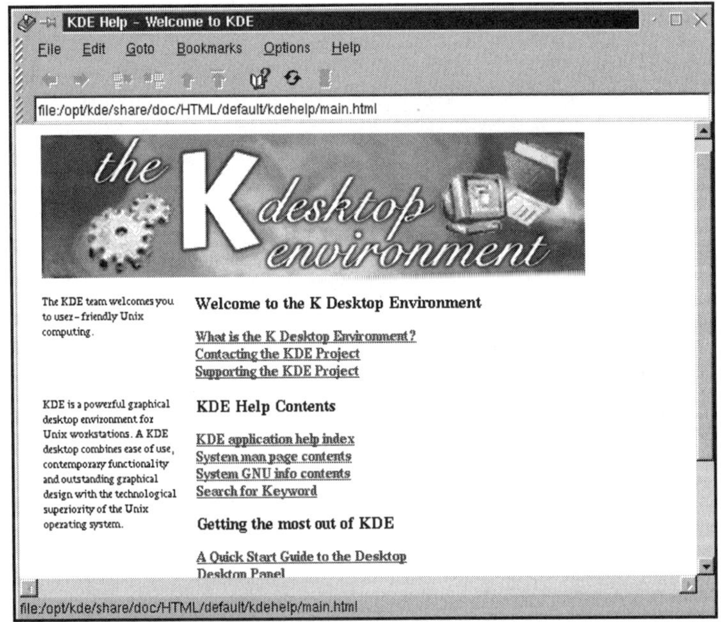

Figure 10.30 *The KDE Help window*

Using KDE Internet Applications

KDE comes with a plethora of Internet applications that are very handy. The most useful for Linux newbies is probably the kppp dialer. This allows you to set up a dial-up connection very easily.

kppp

To set up kppp, do the following:

1. Select kppp from the main KDE Panel menu.
2. Once you've launched kppp, click the Setup button (see Figure 10.31). You can have multiple dial-up accounts, which is very handy for people who use Linux on a laptop.
3. To set up a new account, click the New button. That invokes an account dialog box that enables you to input the phone number, DNS, and other information for your account (see Figure 10.32).

You can get this information from your Internet service provider (ISP). Many ISPs are Linux-friendly, probably because they're running Linux in their shop! However, some, such as AOL, do not support Linux. If you have an AOL account or an account with someone who does not support Linux, you might need to get a new ISP. This is very rare, but there are some ISPs that require Windows programs to log on to their network and do not make available the information to log on to their network using another OS. I've heard tales of non-Linux-friendly ISPs, but unless you live in an area with only one ISP, you should be able to find a Linux-friendly ISP pretty easily.

Figure 10.31 *The kppp utility*

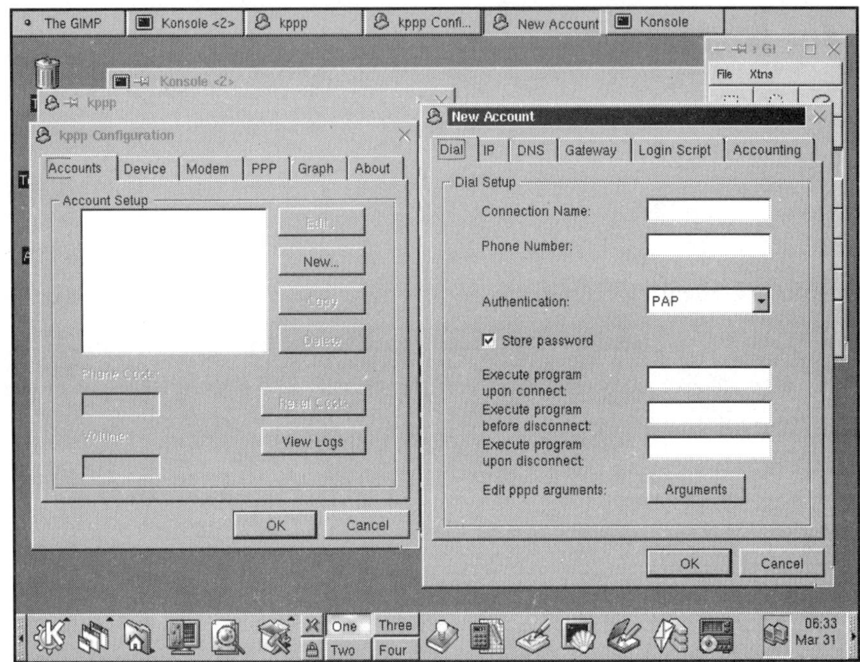

Figure 10.32 *Kppp setup*

Using KDE Utilities

KDE also includes a plethora of utilities that range from extremely useful, like the address book, Kfloppy, Tape Backup Tool, and others, to very silly utilities, such as the mouse pedometer.

You can find the KDE utilities under the main KDE Panel menu by selecting Utilities and then the utility that you'd like to use.

Summary

This chapter provides a brief overview of KDE that should allow you to get up and running. As with any new software, it might take a few days to get used to it, but once you've gotten started with KDE I believe you'll find it just as simple to use as any other GUI.

For more information on KDE or to look for new applications, go to the KDE Web site at http://www.kde.org. You'll find lots of useful background information, as well as other places you can look for help using KDE or new KDE apps or updates to KDE itself.

Chapter 11: Getting Started with GNOME

Joe "Zonker" Brockmeier

Customizing GNOME

GNOME Applications

The GNU Network Object Model Environment (GNOME) is part of the larger GNU project. (See the Introduction for a more complete history of the GNU project.) At the time that the GNOME project was created, the licensing issues behind the KDE Qt libraries meant that KDE was not completely Open Source software. Many Open Source enthusiasts felt that it was necessary to create a wholly Open Source GUI, so the GNOME project was started.

GNOME is a very advanced desktop environment, and the goals for future development in the GNOME project are even loftier than what already has been delivered. It is designed to be easily configurable and includes a large array of standard desktop tools and applications. Furthermore, GNOME's session management capabilities allow it to remember settings from one use to the next so that the desktop environment remains consistent from one session to another.

This chapter applies to the release of GNOME included with Slackware 7. Because Open Source projects are not hindered by artificial release dates or marketing schedules, it is entirely likely that there will be one or more updates in GNOME versions by the time you read this chapter. If you are using a newer version of GNOME, there might be features included with GNOME not discussed in this chapter, but the basics should remain the same. To find out if there's a newer version of GNOME available, visit http://www.gnome.org/.

If you're new to Linux and Open Source software, it might be a new idea to you that there are political issues to software as well as technical ones. Indeed, there are folks, such as Richard Stallman, who would prefer to use inferior software, or none at all, rather than proprietary software such as Windows or the Mac OS. Thus the GNOME project was created. For more on political issues of free software, be sure to read the GNU Philosophy at http://www.fsf.org/philosophy/philosophy.html.

Like many other Open Source software projects, GNOME is the work of dozens or possibly hundreds (I haven't counted) developers around the world. The leading light of the GNOME project is Miguel de Icaza. Miguel is one of the core GNOME developers, as well as the creator of Gnumeric and several other GNOME programs.

Customizing GNOME

GNOME is a flexible environment. You can customize your window manager, background, themes, how your mouse behaves, and much, much more. The default configuration of GNOME might be a bit intimidating for new users, however, so I talk about how to tame GNOME before covering using features.

GNOME Window Managers

GNOME, like KDE, is a full-scale desktop environment. Unlike KDE, however, GNOME does not come with its own window manager. GNOME works with a number of other already available window managers. GNOME works with just about any window manager, but it works best with window managers designed to take hints from GNOME. Some features of GNOME, such as the GNOME pager and session management, might not work properly with all managers.

Several window managers are at least partially GNOME-compliant. The most compatible window managers for GNOME at the time of this writing are Enlightenment, Window Maker, Sawmill, and IceWM. Under the default install of Slackware, you have the choice of Enlightenment, Window Maker, and twm. There really is no best window manager—it's pretty much a matter of personal preference. One of the nice things about Linux is that you have your choice of desktop environments, window managers, and just about everything else!

If you didn't select GNOME as the default desktop environment when you installed Slackware, but it is installed on your system, use a text editor to create a /.xinitrc file in your home directory.

1. Start up vi or your favorite Linux text editor, and name the file ~/**.xinitrc**. The (.) is important! If you leave out the period, the startx script ignores it.

2. If you currently run KDE and want to try out GNOME, enter the following lines in ~/.xinitrc:

```
#exec kde
exec gnome-session
```

3. If you have several other window managers installed, you can put each of them in the ~/.xinitrc like this:

```
#exec kde
exec gnome-session
#exec wmaker
#exec fvwm95
```

GNOME, KDE, and many window managers now support the use of themes. Although themes might mean something slightly different depending on which of the environments or window managers you are in, they basically entail the color scheme, fonts, icons, backgrounds, and sound schemes of the desktop. Using themes allows you to tailor the look and feel of Linux precisely to your liking. You can find out a lot more about themes for KDE, GNOME, Enlightenment, Window Maker, and many other window managers at http://www.themes.org. See Appendix B "Linux Resources" for more on how to make X look really pretty.

4. The number sign tells the startx script the line is a comment, not a command you want carried out. Don't leave more than one line without a comment, or it may confuse the startx script.

5. Save the file and type in **startx** to start GNOME.

Enlightenment

The first time you start GNOME, the Enlightenment window manager should be the default manager. The default Enlightenment theme, ShinyMetal (see Figure 11.1), is a bit difficult for new Linux users to get used to. (Actually, it's a bit hard to get used to for experienced users as well.) If you'd like to try one that's a little less aesthetically pleasing but is somewhat more straightforward and functional, you can use the Enlightenment Configuration Editor to switch themes.

1. To change themes in Enlightenment, or other window manager properties, under GNOME, use the toolbox icon on the GNOME panel to bring up the GNOME Control Center (see Figure 11.2).

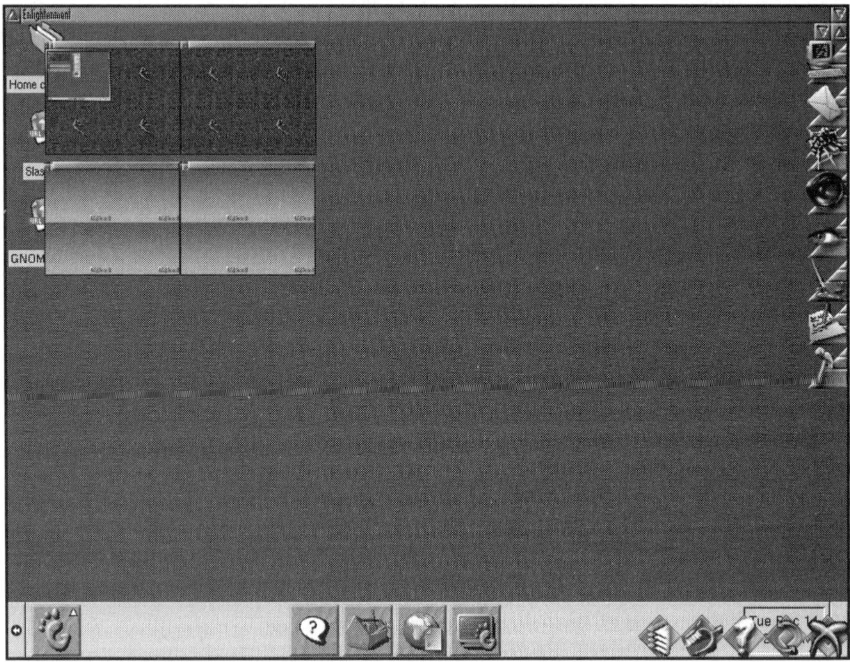

Figure 11.1 *Enlightenment's Default ShinyMetal theme*

Figure 11.2 *GNOME panel and toolbox icon*

2. Choose Window Manager from the selection list in the GNOME Control Center; the right-hand pane of the window should have a Run Configuration Tool for Enlightenment button (see Figure 11.3).

3. Click on the Run Configuration Tool for Enlightenment button, which brings up the Enlightenment Configuration Editor (see Figure 11.4).

4. Select the Themes option from the Enlightenment Configuration Editor by clicking on the Themes text in the left-hand pane of the Configuration Editor window. The ShinyMetal theme should be highlighted (see Figure 11.5).

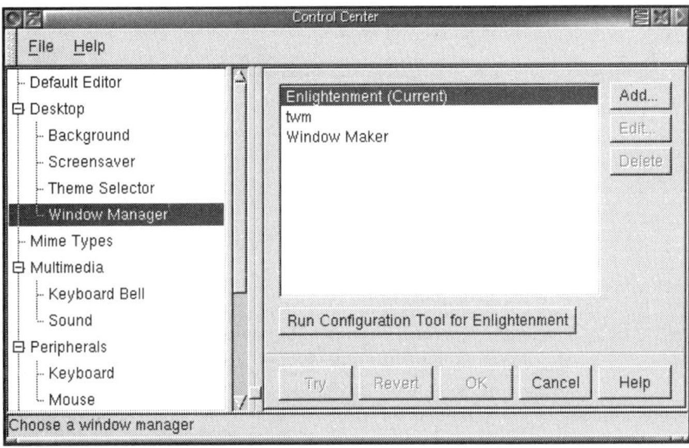

Figure 11.3 *GNOME Control Center*

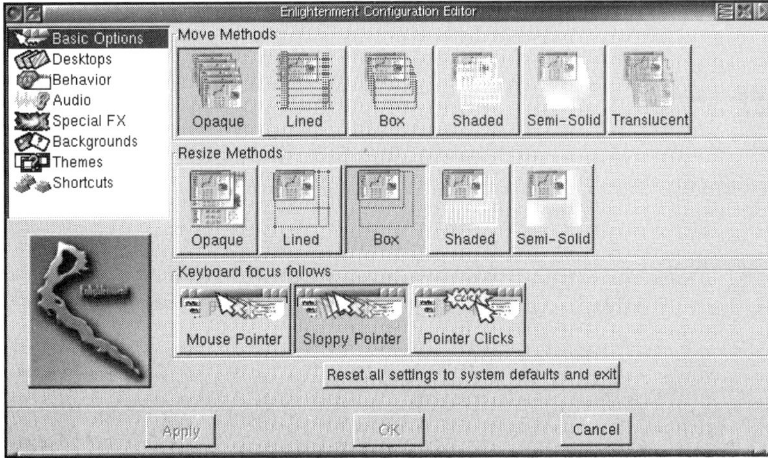

Figure 11.4 *Enlightenment Configuration Editor*

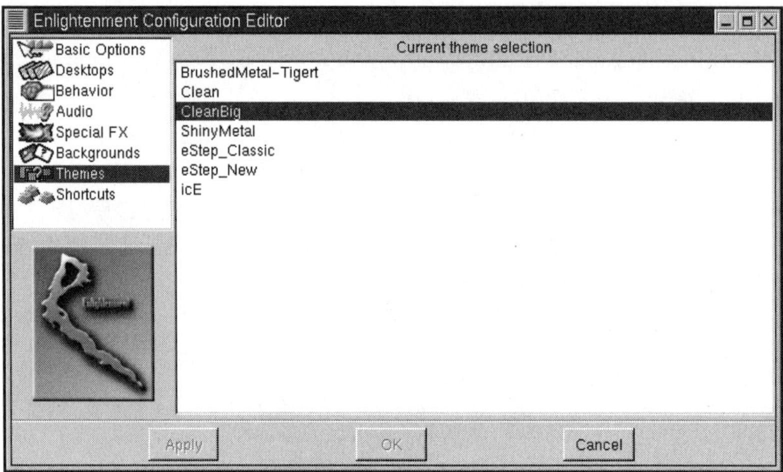

Figure 11.5 *Enlightenment Configuration Editor themes*

5. Select another theme from the Configuration Editor. The CleanBig theme is a good one to try. Click on the theme you want to work with and click Apply. You see an animated stopwatch while Enlightenment is restarting and changing themes.

> You can play with the various themes to find out which one you prefer. I find the CleanBig theme to be the most functional and easiest to use, but tastes vary.

Window Maker

Window Maker is another popular window manager that works well with the GNOME environment. Like Enlightenment, Window Maker also can be used separately from GNOME.

If you'd like GNOME to use Window Maker instead of Enlightenment, you can use the GNOME Control Center to switch from Enlightenment to Window Maker. To do this, complete the following numbered steps.

1. Choose the toolbox icon from the GNOME panel at the bottom of the screen.

2. Select Window Manager from the options on the left-hand side of the Control Center window (see Figure 11.6).

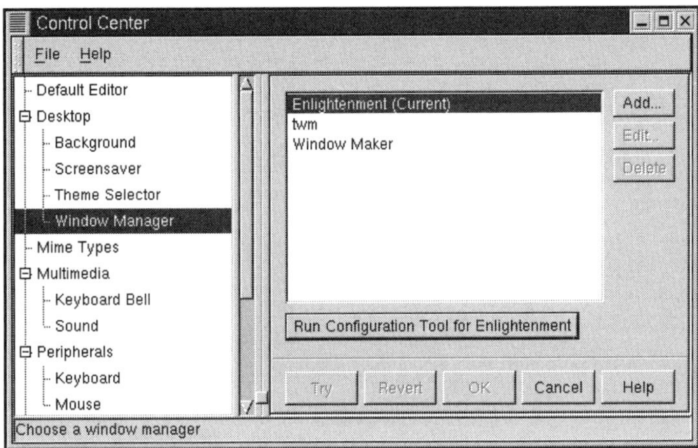

Figure 11.6 *GNOME Control Center*

3. Select Window Maker from the options on the right-hand side of the
   Control Center window. Click on the OK button below the right-hand side
   of the Control Center. Another dialog box pops up after you have changed
   your window manager, asking if you want to save the session now or save the
   session later (see Figure 11.7). It's probably best to go ahead and save your
   changes now.

The rest of the screenshots in this chapter were shot using Enlightenment. If
you are using Window Maker, what you see on your computer screen may
look different than the screenshot in the book, but GNOME should function
the same no matter which window manager is being used.

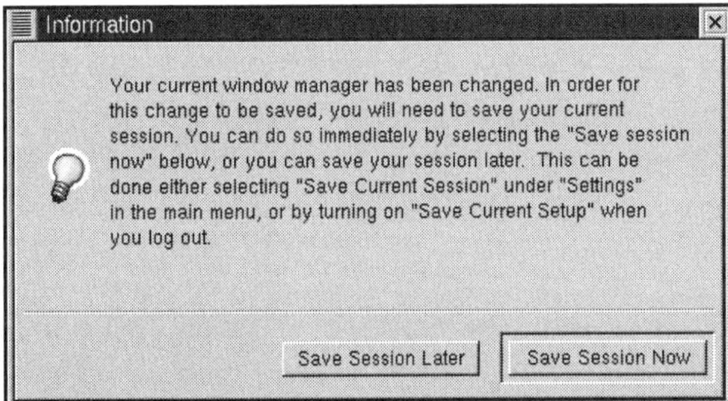

Figure 11.7 *Save Session dialog box*

GNOME Control Center

I've already touched on the GNOME Control Center in changing the default window manager. There are a number of other features the GNOME Control Center allows you to customize as well. These include the following:

- Default Editor
- Desktop
- Background
- Screensaver
- Theme Selector
- Window Manager
- Mime Types
- Multimedia
- Keyboard Bell
- Sound
- Peripherals
- Keyboard
- Mouse
- Startup Programs
- URL Handlers
- User Interface
- Applications
- Dialogs
- MDI

Choosing GNOME's Text Editor

The first selection in the Control Center is the GNOME Editor (see Figure 11.8). GNOME allows you to specify which text editor to use when applications such as the GNOME File Manager are launching a text file. The default editor is Emacs (Emacs is covered in Chapter 13), but you might wish to change this to another editor if you are not familiar with Emacs. Appendix A "A Linux Primer" covers using vi, or you could choose gEdit, the GUI text editor included with GNOME, if you're unfamiliar with vi.

Customizing GNOME's Look and Feel

GNOME has made customizing the look and feel of your Linux desktop much easier than it was in the early days of Linux. With other window managers, such as fvwm95 or twm, you had to customize nearly everything by editing text files—if you could customize at all. GNOME's Control Center allows you to quickly and easily change the background, screensaver, GNOME theme, and even your window manager, as covered earlier in this chapter.

To change the look of your desktop itself, choose Background from the left-hand side of the Control Center (see Figure 11.9).

GNOME gives you the choice between solid desktop colors, color gradients, or a wallpaper image for the desktop. Because many window managers like Enlightenment and Window Maker also allow you to configure the background, you can also tell GNOME to disable background selection so that the GNOME background doesn't override the background chosen by the window manager.

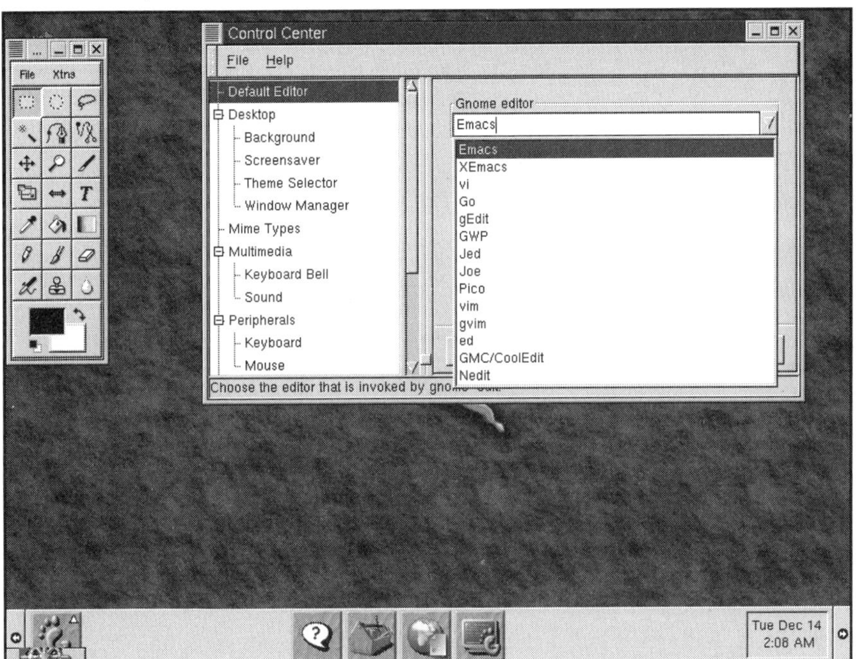

Figure 11.8 *Choose an editor.*

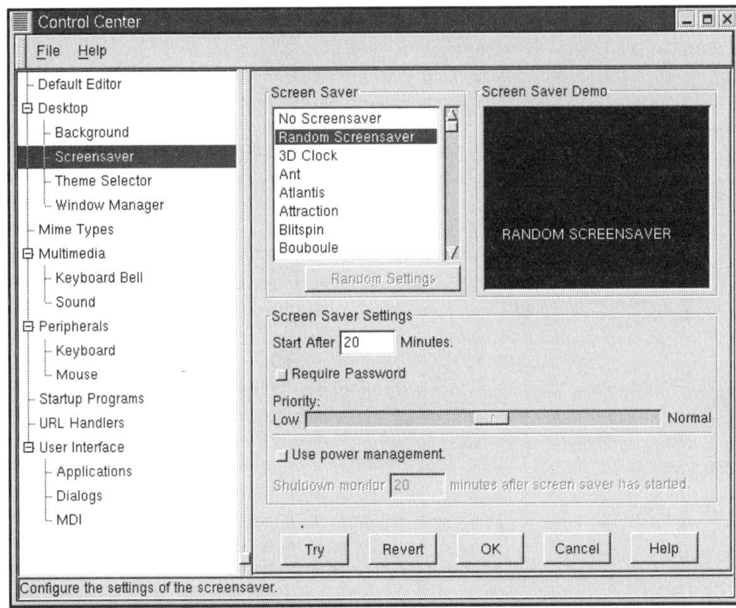

Figure 11.9 *Choose a background.*

Although most modern monitors don't really require screensavers to prevent burn-in if not left on constantly, screensavers are still a lot of fun—especially the ones that come with Linux these days. If no screensaver is selected manually, GNOME simply cycles through all of the screensavers available at random. You can also choose not to have a screensaver, or you can choose to require a password to unlock the screensaver after it begins.

NOTE

The password option is a great feature if you happen to use Linux at work or in a place where your computer is in a public area. This allows you to set the screensaver to start after two or three minutes and no one can read your screen unless they know your password. This way if you're writing a nasty email about your boss and go to lunch, you don't have to worry about him reading it off of your screen. You do still have to worry about him reading it off of the mail server, but that's another story. . . .

Buzzword

GTK stands for Gimp Tool Kit. The Gimp Tool Kit is a widget set that gives the look and feel to applications written with that set of windowing instructions. Basically, a widget set allows application programmers to use a standard tool kit to create things such as buttons, scrollbars, and other common items for a GUI environment without having to rewrite them each time. GNOME uses the GTK widget set, whereas KDE uses the Qt set.

The Theme Selector allows you to customize the look and feel of the buttons, scrollbars, check boxes, and other goodies that are drawn inside applications (see Figure 11.10). This only applies to GNOME-compliant applications that get their look and feel from the GTK tool set.

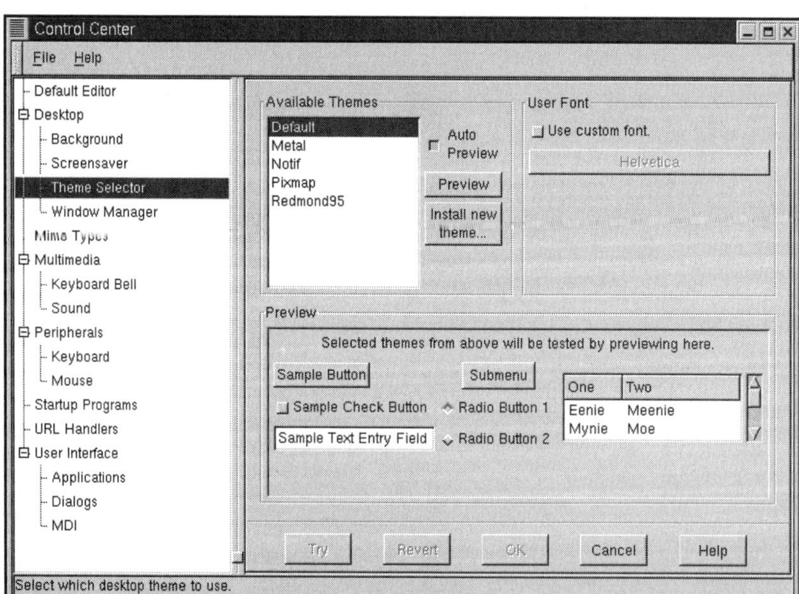

Figure 11.10 *Select a theme.*

There are a number of pre-installed themes that come with GNOME. You can also download more themes for GNOME if you don't have a theme that you really like. See Appendix B "Linux Resources" for places to find GNOME themes.

Choosing a window manager with the Control Center is covered earlier in this chapter. However, you can also add new window managers to the choices in the Control Center if there is another window manager you'd like to use with GNOME.

If you've installed another GNOME-compliant window manager, use the Add button on the right-hand side of the Control Center window to bring up the Add New Window Manager dialog box (see Figure 11.12).

Type in the name of the new window manager, the command to start the window manager, and the command to configure the window manager if it has a configuration tool. If it is GNOME-compliant, check the Window Manager in the Session Managed check box.

Session Management refers to GNOME's abilities to save your work when you exit GNOME. This only functions with GNOME compliant window managers and applications. For instance, if you exit GNOME while using Gnumeric, a GNOME application, Gnumeric reappears in the same place as you left it when you exited GNOME. However, at this time, you still have to save your data manually. It is not automatically saved when you exit GNOME, though that feature is planned for the future. GNOME cannot save the position of applications that are not GNOME-aware.

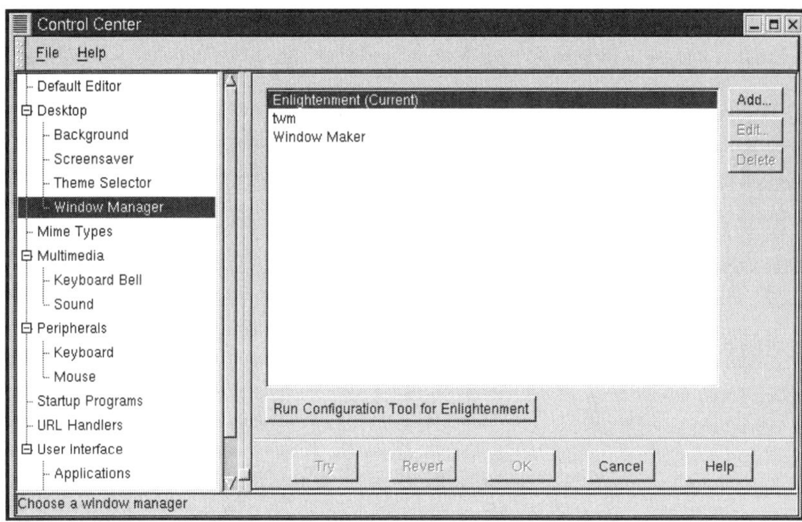

Figure 11.11 *Choose a Window Manager.*

Figure 11.12 *Add New Window Manager dialog box*

Adding a window manager for GNOME is a little beyond the scope of this book, but several other window manager Web sites can be found in Appendix B. Most GNOME-compliant window managers include instructions on how to compile the window manager with use for GNOME.

Defining Actions for File Types

GNOME's Control Center allows you to set actions based on the MIME type of a file. GNOME associates a file with its MIME type by the extension of the file. For instance, a text file typically has a .txt extension under Linux, just as it does under Windows. Such an extension gives the file a "text/plain" MIME type. This allows you to automatically start a program to edit, view, or open a file when you double-click it in the GNOME File Manager, or when you use GNOME's drag and drop capabilities.

To set the actions for a particular MIME type, click on the Edit button on the right side of the Control Center window, and enter the program you want to use to perform the action. GNOME gives you the option of selecting a different program (or no program) to open, view, and edit files. To assign actions to a particular MIME type (see Figure 11.13), follow these steps:

1. Select the MIME type/extension you want to define an action for, or add your own if the type you want to define is not listed in the MIME types available.

2. Click either the Add or Edit button, depending on whether your MIME type is already present.

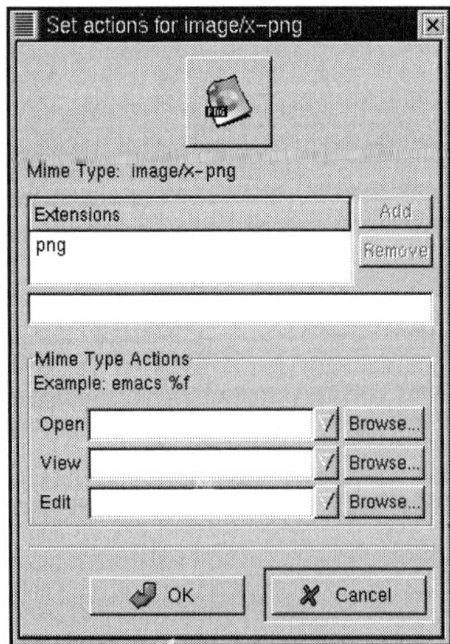

Figure 11.13 *The dialog box for setting MIME Actions.*

3. In the Set Actions for *Application* dialog box, enter the name of the program you want to use to open, view, or edit the files. GNOME requires that you append a %f to the name of the command or program you want to use. GNOME replaces the %f with the name of the file.

4. Click OK to save any changes you have made.

Configuring GNOME Sound Actions

GNOME has tools to set sound events from your PC's system speaker as well as sound generated through the sound card, if the sound card is supported under Linux. See Chapter 7, "Configuring Peripherals: Sound, Printing, and Other Services," for instructions on how to get sound working under Linux.

Regardless of whether your sound card is supported, your PC speaker should function properly as long as it is hooked up. The Control Center allows you to determine the pitch, duration, and volume of the system bell when it sounds (see Figure 11.14).

If your sound card does work with Linux, you can enable sound events under GNOME. If you haven't used this type of feature with Windows or the Mac OS before, sound events are sounds triggered by system events, such as opening a certain program, logging in (or out) of GNOME, program errors, winning or losing one of the GNOME games, button clicks, and other system events under GNOME.

To enable sounds with GNOME, be sure that the Enable Sound Server Startup check box and the Sounds for Events check box is checked in the right-hand side of the Control Center under the Sound—General tab (see Figure 11.15).

MIME is an acronym for Multi-Purpose Internet Mail Extensions. Originally used to allow exchange of data file(s) within text documents such as emails, MIME types have found widespread useage in other applications as well. GNOME uses MIME types to identify files.

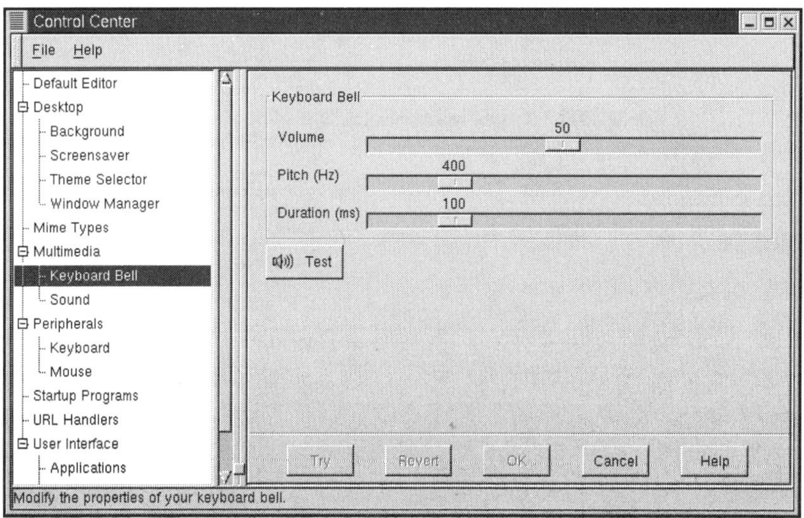

Figure 11.14 *Control Center—Configure System Bell*

The second tab under the Sound category allows you to specify what sounds to be used for predefined events under GNOME (see Figure 11.16). You can specify wave files (.wav), either the ones that GNOME comes with, or download or create your own and then use the Browse button to search for the new files.

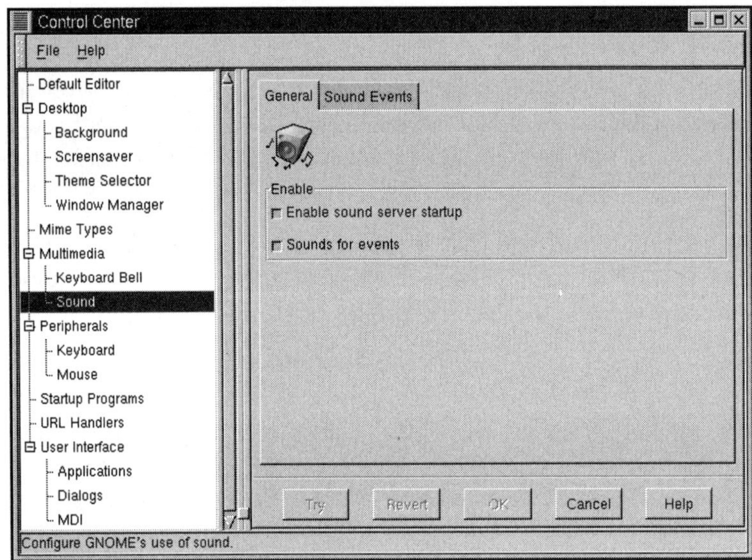

Figure 11.15 *Enable the use of sound.*

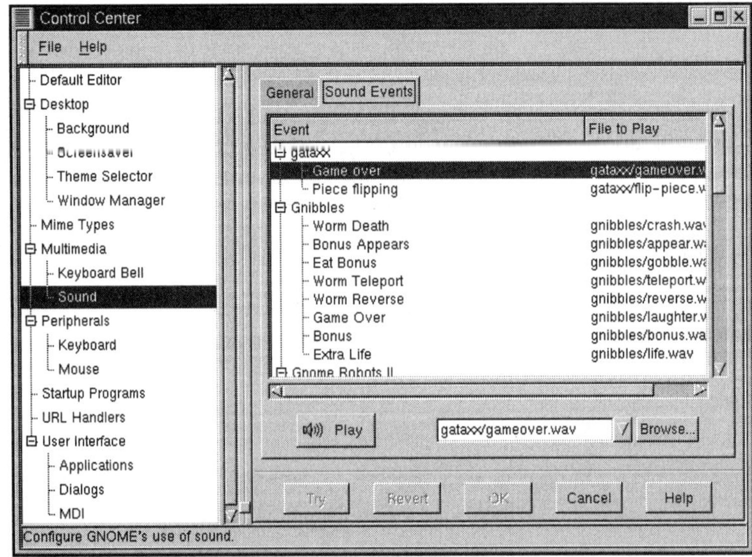

Figure 11.16 *Use sound events.*

Configuring the Keyboard and Mouse under GNOME

The GNOME Control Center also gives you some rudimentary control over the keyboard and mouse behavior under GNOME. The keyboard configuration under GNOME allows the user to specify the repeat rate of keys pressed on the keyboard and the delay between repeated keys (see Figure 11.17). This is especially handy for users who either wish to speed up key repetition when they hold down a key while they're typing or users who need to slow or disable key repetition due to physical handicaps.

Left-handed GNOMErs should be pleased to know that GNOME supports switching the bindings of mouse buttons for left-handed users. To enable left-handed bindings for the mouse, simply change the setting from right-handed to left-handed by clicking the Left Handed radio button (see Figure 11.18). GNOME also allows users to configure how fast the mouse moves in GNOME in relation to the movement of the mouse on your mouse pad.

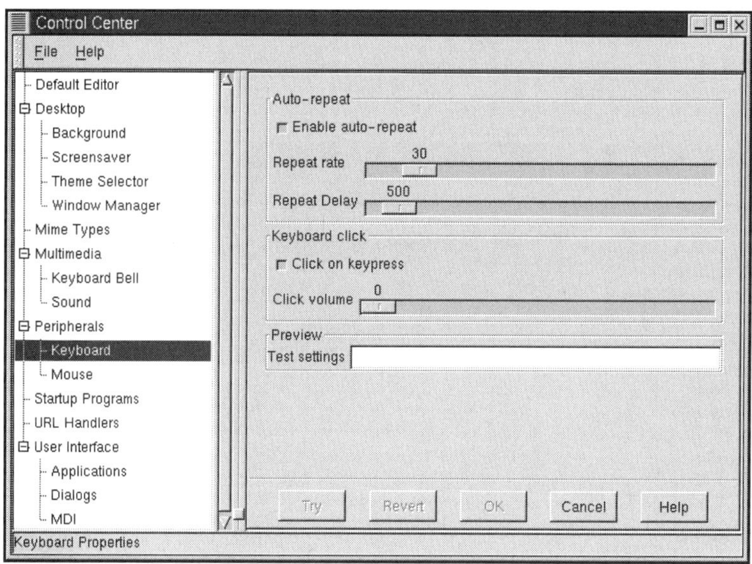

Figure 11.17 *Keyboard options*

Adding Startup Programs to GNOME

To make life a little easier, GNOME allows users to specify programs that they wish to be started whenever they begin a new GNOME session. If, for instance, you use Netscape Navigator and the Gnumeric spreadsheet program every day while you're working in GNOME, you can specify those as startup programs.

To have GNOME launch programs on startup, click on the Add button on the right-hand side of the Control Center under Startup Programs (see Figure 11.19).

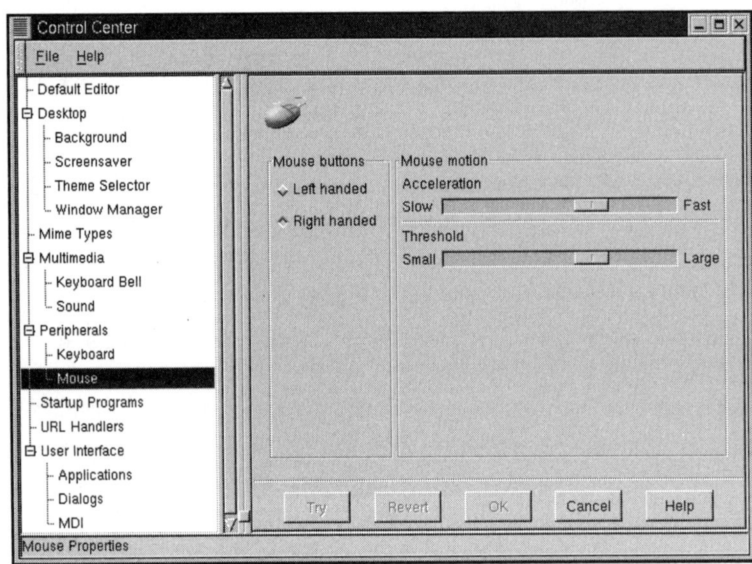

Figure 11.18 *Mouse options*

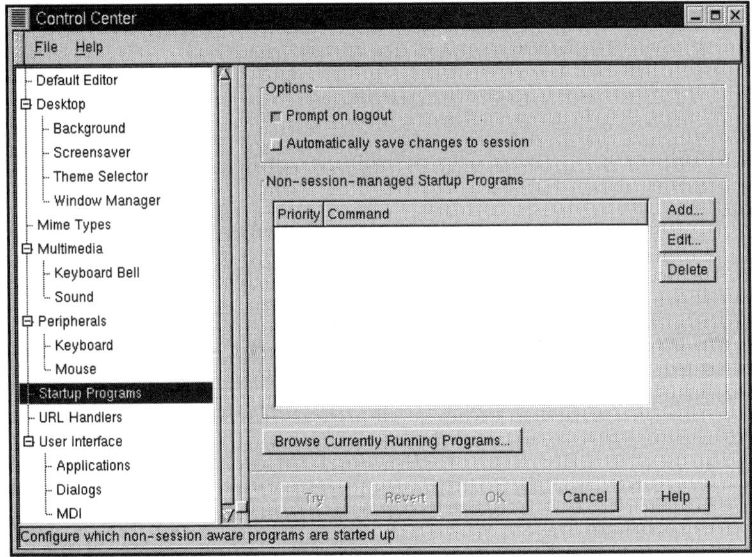

Figure 11.19 *Startup Program options*

The Add Startup Progam dialog box should come up (see Figure 11.20), and you can either type in the name of the command you want to start up automatically, or use the Browse button to search the directory structure for the command or program you want to start each time GNOME starts up.

GNOME also allows you to set the priority of each program to be started. If one application should be started before another one, set its priority number lower than the others being started automatically. If there is no need to have one application launched before another, it's probably best to leave this setting alone.

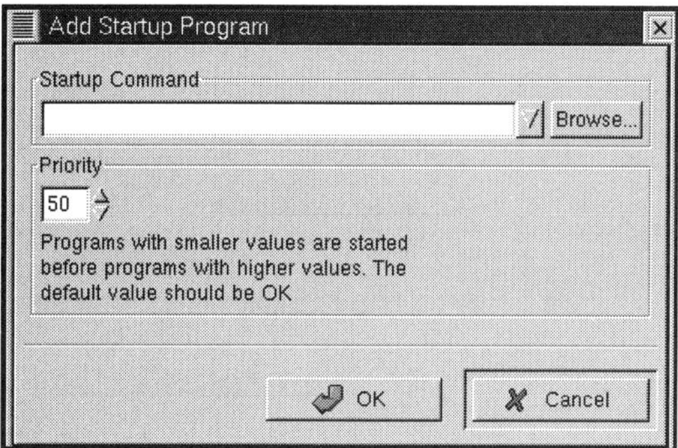

Figure 11.20 *Add a Startup Program.*

Fine-Tuning the User Interface

Under GNOME, many of the user interface issues are handled by the window manager instead of GNOME. However, GNOME does handle menus, toolbars, and dialog box interfaces.

To configure the behavior of menus, toolbars, and status bars drawn by the GTK widget set, use the Control Center's Applications panel shown in Figure 11.21.

The Dialogs panel in the Control Center allows you to configure the behavior of dialog boxes (see Figure 11.22).

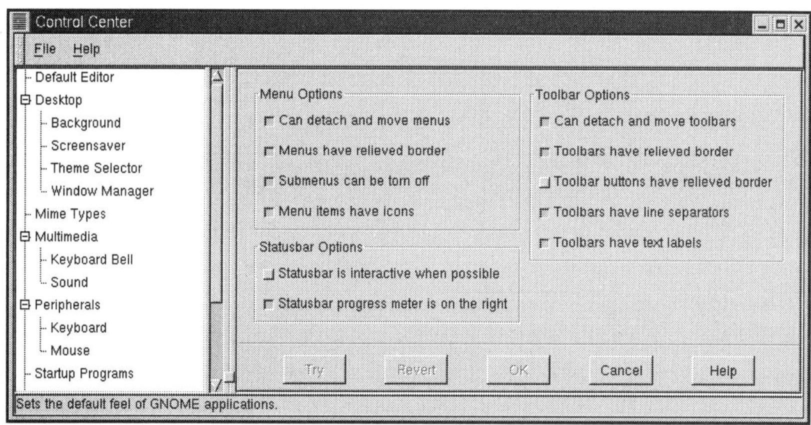

Figure 11.21 *Control Center Applications panel*

Dialog boxes are the pop-up boxes that display choices or error messages under a window manager or desktop environment. The interactive window that comes up when you select File, Open under most programs, that allows you to select a file to open, is an example of a dialog box. So is any error message that requires some input from the user to go on, even if it's just an acknowledgment that the error occurred. For example, "Click Okay to allow your computer to melt down...." Dialog boxes are a ubiquitous part of using a GUI, but they are generally not known by name.

One particularly handy option is to have GNOME position dialog boxes at the mouse cursor so that when a dialog box does pop up you can dispose or deal with it quickly.

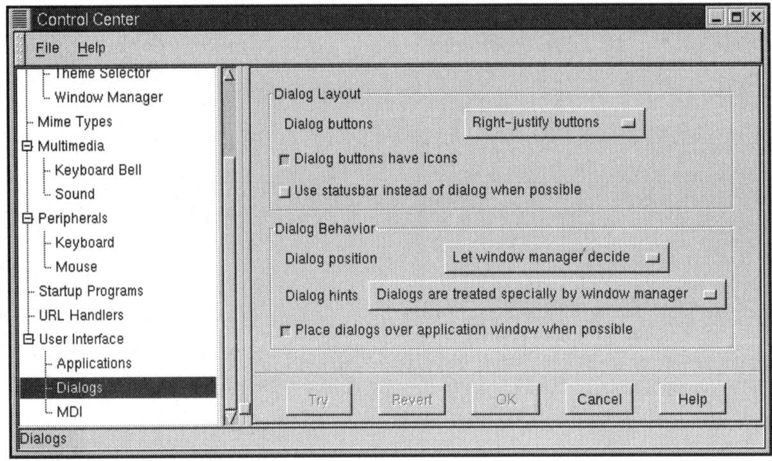

Figure 11.22 *Control Center Dialogs panel*

Using the GNOME Panel

The GNOME panel is one of the most useful parts of the GNOME desktop environment. GNOME's panel is extremely configurable. The panel allows the user to add launcher icons to the panel to start programs, menus, and swallowed applications, and to configure the position and look and feel of the panel. In fact, GNOME allows users to create new panels if they so desire.

Configuring Panel Properties

There's no way to cover all the possible panel permutations in this book without dedicating the entire contents to GNOME rather than Slackware. That being said, I try to cover most of the major configuration options available so that after finishing this section of the book you should be able to strike out on your own and configure GNOME to your heart's content.

There are two ways to bring up configuration dialog boxes for the GNOME panel. Either click the main menu, the one with the GNOME foot on it (see Figure 11.23), or right-click the panel itself (see Figure 11.24). Clicking the main menu brings up the entire menu, whereas right-clicking brings up the context menu for the panel itself.

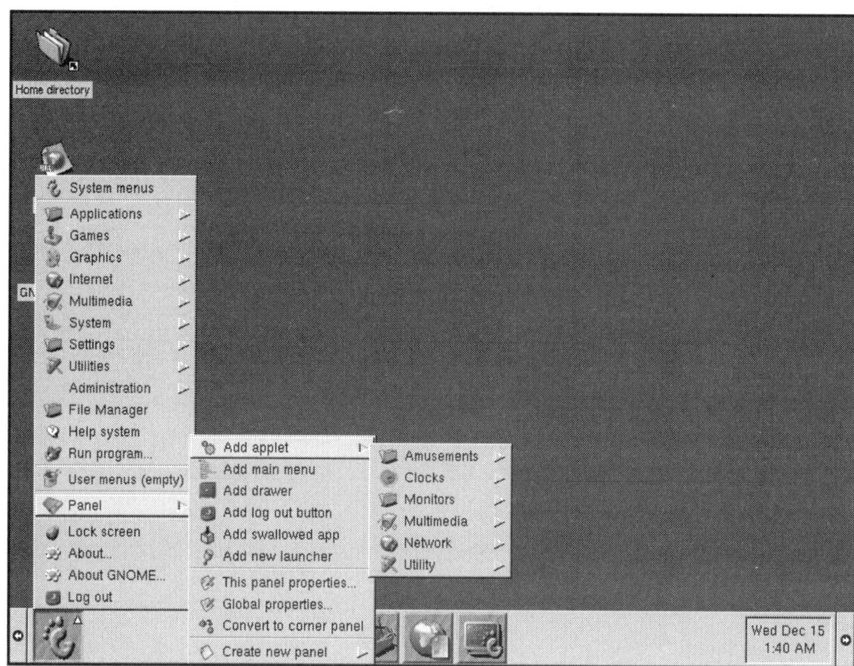

Figure 11.23 *The main GNOME panel menu*

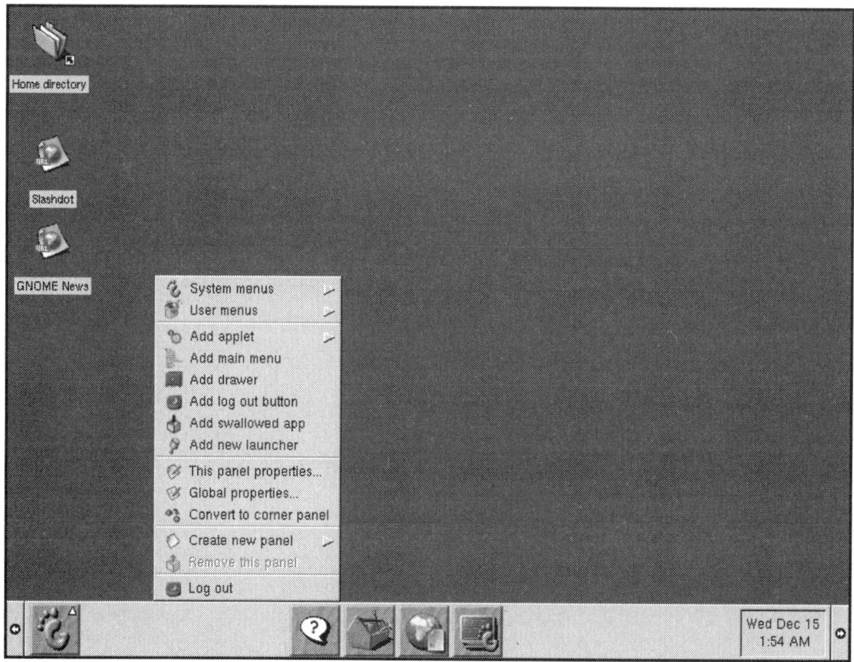

Figure 11.24 *The panel context menu*

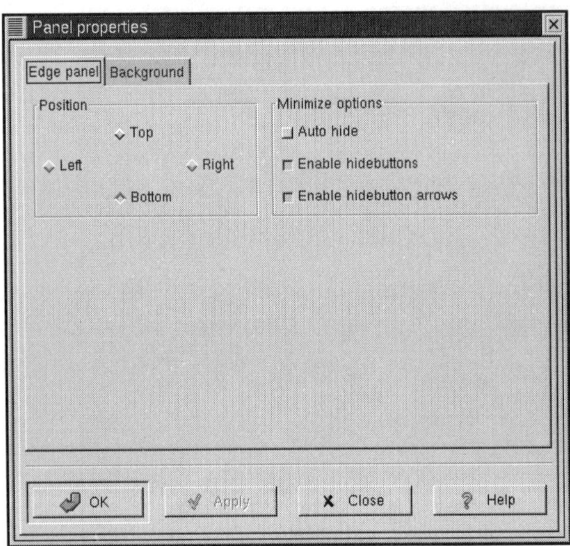

Figure 11.25 *Panel Properties dialog box*

Buzzword

A GNOME drawer is a button on a panel that can hold several GNOME launcher icons.

Whichever menu you call up, you can click on the menu item labeled This Panel Properties to begin configuring the GNOME panel to your liking.

The Panel Properties dialog box allows you to choose background and positioning for the GNOME panel (see Figure 11.25). If your desktop space is limited, you might want to enable the Auto Hide feature of the panel to get it out of the way when it is not being used.

To configure icon backgrounds, GNOME drawer behavior, and other global properties of GNOME panels, choose Global Properties from the panel context menu or main menu (see Figure 11.26). Even if you only use one GNOME panel, you need to configure icon backgrounds, animation speeds, and other features using this dialog box. Unfortunately, there is no way to configure these properties separately if you have more than one panel.

Adding Applets

The GNOME panel allows the user to have applications, or applets, embedded in the panel. There are a wide variety of applets available with GNOME, including various clocks, CPU and memory monitors, CD players, and a few very silly applets like the fish applet, which merely provides an animated fish on your panel.

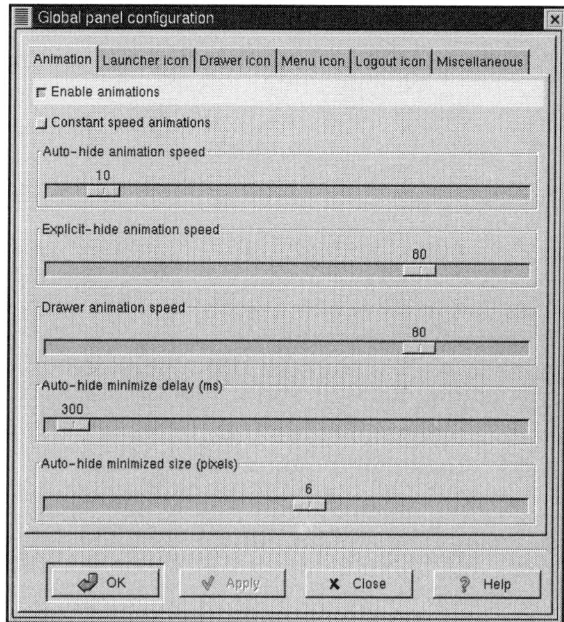

Figure 11.26 *Global Properties*

Adding an applet to the GNOME panel is very easy. To add an applet, such as the Tasklist applet, to the GNOME panel follow these steps:

1. Bring up either the main menu or the Panel context menu.
2. Select Panel, Add Applet, Utility, Tasklist from the menu (see Figure 11.27).

It's that easy! Now the applet is added to the GNOME panel and is available for you to use. GNOME applets remain on the panel until you remove them, so you don't have to re-add the applets every time you restart GNOME.

If you want to configure your applet, right-click it to bring up its context menu (see Figure 11.28). If the applet is configurable, the context menu includes a Properties menu choice. Select Properties and a dialog box appropriate for that applet pops up.

Removing Applets

All good things must come to an end, and sometimes the GNOME panel just gets too crowded. If you want to remove an applet, simply right-click it to bring up the context menu for the applet. It should have a Remove option. Click Remove from Panel, and the applet disappears from the panel unless you re-add it.

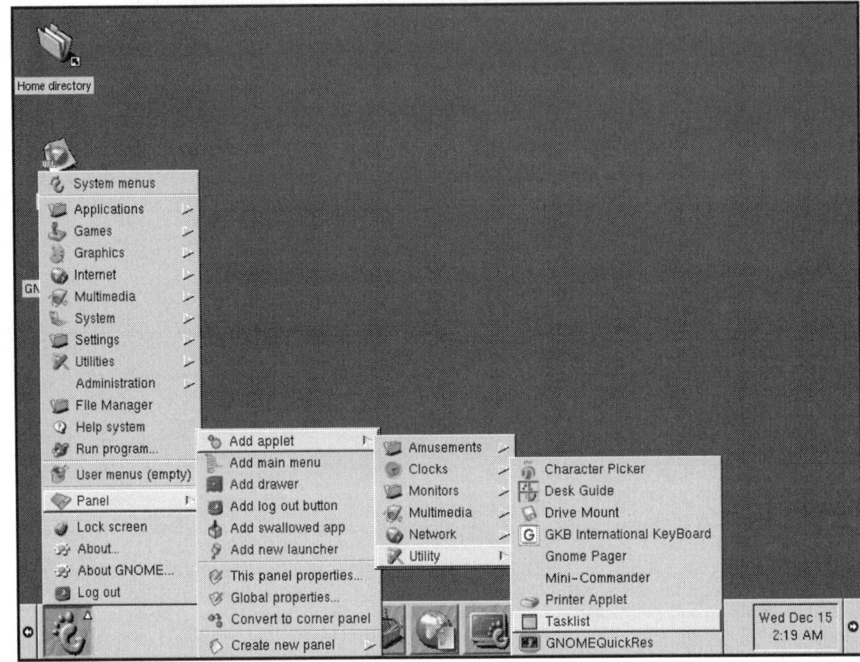

Figure 11.27 *Panel menu*

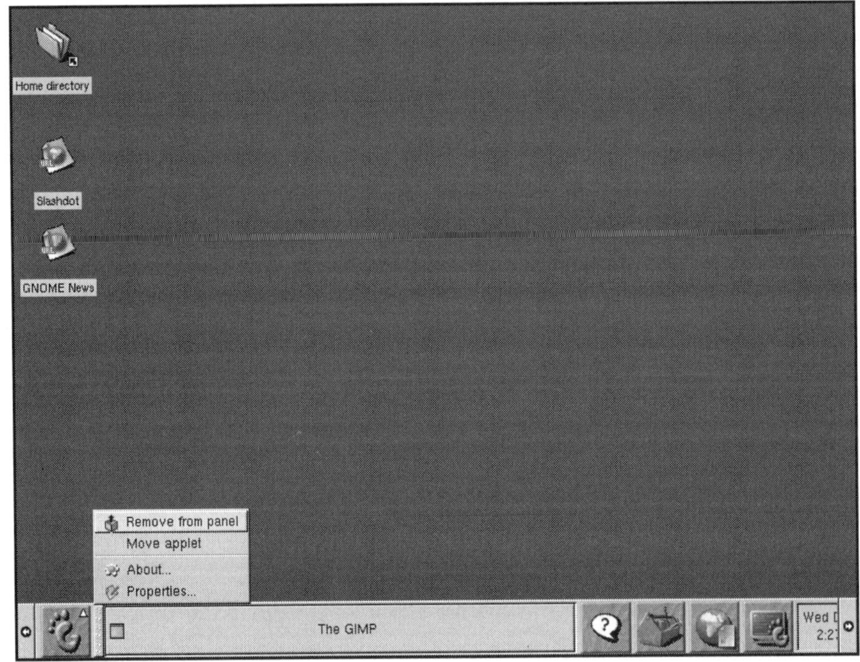

Figure 11.28 *Applet Context menu*

Adding Launchers

Often there are one or two programs you use regularly enough that you want to be able to just click an icon on the desktop or panel rather than having to hunt through the menu every time you want to use it. GNOME allows you to do this very easily.

To add a launcher to the GNOME panel, bring up the Panel context menu and choose the Add New Launcher menu item. You can add a launcher to the GNOME desktop by right-clicking on the desktop and selecting the New and then Launcher menu items from the desktop context menu.

Whether you start from the panel or the desktop, the Create Launcher Applet dialog box appears (see Figure 11.29). The Create launcher dialog allows you to enter a name, comment, and the name of the command or directory you want launched when the applet is used. To select an icon for the program, click the no icon button under the basic tab of the Create Launcher Applet dialog box. If your application is a console program, be sure to check the Run in Terminal check box.

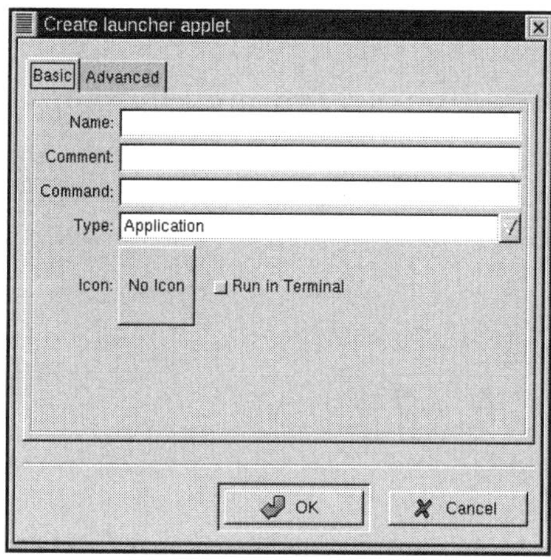

Figure 11.29 *Create new launcher*

GNOME Applications

As a full-featured desktop environment, GNOME comes with a bevy of useful applications and a fair number of games as well. Most of the programs included on the GNOME menu are GNOME-aware programs, meaning they were designed to work with GNOME, use the GTK widget set, and are session-managed by GNOME. That doesn't mean that KDE applications or basic X or console applications in terminal windows don't run just as well under GNOME, but they don't benefit from GNOME's session management, and they might look a bit different from other applications. That doesn't mean they don't run just fine, however.

Although there isn't room to include a complete user's guide to all of the GNOME applications, I describe a few of the more popular GNOME programs.

Gnumeric

Gnumeric is writen by Miguel de Icaza, the same guy who heads up the GNOME project. Gnumeric is a world-class spreadsheet program (see Figure 11.30) that has gotten rave reviews.

Gnumeric is still in development, but it is a stable program. There are a few features that are unimplemented, but from what I've been told there are a number of people using Gnumeric as their main spreadsheet program.

GNOME Calendar

If you're like I am, and I hope you're not, you rely on To Do lists and appointment books to run your life. This is fine, until the appointment books and To Do lists need other To Do lists and appointment books just to keep them straight. Happily, there are now electronic organizers capable of managing an incredible amount of information and even automatically generating alarms to remind you of important events.

The GNOME Calendar is a great personal information minder that handles To Do lists, appointments, and even sets alarms and sends reminder e-mails as well (see Figure 11.31). You can't beat the cost, either.

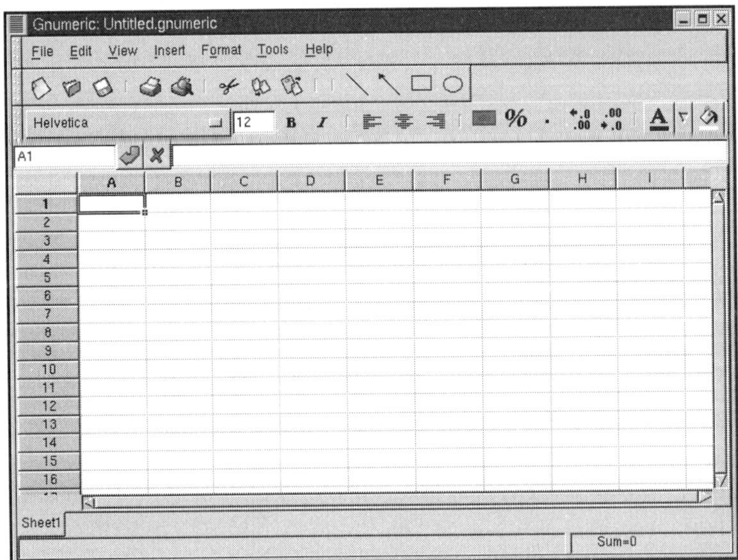

Figure 11.30 *Gnumeric*

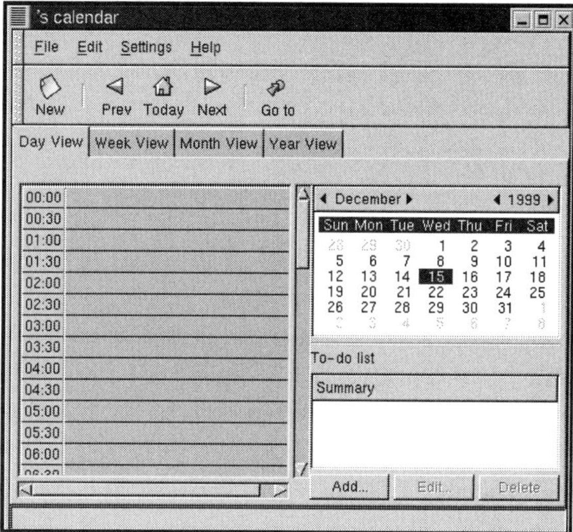

Figure 11.31 *GNOME Calendar*

GNU Midnight Commander

GNOME's file manager is a revved up version of the GNU Midnight Commander, a console application (see Figure 11.32). The GNOME File Manager is similar to the Windows Explorer or the Macintosh Finder applications, except that the GNOME File Manager is a bit more powerful. The Midnight Commander File Manager really makes life easy for Linux newbies by providing an unintimidating GUI interface for the Linux file system.

The Midnight Commander allows for several different views of the file system. These include an icon-only view, a detailed view that includes the full name of the file, file size, and last time the file was accessed, and a custom view that allows you to specify the information you want to see about the files.

The Midnight Commander also includes a file find utility and allows you to copy and move files from place to place without having to memorize the command-line equivalents.

GNOME Help System

Although this chapter tries to cover the major issues you encounter when using GNOME, it cannot cover them all. The GNOME help system (see Figure 11.33) is invaluable for figuring out how to use GNOME. Because GNOME is a free project, the documentation might not always be completely up-to-date. The GNOME project, along with most Open Source projects, tends to lag in documentation. However, the majority of the help system is in place and very well organized.

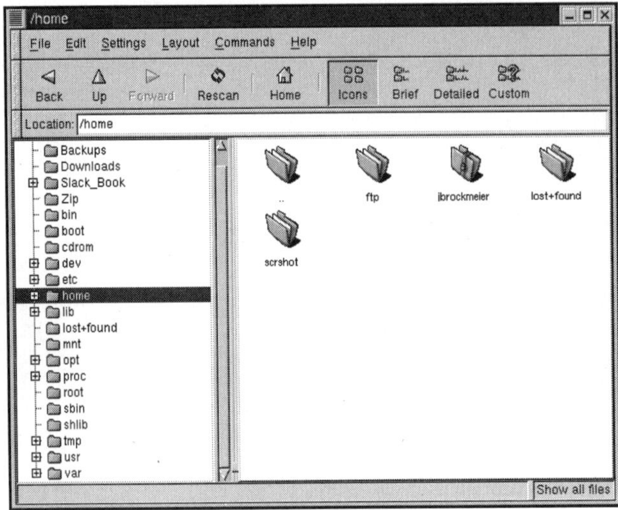

Figure 11.32 *GNU Midnight Commander*

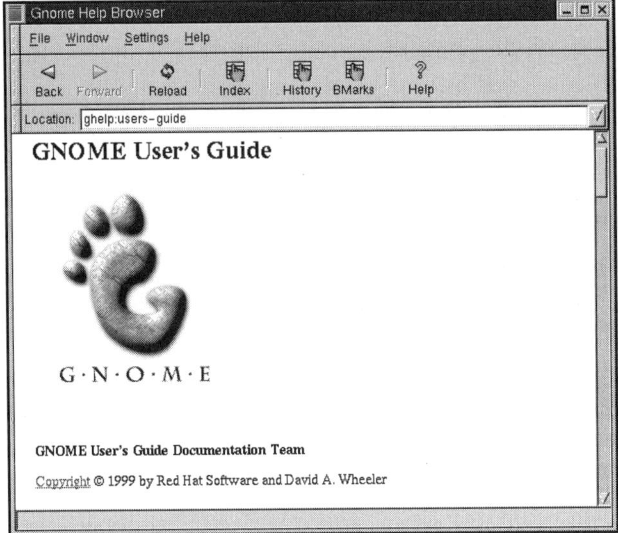

Figure 11.33 *GNOME Help System*

Summary

The GNOME desktop environment is very user-friendly. Usually someone familiar with GUI environments can start using GNOME effectively within minutes. However, fully exploring GNOME and benefiting from all of its features might take a little more time. This chapter is intended to cover the basics of GNOME to allow you to get up and running right away. For more GNOME resources, check out Appendix B.

Charles Coffing

Chapter 12: New Directions

Locating and Installing Applications

Light Office Work

Network and Network Security

Multimedia

y now you've (I hope) gotten your Slackware system installed and configured to your satisfaction. If you are using Slackware as a server, perhaps it is already up and serving files and Web pages. For users of Slackware on the desktop, you've almost certainly acquainted yourself with the command line and found a favorite desktop environment. But however you plan to use Slackware, you might have already wondered what the next step is after you finish this book. What programs are available to help you get the most out of Linux?

Slackware ships with many useful tools and applications, but don't limit yourself to your Slackware CD-ROM or FTP site. The world of Linux extends far beyond your current installation. In this chapter I hope to acquaint you with some of the software gems you might want to use in any of three scenarios: light office work, networking and network security, and multimedia. Linux (and UNIX in general) is well-known for its networking software, but the software in the other two categories might surprise you. On the whole, I hope this chapter helps you get more out of your Linux installation, whether it is in your home, office, or a server room.

Locating and Installing Applications

The list of software I present here is by no means comprehensive. It is simply a set of very useful open-source programs that you owe it to yourself to have a look at. Also remember that there are other possible solutions—Linux is gaining a number of commercial backers. For example, the commercial choices you have among office suites and games are currently blossoming. You can pick up commercial software from a number of companies by browsing the links at http://linux.com/links/ Business/Companies/Vendors. Locating open-source software is done best when you go to one of the application indices available on the Web.

Application Indices

My top picks in this chapter might not be yours. To do your own exploring among the many available Linux applications, visit one of the several Web sites dedicated to cataloging open-source programs. Considering the constantly shifting landscape of the Internet, you might want to start your search at one of the main Linux sites, such as http://www.linux.com or http://www.linux.org. Otherwise, here are some of the most popular application sites:

- **http://freshmeat.net.** The defacto open-source application catalog
- **http://appwatch.com.** A site with a focus similar to freshmeat.net
- **http://happypenguin.org.** A catalog of Linux games

I give home pages for applications only when it seems likely that the page will not move soon. Otherwise, I suggest that you look up the application on one of the above master sites; this should give you the current home page.

Library Issues

The home pages for most applications allow you to download source code. When you are dealing with applications not specifically bundled with Slackware, it's usually best to download the source code and compile it yourself. Chapter 9, "System Upkeep: Administering Your System," explains how to compile and install software from source. As long as you already have the required libraries installed, it's usually quite straightforward.

Sometimes sites also offer precompiled, binary versions of the software so that you don't have to compile it yourself. Chapter 9 also explains how to install these binaries onto your system, even if the program is packaged as an RPM. These binaries should work on your system if they were compiled with the same versions of libraries as you have on your Slackware system. Sometimes, though, things aren't so simple.

If you try to run a precompiled binary and get an error such as this,

```
Segmentation fault
```

or this,

```
gnucash: error in loading shared libraries: libguile.so.4: cannot open shared
object file: No such file or directory
```

there is probably a library problem. The first error message might indicate that the version of the library installed on your system does not quite match the version the program expects. (It also might simply mean the program has a bug.) The second error means you do not have the correct library installed at all.

To decide what library (if any) is causing the error, run the *ldd* command on your binary. It examines the binary and lists all libraries that it requires. If you are missing a library, *ldd* tells you what version you need. For the previous error involving *Gnu-Cash*, here is a sample invocation of *ldd*:

```
ldd `which gnucash`
```

Here's the response:

```
libreadline.so.3 => /lib/libreadline.so.3 (0x4001f000)
libpng.so.2 => /usr/lib/libpng.so.2 (0x40043000)
libjpeg.so.62 => /usr/lib/libjpeg.so.62 (0x40062000)
libz.so.1 => /usr/lib/libz.so.1 (0x40080000)
libm.so.6 => /lib/libm.so.6 (0x40090000)
libXext.so.6 => /usr/X11R6/lib/libXext.so.6 (0x40438000)
libX11.so.6 => /usr/X11R6/lib/libX11.so.6 (0x40445000)
libguile.so.4 => not found
libstdc++-libc6.1-2.so.3 => /usr/lib/libstdc++-libc6.1-2.so.3 (0x4064e000)
/lib/ld-linux.so.2 => /lib/ld-linux.so.2 (0x40000000)
```

Your output will be longer; I removed a number of lines to save space. On the left side of the arrow (=>) is the library required by the binary. The actual file that this maps to on disk is listed to the right of the arrow. Notice that for `libguile.so.4`, no library was found. If the needed version of the library ships with Slackware, install it and try running your new program again.

It's quite easy to figure out if a particular library ships with Slackware, because libraries tend to come in packages with similar names. For example, it's logical to expect to find the Guile library in a package called *guile* or *libguile*.

Even with all the directories on the Slackware CD-ROM, you can quickly find all packages with names similar to what you want. Be sure your CD-ROM is mounted, and then try this command:

```
find /cdrom -name "*guile*.tgz"
```

Of course, you should replace `guile` with the name of the library you're looking for. In this example, the command returned a match:

```
/cdrom/slakware/gtk1/guile.tgz
```

I installed this package to get the library. Usually this is good enough, but not always, as you discover if you keep reading.

In this example, though, I was not so lucky. Slackware does not include the necessary /libguile.so.4 file—it includes a newer version, as I discovered when I ran the following command:

```
ls -l /usr/lib/libguile*
```

Here was the output:

```
lrwxrwxrwx   1 root     root            17 Jul 28  1999 /usr/lib/libguile.so.5 ->
libguile.so.5.0.0
-rwxr-xr-x   1 root     root        542286 Sep 25  1999 /usr/lib/libguile.so.5.0.0
```

You need to do a little legwork of your own when this happens. At this point, you either need to find the required version of the library (either source or binary) and install it, or to recompile the offending program on your system so that it uses your installed version of the library.

Light Office Work

The first class of software I discuss consists of those programs that help with light office work. This includes tasks such as word processing, manipulating spreadsheets, setting appointments, and tracking finances. Don't let my terminology alienate you if you are a home user—this class of software can be useful both in an office and at home.

Office Suites

One thing Linux needed before most people would find it useful on the desktop was a good office suite. Numerous commercial office suites are now available, and open-source suites are starting to appear also. Here are the two open-source endeavors that I think have the most potential.

KOffice

URL: http://koffice.kde.org

Summary: Comprehensive and integrated office suite.

Pros: Many applications that work together.

Cons: Requires new KDE libraries. Still in development.

KOffice is a comprehensive office suite developed to take advantage of KDE's underlying object-embedding technology. KOffice includes a word processor, spreadsheet, database, presentation program, charting program, mathematical formula writing program, and more (see Figure 12.1). Elements from one program can be embedded in another very easily. The developers of KOffice are also working to allow Microsoft Office files (Word, Excel, and PowerPoint) to be imported.

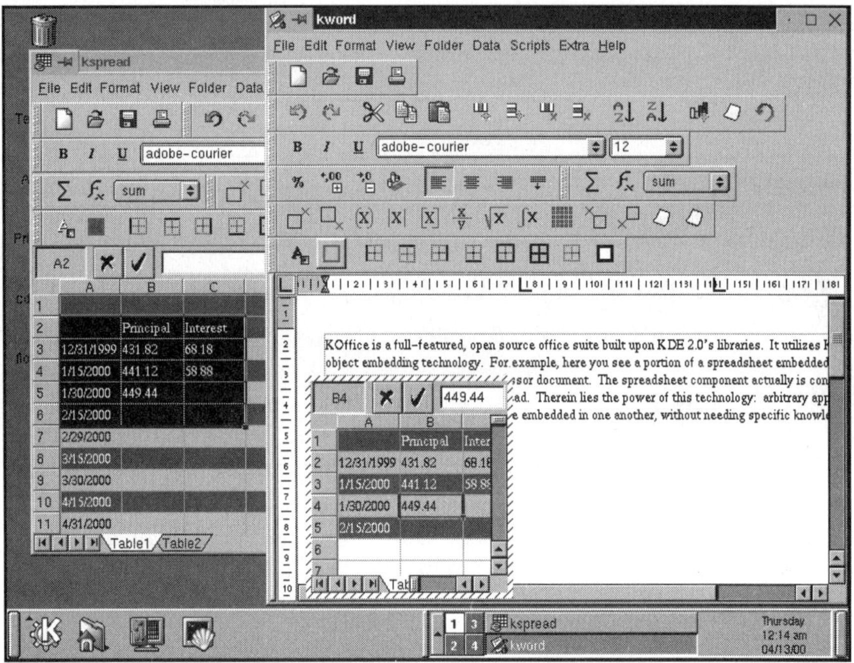

Figure 12.1 KSpread *and* KWord *are components of the KOffice suite.*

Installing KOffice

You don't need to use KDE to use KOffice; you just need to have the KDE libraries installed. However, there is one trick: KOffice requires the libraries from the upcoming KDE version 2, whereas Slackware 7 ships with KDE version 1.1.2. When KDE 2 is released, Slackware will likely include it.

Although some users find KOffice to currently be very usable, you should realize that until KDE and KOffice are officially dubbed version 2.0 and 1.0, respectively, they might have some severe bugs. KOffice covers exciting new ground, but you should exercise caution while it is still in beta.

Until KDE 2 is released, you can get the latest versions of KOffice and the needed KDE 2.*x* and Qt 2.*x* libraries from the binary download section of either http://koffice.kde.org or http://www.kde.org. You should get the kdebase, kdelibs, kdesupport, and Qt packages. Unless you are experienced with compiling very large programs, this is one time that downloading the binary snapshots, rather than source, is probably the easiest and best solution. Table 12.1 shows the libraries required for the KOffice Suite.

Table 12.1 Libraries Required for the KOffice Suite

Library	Optional?	Slackware Package	Purpose
Qt 2.x	No	N/A	GUI
KDE 2.x	No	N/A. Get kdebase, kdelibs, and kdesupport instead.	GUI

Slackware puts the KDE 1.*x* installation in /opt/kde, so pattern your installation after that by placing the new KDE libraries in /opt/kde2. (The tar files might already have this structure; if not, untar the libraries to a temporary location and rename or move the kde directory to /opt/kde2.) As a sanity check, you should end up with these subdirectories in /opt/kde2:

```
bin  include  lib  man  share
```

The Qt package tends to have many files. Some are header files; others are sample code. Unless you are compiling KOffice from source yourself, you only care about one file among all: the actual Qt library. Feel free to unpack the Qt package, move the library in with the other KDE libraries, and then remove everything else like this:

```
cd /tmp
tar -zxvf qt-2.1.0.tar.gz
ls qt/lib/
su
mv qt/lib/qt-2.1.0.so /opt/kde2/lib/
exit
rm -rf qt/
```

Now you are ready to actually install KOffice. As with the KDE libraries, KOffice probably untars to /opt/kde2, but if not, you need to untar it to a temporary directory and then copy the files on top of /opt/kde2.

As a final step, you need to add the /opt/kde2 directory to both your regular path and your library path. You could modify it just for your user, but here I show modifying it globally. Add the line

```
/opt/kde2/lib
```

to /etc/ld.so.conf, after the existing KDE line. After saving the file, run *ldconfig* as root to ensure that all links are correctly set for the libraries. Then you need to add **/opt/kde2/bin** to your path, after the /opt/kde/bin path. Remember that other programs can add to the path through scripts they have put in the /etc/profile.d/ directory. This is how KDE 1.1.2 sets its path. To ensure the KDE 2.*x* path is searched later, put this line at the very end of /etc/profile:

```
export PATH=$PATH:/opt/kde2/bin
```

You can now browse the /opt/kde2/bin directory for the KOffice programs by running the following command:

```
ls /opt/kde2/bin/
```

These are the new programs I have installed:

```
example  kgraph        kimage      kpresenter  kspread
kchart   killustrator  kimageshop  kscript     kword
```

As a bonus, if you install all of KDE 2.*x*, switching between KDE 1.*x* and 2.*x* is as simple as changing the relative ordering of /opt/kde and /opt/kde2 in /etc/ld.so.conf and /etc/profile.

AbiSuite

URL: http://www.abisource.com
Summary: Cross-platform office suite.
Pros: Very small and fast. Program and documents are cross-platform.
Cons: Currently only has a word processor.

AbiSuite is another office suite in development for Linux. AbiSuite, however, has rather different goals than KOffice. Whereas KOffice gains nice features such as object embedding by using KDE's libraries, AbiSuite focuses instead on being small, fast, and cross-platform. This means you can use AbiSuite and AbiSuite documents regardless of your operating system. Windows, BeOS, Linux, and other UNIX variations are all supported. Furthermore, there is a lot to be said for small, efficient programs. In the office suite arena, this seems to be a lost art. Because of these things, AbiSuite certainly deserves a look.

Referring to AbiSuite as an office suite is currently a misnomer. Developing a full suite is the intention, but for now the *AbiWord* word processor (see Figure 12.2) is

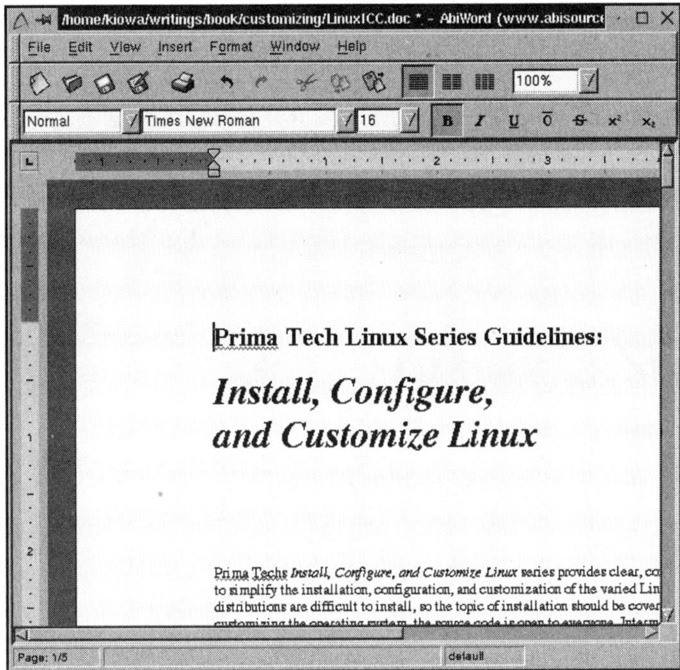

Figure 12.2 *The* AbiWord *word processor*

the only component available. A spreadsheet is in the planning stages, perhaps to be based on an existing GNOME program.

AbiWord is a basic but fully functional word processor. Beyond the standard formatting options, it supports multiple columns and can insert pictures. It also can check the spelling of words as they are typed. *AbiWord* imports Microsoft Word 97, Rich Text Format, and plain-text documents and can export files as Rich Text Format, HTML, and LaTeX. One nice feature is that it can transparently compress its files when it saves them. If you generate lots of documents or are short on disk space, you'll appreciate this feature.

Installing AbiSuite

You can download the source and binaries for a variety of operating systems and hardware types from http://www.abisource.com. AbiSource does a good job of compiling and packaging its software for a number of Linux distributions, so you don't need to compile it yourself unless you want to. Here I assume you are installing the binary, although the library discussion is applicable to the source distribution, also.

When downloading a binary version, you have the choice between statically linked and dynamically linked versions. The dynamic version is smaller because it depends on libraries installed on your system. The static version is an all-in-one program. Because of this, it works regardless of what libraries you do (or don't) have installed, but on the down side, it's larger.

If you download the dynamic binary, you need to ensure you have a number of libraries installed. *AbiWord* depends on the libpng, zlib, and gtkglib packages. Table 12.2 shows the libraries required for the AbiSource Suite.

Table 12.2 Libraries Required for the AbiSource Suite

Library	Optional?	Slackware Package	Purpose
GTK, glib	No	slakware/gtk1/gtkglib.tgz	GUI
PNG	No	slakware/d1/libpng.tgz	Image drawing
Zlib	No	slakware/d1/zlib.tgz	Compression for saved files

The AbiSource Web site has good installation instructions, but these steps should be enough to get you started. The first thing you should do is unpack the *AbiWord* distribution in a temporary directory, because you have to run an installation program that's inside the tar file. You might want to unpack it in the /tmp directory like this:

```
cd /tmp
tar -zxvf abisuite-0.7.8-Linux_i386_dynamic.tar.gz
```

Once it has uncompressed, change into the new directory and run the installation program. You probably want to run it as root so that you can install it into a system directory

```
cd abisuite-0.7.8-Linux_i386_dynamic
./install.sh
```

The installation program guided you. Once it's installed, type **abiword** to start it, and enjoy!

Personal Information Manager

If you're anything like me, you have a ragtag address book with a hundred or so names in it. Appointments and to-do lists get jotted on a piece of paper or in a text file on the computer—whichever is handiest at the moment. A personal information manager, or PIM, could certainly help both of us out. Here are some of my favorites in this category.

GnomeCard

> **URL:** http://www.gnome.org/applist
>
> **Summary:** Address book.
>
> **Pros:** Supports the *vCard* standard. Allows multiple versions of the contact information per person.
>
> **Cons:** Some bugs in the version shipped with Slackware. Compile and install the latest instead.

This little utility is simple, but it does its job well. *GnomeCard* (see Figure 12.3) touts itself as a business card organizer, although I happily use it for my entire address book, both personal and business. It handles all the usual information such as name, address, contact information, and extra comments. One of the most notable features, however, is that it allows multiple addresses, phone numbers, and email addresses to be attached to each person. Also, *GnomeCard* saves its data in the standard *vCard* format, so you should be able to easily share data with other *vCard*-capable address books and mail programs.

Figure 12.3 GnomeCard *address book*

Installing *GnomeCard*

GnomeCard is included with Slackware in the gnome-pim package. However, *GnomeCard* versions as recent as 1.1.5 seem to have several bugs when adding new cards, so you might want to compile it yourself to pick up the latest bug fixes. Browse the software map at http://www.gnome.org to get the source code. Table 12.3 shows the libraries required for *GnomeCard*.

Table 12.3 Libraries Required for *GnomeCard*

Library	Optional?	Slackware Package	Purpose
GTK, glib	No	slakware/gtk1/gtkglib.tgz	GUI
Gnome core	No	slakware/gtk1/gnomlibs.tgz	GUI
Audiofile	Yes	slakware/gtk1/audiofil.tgz	Sound for alarms, for associated PIM programs

Compilation of *GnomeCard* closely follows the method presented in Chapter 9. If the *GnomeCard* source was bundled with other PIM software such as *GnomeCal*, you might need the audiofile library installed so that it compiles.

KOrganizer

URL: http://devel-home.kde.org/~korganiz/

Summary: Calendar and scheduling program.

Pros: Supports *vCalendar* standard. Well written, it includes drag and drop support.

KOrganizer (see Figure 12.4) is a complete calendar and appointment-scheduling program. Some of the nice features include prioritized to-do lists and dragable appointments. It supports the *vCalendar* standard, so you can easily move your data to or from other scheduling programs.

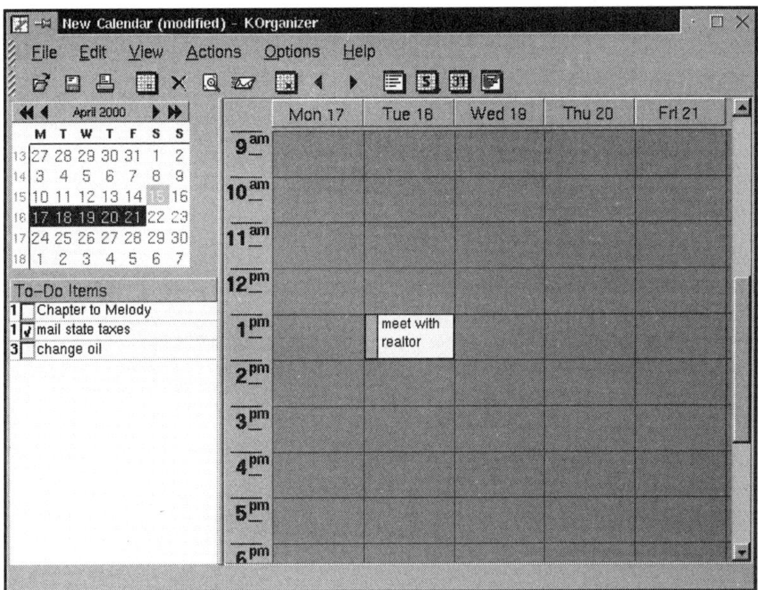

Figure 12.4 *The* KOrganizer *calendar and appointment scheduler*

Installing *KOrganizer*

Like *GnomeCard*, *KOrganizer* is also included in Slackware. To use this version you need to install the *KOrganizer* package, along with the libraries listed in Table 12.4.

Table 12.4 Libraries Required for the *KOrganizer*

Library	Optional?	Slackware Package	Purpose
Qt	No	slakware/kde1/qt_1_44.tgz	GUI
KDE libraries	No	slakware/kde1/kdelibs.tgz	GUI

The version of *KOrganizer* included with Slackware 7 is fully functional, but if you later want to build a more current version from the sources yourself, look at http://devel-home.kde.org/~korganiz/. The compilation and installation sequence is the standard one presented in Chapter 9.

KPilot

URL: Search for "kpilot" on http://freshmeat.net.
Summary: Synchronize a Palm Pilot with Linux.
Pros: Simple to use. Potential support for other PDAs.

If you already own a PDA such as the Palm Pilot, using scheduling software such as *KOrganizer* on your computer might be more of a headache than it is worth because the schedules on the two devices need to be kept synchronized. Thankfully, Linux users can now sync data between their computer and PDA using a program called *KPilot* (see Figure 12.5). *KPilot* was written to replace the functionality of the original Windows-based synchronization program distributed with the Palm Pilots. It supports a number of synchronization features, including synchronizing the date book on the PDA with *KOrganizer*.

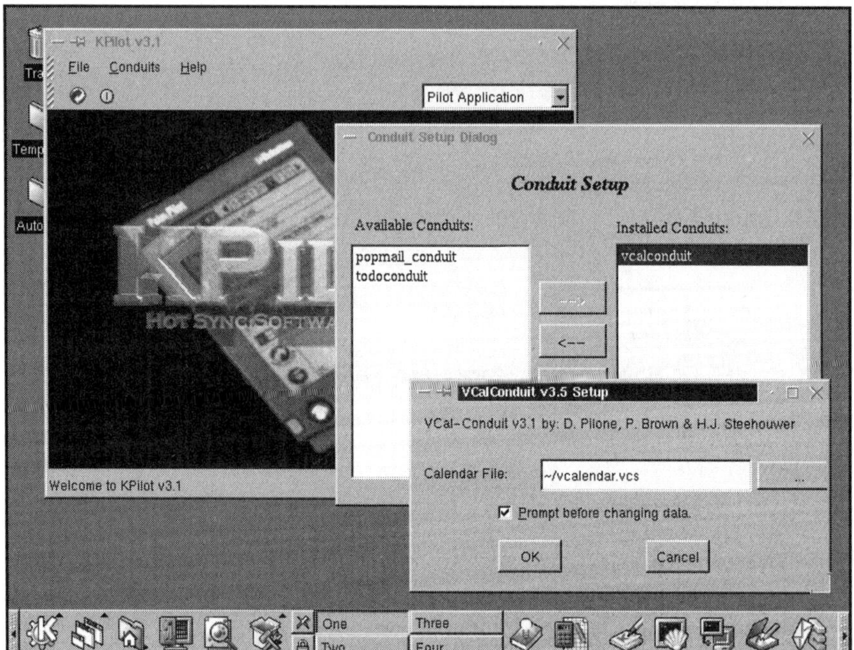

Figure 12.5 *Configuring* KPilot *to synchronize the PDA with* KOrganizer

Installing *KPilot*

KPilot is not included with Slackware, but it's easy to obtain. Search on any of the Linux application sites, such as http://freshmeat.net, for the *KPilot* home page. *KPilot* requires that you install the libraries listed in Table 12.5.

Table 12.5 Libraries Required for *KPilot*

Library	Optional?	Slackware Package	Purpose
Qt	No	slakware/kde1/qt_1_44.tgz	GUI
KDE libraries	No	slakware/kde1/kdelibs.tgz	GUI
Pilot-link	No	N/A	Does the actual data transfer

The pilot-link library is available from the *KPilot* Web site. Compile and install the link library and then *KPilot* itself. When you first run *KPilot*, you need to configure it to use the serial port that your PDA is attached to. You might want to link /dev/pilot to the serial port and have *KPilot* use the symbolic link.

Finance

No office (or home, for that matter) runs without money. Tracking your income and expenses with Linux certainly beats doing it on paper, especially when you need to organize your finances at tax time. Here I present *GnuCash*, an open-source way to manage your money.

GnuCash

URL: http://www.gnucash.org

Summary: Personal finance manager.

Pros: Imports Quicken files. Basic functionality exists, and active development is adding more.

Cons: Relies on a number of external libraries and programs, so building can be difficult.

The most feature-rich, open-source money manager currently available for Linux is *GnuCash* (see Figure 12.6). This program has a number of useful features, such as double-entry bookkeeping, nested accounts, and a general ledger window. It also has more advanced capabilities, such as tracking a stock or mutual fund portfolio and supporting multiple currencies. *GnuCash* also can import QIF (Quicken Interchange Format) files. Most commercial money managers support exporting to QIF files, so migrating to *GnuCash* should be relatively painless.

Installing *GnuCash*

At the *GnuCash* home page (http://www.gnucash.org) you find links to download the source code and sometimes binaries. Compiling and installing *GnuCash* on your own can be difficult because it relies on a number of libraries that are not installed on a Slackware system by default. Thankfully, though, all such libraries are kept on the same FTP server (look for the extra/ directory.) Table 12.6 shows the libraries required for *GnuCash*.

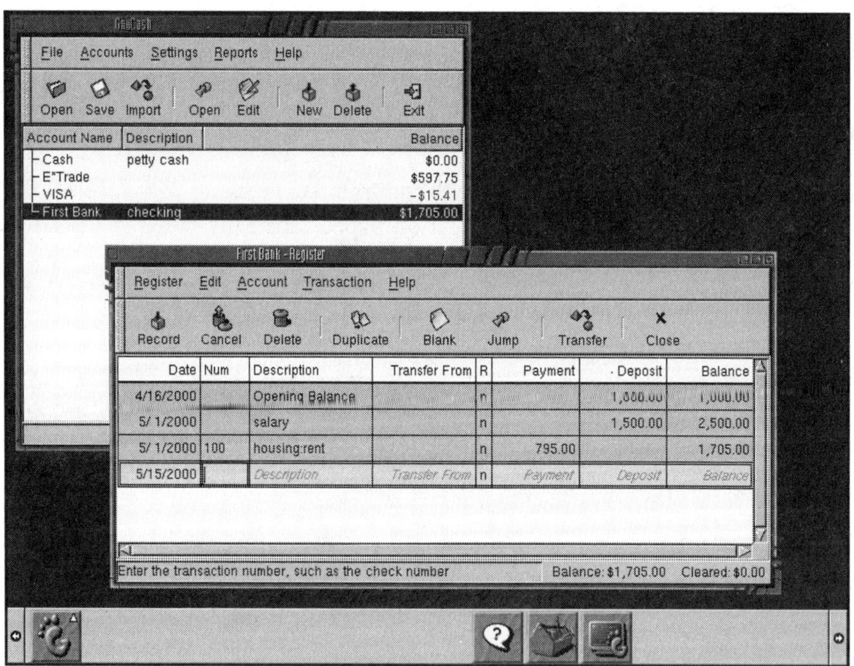

Figure 12.6 *Categories and transactions in* GnuCash

Table 12.6 Libraries Required for *GnuCash*

Library	Optional?	Slackware Package	Purpose
GTK, glib	Yes	slakware/gtk1/gtkglib.tgz	GUI, but Lesstif is an alternative
Guile	No	slakware/gtk1/guilt.tgz	Allows extensible functions such as reports
XmHTML	No	slakware/gtk1/gnomlib.tgz	HTML rendering capability for help and reports
Eperl	Yes	N/A	Allows extensible functions such as reports
Swig	No	N/A	Allows extensible functions such as reports
XPM	No	slakware/x1/xpm.tgz	Needed for image rendering
PMG	No	slakware/d1/libpng.tgz	Needed for image rendering
JPEG	No	slakware/d1/jpeg6.tgz	Needed for image rendering
Print	Yes	slakware/gtk1/gnoprint.tgz	Needed to print checks

Install the packages supplied by Slackware; then download and install the rest. The only oddity about compiling *GnuCash* (once you get the libraries figured out) is that the *make* command gives you a set of choices regarding how to build. You probably want to perform the compilation as

```
make gnome
```

Once you have compiled and installed *GnuCash*, you might want to return to the home page and read the online manual.

Network and Network Security

No matter how you plan to use your Slackware computer, chances are, networking will play a role in it. Whether you are maintaining a company Web server, downloading a game, or chatting with friends online, the tools I list here should make your life easier.

Network Security

Critical servers are often kept behind locked doors for the sake of security. This might be to keep people away from the machine itself and to guard the machine against dangers such as heat and water. Beyond physical protection, such a machine usually has other requirements: It needs an encrypted channel for performing secure remote administration, a method of monitoring the server's health, and automated distribution of files. Even for networked computers that are not so critical as to be locked away in a server room, these sorts of tools can be quite valuable. The first need—secure remote administration—can be satisfied by *OpenSSH*.

OpenSSH

> **URL:** http://www.openssh.com
>
> **Summary:** Secure network connectivity tools.
>
> **Pros:** A single program replaces many insecure programs.

If you are using Slackware as a Web or file server, chances are, at some point, you will want to log in to it remotely to perform administration. Logging in to such a server through the Internet can be risky. Older insecure utilities such as *Telnet* pass your username and password over the network in unencrypted form. If an eavesdropper somewhere on the Internet sees this, your server is in danger of being compromised. Ideally, your username, password, and any data you transfer should be encrypted.

OpenSSH provides this security. It replaces a number of insecure network utilities, including *Telnet*, *FTP*, *rlogin*, *rsh*, and *rcp*. *OpenSSH* is actually created based on an earlier utility called *ssh*. Unfortunately, over time *ssh* became encumbered by a number of patents and restrictive licenses. *OpenSSH* was developed to remove these legal hang-ups.

OpenSSH is a vital utility in any network administrator's toolkit. It can also be useful to the average user. For example, some of us are lucky enough to have a persistent connection to the Internet at home, via technology such as DSL or a cable modem. By using *OpenSSH* in conjunction with a persistent connection, you can access your files even when you are not home. In my case, all my email automatically is forwarded to my Linux machine at home. I can read my email and access any other of my files such as my address book, even while I'm at work or on the road, by using *OpenSSH*. Furthermore, *OpenSSH* allows me to securely assist my Linux-using friends with their computers, even if I am several thousand miles away.

Installing *OpenSSH*

To use *OpenSSH*, you need to download the latest source from http://www.openssh.com. Follow the Linux link and then select an FTP site near you. Legally speaking, if you are outside the United States, you should not download from a United States mirror.

> You could try to find a precompiled binary, but don't worry: *OpenSSH* is easy to compile. Furthermore, if you truly require security, ask yourself this: Do you know you can trust someone else to compile it for you? By compiling it yourself, you have a better idea of what you are getting.

If you are compiling it yourself, you need to get both the *OpenSSH* source and the OpenSSL library. Some OpenSSL RPMs are located on the *OpenSSH* FTP site, in the support/ directory. However, if you want standard tar.gz files, visit http://www.openssl.org and download the latest version from there. Table 12.7 shows the libraries required for *OpenSSH*.

PAM, the pluggable authentication module, allows you to customize how users are authenticated to your system. It is optional, but if you want fine-tuned control, you can download it from http://www.kernel.org/pub/linux/libs/pam/. If you compile *OpenSSH* with support for PAM, you need to correctly configure PAM to get *OpenSSH* working. The PAM distribution contains instructions on how to do this. Table 12.7 lists the libraries required for *OpenSSH*.

Table 12.7　Libraries Required for *OpenSSH*

Library	Optional?	Slackware Package	Purpose
OpenSSL	no	n/a	Encryption
Zlib	no	slakware/d1/zlib.tgz	Compresses data before encrypting for performance
PAM	yes	n/a	Pluggable Authentication Modules

First build and install the OpenSSL library. The steps used to build it differ slightly from those presented in Chapter 9. Instead of configuring the source for your system with a command like this:

```
./configure
```

you run a script called *config*:

```
./config
```

Also, it's a good idea to test it after you have compiled the library but before installing it. After all, security requires a bit of paranoia. Run this command to test the library:

```
make test
```

Assuming the test completes without error, you can finish the installation as normal.

After OpenSSL is installed, you need to compile *OpenSSH*. The compilation steps are similar to the standard ones presented in Chapter 9. Compile and install it on both the server (the machine you wish to remotely gain access to) and any clients.

If *OpenSSH* fails to compile due to complaints of missing OpenSSL header files, check if the OpenSSL installation actually installed the header files. My compilation installed everything but the header files. You can manually put the header files in the right place with these two commands. (Of course, your version of OpenSSL might differ, so change the pathname accordingly.)

```
mkdir /usr/local/include/openssl
cp /usr/include/openssl-0.9.5a/include/openssl/* /usr/local/include/openssl/
```

After finishing the installation on the server, however, you also need to run the following command. This generates the keys needed for encryption:

```
make host-key
```

Once both OpenSSL and *OpenSSH* are correctly compiled and installed on your server and client(s), you need to start the daemon on the server. You can start it immediately by executing the *sshd* command, but you also want to make it start automatically when you turn your computer on. The simplest way to do this is to add these lines to the end of your /etc/rc.d/rc.inet2 file:

```
echo "Starting sshd..."
/usr/local/sbin/sshd &
```

Network Utilities

On a less security-conscious note, quite a number of network utilities exist to automate the maintenance of computers. Slackware includes the standards such as *cron*.

Below I present an interesting utility that can be used as both a tool for some types of maintenance tasks, and as an end-user program.

Pavuk

URL: Search for "pavuk" on http://freshmeat.net.
Summary: Feature-rich Web crawler.
Pros: Supports both command-line and GUI interfaces. Very flexible.
Cons: Complex.

Pavuk means "spider" in the Slovak language, and that's exactly what it is. *Pavuk* can crawl a Web site, downloading all files or just ones matching particular criteria. It has a dizzying array of features and can be used from the command line or within X.

OpenSSH and *Pavuk* have some overlap in their uses, because they both can retrieve files via *FTP*. If security is a concern, use *OpenSSH*. For anonymous downloads (as most are), *Pavuk* is the better choice since it allows the continuation of interrupted downloads.

For one example of how *Pavuk* might be useful to you, consider that some companies have a master Web site that is not accessible to the public. Changes and updates are first made there. Once they are verified, they are then copied over to the real Web server. *Pavuk* can automate this copying process. A nightly *cron* job could invoke *Pavuk* and mirror one Web site over onto another.

Another use of *Pavuk* is to copy some portion of a Web site onto your hard drive so you can browse it off-line at your convenience. Other Web-crawling programs allow this by simply dumping the contents of the Web site to your drive, but few do it so well as *Pavuk*. *Pavuk* can modify the pages as it downloads them, changing the links to be local. This way, you can later browse the pages on your hard drive, without having the browser reference images on the network.

Finally, *Pavuk* can be used as a reliable way of retrieving a single file via *HTTP* or *FTP*. Even if the connection is interrupted, you can resume the transfer later.

Installing *Pavuk*

For such a useful (yet complicated) utility, it's almost ironic how simple *Pavuk* is to get and install. Find the *Pavuk* home page and sources by searching http:// freshmeat.net for "pavuk." *Pavuk* can use a number of optional libraries, but if you don't have them, those features that need them are silently disabled. If any of these features are vital to you, ensure the appropriate libraries are installed before configuring and compiling the *Pavuk* sources. Table 12.8 shows the libraries required for *Pavuk*.

Table 12.8 Libraries Required for *Pavuk*

Library	Optional?	Slackware Package	Purpose
GTK, glib	Yes	slakware/gtk1/gtkglib.tgz	GUI
OpenSSL	Yes	N/A	Encryption for accessing secure Web sites
Gettext	Yes	slakware/d1/gettext.tgz	Internationalization support
Zlib	Yes	slakware/d1/zlib.tgz	Faster decoding of some documents

All these libraries, except for OpenSSL, come with Slackware. If you need to install OpenSSL, refer to the previous discussion on the *OpenSSH* utility.

Once any needed libraries are installed, proceed with the compilation as normal:

```
cd pavuk-0.9p124
./configure
make
make install
```

Configuring *Pavuk*

Pavuk is a powerful tool, but like any other powerful tool it should be treated with the right amount of respect. Used incorrectly, *Pavuk* might crawl from one Web site to another, without limit, slowing down public servers and clogging your local network. In other words, you could get some angry people knocking at your door. Before using *Pavuk* to download more than just a single file, be sure you understand the limits currently in place.

To check the current settings and limits, start *Pavuk* graphically by issuing the ***pavuk -X*** command. Click the Limits button on the toolbar (see Figure 12.7). The window that appears lets you configure where *Pavuk* can and cannot go. The simplest yet most effective restriction is to check the Don't Leave Starting Site option. Now exit this window. You must manually save your settings before the changes are permanent. Pull down the File menu, and select Save Settings to ~/.pavukrc. Now, whether you use *Pavuk* from the command line or GUI, your new settings are used.

From both the command line and the GUI, you can specify options to override your defaults. Once you are comfortable with *Pavuk*, you can get far more control by allowing and disallowing particular sites, Web pages, and document types. But until that time, crawl cautiously.

Figure 12.7 *Using* Pavuk *with the graphical interface*

Network Programs

What fun would the network be if it was only about securing and maintaining computers? Let's talk about some software gems that could be used every day by end users.

Links

URL: Search for "links" on http://freshmeat.net.

Summary: Text-only Web browser.

Pros: Fast and small with many nice features.

Cons: Frames are not fully supported.

Plenty of Web browsers exist for Linux. Some are very feature packed, such as Netscape 4.7, which ships with Slackware. Netscape is a fine browser if your computer has the RAM it demands, and if you can tolerate occasional misbehavior from it. Slackware users as a whole, however, tend to appreciate small, fast, stable systems more than the glitzy graphics that Netscape can offer. Because of this, many migrate towards more minimal text-only Web browsers such as *Lynx*, which is also included in Slackware. *Lynx* is fast, admittedly, but the lack of table support tends to make many Web pages almost unreadable. This is where *Links* comes to the rescue.

> *Lynx* and *Links* are both text-based Web browsers with similar names, but do not confuse them. *Lynx* is a capable program, but little attention has been paid to the interface. *Links* is a relative newcomer, but this new kid on the block presents a nicer interface to the user.

Links is a minimal, text-only Web browser much like its cousin *Lynx*. *Links*, however, goes far beyond what is normally expected of a text-only browser (see Figure 12.8). The first time I used it, I was honestly shocked at how good it was. Not only does it support tables, it partially supports frames. It also lets you navigate with the mouse, regardless of whether you are in X or at the console. *Links* reflows the text on-the-fly if you resize your window. A drop-down menu (accessed by pressing Esc or F10) is a handy feature. Finally, *Links* is fast. It supports persistent connections, and downloads can be put in the background so you can continue browsing. In short, *Links* is a must-have piece of software if Netscape is overkill for your needs.

Installing *Links*

Find *Links* by going to http://freshmeat.net and searching for "links." You need to compile *Links* yourself. Be sure that gpm (mouse support) and ncurses (a screen drawing library) are both installed. These libraries should be installed by default, but you might want to check. Then proceed to compile and install it as normal.

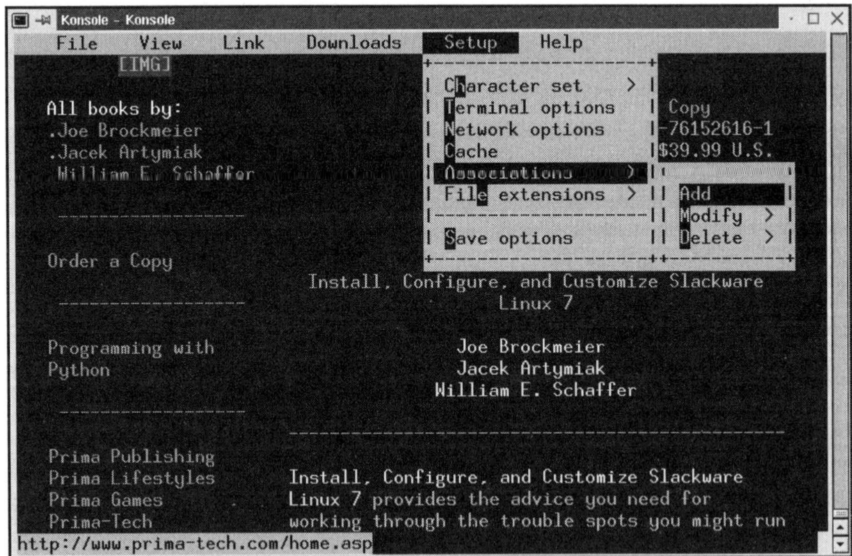

Figure 12.8 *Browsing a Web site with* Links

Table 12.9 Libraries Required for *Links*

Library	Optional?	Slackware Package	Purpose
CPM	Yes	slakware/a1/gpm.tgz	Mouse support
Ncurses	No	slakware/d1/ncurses.tgz	Screen drawing library

EveryBuddy

URL: http://www.everybuddy.com

Summary: Multiprotocol instant messaging.

Pros: Multiple messaging protocols are supported through a single interface.

With this little program, Linux users can chat online with users of AOL's Instant Messenger, ICQ users, and Yahoo chat users. If you don't have any IM account yet, you can get one on at any of these Web pages:

- http://aim.aol.com
- http://www.icq.com
- http://chat.yahoo.com

You don't need to buy or subscribe to anything, nor do you have to download any software; just get an account. *EveryBuddy* can deal with all three protocols. Figure 12.9 shows the *EveryBuddy* interface.

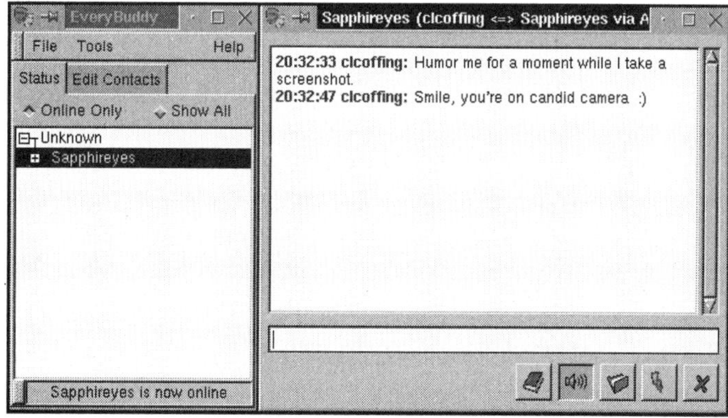

Figure 12.9 *Chatting with people using* EveryBuddy

Installing *EveryBuddy*

EveryBuddy has its own home page at http://www.everybuddy.com. Binaries are available, but not Slackware-specific ones. *EveryBuddy* doesn't depend on much beyond the standard GTK and glib libraries, so these binaries might work for you. Table 12.10 lists the libraries required for *EveryBuddy*.

Table 12.10 Libraries Required for *EveryBuddy*

Library	Optional?	Slackware Package	Purpose
CTK/glib	No	slakware/gtk1/gtkglib.tgz	GUI
ESD	Yes	slakware/gtk1/esound.tgz	Ability to share soundcard

Compiling *EveryBuddy* on your own offers no surprises. *EveryBuddy* supports the Enlightenment Sound Daemon (also known as *ESD*), which allows sounds generated by one application to be mixed with other sounds currently playing. That way, if you are playing music, sound notices due to people sending you an instant message still get played. If you want to mix sounds like this, make sure that the Esound package is installed before configuring and compiling *EveryBuddy*.

Multimedia

No longer does Linux give you only raw processing power, leaving you lacking when it comes to multimedia. New graphics, video, and sound programs have been developed recently, partly spurred by the development of more friendly environments such as KDE and GNOME.

Graphics

For a long time, if the term "graphics" was mentioned in conjunction with UNIX, the only program that came to mind was the venerable *xv*. Thankfully, this is no longer the case. Despite its good points, *xv* is not open source and has not been updated in years. It also uses a proprietary toolkit, so it has its own quirky interface. Graphics manipulation in Linux received a significant boost with the development of *The GIMP*. Although I focus on graphics-editing software here, graphics-viewing programs also have improved recently, due to the interest *The GIMP* generated.

The GIMP

> **URL:** http://www.gimp.org
>
> **Summary:** Flexible image manipulation program.
>
> **Pros:** Feature-rich and extensible.

The GIMP stands for *The GNU Image Manipulation Program*. This program is quite flexible; it can be used as a simple paint program or to create professional images and even retouch photos. *The GIMP* (see Figure 12.10) has been repeatedly compared to Adobe PhotoShop in reviews because of its extensive set of features. These features can be further extended through the use of third-party plug-ins.

Web site designers can appreciate *The GIMP*. The anti-aliasing features can make buttons and images on Web sites appear less grainy and more professional. Home users can enjoy *The GIMP* too. Manipulating large photos can be done even on machines without large amounts of memory because *The GIMP* only loads the portion of the image you are currently working on.

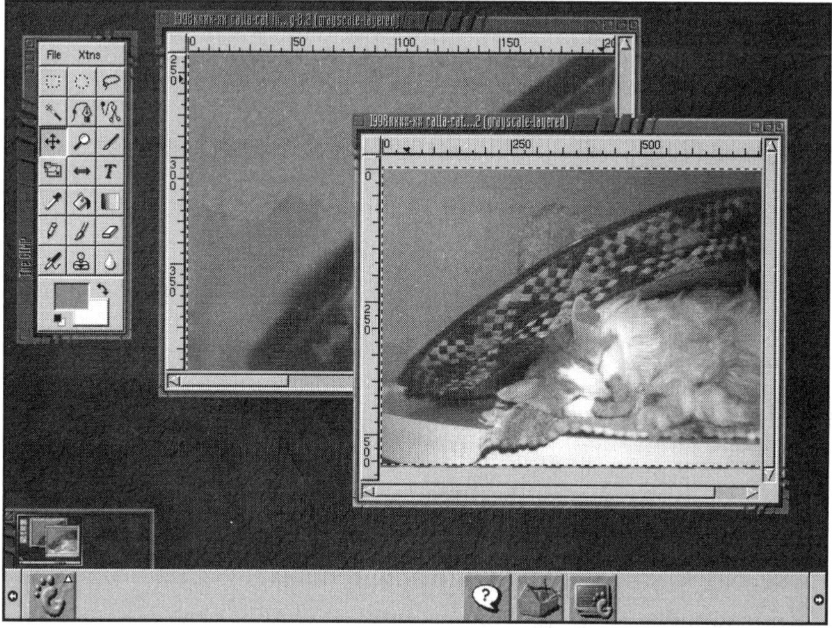

Figure 12.10 *Editing an image with* The GIMP

Installing *The GIMP*

Your Slackware distribution comes with a stable version of *The GIMP*. Installing it, then, should be as simple as installing the package (located in the GTK series) from the CD-ROM or FTP site.

If a new version comes out and you want to compile it, you certainly need the GTK and glib libraries installed. (In fact, GTK and glib were originally developed for *The GIMP*.) You also might want a number of other libraries installed to allow *The GIMP* to handle more types of images (see Table 12.11).

Table 12.11 Libraries Required for *The GIMP*

Library	Optional?	Slackware Package	Purpose
GTK, glib	No	slakware/gtk1/gtkglib.tgz	GUI
AA	Yes	N/A	Support for converting images to ascii art
TIFF	Yes	slakware/d1/libtiff.tgz	Support for TIFF images
PNG	Yes	slakware/d1/libpng.tgz	Support for PNG images
JPEG	Yes	slakware/d1/jpeg6.tgz	Support for JPEG images
MPEG	Yes	N/A	Support for MPEG plug-ins

The compilation and installation of *The GIMP* follows standard method.

Audio

A mute computer isn't all that fun. Here I show you some excellent programs to bring sounds and music to your Linux machine.

Gtk-FMRadio

URL: Search for "fmradio" on http://freshmeat.net.

Summary: FM radio card controller.

Pros: Small. Supports most radio cards via kernel driver.

Cons: Not as flashy as some other tuners.

How many times have you walked into a computer store and looked at a piece of hardware, only to be disappointed when you read on the box that it requires Windows? I used to do that a lot, but then I realized that these so-called requirements were largely a marketing issue. The fact is, many things that claim to require Windows really don't. FM radio cards are one of them. Although radio cards aren't as widespread as sound cards, they are convenient gadgets that help make the personal computer more of a central entertainment system.

Gtk-FMRadio is one of many programs that can act as the control panel for your radio card (see Figure 12.11). Other programs have more features and are flashier, but *Gtk-FMRadio* works with almost all radio cards.

Figure 12.11 *The* Gtk-FMRadio *panel*

Installing *Gtk-FMRadio*

Gtk-FMRadio requires that your kernel has support compiled in for your radio card. The Linux kernel provides support for a wide range of radio cards—but strictly speaking, your kernel does not need to support your card if the tuner program itself does. If you have a popular brand of card and don't want to touch your kernel, go to a Linux application site and search the name of your card. It might be supported natively by a tuner.

Assuming you are proceeding with this particular tuner, first ensure that your kernel has support for your radio card. The kernel that ships with Slackware does support a number of cards, but you must have the modules.tgz package installed. To load support for your card, first view the possible choices by issuing these commands:

```
cd lib/modules/2.2.14/misc/
ls radio*
```

I got this output:

```
radio-aimslab.o    radio-gemtek.o      radio-sf16fmi.o    radio-zoltrix.o
radio-aztech.o     radio-miropcm20.o   radio-trust.o
radio-cadet.o      radio-rtrack2.o     radio-typhoon.o
```

Then load the video subsystem, and then the driver for your radio card:

```
modprobe videodev
modprobe radio-rtrack2
```

> You could, of course, add the last two commands to /etc/profile so the drivers are loaded whenever you boot your computer.

If your current kernel does not have support, you need to recompile it. Chapter 8, "Compiling the Kernel," explains in depth how to recompile your kernel. I just note here that the FM radio drivers in the kernel configuration are not located where you would expect them. Although from the user's point of view these drivers deal with sound, the options are located in the Character Devices, Video for Linux menu. (This placement makes more sense when you realize that the video and radio portions of the Linux kernel have a unified programming interface and are therefore grouped together.)

Once you are using a kernel that supports your card, you need to create special device files in /dev so that you can access the card. Become root and create the device nodes:

```
cd /dev
./MAKEDEV radio
ln -sf radio0 radio
```

By default, the permissions for /dev/radio0 are too restrictive for a normal user to use. You might wish to create a special group such as `audio` or `radio`; add your user name to that group, and give that group read and write permissions to /dev/radio like this:

```
vi /etc/groups
chown root:audio /dev/radio0
chmod 0660 /dev/radio0
```

Table 12.12 lists the required libraries for *Gtk-FMRadio*.

Table 12.12 Libraries Required for *Gtk-FMRadio*

Library	Optional?	Slackware Package	Purpose
GTK, glib	No	slakware/gtk1/gtkglib.tgz	GUI

Now you are ready to try out *Gtk-FMRadio*. Find the sources by searching for "fmradio" on http://freshmeat.net. As you probably guessed from the name, you need the GTK and glib libraries installed. After the usual drill of downloading, compiling, and installing the program, you can continue to explore new Linux software, except now with tunes!

The X Multimedia System

URL: http://www.xmms.org
Summary: A multimedia player that supports numerous audio formats.
Pros: Single interface to play many types of audio. Extensible via plug-ins.

The *X Multimedia System*, or *Xmms* for short, is an extensible multimedia player for X (see Figure 12.12). Besides supporting a number of audio formats (such as MP3, WAV, and Sun's au format), it also supports skins and plug-ins. The skins change its appearance; the plug-ins can change its behavior. Some plug-ins add supports for new audio formats; others go so far as to add a visual representation of audio as it is played.

Installing the X Multimedia System

The source code and some binaries are available at http://www.xmms.org. Compiling *Xmms* holds no surprises, but the functionality you end up with can vary quite a bit depending on what libraries you have installed. Check Table 12.13 and verify that you have installed all the libraries you want before compiling. The mikmod library is available from http://mikmod.darkorb.net/.

Table 12.13 Libraries Required for the *X Multimedia System*

Library	Optional?	Slackware Package	Purpose
GTK, glib	No	slakware/gtk1/gtkglib.tgz	GUI
Mikmod	Yes	N/A	Ability to play module files
Audiofile	Yes, but required by esound	slakware/gtk1/audiofil.tgz	Ability to play WAVE, AIFF, and others
ESD	Yes	slakware/gtk1/esound.tgz	Ability to mix sounds
XML	Yes	slakware/gtk1/libxml.tgz	Ability to display song titles while playing a CD

Figure 12.12 *The* Xmms *panel*

You can find quite a number of enhancements for *Xmms* freely available on the Internet. One repository for skins is on the *Xmms* home page, at http://www.xmms.org/skins.html. You can also find plug-ins nearby, at http://www.xmms.org/plugins.html. Plug-ins are usually compiled and installed much like *Xmms* itself, and they install in the *Xmms* directories. To enable a plug-in, start *Xmms* and press Ctrl+P for the plug-in page. Here you can configure and enable plug-ins.

Summary

This chapter demonstrates a number of programs that run on Slackware. Although a useful system can be built from just the software on the Slackware CD-ROM, I hope I have shown here that there are many more exciting programs available. The programs in this chapter are some of my favorites, but you will certainly find others as good or better if you explore for yourself.

Considering the directions some of these programs are going, it becomes clear that Linux is no longer limited to just servers. The quality of software is increasing, and so is the selection. No matter how you want to use your computer, chances are, someone else has done something similar. Open-source solutions probably already exist to help you if you know where to look. Once you consider commercial software alternatives also, your choices are quite broad indeed.

Chapter 13: Introduction to Emacs

Andy Harris

In this chapter, you examine Emacs, a powerful and popular text editor. You look at many of the features available in Emacs and explore how you can use it to enhance your text-development efforts, whether you are working on simple text documents, managing a Web server, or writing complex programs.

Why a Text Editor?

To those raised on GUI interfaces, it might seem strange to even need a text editor. After all, StarOffice and some of the other commercial materials available can do all that a text editor can and much more. Modern word processors can handle text with formatting, graphics, and a host of special features. All these factors make a program that simply edits text seem out of date or even a little quaint.

Text editing was originally a very large part of computing, and it has never really gone away. Most computer programs still ultimately start out as text files, no matter how elaborate they are when compiled. You might use fancy editors for writing code or for designing Web pages, but eventually it all comes back to text editing. Computer users find themselves constantly needing to edit text files.

Text editors really come into their own when you find yourself needing to access your computer remotely, or when you do not have access to all the graphical features of your editor. This is especially common when you are using your computer as a Web server or when you are doing some kind of programming.

Why Choose Emacs?

Emacs is not the only choice of text editor in the Linux world. A number of other editors are usually included with Linux or UNIX installs. These other editors, especially vi (Visual Editor), are also extremely popular. Linux people are prone to have religious wars about which editor they prefer, but it probably makes sense to know more than one. Golfers have a lot of clubs in their bag because every shot is a little bit different. If you do a lot of text editing, you should know a number of editors because some jobs require a very powerful editor such as Emacs, and some don't. If you think you need some high-powered text editing, it makes a lot of sense to add Emacs to your list of skills.

Emacs is especially useful if you find yourself writing HTML pages or programs in languages such as C, Java, or Perl. In this chapter, you learn how it can help you to efficiently write, test, and debug programs. You also look at some of its exceptionally powerful features, including facilities for searching and replacing text; features that aid in writing, editing, and running macros; modes that let you interact with the Linux environment without leaving your editor; and customization features that let you configure Emacs however you wish.

It is not my goal to turn you into an Emacs fanatic, feeling somehow superior to those unfortunate souls doomed to an eternity with vi or (shudder) pico. I simply want to introduce you to a program that can radically change the way you do certain jobs. Emacs is not a simple application. It has a learning curve, and it requires some effort to master. If you are willing to spend some time with it, you will probably find that it profoundly improves the way you do some of your work.

Understanding Emacs Conventions

I begin by describing some of the assumptions and conventions about Emacs. Emacs assumes the same things about its users that Linux does, in general: Emacs users are smart; they don't mind learning things, but they want excellent performance, solid reliability, and oh, yeah, they want it to be free. In all these ways, Emacs is very much in the same spirit as Linux itself. Although Emacs is available in many forms, including some with GUIs, at heart it is a text-based program. The assumption is that the user might want to use menus occasionally for obscure commands but usually uses keyboard commands.

Do not assume any particular graphical interface, because they are largely irrelevant when you are text editing. In fact, one of the primary reasons you might be interested in Emacs is because it gives you such tremendous power in text mode. This can be very handy if you are using your computer remotely through telnet. If your computer functions as a Web server, you might not even run X. You might only use the text console, or only have access through *Telnet*. (Figure 13.1 shows Emacs from a *Telnet* window; Figure 13.2 shows a graphical version of it designed for X.) Emacs is quite often run from a remote computer or even from a dumb terminal. For this reason, you cannot make any assumptions about how the user is connected, how the keyboard is mapped, or even what kinds of keys the user has on the keyboard. This would seem to be a huge barrier, but Emacs has some clever solutions to this issue, as you see soon.

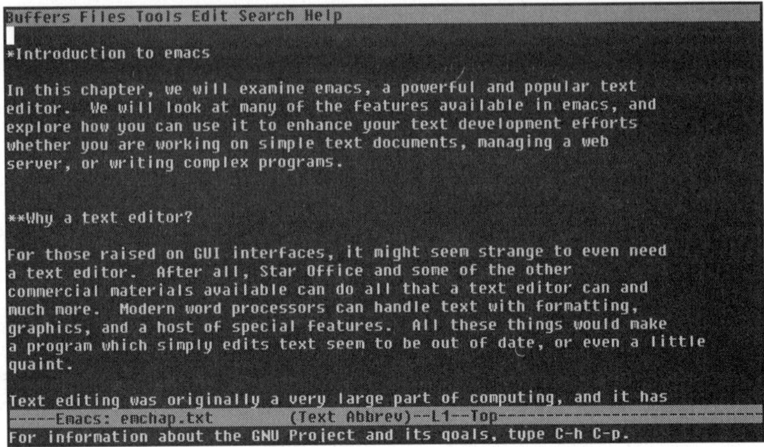

Figure 13.1 *This is how Emacs looks when run from a* Telnet *session. Notice that it is text-only.*

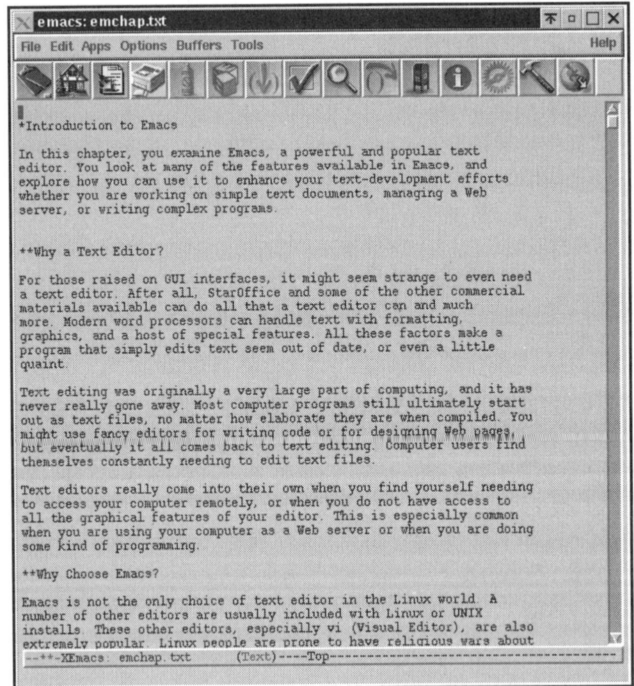

Figure 13.2 *Here is the same file being edited under a graphical version of Emacs.*

Keyboard Commands

Emacs is heavily reliant on keyboard commands for control. Keyboard commands can be difficult to memorize, but this tends to be a smaller barrier than you might think. First of all, most of the common commands have reasonably easy mnemonics, such as Ctrl+F for "forward a character" and Ctrl+B for "back a character." Second, Emacs has a menu system, which you can use when you cannot remember a Control sequence. Third, using keyboard commands can be self-reinforcing because they are so much quicker than using a mouse or a menu. If you are a touch typist, your hands never need to leave the keyboard, even when you are sending complex commands to your editor. Finally, you don't really ever need to make yourself a set of Emacs flash cards to learn your command sequences because the ones you use frequently just etch themselves into your brain and your fingers. After you've had enough practice, you don't even have to think about a particular sequence because it becomes automatic.

Before you get much farther here, there is an important keystroke you should know in case you get into trouble. Emacs has a habit of opening windows on you, and occasionally giving you a strange window or prompt that you don't know what to do with. When you find yourself stuck, try Ctrl+G. This is the "get me out of here" command. It is used much like the Esc key is often used in other programs.

Control Commands

Many of the Emacs commands utilize the Control key. As I mentioned before, Emacs is designed to work on a variety of different keyboards. Fortunately, almost every keyboard made has a Control key. (Even my ancient first love, the TRS-80 model I, had a Control key. I was the envy of my neighborhood with that awesome 16K of memory! Sigh. . . .) In Emacs documentation, a Control sequence is marked with a capital C followed by a dash, so Control+G looks like this: C-g. Though this chapter is meant to get you started with Emacs, you are likely to be using Emacs documentation quite a bit. Therefore, unlike the rest of this book, the remainder of this chapter complies with this style for showing Control commands and Meta commands. (More about Meta commands in just a bit.)

It is not surprising that all the most common commands, including the ones for cursor movement, cutting and pasting, and all the other things that you do the most often, are Control commands. Of course, with a standard keyboard, you still have a limited number of Control combinations. Emacs has a lot of commands, more than can be called with the Control key and a single character, so Emacs uses a number of other tricks for controlling the program. In addition to the normal Control sequences, there are special multikey sequences. For example, all the file-management commands start with C-x. Finding (opening) a file is C-x, C-f; and saving a file is C-x, C-s.

Meta Combinations

Even these multikey sequences are not enough to control the many commands that Emacs supports. In addition to the Control sequences, Emacs supports a second key, called the Meta key. Here's where things get just a little strange. Most keyboards have a secondary Control key, but they aren't all called the same thing. The keyboards in the Intel tradition have an Alt key; Macintoshes have a flower key; and Sun workstations have a diamond key. All of these keys have a common purpose: to invoke another set of control sequences. The problem is that Emacs cannot always recognize these keys. If, for example, the user is running Emacs from a Windows-based *Telnet* program, the Alt key is mapped to the local *Telnet* client, and is not sent across the *Telnet* connection. To avoid this kind of problem, Emacs has multiple ways of reading the Meta key. In a Linux install, you are probably able to use the Alt key as your Meta key. If that does not work, you can use the Esc key instead.

One important thing about using the Esc key as a Meta key: It does not act exactly like the Control key. When you activate a control sequence, you press the Control key down and hold it down as you press another key. If you are using Alt as your Meta key, you can do pretty much the same thing. If you are using the Esc key, it must be pressed and released before you press the next key.

In any case, the Meta key is used for a lot of commands, and in the Emacs documentation, it often appears as M-b, which stands for Meta key and B key.

One very interesting characteristic of Meta sequences is that they tend to amplify Control sequences. For example, C-f means "go forward one character," and M-f means "go forward one word." Likewise, C-y means "yank (or paste) whatever was last cut." M-y means "pull an earlier cut and paste it." I explain these commands later, but the main point here is that Control commands and Meta commands are often related, and the Meta command is usually a more powerful version of the Control command.

M-x Commands

There are a couple other ways to get to commands in the Emacs environment. One of the most powerful is by knowing a command's name. For example, I can never remember what the command sequence for "interactively spell-check the current buffer" is. For me, it is easier to remember the name of the command, *ispell-buffer*. When you can remember the name of a command, you can invoke it directly with M-x. So, to start the spell checker, I type **M-x ispell-buffer**. This works even for commands that do not have a keystroke combination bound to them.

Using the Menus

In addition to all these techniques, Emacs has a set of menus that contain all the most useful commands (see Figure 13.3). In the GUI world, online menus are not anything shocking, but they are very unusual in text-based programs in the UNIX tradition. Most UNIX editors do not have them.

If you are running Emacs within X, you can use your mouse to access the menus in the normal way. If you are in a text mode, the mouse might not work correctly. In most setups, you can use the F10 key to invoke the online menus. If that doesn't work, you can try M-`. Note that ` is the backtick, not the apostrophe. It is often on the same key as the tilde (~) character. If that doesn't work, you can always call up a crude form of menus with this command:

```
M-x tmm-menubar
```

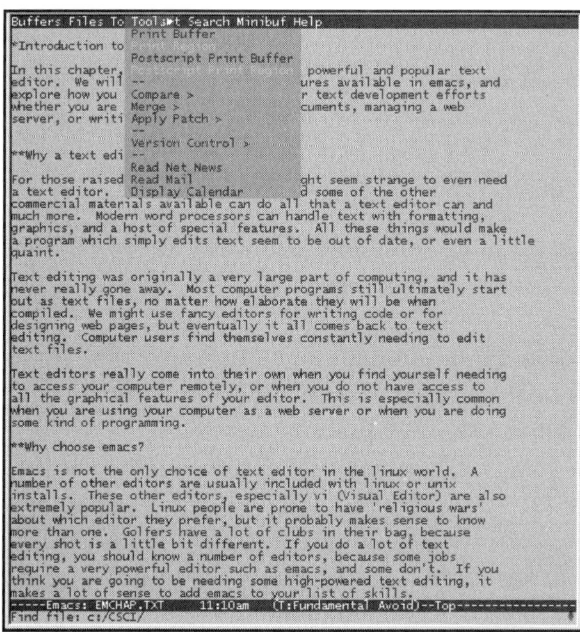

Figure 13.3 *Here is how the menus might look under X.*

In any case, you should see a set of menu items pop up. In text mode, the menus look unusual because they are at the bottom of the screen, but after you play around, you see that they act pretty typically.

In Figure 13.4, you see Emacs run with a text mode menu active. Note that the menu is on the bottom, but all the same commands are available (compared to Figure 13.3). You can access this kind of menu even when you are on a system without a GUI interface.

The Online Help Systems

Emacs is also unusual in the amount of online help it provides. UNIX-style programs are not generally known for excellent help systems, but Emacs has many kinds of help, some of which are pretty useful. All the help commands can be accessed by C-h, and the first one to learn is C-h ?, which brings up a list of other help options. There are a number of choices here, but I go through the most useful for beginners in Table 13.1 and in the following sections.

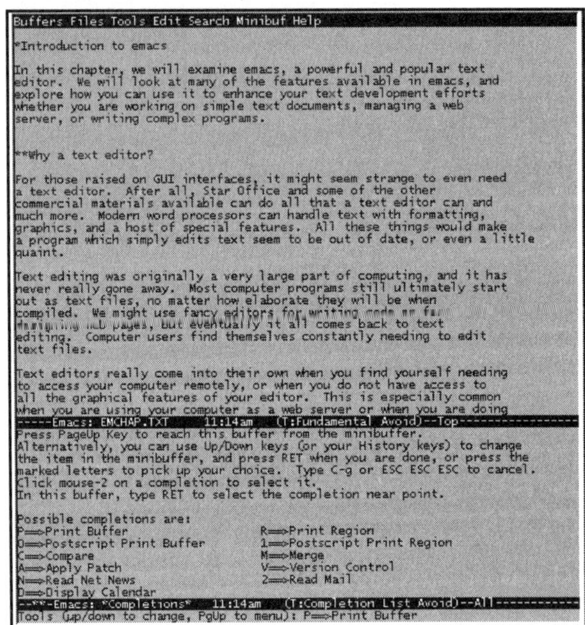

Figure 13.4 *Example of a text mode menu*

Table 13.1 Help Commands

Key	Command	What It Does
C-h ?	*help-for-help*	Shows a list of the help commands
C-h t	*help-with-tutorial*	Runs the online tutorial
C-h a	*command-apropos*	Allows the user to search for a command containing a word
C-h m	*describe-mode*	Describes anything special about the current setup
C-h b	*describe-bindings*	Gives a list of the current key commands
C-h i	*info*	Runs the special info help system
M-` (F10)	*tmm-menubar*	Opens the menu in text mode

C-h t: The Tutorial

Pressing C-h t brings up a window with a text file containing instructions about how to get around in Emacs. If you haven't already done so, you should take a break from reading and run this tutorial. It gets you up and running quickly. You can't hurt anything, so just play around with it to get the basic ideas. The rest of this chapter makes a lot more sense when you've done a little playing on your own. The tutorial takes you through many of the same topics as this chapter and touches on a few other interesting things.

C-h a: Apropos Help

If you want help on some particular topic, you can invoke the apropos help feature with C-h a.

This asks you for a particular keyword and searches for any command name that contains that word. It is like an index system in a more traditional help system. Like those indices, the results can sometimes be exactly what you are looking for, or they can be overwhelming and useless.

C-h b: Finding All the Current Keystrokes

As you have seen, Emacs has a bewildering number of commands. You can use the C-h b command to describe the current key bindings. This displays a little window that contains a list of all the keystroke commands Emacs recognizes and what commands are invoked by each sequence.

C-h i: Getting More Detailed Help

C-h i invokes info mode, which is a full-fledged, hypertext help system. It has a lot of information. It can be overwhelming, but it is as good a help system as you find in the UNIX editor world.

Files, Windows, and Buffers

Basic file management is a critical part of any text editor. Emacs provides all the typical functionality, but adds some special features, such as the ability to work with multiple files at the same time, and to have multiple windows open at once, even in a text-based environment. Table 13.2 outlines the various file, buffer, and window-handling commands, as do the subsequent sections.

Table 13.2 File, Buffer, and Window-Handling Commands

Key	Command	What It Does
C-x C-f	*find-file*	Opens a new or existing file
C-x C-s	*save-buffer*	Saves this file with its existing name
C-x C-c	*save-buffers-kill-emacs*	Exits Emacs
C-x o	*other-window*	Moves to another window (if more than one is visible)
C-x 1	*delete-other-windows*	Makes the current window the only window visible
C-x 2	*split-window-vertically*	Makes another window (full width of the screen)
C-x 3	*split-window-horizontally*	Makes another window (full height of the screen)
M-x shell	*shell*	Makes a UNIX command line in the current window
C-x b	*switch to buffer*	Switches to a buffer (you are prompted for a buffer name)
C-x C-b	*list-buffers*	Displays a buffer menu

Files

Of course, you rarely write text without it being stored somehow in a file. Emacs provides a number of ways to manipulate files, including features for managing multiple files at the same time.

Opening an Existing File

When you are on the Linux command line, you can open up Emacs with a file by typing

```
emacs filename
```

If the file already exists, Emacs starts with the file loaded in. If the file does not already exist, you get a blank screen associated with the filename you chose.

If you are already in Emacs, and you want to load in a file, you can use the *find-file* command (C-x C-f). You are prompted for a filename. Enter it, and it is loaded if it exists; otherwise, you get a blank screen in which to write. If you want to import a file into your current document, you can press C-x i to insert the file. The contents of the file are inserted wherever the cursor is.

Saving a File

Saving a file is very simple. The main way to do this is through the *save-buffer* command, C-x C-s. This command saves the file using whatever name you have assigned. Note that in Emacs, your files always have a name, even if you have never saved them before. If you want to save the file to another name (like you would use a Save As command in Windows), you can use C-x w, which stands for *write-file*.

Windows

Emacs is primarily a text-based program, but it has some of the behavior of its GUI cousins. You have no doubt seen the Emacs screen split into two or more separate areas, with different things in each. These separate areas are called windows. As you have been playing around with Emacs, you have been opening windows all over the place. The help screen opens up a window, as do the text mode menus. One of the most bewildering things about Emacs for beginners is the dozens of windows that seem to keep popping out of nowhere. Emacs can handle more than one file at a time in memory and can even have one file open in two different windows. This can be a powerful but confusing feature.

Opening Multiple Windows

First, let's look at how you open multiple windows without worrying about what goes inside them. Most of the window commands are C-x commands. For example, C-x 2 breaks the current window into two windows stacked on top of each other; C-x 3 breaks the current window into two windows side by side. C-x o (the letter O) moves you to the next window. C-x 0 (the numeral 0) kills the current window, and C-x 1 makes the current window the only visible window.

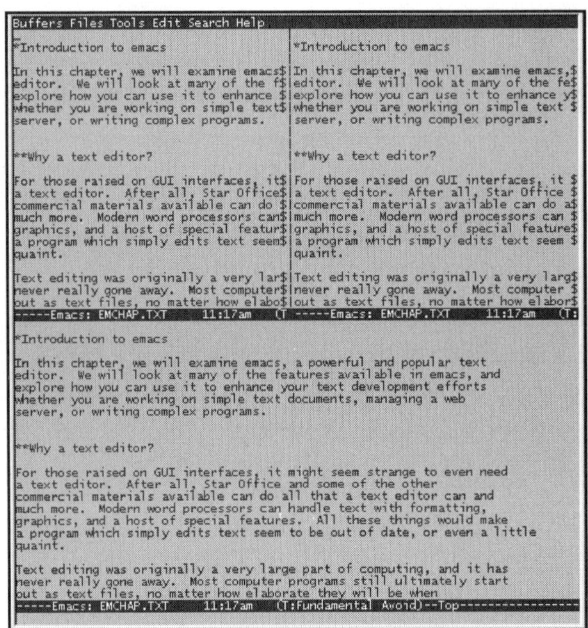

Figure 13.5 *Example of an Emacs session split into three windows*

In Figure 13.5, the Emacs screen has been split into two windows with the C-x 2 command; then the top window has been split again with C-x 3. At this point, all three windows are pointing to the same file and buffer, but they can point to different things if you wish.

Generally, the side-by-side placement of windows is not very satisfying because you can't read the text in either window. The top-and-bottom approach is much better if you find you need two windows. You might not want the windows to be the same size, so you can go into a window and invoke C-x ^ to make that window one line taller. Use the argument feature to make it much larger. For example, C-u 10 C-x ^ makes the current window 10 lines taller, and makes the other window 10 lines shorter. This might be handy when, for example, you want a window pointing out at the command-line shell or running the directory editor. You learn how to do these things in the "Emacs and the UNIX Shell" section of this chapter.

Buffers

So far, the windows you have been using have all pointed to exactly the same file. Whereas this can be interesting, it has limited utility. Emacs allows you to have more than one file open at a time, and you can have different files in different buffers. If you have help open, or one of the other specialty modes, Emacs might have generated a buffer or two for you. It is possible (even likely) that you have more buffers than windows.

How Windows and Buffers Are Related

Essentially, the windows are what the user can see, and the buffers are all of the files (and sometimes some other things) that Emacs currently has in memory. Whenever you use C-x C-f to open a file, you are also opening a buffer. It isn't at all unusual to have five or six buffers open at once if you are working on a project that involves multiple text files.

The easiest way to work with buffers is to invoke the buffer list through C-x C-b. Now type C-x o to change to the list of buffers. You can treat this list like a menu, using the arrow keys to move up and down the list and the Enter key to choose a specific buffer. That buffer is then shown. If you know the name of the buffer you want to go to (it is often the same as the filename), you can instead use C-x b to go to the file directly. C-x b defaults to the last buffer you used, so it is very handy if you are going back and forth between only two buffers. In addition, the C-x b command works on the buffer the cursor is currently in; so you can set up multiple windows with a command such as C-x 2 and then go to each window and press C-x b to specify which buffer you want to show in that window. This can be very handy in certain situations, such as when you are writing shell scripts and you want a UNIX shell available for testing the scripts.

Basic Editing

Well, the point of all this is to edit some text, so let's get going. As complicated as Emacs can be, editing text is very easy. You just type it in, and it appears onscreen.

Cursor Movement

You want to be able to move around in your document, and Emacs gives you a number of ways to do that. You can probably use your arrow keys in the normal way, but you might want to learn some other techniques as well. These other techniques can be used without your hands ever leaving the main keyboard, and they allow for some more flexible options. Table 13.3 summarizes the movement commands.

Table 13.3 Movement Commands

Key	Command	What It Does
C-f (right arrow)	*forward-char*	Move forward one character.
C-b (left arrow)	*backward-char*	Move backwards one character.
C-p (up arrow)	*previous-line*	Move up one line.
C-n (down arrow)	*next-line*	Move down one line.
M-f	*forward-word*	Move forward one word.
M-b	*backward-word*	Move backwards one word.
C-v	*scroll-up*	Move cursor DOWN one screen in the document.
M-v	*scroll-down*	Move cursor UP one screen in the document.
M-<	*beginning-of-buffer*	Go to the beginning of the document.
M->	*end-of-buffer*	Go to the end of the document.
C-a	*beginning-of-line*	Go to beginning of line.
C-e	*end-of-line*	Go to the end of the line.

Character Movement

The easiest kind of movement is a character at a time. Use the arrows to go left, right, up, and down. You can also use Control characters because the arrow commands are not available on every terminal. C-f is forward, C-b is back, C-p is previous line, and C-n is next line. If it's easier for you, remember that p is the last letter in up and n is the last letter in down.

Word and Line Movement

If you want to move more quickly through a file, you can move a word at a time. To go forward a word, you can use M-f, and M-b goes back a word at a time. Notice the relationship between the Control combination and the Meta combination. To go to the beginning of the current line, use C-a. C-e goes to the end of the current line.

Semantic Movement

Emacs has the capability to move in even more powerful ways. You can go forward or back in increments of a sentence, a paragraph, or a screen. Because C-a moves you to the beginning of the line, it shouldn't be surprising that M-a takes you to the beginning of the sentence. Similarly, M-e takes you to the end of the sentence. M-{ takes you to beginning of the paragraph; M-} takes you to the end.

Adding an Argument to a Command

You can also modify the movement commands by adding an argument to the command. Precede the command with C-u and a number to make the command execute that number of times. For example, C-u 8 C-f moves forward eight characters, whereas C-u 4 M-b moves back four words.

Deleting and Inserting Stuff

It is surprising how often the destructive commands come in play when creating text files. Fortunately, Emacs provides a number of ways to delete and reinsert text, as shown in Table 13.4 and in the following sections.

Table 13.4 Insertion and Deletion Commands

Key	Command	What It Does
C-d (Del)	*delete-character*	Delete current character.
Backspace	*backward-delete-character*	Delete previous character.
M-Backspace	*backward-kill-word*	Delete previous word.
C-x Backspace	*backward-kill-sentence*	Delete previous sentence.
C-@ (C-SPACE)	*set-mark*	Set a boundary for copying or deleting.
M-d	*kill-word*	Remove next word, keep it in buffer.
C-w	*kill-region*	Cut from mark to here, keep in buffer.
C-k	*kill-line*	Cut from here to end of line, keep in buffer.
M-k	*kill-sentence*	Cut rest of sentence, keep in buffer.
C-y	*yank*	Paste last thing put in buffer.
M-y	*yank-pop*	Paste previous buffer (C-y must happen first).

Deleting Characters

For the most part, you can use the normal Delete and backspace keys to delete text a character at a time, but these commands do not always work as you suspect when you are accessing Emacs through a *Telnet* session. You might need to set up your *Telnet* to send Delete and backspace characters correctly. In any case, you can always use C-d to delete the current character. C-d acts like the typical Delete key; it deletes the character directly under the cursor, moving all following characters one character to the left. The backspace key deletes the character to the left of the cursor. The characters deleted by using the Delete key, the C-d command, or the backspace key, are really gone; they cannot be yanked back (more on the *yank* command in a few minutes). They can, however, be retrieved by the *undo* command (C-x u).

Deleting Words, Lines, and Sentences

Often you manipulate larger units of text, and you find yourself wanting to delete words, sentences, lines, or paragraphs at a time. Emacs supports a number of commands for doing exactly this.

One note about killing a line: A line usually goes until it reaches a carriage return character. In Emacs, if you hit the C-k command, you delete the entire line, but not the newline character. If you hit C-k again, you delete the newline character as well.

Marking a Region

You can also mark an entire region and kill it all in one command. There are a number of Emacs commands that operate on a region, so it is a good skill to have. Unfortunately, Emacs does not, by default, display in any obvious way which text is in a region, so it can be a tricky concept to get used to.

> It might be easiest to learn how to work with regions if you tell Emacs to always highlight the selected region. To do this, run the command **M-x transient-mark-mode**. If you like this setting and want Emacs to behave this way always, add the line:
>
> ```
> transient-mark-mode t
> ```
>
> to the ~/.emacs file mentioned later.

Basically, here's how it works: you're used to the cursor, which is visible and indicates where the next character you type should go. In addition to this visible cursor, Emacs supports another cursor, which is not visible. This second cursor is called the mark. To work with a region, you do the following:

1. Move the visible cursor to the beginning or end of some text you want to work with (for now, I assume you want to delete the text).

2. Press C-space or C-@ to set the mark at the current cursor position. The two commands mean exactly the same thing, but not all keyboards support C-space.

3. At the bottom of the screen, you see a `Mark Set` message. Move the cursor to the other end of the text you want to manipulate.

4. Activate a region command, such as C-w (*kill-region*). Everything between the current cursor position and the mark is deleted.

> Even if you haven't set Emacs to highlight the region, there is a terrific command for figuring out where the mark currently is. It is C-x C-x, which means *exchange-point-and-mark*. What this command does is move the cursor to wherever the mark was and move the mark to where the cursor was. Use this command twice in a row to see the beginning and the end of a region. It's a really good idea to do this before you run region commands like *kill-region*, because some of the other commands might move the mark without your knowing it has happened.

Yanking (Pasting) Stuff Back

Deleting things can be therapeutic, but there might be times when you do not want something simply destroyed, but moved to another place in the document. Most text editors provide some sort of cut, copy, and paste mechanism; Emacs provides this capability, with a few twists.

Essentially, all the *kill* commands (the ones with *kill* in their Emacs name) are cut commands. What this means is if you delete a word, sentence, line, or paragraph, that text is automatically stored in a buffer that you can access. The only deletion commands that do not behave this way are the ones that work on only one character at a time. In Emacs, pasting is called yanking. (The author of Emacs apparently loved mnemonics so much that he often changed the names of commands so he could make a keystroke that matched!) The standard yank command is C-y. This command pastes the last cut element into the document at the current cursor position.

What makes this interesting is the way that things are added to the kill buffer. Imagine the following line:

```
one two three four five
```

If you went to the beginning of the line and pressed M-d, you would delete one word (the word one), and it would be put in the kill buffer. Now, if you moved somewhere else in the line or document and pressed C-y, the contents of that buffer (the word one) would be pasted at the cursor's position. That's not at all surprising, but here's a twist: what if you started with the same line, put your cursor at the beginning, and hit M-d three times? Clearly, the line would now contain the values

```
four five
```

But the real question is, what is in the buffer? When you press C-y, you see

```
one two three
```

If you do a series of identical *kill* commands, Emacs treats them all as one command and places them together. This is very handy because most of the time you want to move a series of words, lines, or sentences.

The Kill Ring

The kill buffer of Emacs is flexible in another way. In many systems, there is only one buffer for copy and paste. Emacs keeps track of the last thirty deletions (more or less—the exact number can be changed by the user). To yank back earlier text, start by pressing the C-y command, then press M-y until you see the text you are looking for. If you keep pressing M-y, you eventually come back to the last thing killed. Because of this behavior, the kill buffer in Emacs is more accurately referred to as a kill ring, because it can contain many items, and you can go around the ring to find them.

No doubt one of the reasons for Emacs' popularity is how much it adds to the bizarre vocabulary of techies. It's fun to be able to mutter things about "yanking from the kill ring." Sometimes I love being a nerd. . . .

Here's an interesting way to take advantage of the kill ring: If you have some kind of text that is difficult to type and that you use a lot in a document, you can type it once and kill it. Then, whenever you need that phrase, you can yank it from the kill ring. This way you only have to type it once!

More Advanced Editing

You should be able to get by just fine with the editing commands you already know, but soon you might find yourself interested in some of the more powerful editing tools supplied by Emacs. These concepts take some practice to master, but the effort pays off many times in terms of improved efficiency. Table 13.5 shows many of the commands used for advanced editing features.

Table 13.5 Additional Editing Commands

Key	Command	What It Does
C-s	*isearch-forward*	Prompts for a phrase, searches for it interactively.
C-r	*isearch-backward*	Prompts for a phrase, searches for previous instances interactively.
M-%	*query-replace*	Do an interactive search and replace.
M-*	*query-replace-regexp*	Do an interactive regular expression search and replace.
M-x replace-string	*replace-string*	Replaces string without asking.
M-x ispell-buffer	*ispell-buffer*	Run an interactive spell-check.
C-x u	*advertised-undo*	Undo last command.
C-t	*transpose-chars*	Transpose the last two characters.
M-t	*transpose-words*	Transpose the last two words.
C-x C-t	*transpose-lines*	Transpose the last two lines.
M-l	*downcase-word*	Convert current word to all lowercase.
M-u	*upcase-word*	Convert current word to all uppercase.
M-c	*capitalize word*	Convert first character of current word to capital, all other characters to lowercase.

Search and Replace

Editors have had search and replace features from the very beginning, yet people often do not fully take advantage of them. Clever use of search and replace features can often save you a great deal of effort when you find yourself working on some difficult editing problem. Emacs gives you a number of ways of searching for text and replacing it.

Searching for Text

C-s is an *incremental-search-forward* command, which means you can type a phrase and Emacs looks for partial matches as you type. To explain this concept, I experimented on the chapter you are reading now by starting with the cursor at the beginning of the buffer (M-<). I then pressed C-s and started typing the word relationship (it occurs on line 288).

When I typed r, the cursor positioned itself at the r in introduction, the first occurrence of r in the document. When I typed e, the cursor moved to features, the first location of re. As I kept typing letters, the editor found closer and closer words: religious, related, and finally relationship.

Incremental searches start from the current cursor position. You can use this to limit searches to a smaller part of the document, but if you intend to search the entire document, precede the search command with a *beginning-of-buffer* (M-<) command. If you want to find other occurrences of the word, just press C-s again.

The advantage of an incremental search is that you rarely have to type the entire word. You can usually get just the first few letters and Emacs takes you to the word you are looking for.

Although the cursor appears to move when you are doing a sequential search, it doesn't move permanently. To tell the computer you're finished searching, you need to invoke one of the cursor-movement commands. I usually use M-b so I get to the beginning of whatever word I was looking for in the text. If, on the other hand, you decide you don't care about the match you found, you can type C-g and return to where you started.

Searching is a really great way to get around in longer documents. You can use searches on key words, section titles, or unusual words or phrases to get to a particular part of a long document. If you wish, you can search backwards instead of forward. Just use C-r for *incremental-search-backward*, and you can search for previous occurrences of the pattern.

Emacs has more traditional (nonincremental) searching techniques as well, but you probably do not need them unless you are writing macros.

Replacing Text

Searching for text is very useful, but the capability to replace the text can be even handier. This can be used to fix certain common spelling errors or to update a document.

Emacs offers a variety of replace expressions. The most common is *query-replace-string*, invoked by M-%. This command prompts you for a string to search for, and a string to replace it with. It then goes through the document looking for the search string; whenever it finds it, you are asked whether you want to replace the string, ignore it, or quit. There is a version (M-x, the *replace-string* command) that does all the replacements without asking, but this is a prescription for trouble, as it is very easy to make mistakes here. For example, if you decide to change all instances of he to she, then *there* could become *tshere*. Oops—at least the undo command (C-x u) undoes all changes made by this command! It's generally better to do the query form so you can catch these problems.

Using Regular Expressions

Emacs also has support for regular expressions. This is a special feature that has long been a part of the UNIX culture. Regular expressions allow you to search for patterns, rather than specific strings. For example, the regular expression *^hello$* would only match on lines containing nothing but *hello*. The expression *\d\d\d-\d\d\d\d* would match on any phone number, and so on. Regular expression syntax can be a difficult thing to learn, but if you use it enough, it can be an incredibly powerful tool. If you already know regular expressions from some other UNIX tools or from Perl programming, you won't have too much trouble figuring out how Emacs uses them. Regular expressions are one of those things that you could survive just fine without, but once you understand them, you wonder how you ever got along without them.

The commands that support regular expressions usually have *regexp* in their names. For example, to do an incremental search on a regular expression, use the command *isearch-forward-regexp*. Another particularly useful command is *replace-regexp*, which replaces one string (matched by a regular expression) with another.

Checking Spelling

Emacs features a spelling checker that works in a couple of different ways. Both ways rely on the external program *ispell*, so if you do not have that installed, the spelling commands do not work. (It's in the ap1/ispell.tgz package.) To check the spelling of the current word, just move the cursor to the beginning of that word and press M-$. If you want to check the spelling of the entire buffer, move to the beginning of the buffer, press M-x, and type **ispell-buffer**. *Ispell* is an interactive spelling checker, something like spell checkers you have probably used on more formal word processors. When it encounters a word that it cannot find in its dictionary, it gives you a standard set of options, including suggestions for replacement, ignoring the word, or adding it to a custom dictionary.

The Undo Feature

Another really great feature of Emacs is the *undo* command. This is invoked by C-x u, and it undoes the last command. In fact, it can be called multiple times to undo a number of commands. This can really save you when you have made some kind of mistake in your document.

Transposition

Transposition errors are among the most common errors in text editing. To fix such an error, move the cursor to the second of the two letters that need to be swapped, and press C-t to transpose them. There are variations of this command for transposing words (M-t) and for transposing lines (C-x C-t).

Case Changes

Another common editing mistake is misuse of capitalization. For some reason, if I have a word that starts with a *th*, and the *t* is supposed to be capitalized, I often accidentally capitalize the *h* as well, as in *THis*, *THey*, *THe*, and so on.

To fix this, Emacs has some commands to force an entire word to lowercase (M-l), to force an entire word to uppercase (M-u), or to force capitalization of only the first character (M-c). All these commands move the cursor to the end of the word, so they can be used repeatedly to modify a large amount of text quickly.

Editing Modes

By now you might have noticed that Emacs sometimes changes its behavior. For example, if you use Emacs to edit an HTML file, you see an HTML menu appear. If you use Emacs to edit a Java or Perl program, Emacs might put all the comment characters in one color and the keywords in another. If you are in a programming language, you might notice that Emacs automatically indents the code whenever you enter a semicolon (the end-of-line character for many programming languages). One of the things that endears Emacs to high-end users is that it is capable of changing its behavior to manage special forms of editing; this is done through modes. Emacs has two kinds of modes: major and minor.

Major Modes

The major modes generally are related to kinds of editing. There is a major mode for writing plain text (it's called text mode). There are also major modes for HTML, C language programming, typesetting with the Tex and LaTeX languages, and even reading email and playing games!

I generally stick to text mode in this chapter, although it is certainly worth exploring the other modes. There are some very entertaining and useful modes in your implementation of Emacs. To find out which modes are installed in your version of Emacs, press C-h, then a, then search for *mode*. You see a list of modes; select the mode to get a description of its uses and special features. There are literally hundreds of modes. Most of the modes are related to very specific programming languages or other kinds of specialized editing. If you have the LISP sources for Emacs installed, you can view the modes in more logical groupings with C-h p. This gives you a list of packages; press Enter on a package to get a description of the modes and functions offered by it.

Once you are in a particular mode, you see its name on the bottom line of the editor. You can get more information about that mode by typing **C-h m** (*describe-mode*). This gives you an overview of the mode you are in and any special key bindings that might be a part of this mode.

There are two major ways to get into a specific mode. The first way is to simply open up a file. Emacs recognizes a large number of file extensions and automatically opens up the correct mode most of the time. Occasionally, you need to help Emacs along, so you can go directly to a mode by typing its name.

If you want to experiment with an interesting mode, try picture mode. Invoke it with M-x (the *picture-mode* command), and press C-h m to see how it works. I don't want to spoil it for you, but you see that it gives you an interesting way to do ASCII art!

Text Mode

The text mode is actually a pretty boring mode. It adds the ability to use the Tab key and very little else. Surprisingly, text mode does not automatically involve word wrap. This is controlled by a minor mode, as you see shortly. However, the sparseness of text mode is a feature, not a bug. The whole point of working in plain text is to not have any surprises. Text mode is a very clean, very basic mode.

Programming Modes

If you are going to be doing any programming, Emacs is your editor. Programming is a very demanding form of editing, and it has a number of very peculiar needs. I do not have time in this chapter to go through all the programming modes, but it is worthwhile to note what they have in common. The programming modes feature automatic indentation, which can help make it easier to find syntactical errors in your program. They also have syntax coloring, which is a feature that changes the color of text elements based on their meaning. With this feature, your code becomes much easier to read and repair. The programming modes have special features for checking to see that special characters such as parentheses and brackets are matched up correctly. If you've ever done any programming in a language such as C, you know how useful that can be. The programming modes also have a *compile* command, so you can test and run your program without leaving the editor. If you have an error in your program, there are features that help you find the line number where the mistake is reported to be. If you do some programming, Emacs can make your life a whole lot easier.

HTML Mode

Many people use Linux because it is an ideal operating system for running Web servers. Of course, a Web server is pretty boring without some Web pages on it. The HTML mode turns Emacs into a reasonably powerful HTML editor. It does not give you WYSIWYG results, but it can considerably speed up hand-coding of HTML. For example, if you want to add a hyperlink to an HTML document, and you are in HTML mode, you can just press C-c C-c h, and the following is inserted into your document:

```
<a href="http:"></a>
```

The cursor is positioned right after the colon, so you can just start entering the URL. Similar commands are available for all the most common HTML tags. Use of the HTML mode can considerably speed up the creation and modification of HTML documents.

Minor Modes

In addition to the major modes, Emacs also supports a number of minor modes. These are a little bit different from their big brothers. A document can be in only one major mode at a time, but it can have a number of minor modes activated. Whereas major modes can radically change the behavior of Emacs, minor modes are generally subtler and just change a feature or two.

Auto-Fill

By default, Emacs does not place any carriage returns in a file unless you press the Enter key. This is important because in certain kinds of editing, especially programming, a carriage return in the wrong place can spell disaster.

Even so, there may be times when you want word wrap enabled, such as when you're writing an email message or a README file. That's when the auto-fill minor mode comes in handy.

Line Number Mode

Having line numbers visible is sometimes very important; this is especially true in programming when compilers report a problem on a specific line. There should be some easy way of knowing what line you are on, and there should be an easy command to go directly to any given line. Emacs provides a number mode (M-x *line-number-mode*) and a *goto line* command (M-x *goto-line <number>*). (Note: The *goto-line* command works regardless of whether you are in line number mode.) Similar to the line number mode is the column-number-mode.

There are a number of other minor modes available in Emacs. You can learn more about them in the same way you learned about the major modes. Consult the docu-

Fill is what Emacs calls word wrap (I have no idea why); you can turn word wrap on with M-x auto-fill-mode. Incidentally, if you find a paragraph's justification has gotten all messed up, you can invoke the *fill-paragraph* command (M-q) to clean it up. For this to work without surprises, you should keep a blank line between paragraphs.

mentation with C-h p to learn the packages, and when you are in a particular mode, use C-h m to learn about its features. You can also find out more detailed information about the specific modes by using the info browser (C-h i) and searching for a particular mode.

Keyboard Macros

Perhaps the single skill that separates those who just use programs from the true power users is the ability to create and use keyboard macros. Emacs contains features designed to make macros reasonably easy to make, use, and modify. If you have never used keyboard macros before, the basic idea is very simple. You turn on a sort of recorder as you perform a set of keystrokes, and the keystrokes are stored. Once you've created the macro, you can use it to repeat those keystrokes for you at your command. This is really great for doing repetitive jobs. If you find yourself hitting the same key sequence over and over again, such as indenting every line two spaces (this one comes up a lot in programming), it's time for a macro. Table 13.6 covers the macro commands discussed in this section.

Table 13.6 Keyboard Macro Commands

Key	Command	What It Does
C-x (	*start-kbd-macro*	Begin recording a macro.
C-x)	*end-kbd-macro*	Stop recording the macro.
C-x e	*call-last-kbd-macro*	Replay the last macro.
M-5 C-x e	*call-last-kbd-macro*	Replay the macro 5 (or however many) times.
C-x C-k	*edit-kbd-macro*	Prompts for a macro, loads it into an editor screen.
(none)	name-last-kbd-macro	Lets you temporarily assign a new name to a macro.
(none)	*insert-kbd-macro*	Inserts a macro definition into a LISP file.

Defining a Macro

To define a macro in Emacs, simply invoke the *define macro* command with C-x (. Then type your keystrokes, and finish with C-x). Use the open parenthesis to start the macro and the close parenthesis to finish it. If you make a mistake, press C-g to stop recording.

Hints for Useful Macros

Although Emacs makes it reasonably easy to create a keyboard macro, that doesn't mean it is easy to make a macro that performs the way you want. It's easy to make mistakes that can cause your macros to do strange things, so there are a few cautions worth noting.

Use Semantic Commands

It's a good idea to think about exactly what you want a command to do in very general terms, not just on the first line. Say, for example, you want to make a macro that indents a line by two characters. You could record a macro of these keystrokes as in Table 13.7:

Table 13.7 Indentation Macro

Command	Meaning
[space][space]	Insert two spaces.
C-n	Down a line.
C-b C-b	Back two characters.

This works fine on lines that contain at least two characters, but what happens when you try it on a blank line? You should try it yourself and see, but it is not the behavior you wish. Rather than mean simply "go back two characters," you really mean "go to the beginning of the line, however many characters that is." Emacs supplies a command for this, and that is the command you should use. So instead of inserting two spaces, moving down a line, and going back two characters, try inserting two spaces, moving down a line, and returning to the beginning of the current line, as in Table 13.8:

Table 13.8 Improved Indentation Macro

Command	Meaning
[space][space]	Insert two spaces.
C-n	Down a line.
C-a	Beginning of current line.

Sometimes you use commands in macros that you might not use elsewhere, just to avoid this kind of ambiguity. When you are recording macros, you are much more likely to need those movement commands that deal with semantic objects, such as words, sentences, and lines.

Start and End at Related Positions

Macros are most useful when they are repeated. For this reason, it's a very good idea to start a macro at a very recognizable point and to end the macro with the cursor at a similar point. For example, my indent code was careful to put the cursor at the beginning of the next line. This doesn't matter if I'm only going to use the macro once, but most of the time, I have a whole group of lines I want to indent.

It's very common to start and end at the beginning of a line, sentence, or paragraph. The basic rule is: if you want to be able to repeat a macro, you should stop it at the same kind of position you started it. If your macro operates on words, it should start at the beginning of a word and end at the beginning of the next word. If it operates on lines, it should start at the beginning of a line and end at the beginning of the next, and so on.

Test before Using with a Repeat Parameter

If your macro is designed to repeat, it is very tempting to use a repetition parameter on it. For example, to repeat the last keyboard macro five times, you would use C-u 5 C-x e.

Macros can use this parameter just like any other command, but it's a great idea to save your file first, and to test the macro, or you could get some unexpected consequences.

Running a Macro

The basic way to run a macro is with C-x e (*call-last-kbd-macro*). If you want to record more than one macro, record a macro, then press M-x and type **name-last-kbd-macro**. This command prompts you for a name, and that name is attached to that macro. For example, look at the sequence in Table 13.9:

Table 13.9 Recording and Playing Back a Macro

Command	Meaning
C-x (	Start recording a macro.
[space][space]	Two spaces.
C-n	Down a line.
C-a	Beginning of line.
C-x)	End macro recording.
M-x *name-last-kbd-macro*	Name that macro.
indent-2	The new name.
C-u 10 M-x *indent-2*	Indent the next ten lines.

This code records a macro, renames it, and runs it 10 times, indenting the next ten lines in the editor. Even if you record another macro, you can invoke your new command simply by calling its name as an M-x command. The command only stays named as long as this current session is running. If you want to keep it permanently, see the section on customizing Emacs.

Editing a Macro

Keyboard macros are so darn useful that Emacs now includes a specialized editor just for working with them. After you have recorded a macro, use C-x C-k to call up the macro editor. Then, you can type C-x e to have the editor bring up the last keyboard macro you defined, or type M-x and the macro name if it is a macro you have named. The editor has several interesting features; Figure 13.6 shows how it looks.

As you can see, it is typical Emacs. Nothing glamorous here, but it is very functional. You can change the command name by replacing the text after `Command:`, and you can change the keyboard binding so your macro is attached to some specific keystroke. Be careful about this so you don't end up overwriting some existing command. I usually use C-c C-*something* because this is always available, but it still might overwrite something you've already created. If you want to see if a keystroke is available, use C-h k to determine what command, if any, is bound to the keystroke in question.

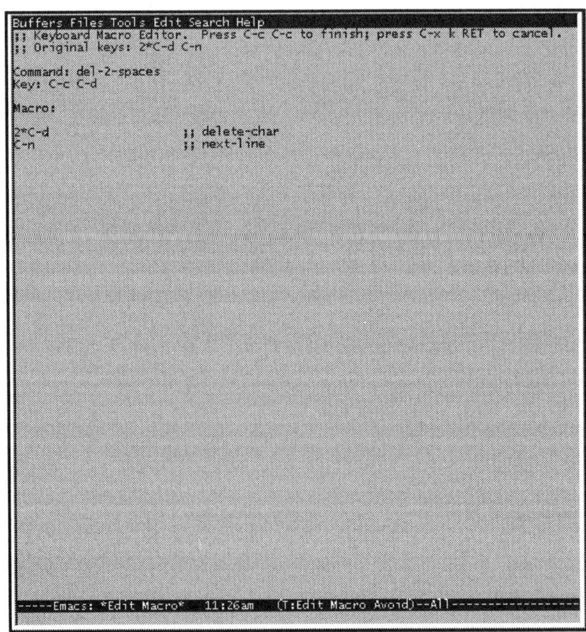

Figure 13.6 *The macro editor manipulating the "delete two spaces" macro*

Note that keystroke bindings can change when you are in different modes, so you might have to reassign a macro if you find yourself in an unusual mode.

Because indenting and deleting indentations come up so often in programming, I have predefined the two macros you have seen here as C-c C-i for *indent-2* and C-c C-d for *del-2*. I have also modified my copy of Emacs so these macros always are loaded whenever I start Emacs up. I cover that in the section called "Customizing Emacs" later in this chapter.

Emacs and the UNIX Shell

Your text editing does not occur in some kind of a vacuum, but in the context of some other sort of work. It is often very handy to be able to communicate with your command line as you are editing. This is particularly handy if you want to change the permissions of files you are making, compile or run programs you are writing, or look around for a particular file to load up or import. Emacs allows a couple of forms of access to the command line.

Managing Files and Directories with Dired

Emacs has a terrific built-in file-management system, called Dired (which stands for *directory editor*). Dired lets you look at a particular directory, search for files using normal Emacs search commands, mark a series of files for batch processing, and has an easy interface to some of the most common commands, such as copying files, renaming them, and changing file permissions.

Starting Dired

There are two main ways to set up Dired. You can press M-x and type **dired**, which is usually bound to C-x d. This causes Dired to open on the current directory. You can also use the C-x C-f command, but rather than specifying a filename, give it a directory. Emacs opens a Dired window on that directory. Figure 13.7 shows an example of a Dired window.

As you can see, it looks a lot like a normal UNIX *ls* command, but there are some important differences. You can use C-n and C-p (and actually N and P, without the Control key) to move up and down the list of files. You can search using the C-s command, just like in a document. If you want to load a file, just move to it and press the Enter key. If you have the appropriate permission, the file is loaded into a buffer for you. To move to a subdirectory, just move the cursor to that directory and press Enter, and a new Dired opens pointing to that directory.

You can rename a file by putting the cursor on its name and pressing Shift-R. You are then prompted for a new name. Likewise, Shift-C allows you to copy a file, and Shift-M prompts you for a new permission set for the file.

```
Buffers Files Tools Search Operate Mark Regexp Immediate Subdir Help
c:/CSCI:
total 4372
-rw-r--r--    1 john_doe root        3862 Mar 27 16:12 #N301Project.html#
-rw-r--r--    1 john_doe root        4294 Mar  7 22:58 #Sorter.java#
-rw-r--r--    1 john_doe root        4618 Mar 27 15:52 #ado.html#
-rw-r--r--    1 john_doe root          44 Apr  9 03:04 #dummy#
-rw-r--r--    1 john_doe root           0 Apr  8 11:05 #sample.html#
drwxr-xr-x    6 john_doe root        3264 May 21  1999 .
drwxr-xr-x   66 john_doe root        3488 Apr 14  1999 ..
-rw-r--r--    1 john_doe root      149504 Mar  1 22:07 100mtS00.doc
-rw-r--r--    1 john_doe root        2243 Jan 27 23:38 ATW~1.HTM~
-rw-r--r--    1 john_doe root        2760 Feb 13 16:51 AdvDHTML.txt
-rw-r--r--    1 john_doe root        1029 Feb 13 16:39 AdvDHTML.txt~
-rw-r--r--    1 john_doe root       60688 Apr 11 05:52 EMCHAP.TXT~
-rw-r--r--    1 john_doe root        5796 Mar  6 13:48 E_R.gif
-rw-r--r--    1 john_doe root       85737 Mar  1 22:05 MidTermS00.doc
-rw-r--r--    1 john_doe root       20992 Mar  1 23:20 N301B.doc
-rw-r--r--    1 john_doe root        3862 Mar 27 16:12 N301Project.html
-rw-r--r--    1 john_doe root         601 Aug 22  1999 PLANES~1.WRL~
-rw-r--r--    1 john_doe root         484 Mar  7 22:55 SORTAP~1.JAV~
-rw-r--r--    1 john_doe root        2586 Mar  4 16:11 SORTER~1.JAV~
-rw-r--r--    1 john_doe root       12140 Feb  3 23:29 SYL~1.HTM~
-rw-r--r--    1 john_doe root         821 Mar  7 22:58 SortAp.class
-rw-r--r--    1 john_doe root         509 Mar  7 22:58 SortAp.java
-rw-r--r--    1 john_doe root         484 Mar  7 22:55 SortAp.java~
-rw-r--r--    1 john_doe root        1345 Mar  6 18:23 Sorter$ML.class
-rw-r--r--    1 john_doe root        3422 Mar  6 18:23 Sorter.class
-rw-r--r--    1 john_doe root          88 Mar  7 22:54 Sorter.html
-rw-r--r--    1 john_doe root        4294 Mar  6 18:23 Sorter.java
-rw-r--r--    1 john_doe root           0 Feb 21 22:56 Sorter.java~
-rw-r--r--    1 john_doe root       16260 Mar  6 13:39 Views.gif
-rw-r--r--    1 john_doe root       10372 Jan  9 16:12 WPSYLF~1.HTM~
-rw-r--r--    1 john_doe root       98304 Jan 22 15:46 Worship1-22-00.ppt
-rw-r--r--    1 john_doe root         912 Feb  7 22:57 adder.html
-rw-r--r--    1 john_doe root      406977 Feb  2 22:58 adder.jpg
-rw-r--r--    1 john_doe root      383087 Feb  5 16:51 adder2.jpg
-rw-r--r--    1 john_doe root       21653 Feb  7 22:31 adderDisplay.jpg
-rw-r--r--    1 john_doe root        4618 Mar 27 15:48 ado.html
-rw-r--r--    1 john_doe root        1420 Mar 27 14:35 ado.html~
-rw-r--r--    1 john_doe root        4138 Apr  4 05:47 avbData.html
-rw-r--r--    1 john_doe root        2088 Apr  4 05:24 avbData.html~
-rw-r--r--    1 john_doe root       13121 Feb 28 17:53 avbmt.mas
-rw-r--r--    1 john_doe root       10581 Feb 28 17:13 avbmt.mas~
-rw-r--r--    1 john_doe root          38 Jul 16  1999 cat.pl
-rw-r--r--    1 john_doe root      159965 Mar 27 17:31 command.html
-rw-r--r--    1 john_doe root        2079 Feb 13 08:55 cookie.html
-rw-r--r--    1 john_doe root        5557 Feb 13 16:16 cookieDB.html
--XX-Dired: CSCI             11:28am   (T:Dired by name Font Avoid)--Top-----
Reading directory c:/CSCI/...done
```

Figure 13.7 *The Dired window pointing to a typical directory*

One of the nicest things about Dired is its capability to mark a series of files. Say you want to change several files to 644 permission so they are visible to the Web server. You can look at a directory file by file, and then press the M (it must be capitalized) key to mark any of the files for which you want to change permission. When a whole series of files is marked, you can then invoke the *m change permission* command and set all file permissions to 644 with one command. This is considerably easier than doing it by hand on the command line, especially if there is no easy UNIX wildcard trick you can use to isolate your set of files. You can also use capital D to mark files; any file marked with the D key is marked for deletion, but the deletion doesn't actually happen until you force it with Shift-D. You can unmark a marked file with the capital U if you made a mistake.

Dired provides even more functionality, but this should give you the basic idea. If you want more information, just go into Dired and call up the mode-specific help (C-h m) for a list of commands.

Running a UNIX Shell inside Emacs

Handy as Dired can be, it still cannot replace the good old Linux shell for some things. There are times when you want to be able to run a command. Of course, Emacs provides a number of ways you can do this.

Running One Linux Command

If you want to just run one command, you can use the *run shell* command by typing M-!. You are prompted for a command, and you can enter in whatever one you wish. The command is executed under your default shell, and the results pop into a new buffer. For example, if you press M-! and type **fortune** (and, of course, fortune is installed on your system), you might find a new buffer containing this gem of wisdom:

```
It pays to memorize the collected poems of Edna St Vincent Millay backwards!!
```

I have no idea what that means.

If you wish, you can also use C-u M-! to automatically put the results in the current buffer.

Running a Shell in a Window

If you wish, you can also run a full-blown Linux shell in another window. This is very handy if you know you're going to be using the shell a lot, such as when you are writing a shell script or compiling a Java program and running it with appletviewer. Just press M-x and type **shell** to generate a shell. You get a new window, and a copy of your default Linux shell runs inside it.

Advantages of Using a Shell under Emacs

This new shell isn't exactly like the original shell, though. It has a few features that make it exceptional. First of all, if you invoke a command like *ls* that has a long output, the output is in an Emacs window you can scroll and search in.

You can invoke M-p and M-n to get at any of the commands you have already typed into the shell. You can also use C-c C-o to clear the output of the previous command. This is a nice way to avoid cluttering up the buffer.

Note that the normal Control sequences you might use with a program running in the shell do not work the same. For example, if you are running some program that is taking too long, in a traditional shell you simply press C-c to end it. Likewise, you are sometimes required to use C-d to mark the end of a file or C-z to suspend a process.

If you need these commands, just precede them with C-c. So, to stop a program, use C-c C-c, and to send a C-d, just type C-c C-d.

Figure 13.8 illustrates a typical use of Emacs. I have the editor split in two, and I have created a small Java program in the top window. The bottom window is a command-line shell, where I have compiled and run the program.

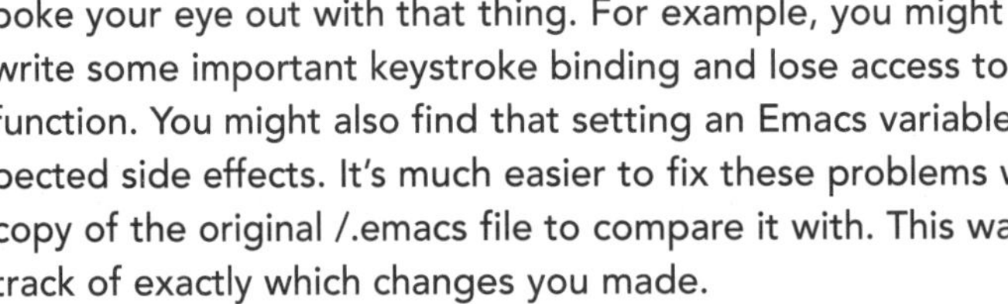

Figure 13.8 *Running a shell in a window*

Customizing Emacs

Once you've been using Emacs for a while, you undoubtedly feel the need to tweak it a little bit so it works exactly the way you like. There's a lot you can do with Emacs. Some of the customization can be quite involved, but you can do a number of very simple things to make your version of Emacs fit your style a little better.

Changing the /.emacs File

Emacs provides a special configuration file called /.emacs, which is normally stored in your home directory. This file might start out empty, or it might already have some code in it that customizes your version of Emacs. To modify your version of Emacs, you can add code to this file. Emacs customizations are written in a dialect of LISP, a language only a computer scientist could love. I don't get into LISP programming here, but there are a number of very interesting things you can do.

Save a backup of your ~/.emacs file before messing around with it. You can poke your eye out with that thing. For example, you might accidentally overwrite some important keystroke binding and lose access to an important function. You might also find that setting an Emacs variable causes unexpected side effects. It's much easier to fix these problems when you have a copy of the original /.emacs file to compare it with. This way, you can keep track of exactly which changes you made.

Remapping Character Combinations

You might also find that you want to change some keystrokes around. This is most common when a command you use a lot has an awkward sequence and one of the easier keystrokes is linked to a command you never use. For example, I love keyboard macros, but the command to play back the last macro, C-x e, is very awkward to do many times in succession. I almost never use the C-l (*recenter*) command. So, I added this line to my /.emacs file:

```
(global-set-key "\C-l" 'call-last-kbd-macro)
```

Essentially, you can use this as a template to map any particular command to any key. Of course, you need to be careful that you don't overwrite some important command sequence like C-x. Note that I used \C to mean control. If you want to map to the Meta key, use \M.

Permanently Storing Macros

If you have a command or two that you really like, you can permanently add them to your Emacs implementation. Just define the macros, make sure they are named correctly, and go to the buffer that contains the /.emacs file. In that file, press M-x and type **insert-kbd-macro**, then type the name of the macro you want to add. This macro now is available by name whenever you start Emacs. If you want to add a keystroke sequence to the command, you can use the *global-set-key* trick. As an example, here's the code in my /.emacs file that adds the *insert* and *delete two spaces* commands:

```
;;Andy's custom macros
(defalias 'insert-2-spaces
  (read-kbd-macro "2*SPC C-n C-a"))
;;map this to C-c C-i when possible
(global-set-key "\C-c\C-i" 'insert-2-spaces)

(defalias 'del-2-spaces
  (read-kbd-macro "2*C-d C-n"))
;;map this to C-c C-d when possible
(global-set-key "\C-c\C-d" 'del-2-spaces)
```

Again, this is not intended as a tutorial in modifying Emacs, but you can see from this example how much you can do if you're willing to study the code a little bit.

Changing Variables

You might want to temporarily change the behavior of Emacs in a number of ways. For example, you might want to change whether Emacs automatically displays the date and time or whether it uses normal or inverse video. These and many of Emacs' other behaviors are controlled by variables. You can look at the info documentation (press C-h i) to see which variables Emacs supports and how you can change them. To change a variable, you need to add a line to your /.emacs file that looks something like this:

```
(setq inverse-video 1)
```

or

```
(setq inverse-video nil)
```

You can get a lot of mileage out of this simple trick by digging through the online documentation. You can change all kinds of other things by manipulating variables, including whether Emacs makes a bell sound or flashes on an error, whether matching parentheses blink, whether searches are case-sensitive, and a lot more.

Example of Emacs LISP Programming

Finally, as an example of the things you can do when you decide to go all out and learn to program Emacs with LISP, I show you a couple of other things I added to my ~/.emacs file. These examples use a language called LISP. LISP is not terribly difficult to learn, but it is a very old language, and it isn't as clean to work with as some of the newer languages. In any case, here are some simple examples:

Applet Page

This code is very basic, but it is handy nonetheless.

```
; default applet html macro
(defun html-applet()
  "creates basic HTML page with an applet"
  (interactive)
  (setq
    applet-name
    (read-string "Applet name? ")
```

```
  )
  (insert "
<html>
<head>
<title>" applet-name "</title>
</head>

<body>
<center><center>
<h1>" applet-name "<br></h1>
<applet code = " applet-name ".class
        height = 200
        width = 200>
This page requires a java-capable browser
</applet>
</center>
<hr>
<a href = " applet-name ".java>Source code of " applet-name "</a>
</body>"
  ); end insert
); end func def
```

HTML Template

The code shown in Figure 13.9 asks the user for the title of a page and generates a simple HTML page with the title automatically placed and with a centered heading. The page also contains my email and Web information so I don't have to add it to every page I write. Notice especially the way you can get input from the user with the *read-string* command and how you can print out a multiline string. This is probably my favorite LISP program. Simple as it is, I use it all the time.

Link Maker

I use the macro shown in Figure 13.10 to automate the creation of Web pages that show some external file. Because I teach various forms of programming, I frequently want to be able to write an HTML page that contains a link to a file and then the source code of that file within <pre></pre> tags. This little program does that for me.

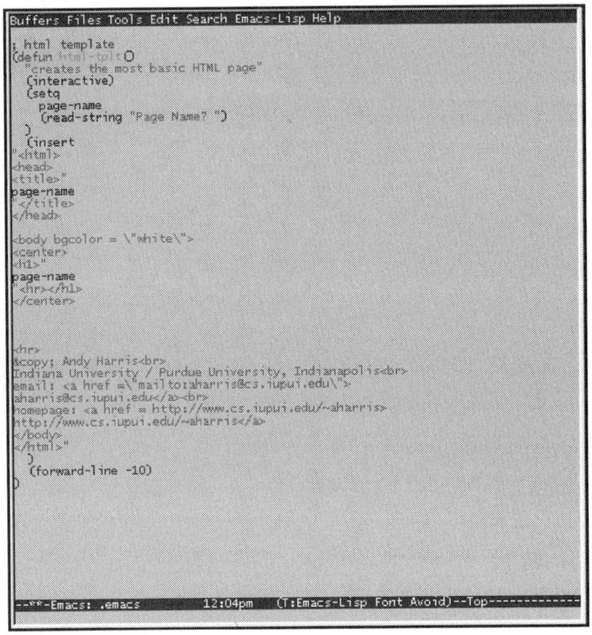

```
Buffers Files Tools Edit Search Emacs-Lisp Help

; html template
(defun html-tplt ()
  "creates the most basic HTML page"
  (interactive)
  (setq
   page-name
    (read-string "Page Name? ")
  )
  (insert
"<html>
<head>
<title>"
page-name
"</title>
</head>

<body bgcolor = \"white\">
<center>
<h1>"
page-name
" <hr></h1>
</center>


<hr>
&copy; Andy Harris<br>
Indiana University / Purdue University, Indianapolis<br>
email: <a href =\"mailto:aharris@cs.iupui.edu\">
aharris@cs.iupui.edu</a><br>
homepage: <a href = http://www.cs.iupui.edu/~aharris>
http://www.cs.iupui.edu/~aharris</a>
</body>
</html>"
  )
  (forward-line -10)
)

--**-Emacs: .emacs       12:04pm   (T:Emacs-Lisp Font Avoid)--Top-----------
```

Figure 13.9 *The HTML template* LISP *program*

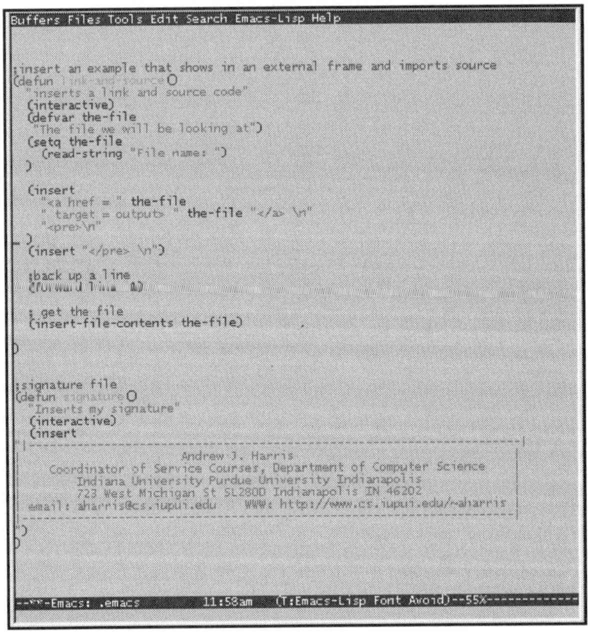

```
Buffers Files Tools Edit Search Emacs-Lisp Help


;insert an example that shows in an external frame and imports source
(defun link-and-source ()
  "inserts a link and source code"
  (interactive)
  (defvar the-file
    "The file we will be looking at")
  (setq the-file
    (read-string "File name: ")
  )

  (insert
    "<a href = " the-file
    " target = output> " the-file "</a> \n"
    "<pre>\n"
  )
  (insert "</pre> \n")

  ;back up a line
  (forward-line -2)

  ; get the file
  (insert-file-contents the-file)

)


;signature file
(defun signature ()
  "Inserts my signature"
  (interactive)
  (insert
"|-----------------------------------------------------|
             Andrew J. Harris
   Coordinator of Service Courses, Department of Computer Science
         Indiana University Purdue University Indianapolis
         723 West Michigan St SL280D Indianapolis IN 46202
  email: aharris@cs.iupui.edu    WWW: http://www.cs.iupui.edu/~aharris
                                                                      |"
  )
)

--**-Emacs: .emacs       11:58am   (T:Emacs-Lisp Font Avoid)--55%-----------
```

Figure 13.10 *My ~/.emacs file with two interesting* LISP *functions visible*

More Interesting Things to Investigate

As you can see, there is plenty to Emacs, and you've barely scratched the surface. As a little bonus for getting this far, I suggest you try a few other modes in Emacs. I think you'll find some of them a lot of fun. Don't forget to use the C-h m command to find out mode-specific help!!

- M-x *blackbox*
- M-x *calendar*
- M-x *dissociate*
- M-x *doctor*
- M-x *dunnet*
- M-x *gomoku*
- M-x *hanoi*
- M-x *life*
- M-x *solitaire*

Summary

As you can see, Emacs provides a lot of power and flexibility. In this chapter, you have looked at the basic manipulation of Emacs and essential text editing. You have also examined some of the more powerful functions of Emacs, including the search and replace functions, editing modes, and use of multiple windows and buffers. You have also looked briefly at how to customize Emacs to suit your own preferences by writing keyboard macros and by examining some simple Emacs LISP functions. Emacs is a very complex program, and it can take a lot of time to learn everything it can do. However, you might find that once you spend the energy learning this program, it becomes one of your most important tools. The humble text editor can actually be one of the most powerful tools in computing. If you take advantage of Emacs' capabilities, it rewards you by helping you maximize your computing skills.

PART III
Appendixes

Joe "Zonker" Brockmeier

Appendix A: A Linux Primer

Getting Started: The Login Prompt

Getting Familiar with Multi-User Operating Systems

Working at the Shell Prompt

Common Commands

Directory Structure

Using vi to Edit Text

Now that you've successfully installed Linux on your computer, it's time to log on to your system and start getting acclimated to working in Linux. You're probably already familiar with using a GUI and can find your way around unfamiliar GUIs such as KDE or GNOME pretty easily. After all, you just experiment with pointing and clicking on icons or menus until you find one that does what you want. With a command-line interface (CLI), however, you might have a little more trouble getting around if you don't know what's going on.

Getting Started: The Login Prompt

When you start your computer, and Linux has finished booting, you get a prompt to log in that looks something like this:

```
Welcome to Linux 2.2.6.
Odin Login:
```

The name in front of `Login` is the name you've given your computer when you set up networking. If you haven't given your computer a name (shame on you), the default is `Darkstar`.

If you've set up a regular account for yourself, type in your username at the prompt. If you haven't set up a normal user account for yourself, however, type in **root**.

It is a bad idea to do all of your work on your system as root if you aren't very familiar with Linux. Actually, it's a bad idea to do all of your work as root even if you are very familiar with Linux. Linux is an obedient operating system—it does whatever you tell it to do if you have the proper permissions to do so. This means it is possible to delete your entire directory tree without any fuss from the system. Consider yourself warned.

Using Passwords

After typing in your username, you are prompted to type in your password. For security reasons, your password does not display as you type. Furthermore, if your computer is exposed to other users—even if just through a dial-up Internet connection—you probably should change your password from time to time and use a password that includes numbers as well as letters. Passwords made up of regular words are considered weak because they can be found in a dictionary and are therefore vulnerable to what is known as a dictionary attack. Don't be so clever with your password that you forget it, though—especially if you don't use Linux every day. On a dual-boot system it's very easy to install Linux, forget about it for a while, and then go back to find you've forgotten your password! There are ways to fix this, but it's easier not to worry about it in the first place.

> If you are having trouble with your password, but you're sure you're typing it correctly, make sure that the Caps Lock key is not toggled. Linux passwords are case-sensitive. You'd be surprised how often this happens.

Now that you're logged in to the system, it's time to start getting familiar with how to navigate the Linux OS from the command line.

Getting Familiar with Multi-User Operating Systems

Linux is a multi-user operating system. That means you can have several people logged in to one Linux machine who are all working simultaneously. Typical desktop operating systems are only designed to handle one user at a time. A typical Linux machine can have one user logged in locally and several other users logged in remotely over a network connection.

Using Virtual Terminals

Another way to make use of Linux's multi-user functionality is to log in to multiple virtual terminals. While you're logged in to the system, press Alt+F2 and you are shown another login screen. This enables you to work on several things at the command line simultaneously, just by alternating between virtual terminals.

You can be logged in to several virtual terminals at a time, which is very useful. If you find you need to do something as root, for example, you can log in to a virtual terminal and execute the commands you need to as root. Once you finish with the system administrator stuff, you can log out again so you aren't tempted to work as root on everyday tasks.

Using the whoami Command

If you're logged in to five virtual terminals, some as yourself and some as root, what if you forget which is which? Easy. At the shell prompt, type in **whoami** and the system tells you who you are logged in as at that terminal. Figure A.1 shows an example of the output of the *whoami* command.

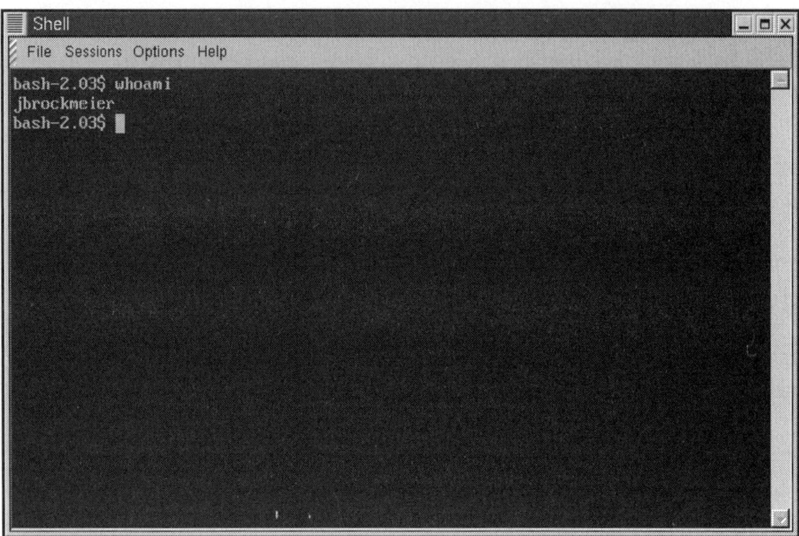

Figure A.1 *An example of the output from the* whoami *command*

Another sign to look for is the shell prompt. Under bash, the shell prompt is a dollar sign ($) when you are logged in as a regular user. When logged in as root, the shell prompt is a pound sign (#) instead.

Understanding and Using File Permissions

The key difference between the root user and the typical user on a Linux system is the permissions each has on the system. As the name implies, permissions indicate what a particular user is allowed to do. If you have permission to manipulate a file, Linux lets you do so. If you do not, however, the system returns a `permission denied` error message.

Permissions are very important for a multi-user operating system. They prevent unauthorized users from accessing files vital to the system, and they prevent users from accessing or accidentally overwriting each other's files.

This also makes Linux a great OS for home use. When a family shares a computer, Mom, Dad, and the kids each have separate home directories where they can save their own files without worry. With legacy operating systems, such as Windows, files belonging to one family member often get misplaced or deleted by another family member who doesn't realize the files are important. This often has the effect of contributing to Dad's ulcer when his report due Monday morning has been deleted to make more room for a game Junior downloaded.

There are three types of permissions: read, write, and execute. These permissions can apply to the owner of the file (the user), the group to which the file belongs (the group), and all other users (the others). By making a file owned by a particular user and group, and then setting permissions for the user, the group, and the others, you can control precisely who can access the file.

Table A.1 Meanings of Permissions

Permission	File	Directory
Read	File can be read.	Directory contents can be listed.
Write	File can be modified.	Files can be created and deleted in the directory.
Execute	File can be executed.	Directory can be opened.

Typically, a new file is owned by the user who created it. The file has read and write permissions for that user and read access for anyone else. If you don't want anyone else to be able to read the file, be sure to remove the read option from the file for the group and for all other users. To do this, execute the following command:

```
chmod 600 file
```

Running the *chmod* (change mode) command on a file changes the mode of access to the file, depending on the arguments you pass to the file when you run it. In the preceding example, you pass the octal notation for the level of permissions allowed for that file. The first digit describes the permissions for the user, the second digit is for the group, and the last is for all other users. Also, note that no matter what permissions are set on a file, the root user can always access a file.

The octal notation, 0-7, represents the file permissions numerically. 0 indicates no permissions, 1 indicates execute permission, 2 indicates write permission, and 4 indicates read permission. When you add the numbers together, you have between 0 and 7. So, if you have read and write permission, the number would be 6, for example. For some people, it is easier to remember number schemes than the other way round.

It's also possible to tell *chmod* only what permissions to change, rather than give it an entirely new set of permissions. For example, if you wanted to allow everyone in the file's group to write to it, you could use this command:

```
chmod g+w file
```

You refer to the user, group, and others with the letters u, g, and o. A plus sign sets the permissions; a minus sign clears them. The permissions themselves are indicated with r for read, w for write, and x for execute. You can specify multiple letters at once.

To find out what permissions are currently set on a file, run the *ls* command with the *-l* argument, as follows. I use my own screen name as a placeholder for these examples.

```
$ ls -l testfile
-r——   1 zonker    users            0 Sep 26 15:28 testfile
```

The first - is not related to permissions; the next three are related to my (Zonker) permissions; the next three are related to my group's permissions; and the final three are related to the permissions of all users. As you can see, I only have read access to the file, and no one else can read the file. If I had read, write, and execute access, the output would look like this:

```
-rwx——   1 zonker    users            0 Sep 26 15:28 testfile
```

Files stored under MS-DOS or Microsoft Windows can also have permissions, but you'll have fewer options since those are not multi-user operating systems.

Finding Hidden Files

Unlike MS-DOS files, which can have a flag set to make them hidden, Linux files are hidden when they begin with a dot (period).

Many common configuration files are stored in dotfiles in each user's home directory. You normally don't see these files unless you ask to see them, as in this example:

```
$ ls -a
./    .Xdefaults    .bash_profile    .emacs   .mailcap   .zshrc     tmp/
../   .bash_logout   .bashrc          .kderc   .vimrc     Desktop/
```

Linux files that begin with a dot are hidden. These are commonly called dotfiles.

Working at the Shell

The default command shell under Slackware Linux is the GNU BourneAgain Shell, or bash. The shell is the command interpreter for Linux, much like command.com is for MS-DOS or its GUI equivalent, the Windows Explorer, under MS Windows. The bash shell executes commands from standard input or from a script. Shell scripts under Linux are the functional equivalent of batch files under MS-DOS, except that they are much more powerful than the average batch file.

The bash shell is not the only command shell available for Linux. Three other popular shells are csh, which is similar to the Berkley UNIX C Shell, and the enhanced version of csh, tcsh, as well as the Z shell, zsh.

As is often the case in Linux, there is a dizzying variety of options, far too many to cover in a book concerned with brevity and simplicity. Generally, the Bourne Again Shell is probably the only shell you ever need to know. However, there are plenty of other shells available if you find you want to experiment.

You do not need to do anything to initialize the bash shell; it is available after you install Slackware and runs whenever you log in to the computer. However, there are options for the bash shell you can use to configure the way bash behaves. When you log in to Linux, bash looks for a file called /.bashrc in your home directory. If this exists, bash reads the file and executes the commands that you put in the file.

Under Slackware Linux, ~/.bashrc is not created by default. However, if you wish to customize bash, you can easily create your own /.bashrc. Remember, /.bashrc is not the same to Linux as bashrc. The /.bashrc file is a dot file, which means it is normally a hidden file. Most configuration files under Linux are dotfiles found in the user's home directory.

Understanding the Linux Philosophy

You probably notice that I mention piping and redirecting output and input several times in explaining commands in this primer. The reason is that the UNIX philosophy is that every command should be a filter and operate on input and output. Almost any command's output can be piped or redirected into a file, a device, or another command. Linux follows the basic idea of UNIX in this fashion. I explain a few simple ways to utilize this in this appendix, but I barely can touch the surface of the capabilities of Linux. You should experiment with redirection and pipes a little on your own. You might be surprised what kind of timesaving shortcuts you discover.

Piping Input and Output

Piping is taking the output of one command and making it input for another command. For example, to pipe the output of the *ps* command to the *grep* command to search for a process ID, issue this command:

```
ps -ax | grep netscape
```

The | is the pipe symbol. If there is a Netscape process running, *grep* outputs the lines with *netscape* in them to standard out (the monitor).

Using Direction and Redirection

You can redirect input or output with the symbols > and <. The > symbol redirects output to a file or device. The < symbol changes a command's input to come from a file or device rather than from the keyboard.

You can use the > symbol to create a file by redirecting output from a command to a filename. Be careful not to overwrite an existing file with this redirection. If you would rather append the output to an existing file, use >>, which tells the shell not to clobber the file, but instead append to it. If you want to overwrite a file, use >|, which tells the shell to go ahead and overwrite the file without asking. Some shells treat > and >| the same, never asking you if it is okay to overwrite the file.

As always, be careful with redirection symbols. You can easily overwrite an important file.

Common Commands

There are quite a few common commands that you should familiarize yourself with in order to get around in Linux. Even if you plan on spending most of your time in KDE, GNOME, or one of Linux's other GUIs, you find using these commands in an xterm or at the console very useful. You will also find you are able to combine commands with each other to simplify everyday tasks.

Some commands have a large number of options, and they might not all be covered in this text if they aren't likely to be used in normal situations. For a complete list of options, you can consult the command's man page.

Copying Files: The cp Command

Name: *cp*

Function: To copy files and directories.

Syntax: `cp [options] file(s) destination`

Description: The *cp* command is similar to the MS-DOS command *copy;* it's used to copy files or directories from one place to another. You can copy one file to a new file, one file to another place, or a large number of files all at once to a new place. When you copy a file, you do not delete the original file by default. If you wish to move a file rather than make a copy of it, use the *mv* command instead.

Usage: To use the *cp* command, type **cp**, followed by any options, and then type the directory or filename(s) you want to copy, followed by the destination. If you want to copy multiple files, you can use wildcards, or you can list multiple files separated by spaces.

Options:

-f Force. Remove any existing files of the same name.

-i Interactive. Prompt the user if there is an existing file of the same name in the destination directory.

-p Preserve. This option tells the *cp* command to preserve the original file's permissions, if possible.

-R Recursive. Copy directories located under the starting directory. The default is not to copy subdirectories.

Example 1: Copying a File into Another Directory

Let's say you download a /.tgz file called ~/program.tgz—which contains source code—into your home directory, and you want to unzip and untar it, but you don't want to do it in your home directory. You can *cp* the file into the /tmp directory and work with it there. To do this, type in the following:

```
cp program.tgz /tmp
```

Note that you do not get an error message if the file already exists unless you use the interactive option. If the file exists, you are asked whether you want to overwrite the file or not, like this:

```
cp -i program.tgz /tmp
cp: overwrite  /tmp/program.tgz'?
```

If you answer y, the file is overwritten; if n, the file is not overwritten.

Example 2: Copying Multiple Files into Another Directory

If you have a group of files you want to move into another directory without having to type each filename individually, you can use wildcards. If you want to copy all files in the current directory to another directory, type

```
cp * /tmp
```

This copies all files in the directory to the /tmp directory; however, it does not copy directories unless specifically told to. To copy files and directories, use the recursive option.

```
cp -R * /tmp
```

Note that *-r* and *-R* are not equivalent. Unlike MS-DOS and Windows, Linux is case-sensitive. Be careful when typing commands under Linux, as interchanging uppercase and lowercase letters might cause unwanted and possibly disastrous results!

If you'd like to copy all files with a specific extension to another directory, you can use wildcards to selectively copy groups of files like this:

```
cp *.jpg *.gif images
```

This copies all JPEG and GIF files to the image directory, without copying any other files with them. You can also use the question mark character (?) to match a single character rather than a group of characters.

Moving Files: The mv Command

Name: *mv*

Function: To move or rename files and directories.

Syntax: `mv [options] file(s) destination`

Description: The *mv* command can be used to move a file or files to another directory, or to rename a file or files. The *mv* command is similar to the *MOVE* command under MS-DOS, but the *mv* command is much more powerful than its MS-DOS equivalent. The *mv* command does delete the original file that is being moved, so be sure to use the command carefully. The *mv* command is also used to rename files under Linux, so it also takes the place of the *REN* command under MS-DOS.

Usage: To move a file, type **mv**, followed by any options, then the name of the file(s) or directories to be moved, and then the destination to which you want the file(s) moved. As with the *cp* command, you can use wildcards to move multiple files rather than typing individual filenames.

Options:

-b Backup. The backup option creates a backup file of any files that would be overwritten by moving a file. By default backup files have a tilde character (~) extension.

-f Force. Removes any files of the same name when trying to move a file without prompting the user.

-i Interactive. The interactive mode of *mv* prompts the user if moving the current file will overwrite another file. If there are no conflicting files, *mv* simply moves the file with no complaint.

-S Suffix. Appends a suffix to any backup files. By default, the tilde suffix is applied, but you can specify any type of suffix, such as .bak or .tmp.

Example 1: Moving a File to Another Directory

To move the file index.html to another directory without making a backup or being prompted in the event of an overwrite, use the *mv* command, followed by the name of the file and its destination:

```
mv index.html /home/zonker/backup/
```

If you're not certain whether a file of the same name already exists, use the interactive mode of *mv*. If the file already exists, your output looks like this:

```
mv -i index.html /home/zonker/backup/
mv: replace /home/zonker/backup/index.html'?
```

Example 2: Moving Multiple Files to Another Directory

You can use wildcards to move more than one file to another directory. Be careful! The *mv* command can move directories as well as regular files. Be sure you actually want to move everything under a directory before using the wildcard (*).

If you want to move all of the .html files in the current directory to the /home/httpd/ directory, you use this command:

```
mv *.html /home/httpd/
```

The *.html specifies that you want to move all files that end in .html to another directory. If you want to move all files in the current directory to the /home/httpd/ directory, you type

```
mv * /home/httpd/
```

This moves all files in the current directory, except any dotfiles. To move dotfiles, you have to be more explicit:

```
mv .* /home/httpd/
```

Example 3: Renaming Files with mv

Linux does not have a separate rename command, so the *mv* command is used to rename files. If you want to rename index.html to index.html.old, for instance, you use the *mv* command like this:

```
mv index.html index.html.old
```

As far as Linux is concerned, moving a file and renaming it are the same thing.

Creating Directories: The mkdir Command

Name: *mkdir*

Function: To create new directories.

Syntax: `mkdir [options] directory`

Description: The *mkdir* command is pretty straightforward. It behaves the same way that the MS-DOS command *MKDIR* works. The Linux command does have some additional functionality—you can set the permissions of the directory when it is created.

Usage: To create a new directory simply type **mkdir** and any options and then the name of the directory you wish to create.

Options:

-m Mode. To create a directory with specified permissions.

Example 1: Creating a New Directory

To create a new directory called /html under the current directory, use the *mkdir* command followed by the name of the new directory:

```
mkdir html
```

If you want to create a new directory called download under the /tmp directory that has read-only permissions for other users and members of your group, and read and write permissions for you, use the *mkdir* command plus the proper octal mode:

```
mkdir -m 644 /tmp/download
```

This creates a directory named download under the /tmp directory. You do not need to be in the /tmp directory to create a subdirectory for it. If a file or directory named /download already exists in the /tmp directory, you receive the following error message:

```
mkdir /tmp/download
mkdir: cannot make directory  download': File exists
```

Listing and Finding Files with ls

Name: *ls*

Function: To list the contents of a directory.

Syntax: `ls [options] [directory or file(s)]`

Description: The *ls* command lists the contents of a directory. This command is similar to the MS-DOS command *DIR*. In fact, typing *dir* under Linux is the same as typing *ls -c*. The *ls* command is one of the commands you use the most under Linux. You can also use the *ls* command to get information about a specific file in a directory.

Usage: To use the *ls* command, you simply type the command, followed by any options you want to invoke and any filenames (including wildcards) that you want to specify.

Options:

-a All. Using the *-a* option lists all files in a directory, including hidden files.

-A Almost all. Lists all files in a directory, except for . and ...

-i Inode. Prints inode number of each file.

-l Long. In addition to the filenames, lists the file type, permissions, owner name, size of the file and the last time the file was modified. Also known as the verbose mode.

-r Reverse. Lists the directory contents in reverse order.

-sk Kilobytes. Lists file sizes in kilobytes. The *s* specifies that, yes, you want to see the sizes.

-X Extension. Sorts files by their extension; files with no extension will be sorted first.

Example 1: Listing Files in Your Home Directory

You probably want to know what files are in your home directory from time to time, so it's a good idea to know how to check. To list the files in your home directory, type the following command:

```
ls ~
```

That's all you need to type. The ~ character is a shortcut that refers to your home directory. The output for the command looks something like Figure A.2.

Did you notice on your screen that not only are the files in the current directory listed, but that they're in color? That's one of the ways Linux makes your life a little bit easier.

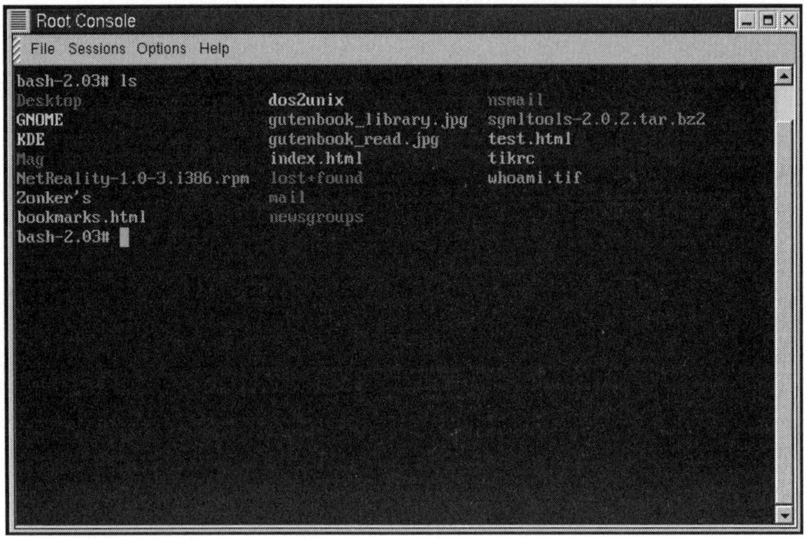

Figure A.2 *Output of the* ls *command*

Example 2: Listing Hidden Files in a Directory

If you decide you want to edit resource files, you probably have to find some hidden files. To list all files in a directory, type in the following:

```
ls -a
```

When listing all of the files in your home directory, you find there are quite a few more files than you might have thought.

Example 3: Listing All Files and Their Attributes

If you want to see all of the files in a directory and their attributes, combine the *-a* and *-l* options, as follows:

```
ls -al
```

You see a listing of all files in the directory, as well as their permissions, modification dates, whom they belong to, and the size of the files. The first letter indicates whether it is a file, directory, link, or other. A file is a dash (-), a directory is d, a symbolic link is an l, and a hard link is represented as a regular file. Other characters indicate it is a special type of file. After that letter comes the permissions. There are three groups of three letters. The first set is the permissions given to the owner of the file. The next set of three is for the group of the file, and then finally the permissions for everyone else. Then you see the owner of the file, followed by the group to which the file belongs. By default, the size of each file is displayed in bytes. Next in the listing is the last time the file was modified, or touched, and then the name of the file itself.

> The expression touch is not one I coined. On UNIX-style operating systems, a file is said to be touched when it is modified by a user in some way. A file is not touched when you just list the contents of a directory the file is in, or view the contents of the file.

Making Links

Name: *ln*

Function: To create a hard link or symbolic link to a file.

Syntax: `ln [options] source [linkname]`

Description: The *ln* command creates a link to a file or directory. By using the *ln* command you can create either a symbolic link or a hard link. A symbolic, or soft, link is a special file that contains a pathname. Hard links are actually another name for a file, rather than a pointer to that file like symbolic links. As long as a name (that is, a hard link) for a file exists, it remains on disk. Even if you create a file, create a hard link to it, and then delete the original file, the data remains safely on disk. If you create a symbolic link pointing to a file and delete the original file, the file ceases to exist and the soft link is left pointing to nothing.

The other major difference between symbolic links and hard links is that symbolic links can cross filesystems. Hard links can only point to files on the same filesystem. For instance, if you have your /home directory on one hard drive partition, and the /opt directory on another, you could not create a hard link from something in the /home directory to something in the /opt directory. However, you could create a symbolic link between the two with no problem.

Usage: Use the *ln* command to create symbolic or hard links to files or directories. If you do not specify the name of the link, *ln* attempts to create a link with the same name as what you're linking to.

Options:

-f Force. Removes files if they already exist with the link's name.

-i Interactive. Prompts the user if files exist.

-s Symbolic. Makes a symbolic link rather than a hard link.

Example 1: Creating a Symbolic Link to a Directory

Let's say you do a lot of work in the /home/httpd/Webpages/uri/ directory, but don't feel like typing the entire directory name each time you want to change to that directory. You can create a symbolic link to that directory in your home directory called /Web and then you only have to type **cd Web** to change to the /home/httpd/Webpages/uri/ directory. To create that link, use the following command:

```
ln -s /home/httpd/Webpages/uri/ ~/Web
```

As long as there are no files in your home directory called /Web, you have created a symbolic link to the proper directory. This can be very useful and save quite a bit of typing!

Moving around the Command Line Interface: cd

Name: *cd*

Function: change the working directory.

Syntax: `cd [directory]`

Description: The *cd* command changes your working directory to another directory that you specify. This command is used to navigate the directory structure in Linux. Typing only *cd* returns you to your home directory. The *cd* command works similarly to the *CD* command under DOS. However, the *cd* command is a little more flexible in that it allows you shortcuts to change between your home directory and the previous working directory.

Usage: Use the *cd* command to change directories. Specifying no directory returns you to your home directory.

Options: none

Example 1: Changing to the Parent Directory of the Current Working Directory

As in DOS, the parent directory is always .. . To go up one level in the directory structure, simply type the following:

```
cd ..
```

You must have a space between the .. and cd. If you type cd.. with no space (as you might be used to doing under DOS), you get an error message telling you that the command cd.. is not found.

If you want to go up several levels in the directory structure, you can do so by typing this:

```
cd ../../
```

This moves you up two levels from your current directory.

Example 2: Changing to a Specific Directory

To change to a specific directory you issue the *cd* command, and then the name of the directory you wish to change to. If you're working in your home directory and decide to switch to the /tmp directory, you use this command:

```
cd /tmp
```

> It is important to note that /tmp and tmp are not the same in this instance. The /tmp tells the shell you want to go to the tmp under the / (root) directory and not a tmp directory under the present working directory.

Example 3: Going Home Quickly

To get to your home directory quickly, simply use the *cd* command with no arguments, like this:

```
cd
```

If you do not specify a directory, the bash shell assumes you wish to go back to your home directory. You can also use the tilde (~) symbol to specify your home directory, as in the following example:

```
cd ~
```

Example 4: Going Back to the Previous Working Directory

If you want to quickly jump back to the directory you were last in, without typing the full pathname of that directory, type this shortcut:

```
cd -
```

Once you get the hang of the *cd* command, and Linux's directory structure, you find that using the command-line interface is not as unfriendly as you might have thought when you first started using Linux. If you try using DOS after using Linux for a while, you really find yourself missing Linux.

Where the Heck Am I? Using pwd

Name: *pwd*

Function: To print the name of the present working directory.

Syntax: pwd

Description: The command *pwd* is about as straightforward as you can get. It's a one-trick pony. If you have lost track of where you're at in the directory structure, you simply use *pwd* to get the shell to print the present working directory to standard out.

Usage: Use the *pwd* command to find the present working directory.

Options: None.

Example 1: Using pwd to Find the Present Working Directory

At the command shell, type in

pwd

The output is the current working directory. The *pwd* command does not take any options or arguments.

Mounting Filesystems

There are two commands under Linux that are pertinent to accessing filesystems: *mount* and *umount*. The *mount* command is used to mount a filesystem, and not surprisingly, the *umount* command is used to unmount a mounted filesystem.

Name: *mount*

Function: To make available, or mount, a filesystem.

Syntax: mount [options] device [directory]

Description: Unlike other operating systems you might be used to, Linux requires that you mount a filesystem before you can use it. Generally, most of this happens during the boot-up procedure, and you don't do it manually. CD-ROMs and floppies have to be mounted as you wish to use them, and unmounted when you are finished. Normally you have to be the superuser (root) to issue the *mount* command. You do not normally need to specify the filesystem type or the directory to mount in if the device is already listed in the /etc/fstab file. If you want to make a device mountable by a user, or all users, include that information on the device line in /etc/fstab. Open your favorite text editor and put an entry in the /etc/fstab file like this:

```
/dev/hdd /cdrom iso9660 ro,user
```

From left to right, that line includes the name of the device, the directory it should be mounted under, the filesystem type, an option specifying read-only, and an option specifying that non-root users can mount the device. Be sure to separate the options only with commas but no spaces, otherwise Linux doesn't understand what you're saying.

Currently mounted filesystems can be found in the /etc/mtab file. Do not edit the /etc/mtab file by hand, because it is updated dynamically by your system. It is useful to be able to read the /etc/mtab file, however, to see what devices are currently available and what filesystems they are mounted as.

Usage: To use the mount command, type **mount** followed by any options, and then the device name you wish to mount and optionally the directory you want the device mounted under. In Slackware Linux, the default directory for the CD-ROM is /cdrom. If you have additional devices you need to access, you can create directories for them under the /mnt directory (or wherever else you like, but the /mnt directory is the standard location).

Another nifty thing about Linux (and there are plenty!) is that it can handle quite a few filesystem types. Linux can read disks in its own native format (ext2), the FAT16 and FAT32 formats used by MS-DOS and Windows 9x, the Macintosh filesystem HFS, the Joliet filesystem used by Windows 9x for CD-ROMs and the standard ISO9660 CD-ROM format, as well as many others. I found this very handy when I was sent a Zip disk with art files in Macintosh format. Using Windows I would have had to buy an expensive program to read files from a Mac disk; using Linux I just had to recompile the kernel to support HFS and mount the disk like any other Zip.

Options:

-a Auto. Determines filesystem type automatically, if possible.

-n No write. Mounts the device without writing in /etc/mtab. Useful if /etc/mtab is a read-only file.

-t Type. Specifies the filesystem type. The following filesystem types are common:

- *ext2*—The native Linux filesystem
- *msdos*—FAT16 filesystem
- *umsdos*—UMSDOS filesystem
- *vfat*—The FAT32 filesystem
- *minix*—The Minux filesystem

- *nfs*—Network filesystem
- *smbfs*—SMB shares from Windows or Samba
- *iso9660*—Standard CD-ROM filesystem
- *hfs*—Standard Macintosh filesystem

-v Verbose. Prints any messages to standard out.

-o Options. Filesystem-specific options are specified by *-o* followed by a comma-separated list of options. Note that I am only listing the most common options. Most of these apply to all filesystem types, but some filesystems may support additional options.

- *auto*—Can also be specified by *-a*
- *defaults*—Uses the default options (*rw, suid, dev, exec, auto, nouser, async*)
- *exec*—Permits the execution of binaries on the filesystem
- *noexec*—Does not permit the execution of binaries on the filesystem
- *ro*—Mounts the filesystem read-only, does not allow writing to the filesystem
- *rw*—Mounts the fileystem read-write, allows writing to the filesystem if the user has the privileges

Example 1: Mounting a CD-ROM

To use a CD-ROM you need to mount it. By default, Slackware Linux comes with a /cdrom directory. To mount a typical CD-ROM, type this command:

```
mount -t iso9660 /dev/hdd /cdrom
```

This tells the system that the filesystem type (-t) is iso9660, the CD-ROM standard, and that your CD-ROM is located on the fourth IDE channel (hdd). Typically, your hard drive is hda; if you have a second it usually is hdb, and so on. On most PCs there are two IDE controllers that can each have two devices, allowing for hda through hdd. The master device on the first controller is hda; the slave device is hdb. The master device on the second controller is hdc, and the slave device is hdd. The final argument to the *mount* command is the directory you want the CD-ROM mounted under. Now, unless there are errors, you can access the CD-ROM from that directory.

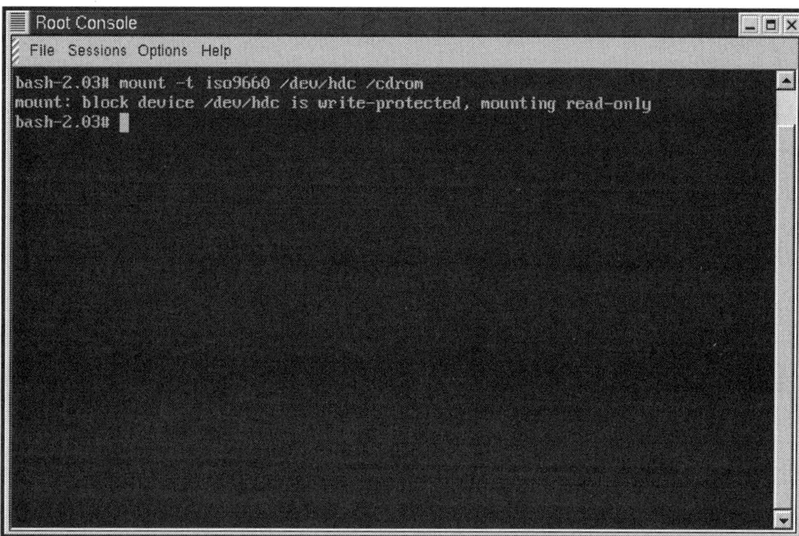

Figure A.3 *Typical output from the* mount *command*

Example 2: Mounting a Floppy

To mount a MS-DOS floppy in what would be drive A under MS-DOS, use the *mount* command like this:

```
mount -t msdos /dev/fd0 /floppy
```

This mounts an MS-DOS (FAT16) floppy under the /floppy directory. By default it allows read and write access. If you do not want to allow write access to the floppy, you can specify that with the *-o rw* option, like this:

```
mount -t msdos -o rw /dev/fd0 /floppy
```

If your /etc/fstab file is set up correctly, you can save typing. You only have to tell the *mount* command what device to mount; it tries to assume the rest by reading /etc/fstab. So to mount your floppy, usually all you really need to type is this:

```
mount /dev/fd0
```

Unlike Windows, Linux does not assign drive letters to devices. Devices become part of the filesystem when mounted. Although this probably seems foreign to you at first, it actually tends to make more sense. For one thing, you're not limited to 26 devices on your system! Okay, you probably won't hit this limit at home, but it is a real concern in a networked environment.

Unmounting Filesystems

When I first started using Slackware, I kept trying to unmount CD-ROMs and floppies using *unmount* instead of *umount*. It's a common mistake. I eventually started remembering that it was *umount* instead of *unmount*, but you don't have to. If you want to type a more logical command, go to the /bin directory and make a symbolic link to *umount* called *unmount*, like this: **ln -s umount unmount**. Then the system finds a command called *unmount* after all. The -s provides a symbolic link to the command *umount*, thus providing for those who think *unmount* is more logical.

Name: *umount*

Function: To unmount a device attached to the filesystem.

Syntax: `umount [options] directory`

Description: The *umount* command unmounts a mounted device. You probably only need to use *umount* on devices such as your CD-ROM drive or floppy drive, though it can also be used to unmount any device on the system that is not currently being used. It is the opposite of the *mount* command.

Usage: To use the *umount* command, type **umount** followed by any options and then the directory name the device is mounted under. You can also use the device name instead of the directory, but it's usually easier to type the directory name.

Note that if the filesystem is in use, Linux does not allow you to unmount it. If you are in the /cdrom directory, for instance, it does not let you unmount a CD-ROM mounted under that directory.

Options:

-n No write. Unmounts without writing in the /etc/mtab file.

-r Read only. If unmounting fails, this will try to remount read-only instead.

Example 1: Unmounting the CD-ROM

To unmount a CD-ROM mounted under the /cdrom directory, type

```
umount /cdrom
```

As long as no one is currently accessing /cdrom or is in that directory, the device is unmounted with no error messages or other output.

Example 2: Unmounting the Floppy

The syntax for unmounting a floppy is the same. Type

```
umount /floppy
```

Deleting Files

Name: *rm*

Function: To remove files and directories.

Syntax: `rm [options] file(s)`

Description: The *rm* command is similar to the *DEL* command under MS-DOS, but it is much more powerful.

Unlike MS-DOS, Windows, or the Mac OS, Linux assumes you know what you're doing. This means if you have the permissions to remove files, Linux lets you and it doesn't complain that it might damage the system. Be very careful when removing files under Linux; once they're gone, they're gone. There is no undelete command under Linux, so be sure to exercise this command with caution. You can wipe out your entire directory tree and Linux happily lets you. This is a good reason not to do your work when you are logged in as root. Normal users don't have the permissions to really mess up the entire system. The root user, on the other hand, can delete the entire filesystem with one command.

Usage: To remove a file, type **rm**, then any options, and then the name of the file to be removed.

Options:

-f Force. Do not prompt the user for confirmation, and give no error messages for nonexisting files.

-i Interactive. Ask before removing each file.

-r,-R Recursive. Remove directories and their contents recursively.

-v Verbose. Print the names of files being removed.

Example 1: Removing a File

To simply remove a file use the *rm* command with no options, and only one argument—the name of the file you wish to remove, like this:

```
rm file
```

This removes the file with no error message or output of any kind as long as the file does exist and you have permissions to remove it. If the file doesn't exist or you don't have permissions, *rm* produces an error message.

Example 2: Removing a Directory and All Files under It

To remove an entire directory and any contents in the directory, use the *rm* command along with the recursive (*-r* or *-R*) option and the name of the directory, like this:

```
rm -r tmp/
```

As long as you have the proper permissions, and the directory exists, there is no prompting or messages; Linux simply removes the directory and all of its contents. This is a good argument for using the interactive option as well, like this:

```
rm -ri tmp/
```


Figure A.4 *Using* rm *interactively*

As you can see from the Figure A.4, you have several chances to change your mind about removing the file under the tmp directory, and removing the directory itself. Unless you are very sure of yourself, and even if you are, I recommend using the interactive option of the *rm* command. It takes a little longer, but there's less chance of deleting a important file. Granted, deleting a vital part of your system helps you build valuable troubleshooting skills, but that's probably not the way you want to build them.

Example 3: Deleting Multiple Files with Wildcards

You can use wildcards to delete multiple files at once without having to type individual filenames.

> Be very careful with wildcards. You can very easily destroy files you do not want to delete.

If you have multiple files that only differ by one character, you can use the ? wildcard to represent only one character, like this:

```
rm -i temp?
```

That command deletes any file named temp1, temp2, and so on. It does not delete a file named temp22, stuff, or just plain temp.

The * wildcard in the next example deletes any file that begins with temp in the current directory. You can use the * wildcard to match a few files, like this:

```
rm -i temp*
```

Or you can use the * wildcard to match all files in a directory, like this:

```
rm -i *
```

> The interactive option is not necessary, but I'm putting it in the examples to encourage you to use it, at least until you're very familiar with Linux.

Example 4: Utter Insanity

If you're just fed up with your system, you can delete the entire directory tree with the following command executed as root under the / directory. Be sure you've got installation disks ready to go.

```
rm -rf *
```

Do not try this at home, and no, I haven't tried it to make sure it works.

Viewing and Manipulating Files with cat

Name: *cat*

Function: Concatenate files and print on standard out.

Syntax: `cat [options] [file(s)]`

Description: The *cat* command basically takes a file (or standard input, if you don't specify a file) and prints it to standard out. This is somewhat useful for quickly viewing files such as /etc/fstab or one of the other configuration files. The *cat* command really becomes useful in conjunction with other commands, either by piping the output of *cat* to other commands, or creating files with the output.

Usage: To concatenate a file to standard output, type **cat** followed by any options, and the name of the file. Generally *cat* is used with some sort of redirection.

Options:

–b Number. Number all lines that are not blank.

–s Squeeze. Replace multiple blank lines with one blank line.

–n Number all. Number all lines.

v Show nonprinting. Show nonprinting characters as well as regular characters.

–T Tabs. Show tabs in a file.

Example 1: Concatenating a File to the Display

The simplest use of *cat* is to display the contents of a file to the screen, with no options. This can be useful to quickly view the contents of a file, without opening the file in vi or Emacs. To see what filesystems are currently mounted you can *cat* the contents of /etc/mtab to the display (standard out), like this:

```
cat /etc/mtab
```

This is somewhat useful, but *cat* becomes very useful when you redirect the output of the command to a file or another command.

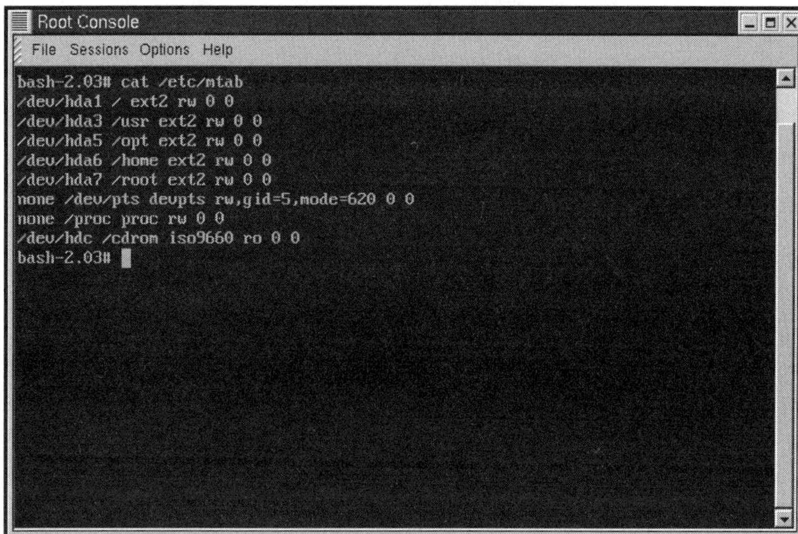

Figure A.5 *The output of cat /etc/mtab*

Example 2: Redirecting the Output of a Concatenation

To redirect the output of *cat*, you should either pipe the output of *cat* to another command, or redirect the output into a file. Here's how you redirect output from *cat* into another file.

```
cat file > file2
```

The preceding command overwrites the contents of the file if it already exists, and creates the file if it doesn't exist. Basically, this is a poor man's copy.

If you want to append the contents of one file onto another, without overwriting the original contents, you can use the following command:

```
cat file >> file2
```

This tells the shell to append the output of *cat* to the file rather than overwriting it.

cat is also used frequently in conjunction with the *less* command and the *grep* command. Say you have a text file where you save all of your friends' names and addresses, phone numbers, and email addresses, and you want to find one quickly (see Figure A.6). You can *cat* the file and pipe the output to *grep* and use *grep* to search for your friend's name. For instance

```
cat phonenumbers.txt | grep Bob
```

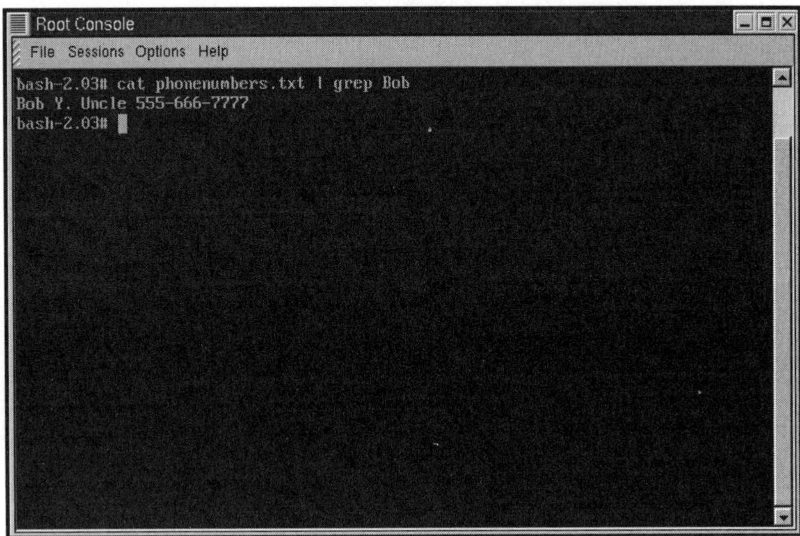

Figure A.6 *Using* cat *and* grep *to find phone numbers*

The preceding command outputs every line with Bob in it, saving you the hassle of searching through all of your friends' information in that file. You can even create a file just for Bob by redirecting the output to /Bob.txt, like this.

```
cat phonenumbers.txt | grep Bob > Bob.txt
```

Viewing Files with less

The *less* command is also useful to view files, especially longer files. It also enables you to navigate files in a way that *cat* does not.

Name: *less*

Function: The *less* command reads a file (or standard input, if no file is given) to standard output. It is similar to the *more* command, but allows forward and backward movement.

Syntax: `less [options] [file]`

Options:

-E End. Tells *less* to exit when it reaches the end of a file.

-f Force. Forces non-regular files to be opened. No error message is given when opening a binary file.

-i Ignore. Causes searches to ignore case.

-p Pattern. Starts *less* on the first instance of a given pattern.

-s Squeeze. Display multiple blank lines as one blank line.

-S Chop lines. The *-S* option causes long lines to be truncated rather than wrapped. In other words, lines too long for the display are chopped to fit and the remainder is discarded.

-u Printable. Carriage feeds and backspaces to be treated as printable characters.

Example 1: Displaying a File with less

```
less /etc/rc.d/rc.modules
```

The preceding displays the file /etc/rc.d/rc.modules and enables you to navigate the file without having to open a text editor.

To move around in *less*, use the following keys:

- *Enter*—Move one line forward.
- *d* or Ctrl+*D*—Move forward one-half screen at a time.
- *b* or Ctrl+*B*—Move backward one-half screen at a time.
- *Left arrow*—Move horizontally to the left.
- *Right arrow*—Move horizontally to the right.
- *F*—Scroll forward.
- *g*—Go to the beginning of the file, or if preceded by a number, go to that line.
- *G*—Go to the end of the file, or if preceded by a number, go to that line.
- *h*—Display a summary of *less* commands.
- *Space*—Scroll forward an entire screen.

Viewing Running Processes with ps

Name: *ps*

Function: Display running processes.

Syntax: `ps [options] [pid(s)]`

Description: The *ps* command displays process status to standard out. You get a static report of what processes are currently running. The *top* command is similar but provides a continually updating report of processes and their status. The *ps* command is useful to see what processes are running, who has created the process, and what the process statuses are.

Usage: To use *ps*, type **ps** followed by any options, and a process ID if you want to check a specific process and know its ID. If you don't know the ID of the process, you can run *ps* to find out!

Options:

-l Long. Give lots of information.

-u User. Give username and start time of processes.

-m Memory. Give memory usage.

-a All. Show processes created by other users as well.

-x Detached. Show processes that are not associated with a terminal.

-C Command. Show processes with the given command name.

-w Wide. Don't truncate output to fit on one line; display full information.

-r Running. Only show running processes.

pid(s) Process IDs. Show only the process IDs given. If you specify several process IDs, separate them with spaces.

Example 1: Show User's Current Processes

To show your processes, use the simple *ps* command:

```
ps
```

This only displays processes owned by the user who runs the *ps* command. The *ps* command also appears on the list of running processes.

Example 2: Show All Processes

To display all currently running processes, use the *ps* command with the *-a* and *-x* options (see Figure A.7):

```
ps -ax
```

The first number in the output is the process ID (pid). The next column in the output is the terminal from which the command is being run, and the third column displays the status of the command. Processes can have a status of running (R), sleeping (S), stopped (SW), or zombie (Z). The fourth column displays the amount of time the process has been running, and the final column displays the command name.

```
Root Console                                              _ □ X
 File  Sessions  Options  Help
3257 tty1      S      0:00 xinit /root/.xinitrc --
3258 ?         S      0:12 /usr/X11R6/bin/X :0
3260 tty1      S      0:00 gnome-session
3263 ?         S      0:00 esd -terminate -nobeeps -as 2 -spawnpid 3261
3266 tty1      S      0:00 gnome-smproxy --sm-config-prefix /.gnome-smproxy-z2iH
3268 tty1      S      0:02 enlightenment -theme /usr/share/enlightenment/themes/
3283 tty1      S      0:01 panel --sm-config-prefix /panel.d/Session-MDbWDU/ --s
3286 tty1      S      0:00 xscreensaver -no-splash -timeout 20 -nice 10
3287 tty1      S      0:00 gmc --sm-config-prefix /gmc-EulWyR/ --sm-client-id 11
3289 ?         S      0:00 gnome-name-service
3297 ?         S      0:00 gen_util_applet --activate-goad-server gen_util_apple
3300 ?         S      0:00 quickres_applet --activate-goad-server quickres_apple
3303 ?         S      0:00 multiload_applet --activate-goad-server multiload_app
3307 ?         S      0:00 tasklist_applet --activate-goad-server tasklist_apple
3316 tty1      S      0:01 konsole
3317 pts/0     S      0:00 /bin/bash
3319 pts/1     S      0:00 bash
3321 pts/2     S      0:00 sh
3325 tty1      S      0:02 gimp
3326 tty1      S      0:00 /usr/lib/gimp/1.0/plug-ins/script-fu -gimp 8 7 64 64
3335 pts/3     S      0:00 bash
3377 pts/3     R      0:00 ps -ax
bash-2.03#
```

Figure A.7 *Output of ps -ax*

Stopping Processes with kill

Name: *kill*

Function: The *kill* command sends a signal to a process. By default, *kill* sends the SIGTERM (terminate) signal.

Syntax: `kill [option] pid(s)`

Description: Generally, the *kill* command is used to terminate a process that does not terminate in another fashion. *kill* can send other signals to a process as well. The *kill* command can also list the signal names.

Options:

-s Signal. Specify which signal to send, which can be given as a name or number.

-p Print. Tells *kill* not to send a signal to the process, but only to print the *pid* of the process.

-l List. List the signal names and numbers.

pid(s) Process IDs. Specifies the processes to which the signal should be sent. If you want to send the signal to several processes, separate the IDs with spaces.

Example 1: Killing an Errant Process

If a process has stopped responding, you can use the *kill* command to stop the process. If the process ID you want killed is 212, the following should stop the process. Note that you can only kill a process you did not create if you are the superuser on the system.

```
kill 212
```

This tells the process to exit, but it first gives it a chance to clean up—perhaps it will save any data it has before exiting.

If the default signal sent by *kill* does not terminate the process, signal 9 (SIGKILL) should always terminate the process.

```
kill -9 212
```

You should use *kill -9* only when a normal kill won't do it, because this method forcefully terminates the process without giving it a chance to clean up.

> Be very careful using *kill*. If you terminate the wrong process ID while you are root, you could very easily cause problems for yourself or other users on the system.

Getting Help with the man Command

Name: *man*

Function: Displays the man (manual) page for a command.

Syntax: `man [options] command`

Description: The man command is your friend. Really. If you learn no other Linux commands, that is, commit no other command to memory, learn this one. If you know the name of a command, the man page tells you how to use it, providing the man page is installed on your system. (Hint: Don't save diskspace by not installing documentation; you'll need it later!)

There are nine sections of man pages. They are:

1. Commands—Commands a user can execute from a shell.
2. System calls—System calls available from the Linux kernel. These are usually only useful to programmers.
3. Library calls—Functions available in libraries. These are usually only useful to programmers.

4. Special files—Pages for files found in /dev.

5. File formats—The format of files such as /etc/fstab and other useful files.

6. Games and demonstrations—Nuff said.

7. Other—Things like the *man* man page.

8. System commands—Commands only root can execute.

9. Kernel information—A manual section that contains information about kernel code.

Usage: Using *man* is simple. Just type **man** followed by the name of the command or file you want help with.

Options:

-f Output. Equivalent to the *whatis* command.

-h Help. Displays a brief help message.

1–9 Manual section. Specifically names the man page section to search. Useful if the same command appears in multiple sections.

Example 1: Displaying the man Page for cp

To display *cp*'s man page (see Figure A.8), simply type **man**, followed by the command you want displayed—*cp*, in this case.

```
man cp
```

Figure A.8 *The* cp *man page*

The man pages are a bit cryptic—they're not necessarily written for non-Linux or nongeek types. However, the man pages display and explain, sometimes tersely, the options and syntax for each command. They're extremely helpful in a pinch.

Directory Structure

The directory structure under Linux is much different from that of the directory structure of typical desktop operating systems. Linux's directory structure is patterned after UNIX—everything is in a single directory *tree*. This tree includes all your files, your hardware devices, any devices you have mounted, and even dynamically generated information about your system.

The / Directory

The / directory is typically called the root directory, not to be confused with /root, which is actually the home directory of the root user. All other directories fall under the root directory. Under Slackware, this includes the following top-level directories:

- /bin
- /boot
- /cdrom
- /dev
- /etc
- /home
- /lib
- /lost+found
- /mnt
- /opt
- /proc
- /root
- /sbin
- /tmp
- /usr
- /var

You also can create other directories under the root directory if you want, although you should exercise some restraint. On systems that have Microsoft Windows or MS-DOS, I usually mount the DOS filesystem under /C or /Fat-C so I can use files between Linux and Windows when I need to. Remember, Linux can read FAT and FAT32 filesystems, but you won't be able to see your ext2 filesystems under Windows or MS-DOS. It's probably a good idea to store all of your personal files under your home directory rather than just piling them under the root directory. This helps you keep your system well organized and keeps clutter to a minimum.

The /bin Directory

The /bin directory is where the most basic binary executable files that are used system-wide are stored. As you may have guessed, /bin is short for binary. Executable files are often referred to as binaries on UNIX-style systems, which is probably a bit misleading. If you use WordPerfect under Linux, for example, the files are stored in a binary format, but they're not executable. Also, shell scripts are ASCII files that are flagged as an executable file, but they aren't stored in binary format.

Under the /bin directory you find most of the common commands like *ls*, *touch*, *mount*, *cd*, and other commands used by all users on the system. These fundamental commands are kept in this directory, separate from other programs (such as Emacs or games,) to make it easier to recover a sick system.

The /boot Directory

Not surprisingly, the /boot directory contains files related to booting your Linux system. There is nothing very interesting in this directory, and it is probably best to leave it alone. You only modify files in this directory if you compile your own kernel.

The /dev Directory

The /dev directory is not a typical directory. It contains special files that represent devices attached to your system. Some of these are block devices, meaning they deal only in big chunks of data. Your hard drive is a block device. Others, such as your mouse, are character devices that only give and take a single character at a time. By reading and writing to and from these files, programs can communicate with your hardware. For example, the input from your mouse usually comes in to Linux from the file /dev/mouse. For a little fun, go to the /dev directory, type in **cat mouse**, and move your mouse around a bit (see Figure A.9).

```
cd /dev
cat mouse
```

If you follow the previous steps, you start seeing a bunch of gibberish on the screen, because instead of directing your mouse input to the normal destination, you're directing it to standard output—namely your screen. Don't worry, you haven't broken your computer. Type in Ctrl+C to quit sending the mouse signal to standard out. See what your computer has to put up with?

If what you type is now gibberish too, blindly type **reset** and hit Enter to restore sanity.

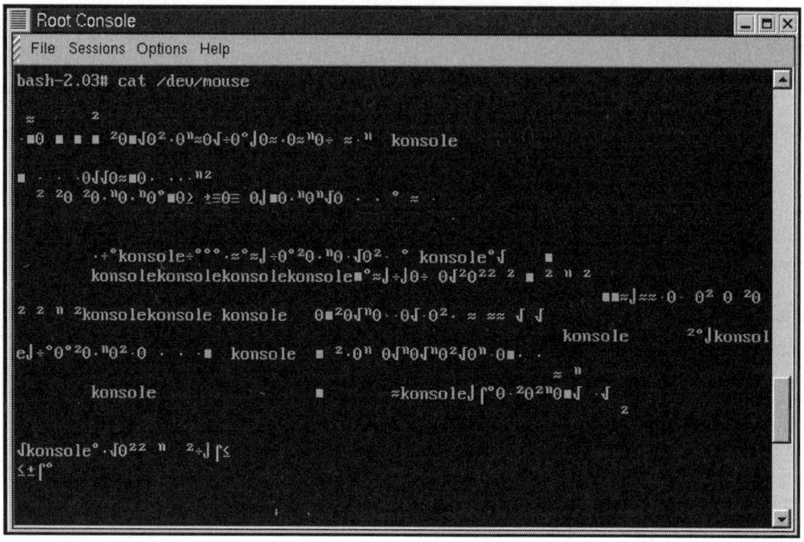

Figure A.9 *Playing cat 'n' mouse*

Your hard drive is represented in this directory. It probably is /dev/hda. You used this device when you configured partitions during installation. Advanced users might even read and write directly to these devices to make byte-for-byte copies of the hard drive.

Another popular destination under the /dev directory is /dev/null. This is basically the same as "File 13"—anything sent to /dev/null basically is being thrown away. This is sometimes useful for programmers to send output to /dev/null rather than write it to disk when there is output that has to go somewhere.

A final interesting device in this directory is /dev/zero. Like /dev/null, this isn't an actual physical piece of hardware, but Linux treats it as if it were one. This device continually spits out zeroes. What good is that? For any politicians out there looking for a modern paper shredder, here's a quick way to totally blank a floppy:

```
cat /dev/zero > /dev/fd0
```

You probably don't have to worry about /dev too much, but there might be occasions when you can find use for directing input from a device to a file rather than to its normal destination—mostly for troubleshooting purposes. You also should be familiar with this directory when you are configuring new hardware.

The /etc Directory

The /etc directory, usually pronounced "etsee," contains configuration files and several other directories that contain more configuration files. Some of the more important files contained in /etc are the /XF86Config file, the /fstab and /mtab config files and the /rc.d directory. The /XF86Config file contains the configuration information for XFree86, including which X server it should use, the refresh rate of your monitor, and information about your mouse and keyboard. You probably never need to edit this file directly, but it is there if you do need to edit it.

The other two files, /fstab and /mtab, are short for Filesystem Table and Mount Table, respectively. The /fstab is created when you install Slackware. If you add a hard drive or other storage device, you have to manually add a line for it to the /fstab. The /mtab is updated dynamically, depending on which devices currently are mounted on the system. For instance, if you mount a MS-DOS floppy (*mount -t msdos /dev/fd0 /floppy*), the /mtab gains a new line:

```
/dev/hda3 / ext2 rw 0 0
/dev/hdb1 /usr ext2 rw 0 0
/dev/hdb2 /opt ext2 rw 0 0
none /proc proc rw 0 0
/dev/fd0 /floppy msdos rw 0 0
```

The first entry /dev/hda3 / ext2 rw 0 0 is my root partition, which is located on the third partition on my first IDE hard drive. It is an ext2 filesystem that is mounted with read and write enabled.

The /usr and /opt directories are actually mounted on separate physical partitions on my second IDE hard drive. They are also ext2 filesystems, mounted with read and write enabled. The floppy is device /dev/fd0 mounted under /floppy and is an MS-DOS (FAT16) filesystem. If I had a second floppy drive, it would be /dev/fd1, and so on. If I unmount the floppy drive, the /mtab drops that entry. The /mtab exists for programs to read to see what devices are mounted.

The /etc/rc.d directory contains configuration scripts for the different runlevels under Linux, as well as the files that control the console font, Samba, the serial port, and other fun things. You also find the ppp directory, which is where the config files for ppp are found. You might need to edit these to use ppp on your system.

One of the ways that Slackware differs from other Linux Distributions is that Slackware does not use an /etc/init.d directory; instead, it uses /etc/rc.d. This can create some headaches when installing software if the install script looks for an /init.d directory.

The /home Directory

The /home directory contains the home directories of all users on the system, (with the exception of the root user, whose home directory resides in /root.) If your username is bsmith, for example, your home directory would be /home/bsmith.

Because Linux is a multi-user system, having separate home directories for each user is a necessity. Other desktop operating systems allow users' files to be intermingled. Linux forces them to stay separate, giving you a bit of privacy and security.

The /ftp and /httpd directories are under the /home directory as well. If you are running an FTP or Web server, these directories contain the files visible to the outside world.

The /lib Directory

Under the /lib directory you find library files. Library files are files that are required when compiling or running many programs under Linux. Library files are similar to DLL files under Windows. This is another directory that it's best not to muck about in unless you need to and know what you're doing.

The /lost and found Directory

The /lost+found directory generally is empty. If your computer shuts down without properly unmounting the drives, Linux does a filesystem check (fsck). Any file fragments that aren't properly accounted for are put in the /lost+found directory. In general, as long as your system is healthy, this directory is unnecessary.

The /mnt Directory

Unless you create directories under /mnt, it remains empty. Some distributions put things like the CD-ROM or floppy drive directories under /mnt, but Slackware does not. I use the /mnt directory to mount network filesystems with my laptop computer.

The /opt Directory

The /opt directory contains optional programs—generally large programs. If you download a new version of Netscape, it might install here. The K Desktop Environment installs in the /opt directory by default as well.

The /proc Directory

The /proc directory does not contain actual files; it is generated on the fly by Linux. It contains information about running processes and the status of the hardware. You can get information about hardware devices or running processes by using the *cat* command on these files. For instance, you can find out what filesystems your kernel supports by running the following command:

```
cat /proc/filesystems
```

Or, you can find out what interrupts your hardware devices are using by running this command:

```
cat /proc/interrupts
```

Generally, the /proc directory is an area for powerusers only, but on occasion you might be instructed to get information from the /proc directory in order to troubleshoot or configure devices.

The /root Directory

The /root directory is the home directory for the root user. When logged on as root, the *cd* command brings you to this directory. It is kept separate from the home directories in /home so that the root user can maintain the system, even if the /home directory gets destroyed.

The /sbin Directory

The /sbin directory contains more binary files. This directory is similar in purpose to /bin, except /sbin contains *system* binaries. Most are related to system upkeep. Typically, you must be root to use these binaries.

The /tmp Directory

The /tmp directory contains temporary files. This is a good place to stick a file you plan to delete. Many programs automatically create temporary files in the /tmp directory. KDE creates files in /tmp for the K File Manager and a few other programs while it is running, so it's a good idea not to delete anything in the /tmp directory while you're in KDE or X Windows.

The /tmp directory is a handy place to decompress and compile programs that you've downloaded. Once you've compiled and installed a program you should be able to delete all of the remaining unnecessary files from the /tmp directory. Be sure to keep an archived copy of the .tgz files you download in another area, though.

The /usr Directory

The /usr directory and its subdirectory /usr/local are often kept on separate partitions because of their size. The /usr directory is one of the larger directories, because it contains the majority of software on your system: the X11 directories, development tools, library files, and games.

The directory layout within /usr/local mimics what you see in /usr. Usually, Slackware packages install in /usr. If you compile your own software, it goes in /usr/local.

The /var Directory

The /var directory contains variable files, mostly system logs. As a general rule, files under /var aren't of much interest unless you want to monitor the health of Linux or a Web server.

Directory structure under Linux is a bit more complex than under MS-DOS/Windows, but in the end it also makes more sense. Under DOS and Windows, directory structure tends to be a bit haphazard, and many third-party programs put program directories wherever they feel like it, with little rhyme or reason. There is actually a method to the madness under UNIX-style OSes, which should comfort you when you're getting used to the system.

Using vi to Edit Text

Editing text under Linux is not something to be taken lightly. If you wish to configure your system at all, you need to learn to cozy up with a text editor. Almost all configuration files used in Linux are plain ASCII text files meant to be edited by hand, unlike the binary files that are often used for configuration under Windows or the Mac OS.

There are GUI text editors available under KDE, GNOME, and other window managers, but vi has more functionality (and more of a learning curve) compared to the GUI editors. The more vital reason to learn a console-based text editor is that you have access to it even if you cannot get into your GUI for some reason. I don't take a great deal of time to explain the use of the GUI text editors because they are sufficiently self-explanatory to anyone who has used a text editor or word processor under Windows or the Mac. A word of caution, however: be sure, if you use a text editor or word processor of any kind to edit configuration files, that you are saving your files in plain ASCII text and that the program does not insert line breaks when not explicitly instructed to do so.

> Another reason I've found to learn to use a console-based text editor instead of any kind of word processor is that, at least in my experience, a console-based text editor is less distracting. My first real experiences writing long papers were not on a computer, but on a word processor that was basically nothing but a typewriter with a monitor. I hammered papers out right and left on it, but going to a PC-based word processor, such as Word or Word-Perfect, slowed my writing down considerably, because I was suddenly faced with all these lovely fonts and formatting options, not to mention all of the games accessible when I was in an GUI environment. . . . Anyway, if you're serious about writing, I think you'll find a text editor a much better choice. You can always save a file as plain ASCII text and not have to worry about formatting until you're finished.

There are, of course, more choices other than vi console-based text editing. In fact, there are several versions, or clones, of vi that are in popular use by Linux users. For the most part, if you know the key bindings for any of the vi clones you'll be able to use all of the clones.

vi versus Emacs

Most Linux users have very strong opinions about which text editor is the best. Frighteningly strong opinions, actually. The adage about not discussing religion or politics in polite conversation should probably extend to include text editors in the Linux community.

Which text editor is best is really dependent on the individual using the editor. I prefer vi because it is simpler than the Emacs variants and is also lighter on system resources. Also, due to its low system requirements, vi is usually an option when you need to do system repair, and Emacs generally is not.

About vi

vi (pronounced "vee-eye") is the standard editor on many UNIX systems. The name vi is derived from *vi*sual editor. However, the original vi itself is not actually available on Linux. There are several clones of vi that are available on Linux, though. Most Linux users simply refer to their vi clone as vi rather than differentiate between the clone and the original vi. The features in the standard vi are actually defined by a

POSIX is the Portable Operating System Interface— a description of the standard interfaces for UNIX-based operating systems such as Linux. Linux is not 100-percent POSIX-compliant, but does conform to most POSIX standards. The idea behind POSIX is to allow programs to be ported from one flavor of UNIX to another without massive rewriting of code. POSIX standards define things such as standard shell interfaces and an application programming interface in C.

POSIX specification for shell utilities under UNIX, and most clones support all of the standard features plus a number of extras that are not compatible with the original vi, but are marked improvements over the original.

Slackware's default vi clone is *elvis,* one of several clones for vi that are available. When you type vi at the shell prompt, you are brought into elvis, unless you change the symbolic link that points to elvis. Another vi clone that is available with Slackware is VIM (Vi IMproved). If you decide you'd rather use VIM than elvis, you can point the symbolic link for vi to VIM instead of elvis by doing the following:

1. You need to be logged in to the system as root. You can do this without logging out by running the *su* command with no arguments and typing in the root password.

2. Change to the /usr/bin directory.

3. Check to see which binary the symbolic link vi is pointing to by using the *ls* command.

   The output should look like this:

   ```
   lrwxrwxrwx   1 root      root         3 Oct  7 12:18 vi -> elvis*
   ```

4. Because a symbolic link named vi already exists, it has to be removed to allow a symbolic link to be created that points to VIM. There are two ways to do this: either remove the link, and then create a new link, or use the *-f* (force) switch for the *ln* command. The *-f* switch tells the shell to remove an existing file if there is one, and then create a new file by that name. Your command should look like this:

   ```
   ln -sf vim vi
   ```

   This command removes the existing symbolic link and creates a new one pointing to VIM. To be sure you've created a new link, go ahead and run the *ls* command again to see that the new link exists.

   ```
   ls -l vi
   ```

   Your output should look something like this:

   ```
   lrwxrwxrwx   1 root      root         3 Nov 27 23:24 vi -> vim*
   ```

   Now when you type **vi**, you bring up the VIM text editor rather than elvis.

5. Once the changes are finished, you should log out as root and resume working as a regular user so that there are no nasty accidents!

   ```
   exit
   ```

Using vi

vi is what is known as a modal editor. While using vi, you are in either the command mode or the insert mode, but unlike most text editors you don't use both modes at the same time. vi is designed to enable the user to keep his or her hands on the home keys of the keyboard while using the editor. This design enables users to improve their speed greatly because their hands don't have to leave the home keys, and thus a user spends less time trying to use odd keys, such as function keys or meta keys. Users can delete, cut, paste, search, navigate, and more by using the standard keys. This requires that the program differentiate between when the user is in an insert mode and when the user is in a command mode.

> Actually, some would say that vi has three modes: insert mode, command mode, and ex mode—or as the Getting Started Guide from the Linux Documentation Project calls it, the last line mode (ex commands are entered on the bottom of the screen). Many commands in vi are actually associated with the ex editor. VIM and elvis, however, both combine ex and vi into one handy text editor, so why complicate matters? However, if it ever comes up in a game of Trivial Pursuit, you'll be prepared.

Starting vi

To begin, putter around in vi a little bit to get the hang of it. Type **vi** at the shell prompt, either at the console or in an xterm or its equivalent. Once you enter vi with an empty buffer, you can type **i** to begin inserting text. You are now in vi's insert mode. To leave the insert mode and return to command mode, hit the Esc key.

Now that you're in vi, try doing a little editing to get the hang of it.

1. If you're not in insert mode already, type **i** to enter vi's insert mode. If you're in the vi clone elvis, you see an asterisk (*) appear in the lower-right corner of the screen. If you're in VIM, there is no visual indication that you have changed modes. The i that you've typed doesn't appear unless you type it a second time.

2. Once in the insert mode, type in a little text so that you have something to mess around with.

When you edit text in vi, whether you're creating a new file or editing an existing file, it is stored in a *buffer*—basically a space in memory—until you write the changes to a file or discard them. If you start vi without opening a file to edit, it creates an empty buffer to begin working in. vi also stores existing files in a buffer rather than working directly on them, and commits changes to the file once the write command is given.

3. Now that you have some text to play around with, hit the Esc key to re-enter command mode.

4. Practice moving around a little bit. You can usually move around using the arrow keys, but sometimes if you're using vi on a remote machine with telnet, the arrow keys are not recognized properly. Because vi was originally designed for machines with keyboards that didn't have arrow keys, you can navigate using regular keys. Use the following keys for navigating in vi:

h   Left one character

j   Down one line

k   Up one line

l   Right one character

w   Forward one word

b   Backward one word

Try moving forward and back a little bit. If you've played some of the text-based games that come with Linux, or some other popular games on other platforms, you may already be familiar with moving using the hjkl keys.

In general, typing a number before a command makes the command repeat that many times. Typing **6h** moves you left six characters, and typing **3j** moves you down three lines.

vi does not break lines by default because it is designed to edit code as well as typical text. Thus, a line can be much longer than the width of the screen on which it is displayed. vi automatically wraps text while it is being typed, but it does not insert line breaks by default.

> As with most things in Linux, vi commands are case-sensitive. If you are experiencing weird behavior, it might be because the Caps Lock key has accidentally been toggled.

5. Because you're only dealing with one sentence, moving one word at a time is probably sufficient. However, vi is designed to edit large files as well as small. There are shortcuts for moving quickly through a file. The following keys and key combinations move you more quickly through a file:

^   Moves the cursor to the beginning of a line.

$ Moves the cursor to the end of a line.

nG   Moves the cursor to a specific line number. Line 0 is treated as the end of the file.

n%   Moves the cursor to a certain percentage of the file.

6. After you've moved around, try editing the text a little. The following keys delete, cut, paste, and otherwise massage text. Remember, if you are in insert mode, you have to hit the Esc key to return to command mode.

i	Enter insert mode.
a	Enter insert mode, except insertion begins next to the cursor, rather than directly where the cursor is placed.
x	Deletes the character that the cursor is currently on.
nx	Deletes n characters.
dd	Deletes the entire line that the cursor is on.
ndd	Deletes *n* lines.
das	Deletes a sentence, not the entire line.
dw	Deletes a word.
cw	Changes a word. This deletes the word that the cursor is currently on and places you in insert mode so that you can replace the word.
y	Yanks a line. This copies the current line so it can be pasted later.
ny	Yanks a number of lines.
p	Pastes text below the current line.
P	Pastes text above the current line.
o	Inserts a blank line, and moves to the beginning of it.
J	Joins two lines of text.
.	Repeat last command.
u	Undo last command.

7. After a little editing, you're ready for the next step, which is actually saving the buffer that you're working on to a file. To write a new file, or to save to an existing file, use the last line mode of vi. Entering last line mode is similar to command mode. Type the Esc key if you're not already in command mode, and then type a colon (:) to enter the last line mode. The commands for saving files work only in the last line mode:

:w filename	Write to a new file.
:w!filename	Overwrite an existing file.
:wq filename	Write to file and then quit vi.
:wq	Write to file and quit vi, if a filename is already assigned.
:q!	Quit without saving.
:q	Quit.

Buzzword

Here's another little piece of Linux trivia that might come in handy someday. The exclamation point (!) character is often referred to as bang when reading a command out loud. For instance, if you were instructing someone how to quit vi, you'd say "Type colon, q, bang, and hit Enter."

That covers most of the basic capabilities of vi. It might take a few days of playing around with the keystrokes to navigate and do basic operations within vi, but once you get the hang of it, you find you can get around quite quickly and be very productive in vi.

Opening Files

Opening a file with vi is pretty straightforward. Typing **vi** *filename* either opens an existing file or creates a file if there was not a file by that name previously.

You can also start at a specific part of a file by using one of the following methods. Typing **vi +102** *filename* opens the named file and places the cursor at the beginning of line 102. You can also search the file for the first instance of a given term by using **vi +/term** *filename*. This uses vi's search capability to place the cursor at the first instance of the search keyword.

Advanced vi

This appendix mostly has covered very basic functions within vi. The advanced functions of vi can, and have, been the subject of entire books. I don't attempt to cover all of the features of vi here, but there are a few features that shouldn't be overlooked. I discuss these features in the following sections.

Searching Text with vi

To search through a file for instances of a string of text, you need to be in vi's last line mode. Instead of using the colon, however, you use either the forward slash (/) or question mark (?) to search through the text. Here are some of the commands you can use to search text with vi.

/text	vi searches forward through the buffer for text.
?text	vi searches backward through the buffer for text.
n	vi searches forward for the next occurrence of the preceding search term.
N	vi searches backward for the next occurrence of the preceding search term.

Search and Replace with vi

vi allows for advanced search and replace. To use search and replace with vi, enter the last line mode by typing a colon. Then enter the search term and replacement text, like this:

```
%s/original/replacement/gc
```

The preceding command tells vi to search for original and replace it with replacement if found, but to ask for confirmation first. The / character is a separator. The g in the command tells vi that it is a global search and replace—it won't stop after just one replacement. The c in the command tells vi that you wish to confirm before replacing the first text for the second.

Inserting Another File

To insert the contents of another file into the current buffer at the current cursor position, follow these steps:

1. Enter vi's command mode by pressing Esc.
2. Enter the last line mode by typing the colon (:).
3. Use the following syntax to tell vi the name of the file to open:

```
:r filename
```

or

```
:r/directory/filename
```

for a file not in the current directory.

This inserts the contents of the named file into the current buffer. You can use this feature for cutting and pasting between files or for inserting system files into another file for editing or modifying.

> Unless you really know what you're doing, it's much smarter to always edit a copy of a system configuration file rather than the original file. Actually, even if you do know what you're doing, it's still safer. If you don't, editing an original file is nearly suicidal.

Though this hasn't been an exhaustive look at vi, it should get you started. If you're interested in learning the more advanced features available, try using either the elvis or VIM man pages or some of the Web sites dedicated to vi clones. You can find a listing of those sites and other great resource sites in Appendix B "Linux Resources." I think you'll find yourself addicted to vi if you give it a try!

Summary

This Linux Primer should give you a good idea of how to get around in the Linux CLI. Most users who are new to Linux and just want to use Linux as a workstation or desktop operating system probably don't need to be gurus at the shell prompt, but it never hurts to have an idea of how to get around the shell if needed. You might even find that using the CLI is better in many cases. The nice thing about Linux is that you don't need to make a choice between GUI and CLI; you can fire up KDE (or whatever your favorite window manager/desktop environment is) and open several console windows and go to town!

Appendix B: Linux Resources

Joe "Zonker" Brockmeier

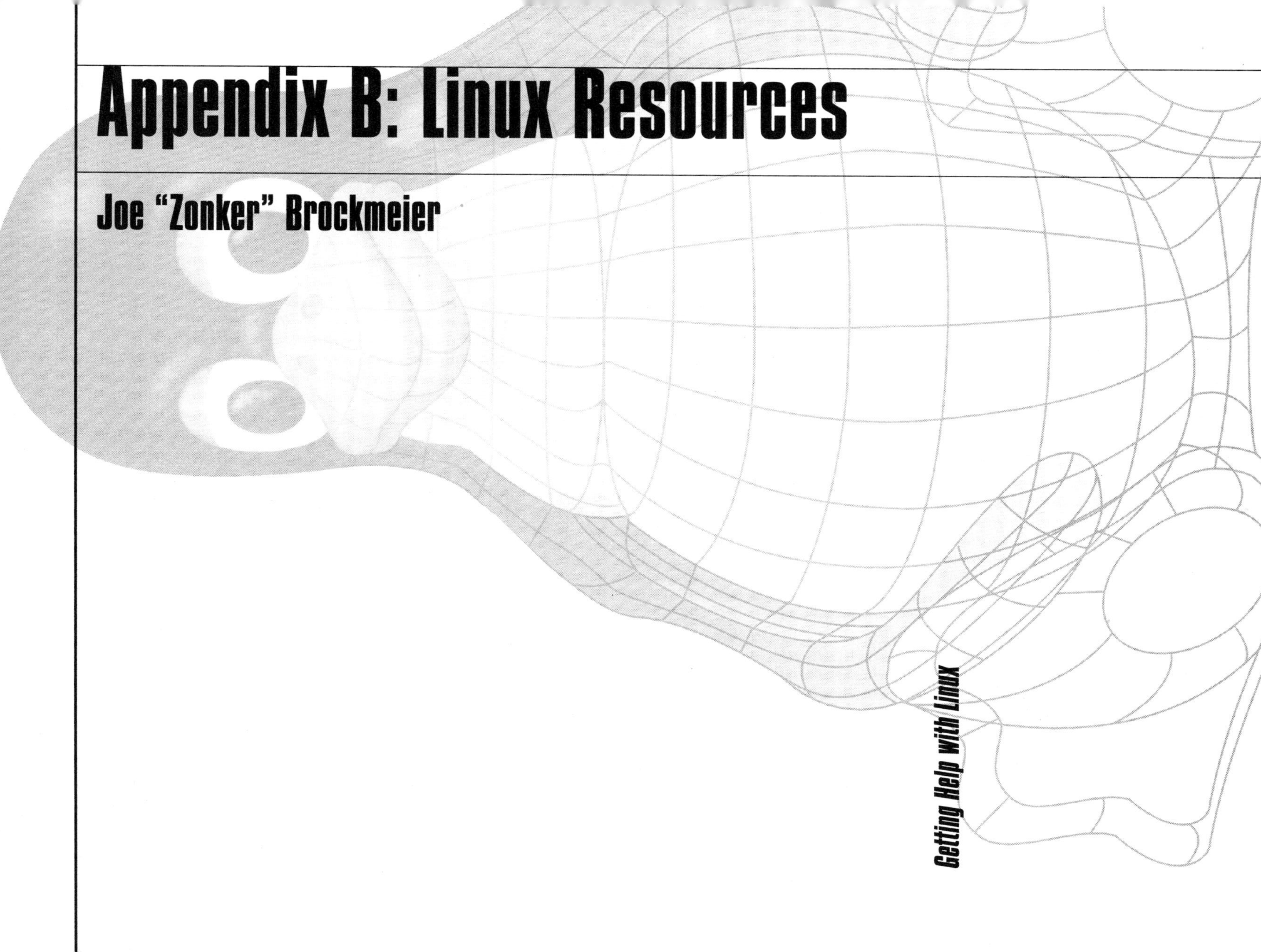

One of the best things about Linux is the fact that the Linux community has built a wonderful support infrastructure that is available to anyone—for free, no less! Slackware Linux itself comes with a huge number of help documents, HOWTO documents, and various other sources of information. These are all available online while you're using Slackware Linux.

Both KDE and GNOME have extensive online help systems. GNOME's help system includes not only GNOME-specific help, but man pages and GNU info pages as well. The GNU info pages and the man pages are also available at the console to give you assistance while you're toiling away at the command line.

In short, getting help with Linux isn't hard—it's only a matter of where to look. Where to look is what this appendix is all about.

Getting Help with Linux

Linux is mostly a DIY (do-it-yourself) operating system. The people who have been making Linux popular for the last couple of years are do-it-yourselfers and aren't averse to spending a lot of time figuring out problems. This differs a little from the mentality of the average computer user, who just wants it to work right now and doesn't want to have to learn anything in the process of making the computer work.

Because you've taken the time (and money, thank you!) to buy this book and read this far, I assume you do want to learn something. Luckily, the do-it-yourselfers who have been struggling and taming Linux over the years have often paused before tackling the next arduous task to actually write down how they accomplished the last arduous task. This is a good thing. This means that there's a trail through the woods for you to follow.

If you do find yourself on an unblazed trail, don't be afraid to try to figure it out yourself first. You'd be surprised what a little persistence, a bit of educated guessing, and a little blind luck can do. If you come across insurmountable problems, though, don't be afraid to ask if you can't find any documentation on what you're looking for.

A few words of caution, however. Before wandering onto a newsgroup or IRC channel or sending "help me" e-mail to Linus, make sure you have done your homework. If you ask a question of people, be sure to give them enough information to answer the question. For example, if you're having trouble with a video card, be sure to provide the important information, such as the type of video card, chipset, amount of RAM on the card, version of Linux you're using, and type of computer the video card is in. You might even want to describe any other peripherals attached to the system and what type of processor, motherboard, and how much RAM your main system has too. This is just common courtesy so that anyone trying to figure out your problem has the information they need to do so. If you post something such as "Hey, does anyone know why I can't get the X Windows System to work on Slackware Linux?" to a major newsgroup or IRC channel, be prepared to be ignored at best and at worst to need asbestos underwear for all the flames that come your way.

Using Online Docs

The first step is to access what you have readily available. The man pages (discussed in more detail in Appendix A, "A Linux Primer") and GNU info pages are available any time you can access your system.

Using man

Linux comes with lots of documentation. At the command-line interface, you have man pages and GNU info pages. To access a man page, simply type **man** and the name of the command or program you want to read the manual page on.

To view the man page for the *man* command, for example, you type the following:

```
man man
```

What you see is something like what is shown in Figure B.1.

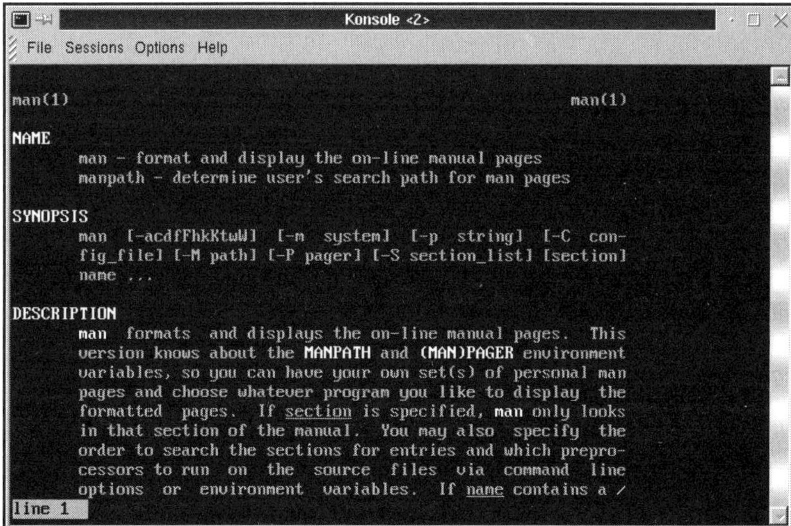

Figure B.1 *The* man *command's manual page*

Man pages are available for most commonly used commands, such as *mv*, *ls*, *less*, *cp*, and so on. You can also find man pages on many common configuration files and more complicated programs, such as *XFree86*.

To quit the man program, simply type **q**.

Using GNU Info

To start the GNU hypertext info system, just type the word **info** at the shell prompt. What you see looks something like what is shown in Figure B.2.

GNU info is a little more difficult to navigate at the console than man pages. The interface for GNU info is similar to the interface for Emacs, which is to say, it's not self-explanatory.

To move forward a page, press the spacebar. To move backward, use either the Delete key or the backspace key, depending on the type of terminal you are using.

To return to the top of the directory structure in GNU info, type **d**. To quickly go to one of the hypertext nodes, type **g**, followed by the name of the node in parentheses.

For example, at the introductory page, you see a listing of available nodes. One of the nodes is about the GNU C compiler, or GCC. To get to the GCC node, type **g** (gcc) and info brings up the GCC node. To exit from info, type **q**.

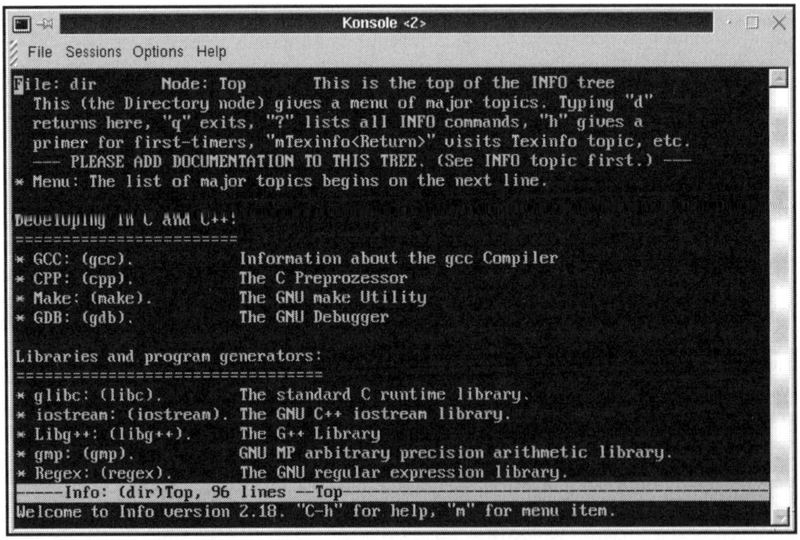

Figure B.2 *GNU info*

Finding Other Online Docs

If you do the full installation, Slackware also installs all of the Linux Documentation Project HOWTOs and mini-HOWTOs, as well as a ton of other documentation for various programs in the /usr/doc/ directory. To access the LDP HOWTOs, go to the /usr/doc/Linux-HOWTOs/ directory. All of the HOWTOs are stored in plain text, and the mini-HOWTOs are stored in the /usr/doc/Linux-mini-HOWTOs/ directory in plain ASCII text. You can use vi or Emacs to view the files or the GNU program *less*, described in Appendix A.

Essential Web Sites

Linux Web sites are multiplying like rabbits on Viagra right now. There have been good sites for Linux online for quite a while, but recently the signal-to-noise ratio has gotten pretty bad.

I try to list the cream of the crop. From there you might find other sites that also pique your interest.

Although every effort has been made to verify that these URLs are accurate and live at the time of this writing, the Web moves pretty quickly. It's entirely possible that documents might move or sites go black. Feel free to notify Prima Publishing if this happens so future editions of this book are accurate.

Documentation Sites

The mother of all Linux documentation sites is the Linux Documentation Project. The LDP, as it is affectionately known, houses HOWTOs, mini-HOWTOs, Guides, FAQs, and other assorted documentation guaranteed to help you learn more about Linux and quite possibly solve a problem you're currently having with Linux, if there are any.

The LDP's main site can be found at http://www.Linuxdoc.org.

The Linux Gazette is another great resource for Linux. Basically an online Linux magazine (not to be confused with Linux Magazine) the Linux Gazette is a repository of a huge number of articles and assorted goodies for the Linux enthusiast.

The Linux Gazette is published by SSC and can be found at http://www.linuxgazette.com.

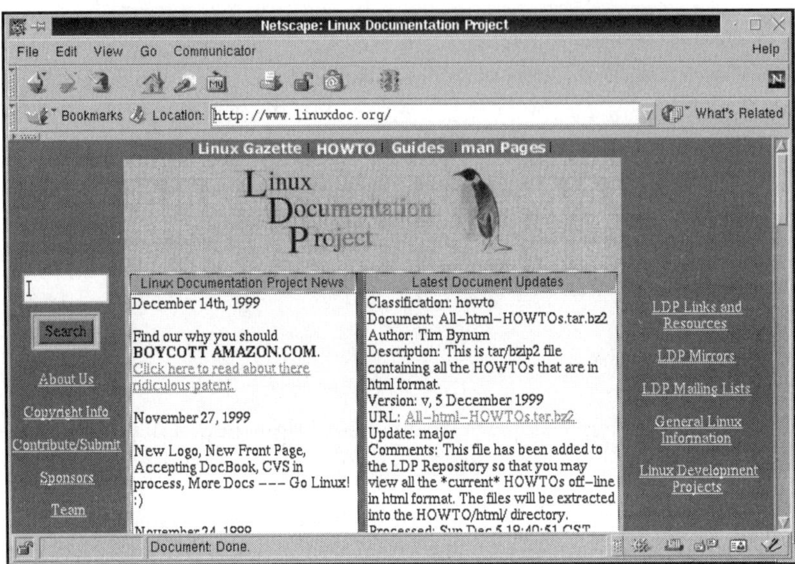

Figure B.3 *The Linux Documentation Project Web site*

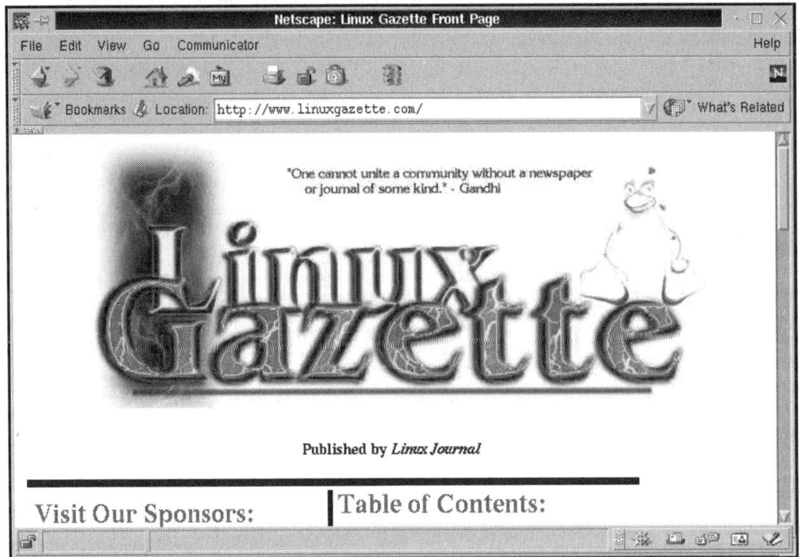

Figure B.4 *The Linux Gazette*

Another great site for "Everything Linux" is http://LinuxMall.com. Okay, I have to admit that I do work for LinuxMall.com, but it really is a great site to get started with Linux. It offers tons of Linux-related products and such and also features news and information about Linux. LinuxMall.com has a resources section, news section, and a lot more.

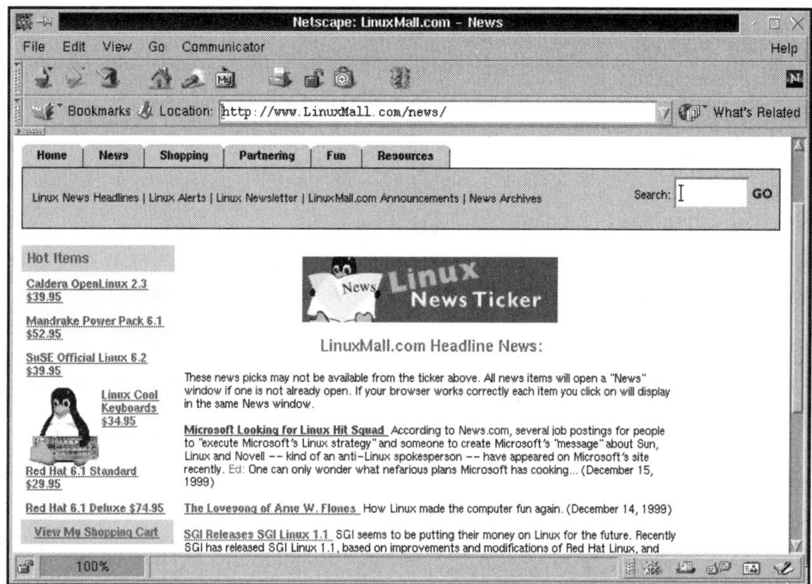

Figure B.5 *LinuxMall's Web site*

Of course, the best place on the Web to get information about Slackware Linux is none other than Slackware's home page. At http://www.Slackware.com, you find user forums, mirrors, and links to the current development tree of Slackware.

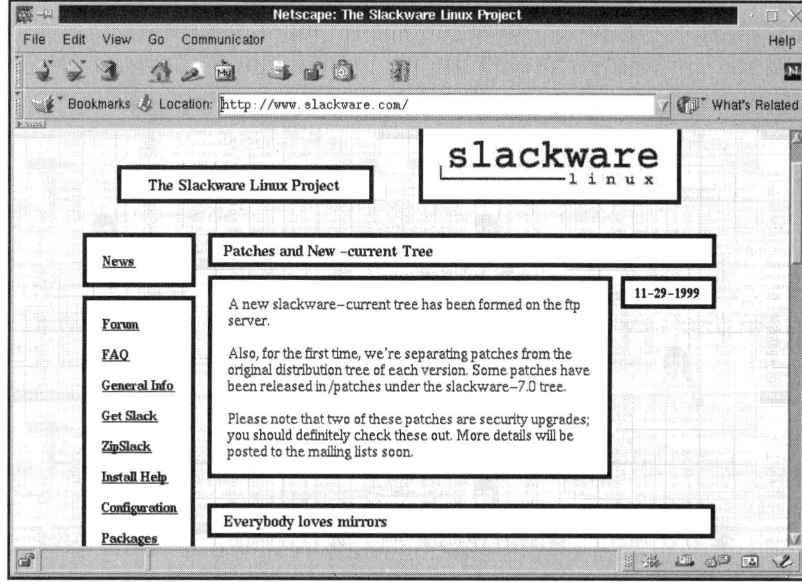

Figure B.6 *Slackware's Web site*

The Open Source Writers Group is a fairly new project, but it already has a lot of steam behind it. The OSWG is seeking to assist open source projects in teaming up with authors who want to contribute to the open source movement. The OSWG is sponsored by the Puffin Group and headed by Deb Richardson.

You can find the OSWG at http://www.oswg.org.

One of my favorite sites is the vi Web site, which is, to quote the site, "all about vi and its clones." As an avid vi user, I find this page very useful. You can find it at http://www.math.fu-berlin.de/~guckes/vi/.

Another great vi site is the VIM home page, which is dedicated to that particular clone of vi. At the VIM Web site, you can not only find great documentation for VIM and links to other sites with information about VIM and vi clones, you can also download the latest release of VIM, not just for Linux but for Windows, DOS, the Mac OS, and a few other major OSes. Just in case you can't use Linux at work, at least you can get your vi fix.

The VIM home page is located at http://www.vim.org.

The Linux Magazine Web site, the virtual equivalent of the *Linux Magazine*, is a great resource for Linux users. *Linux Magazine* has begun to archive past issues at the site and has a lot of great articles and such.

You can find the Linux Magazine home page at http://www.Linux-Mag.com.

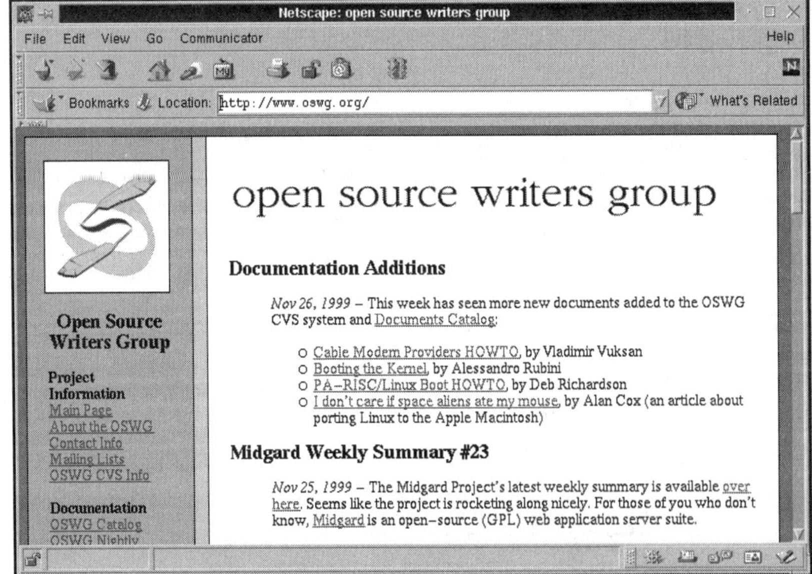

Figure B.7 *Open Source Writers Group Web site*

News Sites

There are a few really good news sites for Linux. My favorite Linux news site is the Linux Weekly News. The Linux Weekly News is a distillation of the last week of events in Linux, along with intelligent commentary and editorial comment. The folks at LWN don't post everything; they only cover what is really newsworthy, and they deserve the title of a news site.

You can find the Linux Weekly News site at http://www.lwn.net.

Another Linux news site is Linux Today. Linux Today is the site to go to for everything that has made the news about Linux. They pretty much post all submissions, which makes them the most complete Linux news site on the Web. Unfortunately, some of the content isn't, in my opinion, really worth reading, but if you look you find a few good stories or features there every day.

You can find Linux Today at http://www.LinuxToday.com.

Of course, no mention of online Linux news would be complete without mentioning Slashdot. Slashdot is not only a Linux news site, but also covers a fair bit about Linux and other open source news. Slashdot is the site for "News for Nerds" and presents quite a few interesting stories on a regular basis.

Slashdot is located at http://www.slashdot.org.

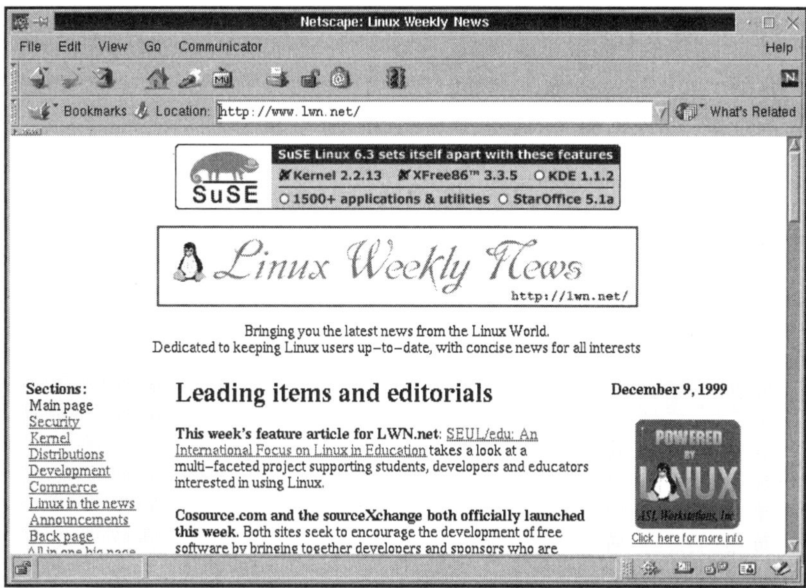

Figure B.8 *Linux Weekly News Web site*

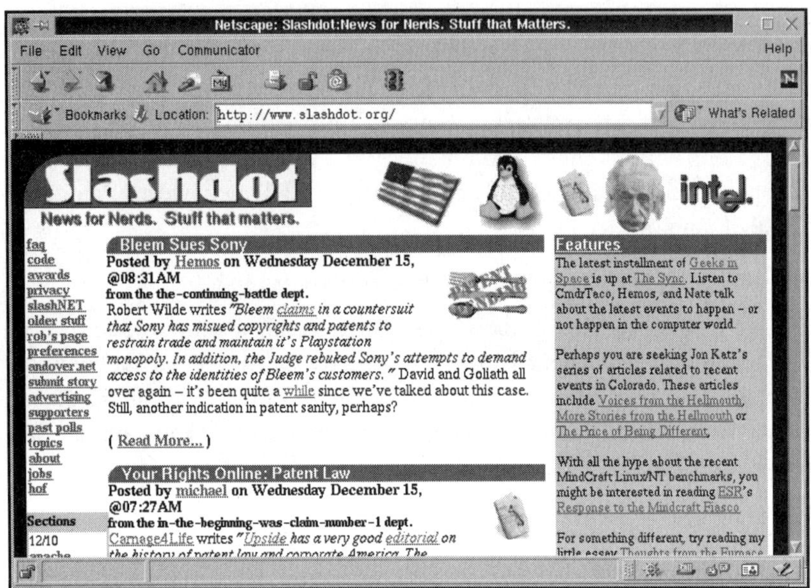

Figure B.9 *Slashdot Web site*

Community Sites

There are a fair number of Web sites dedicated to Linux that don't necessarily host news or documentation, but they're still important resources. You can find a lot of good information or software online if you're willing to look for a little while.

One of the longest-running Linux community sites is Linux Online. Linux Online is mainly a collection of links to other Linux sites with a little information thrown in for good measure. You can find Linux Online at http://www.Linux.org.

Another great Linux community site is http://www.Linux.com. Linux.com is sponsored by VA Linux Systems and is run by Trae McCombs. Linux.com has tons of information, feature articles, resources for Linux User Groups, tutorials, and much more. It's an awfully spiffy site, too.

If you're looking to download software, you might want to try Freshmeat. Freshmeat is the site to find open-source software to make your computer happy. Freshmeat maintains a huge database of software for Linux and FreeBSD. You can find Freshmeat at http://www.freshmeat.net.

Another important site for Linux is the GNU Project Web site. The GNU site links to GNU projects, the Free Software Foundation, the GNU Manifesto, documentation, and a ton of other goodies. You can find the GNU Web site at http://www.gnu.org.

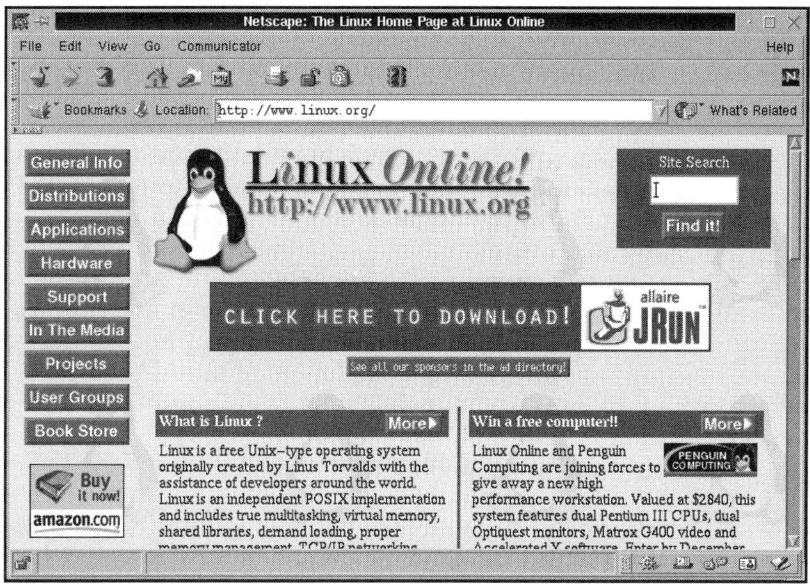

Figure B.10 *Linux Online Web site*

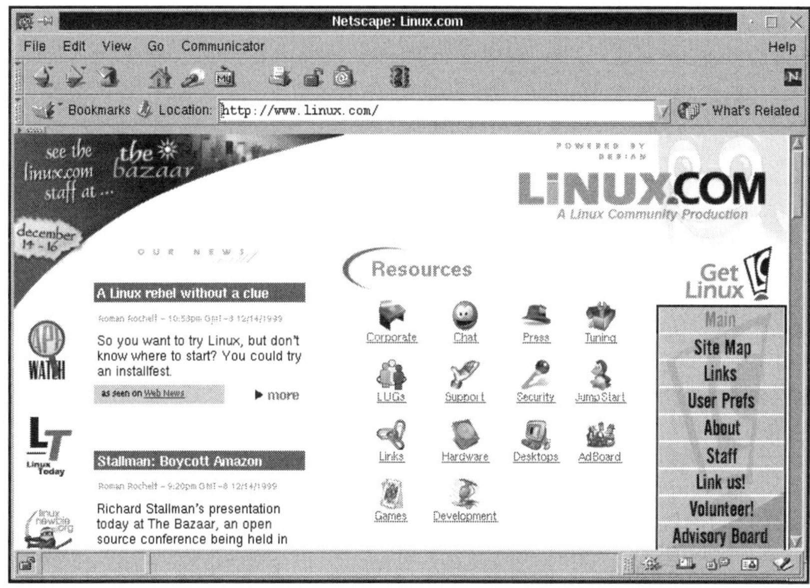

Figure B.11 *Linux.com Web site*

Newsgroups

Newsgroups are one of the best places to find information about using Linux. Be careful, however, to ask intelligent questions and provide plenty of background information when asking a question. Also, be sure that your questions are relevant to the group at hand. Posting questions about Slackware to alt.redhat.discussion, for instance, probably doesn't net you any useful information, unless you count broadening your vocabulary as a useful thing.

There are far too many Linux newsgroups to list, but here's a starter list for people new to Linux:

- alt.os.linux
- alt.os.linux.slackware
- comp.os.linux.answers
- comp.os.linux.hardware
- comp.os.linux.help
- comp.os.linux.networking
- comp.os.linux.setup
- comp.os.linux.x

If you post intelligent questions to these lists, you're almost guaranteed to get back helpful answers in a timely fashion. One caveat, however: don't expect miracles. If you're asking, "How can I get my Commodore 64 to run Slackware?" or "How can I get my Winmodem to work with Linux?" you'll probably be disappointed. It's not that Linux users don't like to help, but there are some problems that just aren't fixable.

IRC

IRC is another very popular support medium for Linux. If you've got questions about any aspect of Linux, find a friendly Linux IRC channel like #linuxhelp or #linuxnewbie to ask questions on. You'll find IRCers stumbling over each other to be the first to solve your problem.

Linux User Groups

If you just can't find help online, don't sweat it. Look for a local Linux User Group. Odds are, if you live in a well-populated area, there's probably a Linux User Group near you. Linux User Groups exist to give Linux users a chance to meet with each other, pick each other's brains, and help advocate Linux to people who aren't yet familiar with Linux.

If you're not sure if there's a Linux User Group in your area, try the Linux User Groups World Wide listing at http://www.linux.org/users/. There are more than 308 LUGs listed from around the world, with 131 in the United States alone. You can also find a LUG at http://www.linux.com/lug/. If you really want to learn about Linux quickly, try joining a LUG.

Summary

This appendix is just a brief overview all the available Linux resources. To list all of them would take, well, a book. If you start by perusing the Linux Documentation Project and visiting a few of the other Linux community sites, you should quickly get a feel for what is out there. I really recommend paying a visit to a LUG meeting as well. There's nothing like the enthusiasm of others to help you maintain a healthy level of interest in learning more about Linux.

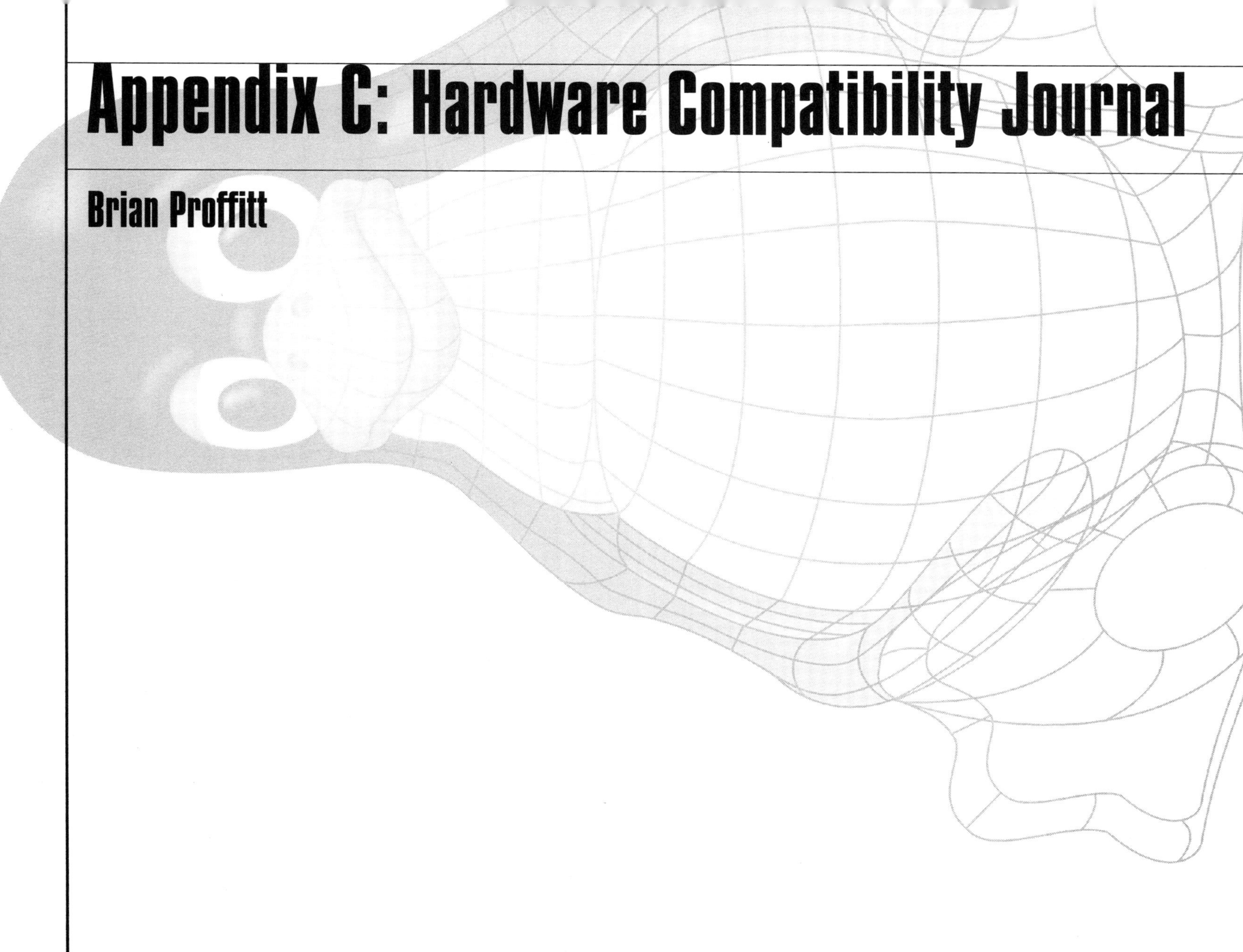

Appendix C: Hardware Compatibility Journal

Brian Proffitt

As you gather hardware information about your PC, feel free to fill out this form as a journal of the data you find.

CPU ____

Manufacturer _______________________________________

Model ____

Speed ____

Motherboard _______________________________________

Manufacturer _______________________________________

Model ____

Buses ____

Manufacturer _______________________________________

Model ____

Memory (RAM) _____________________________________

Size ____

Video Card ____

Manufacturer _______________________________________

Model ____

Video RAM size _____________________________________

Monitor ____

Manufacturer _______________________________________

Model ____

Horizontal Synchronization Rate ____________________

Vertical Synchronization Rate ______________________

Hard Drive _______________________________________

Manufacturer _______________________________________

Model _______________________________________

Size _______________________________________

Type _______________________________________

      SCSI _______________________________________

      IDE _______________________________________

Network Card _______________________________________

Manufacturer _______________________________________

Model _______________________________________

CD-ROM Drive _______________________________________

Manufacturer _______________________________________

Model _______________________________________

Size _______________________________________

Floppy Drive _______________________________________

Manufacturer _______________________________________

Model _______________________________________

Size _______________________________________

Modem _______________________________________

Manufacturer _______________________________________

Model _______________________________________

Transmission Speed _______________________________________

Printer _______________________________________

Manufacturer _______________________________________

Model _______________________________________

Mouse ____

Manufacturer ____

Model ____

Type ____

      PS/2 ____

      Serial ____

Keyboard ____

Manufacturer ____

Model ____

Number of Keys ____

Language ____

SCSI Card and Devices ___________________________________

Manufacturer ____

Model ____

Type of Device Controlled ________________________________

IDE Adapters ____

Manufacturer ____

Model ____

Type of Device Controlled ________________________________

Zip/Jaz Drive ____

Manufacturer ____

Model ____

Size ____

Tape Drive ____

Manufacturer ____

Model ____

Size ____

Sound Card ____

Manufacturer ____

Model ____

Scanner ____

Manufacturer ____

Model ____

Infrared Device ____

Manufacturer ____

Model ____

Type of Device Controlled ____

Joystick ____

Manufacturer ____

Model ____

Serial Device ____

Manufacturer ____

Model ____

Type of Device Controlled ____

Parallel Device _______________________________________

Manufacturer ____

Model ____

Type of Device Controlled ________________________________

PCMCIA ____

Manufacturer ____

Model ____

Card Type ____

BIOS Settings ____

Network Settings _____________________________________

With the right provider, your site launch is a no-brainer.

f we can take care of NASA, M.I.T., Duke Jniversity, Conoco, and Motorola, we hink we can help you. Our Linux-based veb clusters come complete with hardware, software, installation and support.

We offer turnkey systems or incremental load-balancing capacity. And since we've been around forever (1994) you know we're here for the long run.

atípa
LINUX SOLUTIONS
LEADING LINUX™

www.atipa.com
800.360.4346

DISCOVER LINUX!™

LinuxMall.com is the premier Web site for the Open Source operating system that's taking the world by storm. Visitors to LinuxMall.com can find technical information, the latest news, upcoming Linux Community events, links to online resources, and of course, an unbeaten selection of Linux-related products to buy.

LinuxMall.com offers a special deal to readers of PRIMA TECH titles. Simply visit **www.LinuxMall.com/iccs_coupon** and buy at least $50 worth of products, and a $10 discount will be applied at checkout time!

So, if you're ready to discover Linux, come and make your discovery at LinuxMall.com!

Save! Save! Save!

$10.00 OFF

your $50.00 purchase

Put away your scissors —it's an online coupon!

LEADING THE LINUX RESOURCE REVOLUTION

PRIMA TECH's LINUX® SERIES

Are you ready for Linux?

We are. PRIMA TECH's Linux Series has what you need. Because each distribution of Linux has its own unique features, the series consists of books in four categories—programming and development, networking and administration, installation and configuration, and applications—for each of the most popular Linux flavors—Red Hat, Caldera, SuSE, and Slackware. PRIMA TECH's Linux Series provides innovative resources for users of today's OS technology leader.

PHP Essentials
0-7615-2729-X ◆ $39.99 U.S. ◆ $59.95 Can.

CorelDRAW for Linux
0-7615-2925-X
$39.99 U.S. ◆ $59.95 Can.

Guerrilla Guide to Great Graphics with the GIMP
0-7615-2407-X
$39.99 U.S. ◆ $59.95 Can.

Install, Configure, and Customize Corel Linux
0-7615-2786-9
$39.99 U.S. ◆ $59.95 Can.

Install, Configure, and Customize Red Hat Linux
0-7615-2306-5
$39.99 U.S. ◆ $59.95 Can.

Install, Configure, and Customize Slackware Linux 7
0-7615-2616-1
$39.99 U.S. ◆ $59.95 Can.

Install, Configure, and Customize SuSE Linux
0-7615-2308-1
$39.99 U.S. ◆ $59.95 Can.

Integrate Linux Solutions Into Your Windows Network
0-7615-2791-5
$39.99 U.S. ◆ $59.95 Can.

Integrating Your Network with Caldera OpenLinux
0-7615-2301-4
$49.99 U.S. ◆ $74.95 Can.

Linux for Your Laptop
0-7615-2816-4
$39.99 U.S. ◆ $59.95 Can.

Programming with Python
0-7615-2334-0
$39.99 U.S. ◆ $59.95 Can.

Red Hat Linux Administrator's Guide
0-7615-2157-7
$49.99 U.S. ◆ $74.95 Can.

Sun StarOffice 5.1 for Linux
0-7615-2454-1
$29.99 U.S. ◆ $44.95 Can.

VMware 2.0 for Linux
0-7615-2764-8
$39.99 U.S. ◆ $59.95 Can.

PRIMA TECH
A Division of Prima Publishing
www.prima-tech.com
Call today to order!
1.800.632.8676, ext. 4444

Applications
Install/Configure
Networking/Administration
Programming/Development

License Agreement/Notice of Limited Warranty

By opening the sealed disk container in this book, you agree to the following terms and conditions. If, upon reading the following license agreement and notice of limited warranty, you cannot agree to the terms and conditions set forth, return the unused book with unopened disk to the place where you purchased it for a refund.

License:
This book includes a copy of the downloadable version of Slackware Linux 7. Slackware is free software; you can redistribute it and/or modify it under the terms of the GNU General Public License as published by the Free Software Foundation; either version 2 of the License, or (at your option) any later version. A full version of the GPL is included on the CD.

Notice of Limited Warranty:
The enclosed disk is warranted by Prima Publishing to be free of physical defects in materials and workmanship for a period of sixty (60) days from end user's purchase of the book/disk combination. During the sixty-day term of the limited warranty, Prima will provide a replacement disk upon the return of a defective disk.

Limited Liability:
THE SOLE REMEDY FOR BREACH OF THIS LIMITED WARRANTY SHALL CONSIST ENTIRELY OF REPLACEMENT OF THE DEFECTIVE DISK. IN NO EVENT SHALL PRIMA OR THE AUTHORS BE LIABLE FOR ANY OTHER DAMAGES, INCLUDING LOSS OR CORRUPTION OF DATA, CHANGES IN THE FUNCTIONAL CHARACTERISTICS OF THE HARDWARE OR OPERATING SYSTEM, DELETERIOUS INTERACTION WITH OTHER SOFTWARE, OR ANY OTHER SPECIAL, INCIDENTAL, OR CONSEQUENTIAL DAMAGES THAT MAY ARISE, EVEN IF PRIMA AND/OR THE AUTHOR HAVE PREVIOUSLY BEEN NOTIFIED THAT THE POSSIBILITY OF SUCH DAMAGES EXISTS.

Disclaimer of Warranties:
PRIMA AND THE AUTHORS SPECIFICALLY DISCLAIM ANY AND ALL OTHER WARRANTIES, EITHER EXPRESS OR IMPLIED, INCLUDING WARRANTIES OF MERCHANTABILITY, SUITABILITY TO A PARTICULAR TASK OR PURPOSE, OR FREEDOM FROM ERRORS. SOME STATES DO NOT ALLOW FOR EXCLUSION OF IMPLIED WARRANTIES OR LIMITATION OF INCIDENTAL OR CONSEQUENTIAL DAMAGES, SO THESE LIMITATIONS MAY NOT APPLY TO YOU.

Other:
This Agreement is governed by the laws of the State of California without regard to choice of law principles. The United Convention of Contracts for the International Sale of Goods is specifically disclaimed. This Agreement constitutes the entire agreement between you and Prima Publishing regarding use of the software.